DANIEL C. DENNETT

Intuition Pumps and Other Tools for Thinking

ALLEN LANE
an imprint of
PENGUIN BOOKS

ALLEN LANE

Published by the Penguin Group
Penguin Books Ltd, 80 Strand, London WC2R ORL, England
Penguin Group (USA) Inc., 375 Hudson Street, New York, New York 10014, USA
Penguin Group (Canada), 90 Eglinton Avenue East, Suite 700, Toronto, Ontario, Canada M4P 2Y3
(a division of Pearson Penguin Canada Inc.)
Penguin Ireland, 25 St Stephen's Green, Dublin 2, Ireland (a division of Penguin Books Ltd)
Penguin Group (Australia), 707 Collins Street, Melbourne, Victoria 3008, Australia
(a division of Pearson Australia Group Pty Ltd)
Penguin Books India Pvt Ltd, 11 Community Centre, Panchsheel Park, New Delhi – 110 017, India
Penguin Group (NZ), 67 Apollo Drive, Rosedale, Auckland 0632, New Zealand
(a division of Pearson New Zealand Ltd)
Penguin Books (South Africa) (Pty) Ltd, Block D, Rosebank Office Park, 181 Jan Smuts Avenue,
Parktown North, Gauteng 2193, South Africa

Penguin Books Ltd, Registered Offices: 80 Strand, London WC2R ORL, England

www.penguin.com

First published in the United States of America by W. W. Norton & Company, Inc. 2013
First published in Great Britain by Allen Lane 2013

003

Copyright © Daniel C. Dennett, 2013

The moral right of the author has been asserted

Printed in Great Britain by Clays Ltd, St Ives plc

A CIP catalogue record for this book is available from the British Library

ISBN: 978-1-846-14475-2

www.greenpenguin.co.uk

ALWAYS LEARNING   PEARSON

FOR TUFTS UNIVERSITY, MY ACADEMIC HOME

CONTENTS

PREFACE

Tufts University has been my academic home for more than forty years, and for me it has always seemed to be just right, like Goldilocks's porridge: not too burdened, not too pampered, brilliant colleagues to learn from with a minimum of academic prima donnas, good students serious enough to deserve attention without thinking they are entitled to round-the-clock maintenance, an ivory tower with a deep commitment to solving problems in the real world. Since creating the Center for Cognitive Studies in 1986, Tufts has supported my research, largely sparing me the ordeals and obligations of grantsmanship, and given me remarkable freedom to work with folks in many fields, either traveling afar to workshops, labs, and conferences or bringing visiting scholars and others to the Center. This book shows what I've been up to all these years.

In the spring of 2012, I test-flew a first draft of the chapters in a seminar I offered in the Tufts Philosophy Department. That has been my custom for years, but this time I wanted the students to help me make the book as accessible to the uninitiated as possible, so I excluded graduate students and philosophy majors and limited the class to just a dozen intrepid freshmen, the first twelve—actually thirteen, due to a clerical fumble—who volunteered. We led each other on a rollicking trip through the topics, as they learned that they really could stand up to the professor, and I learned that I really could reach back farther and explain it all better. So here's to my young collaborators, with thanks for their courage, imagination, energy, and enthusiasm: Tom Addison, Nick Boswell, Tony Cannistra, Brendan Fleig-Goldstein, Claire Hirschberg, Caleb Malchik, Carter Palmer, Amar Patel, Kumar Ramanathan, Ariel Rascoe, Nikolai Renedo, Mikko Silliman, and Eric Tondreau.

The second draft that emerged from that seminar was then read by my dear friends Bo Dahlbom, Sue Stafford, and Dale Peterson, who provided me with still further usefully candid appraisals and suggestions, most of which I have followed, and by my editor, Drake McFeely, ably assisted by Brendan Curry, at W. W. Norton, who are also responsible for many improvements, for which I am grateful. Special thanks to Teresa Salvato, program coordinator at the Center for Cognitive Studies, who contributed directly to the entire project in innumerable ways and helped indirectly by managing the Center and my travels so effectively that I could devote more time and energy to making and using my thinking tools.

Finally, as always, thanks and love to my wife, Susan. We've been a team for fifty years, and she is as responsible as I am for what we, together, have done.

DANIEL C. DENNETT
Blue Hill, Maine
August 2012

Intuition Pumps

AND OTHER
TOOLS FOR THINKING

I. INTRODUCTION: WHAT IS AN INTUITION PUMP?

You can't do much carpentry with your bare hands and you can't do much thinking with your bare brain.

—Bo Dahlbom

Thinking is hard. Thinking about some problems is so hard it can make your head ache just thinking about thinking about them. My colleague the neuropsychologist Marcel Kinsbourne suggests that whenever we find thinking hard, it is because the stony path to truth is competing with seductive, easier paths that turn out to be dead ends. Most of the effort in thinking is a matter of resisting these temptations. We keep getting waylaid and have to steel ourselves for the task at hand. *Ugh.*

There is a famous story about John von Neumann, the mathematician and physicist who turned Alan Turing's idea (what we now call a Turing machine) into an actual electronic computer (what we now call a Von Neumann machine, such as your laptop or smart phone). Von Neumann was a virtuoso thinker, legendary for his lightning capacity for doing prodigious calculations in his head. According to the story—and like most famous stories, this one has many versions—a colleague approached him one day with a puzzle that had two paths to a solution, a laborious, complicated calculation and an elegant, *Aha!-*

type solution. This colleague had a theory: in such a case, mathematicians work out the laborious solution while the (lazier, but smarter) physicists pause and find the quick-and-easy solution. Which solution would von Neumann find? You know the sort of puzzle: Two trains, 100 miles apart, are approaching each other on the same track, one going 30 miles per hour, the other going 20 miles per hour. A bird flying 120 miles per hour starts at train A (when they are 100 miles apart), flies to train B, turns around and flies back to the approaching train A, and so forth, until the two trains collide. How far has the bird flown when the collision occurs? "Two hundred and forty miles," von Neumann answered almost instantly. "Darn," replied his colleague, "I predicted you'd do it the hard way, summing the infinite series." "Ay!" von Neumann cried in embarrassment, smiting his forehead. "There's an easy way!" (Hint: How long until the trains collide?)

Some people, like von Neumann, are such natural geniuses that they can breeze through the toughest tangles; others are more plodding but are blessed with a heroic supply of "willpower" that helps them stay the course in their dogged pursuit of truth. Then there are the rest of us, not calculating prodigies and a little bit lazy, but still aspiring to understand whatever confronts us. What can we do? We can use thinking tools, by the dozens. These handy prosthetic imagination-extenders and focus-holders permit us to think reliably and even gracefully about really hard questions. This book is a collection of my favorite thinking tools. I will not just describe them; I intend to *use* them to move your mind gently through uncomfortable territory all the way to a quite radical vision of meaning, mind, and free will. We will begin with some tools that are simple and general, having applications to all sorts of topics. Some of these are familiar, but others have not been much noticed or discussed. Then I will introduce you to some tools that are for very special purposes indeed, designed to explode one specific seductive idea or another, clearing a way out of a deep rut that still traps and flummoxes experts. We will also encounter and dismantle a variety of bad thinking tools, misbegotten persuasion-devices that can lead you astray if you aren't careful. Whether or not you arrive comfortably at my proposed destination—and decide to stay there with me—the journey will equip you with new ways of thinking about the topics, and thinking about thinking.

The physicist Richard Feynman was perhaps an even more legendary genius than von Neumann, and he was certainly endowed with a world-class brain—but he also loved having fun, and we can all be grateful that he particularly enjoyed revealing the tricks of the trade he used to make life easier for himself. No matter how smart you are, you're smarter if you take the easy ways when they are available. His autobiographical books, *"Surely You're Joking, Mr. Feynman!"* and *What Do You Care What Other People Think?*, should be on the required reading list of every aspiring thinker, since they have many hints about how to tame the toughest problems—and even how to dazzle an audience with fakery when nothing better comes to mind. Inspired by the wealth of useful observations in his books, and his candor in revealing how his mind worked, I decided to try my own hand at a similar project, less autobiographical and with the ambitious goal of persuading you to think about these topics *my way*. I will go to considerable lengths to cajole you out of some of your firmly held convictions, but with nothing up my sleeve. One of my main goals is to reveal along the way just what I am doing and why.

Like all artisans, a blacksmith needs tools, but—according to an old (indeed almost extinct) observation—blacksmiths are unique in that they make their own tools. Carpenters don't make their saws and hammers, tailors don't make their scissors and needles, and plumbers don't make their wrenches, but blacksmiths can make their hammers, tongs, anvils, and chisels out of their raw material, iron. What about thinking tools? Who makes them? And what are they made of? Philosophers have made some of the best of them—out of nothing but ideas, useful structures of information. René Descartes gave us *Cartesian coordinates*, the *x*- and *y*-axes without which *calculus*—a thinking tool *par excellence* simultaneously invented by Isaac Newton and the philosopher Gottfried Wilhelm Leibniz—would be almost unthinkable. Blaise Pascal gave us *probability theory* so we can easily calculate the odds of various wagers. The Reverend Thomas Bayes was also a talented mathematician, and he gave us *Bayes's theorem*, the backbone of Bayesian statistical thinking. But most of the tools that feature in this book are simpler ones, not the precise, systematic machines of mathematics and science but the hand tools of the mind. Among them are

> *Labels.* Sometimes just creating a vivid name for something helps you keep track of it while you turn it around in your mind trying to understand it. Among the most useful labels, as we shall see, are warning labels or alarms, which alert us to likely sources of error.

> *Examples.* Some philosophers think that using examples in their work is, if not quite cheating, at least uncalled for—rather the way novelists shun illustrations in their novels. The novelists take pride in doing it all with words, and the philosophers take pride in doing it all with carefully crafted abstract generalizations presented in rigorous order, as close to mathematical proofs as they can muster. Good for them, but they can't expect me to recommend their work to any but a few remarkable students. It's just more difficult than it has to be.

> *Analogies and metaphors.* Mapping the features of one complex thing onto the features of another complex thing that you already (think you) understand is a famously powerful thinking tool, but it is so powerful that it often leads thinkers astray when their imaginations get captured by a treacherous analogy.

> *Staging.* You can shingle a roof, paint a house, or fix a chimney with the help of just a ladder, moving it and climbing, moving it and climbing, getting access to only a small part

of the job at a time, but it's often a lot easier in the end to take the time at the beginning to erect some sturdy staging that will allow you to move swiftly and safely around the whole project. Several of the most valuable thinking tools in this book are examples of staging that take some time to put in place but then permit a variety of problems to be tackled together—without all the ladder-moving.

And, finally, the sort of thought experiments I have dubbed *intuition pumps*.

Thought experiments are among the favorite tools of philosophers, not surprisingly. Who needs a lab when you can figure out the answer to your question by some ingenious deduction? Scientists, from Galileo to Einstein and beyond, have also used thought experiments to good effect, so these are not just philosophers' tools. Some thought experiments are analyzable as rigorous arguments, often of the form **reductio ad absurdum**,* in which one takes one's opponents' premises and derives a formal contradiction (an absurd result), showing that they can't all be right. One of my favorites is the proof attributed to Galileo that heavy things don't fall faster than lighter things (when friction is negligible). If they did, he argued, then since heavy stone A would fall faster than light stone B, if we tied B to A, stone B would act as a drag, slowing A down. But A tied to B is heavier than A alone, so the two together should also fall faster than A by itself. We have concluded that tying B to A would make something that fell both faster and slower than A by itself, which is a contradiction.

Other thought experiments are less rigorous but often just as effective: little stories designed to provoke a heartfelt, table-thumping

---

* Words and phrases in boldface are the names of tools for thinking described and discussed in more detail elsewhere in the book. Look in the index to find them, since some of them do not get a whole piece to themselves.

intuition—"Yes, of course, it has to be so!"—about whatever thesis is being defended. I have called these *intuition pumps*. I coined the term in the first of my public critiques of philosopher John Searle's famous **Chinese Room** thought experiment (Searle, 1980; Dennett, 1980), and some thinkers concluded I meant the term to be disparaging or dismissive. On the contrary, I love intuition pumps! That is, some intuition pumps are excellent, some are dubious, and only a few are downright deceptive. Intuition pumps have been a dominant force in philosophy for centuries. They are the philosophers' version of Aesop's fables, which have been recognized as wonderful thinking tools since before there were philosophers.* If you ever studied philosophy in college, you were probably exposed to such classics as Plato's cave, in *The Republic*, in which people are chained and can see only the shadows of real things cast on the cave wall; or his example, in *Meno*, of teaching geometry to the slave boy. Then there is Descartes's evil demon, deceiving Descartes into believing in a world that was entirely illusory—the original Virtual Reality thought experiment—and Hobbes's state of nature, in which life is nasty, brutish, and short. Not as famous as Aesop's "Boy Who Cried Wolf" or "The Ant and the Grasshopper," but still widely known, each is designed to pump some intuitions. Plato's cave purports to enlighten us about the nature of perception and reality, and the slave boy is supposed to illustrate our innate knowledge; the evil demon is the ultimate skepticism-generator, and our improvement over the state of nature when we contract to form a society is the point of Hobbes's parable. These are the enduring melodies of philosophy, with the staying power that ensures that students will remember them, quite vividly and accurately, years after they have forgotten the intricate surrounding arguments and analysis. A good intuition pump is more robust than any one version of it. We will consider a

---

* Aesop, like Homer, is almost as mythic as his fables, which were transmitted orally for centuries before they were first written down a few hundred years before the era of Plato and Socrates. Aesop may not have been Greek; there is circumstantial evidence that he was Ethiopian.

variety of contemporary intuition pumps, including some defective ones, and the goal will be to understand what they are good for, how they work, how to use them, and even how to make them.

Here's a short, simple example: the Whimsical Jailer. Every night he waits until all the prisoners are sound asleep and then he goes around unlocking all the doors, leaving them open for hours on end. Question: Are the prisoners free? Do they have an *opportunity* to leave? Not really. Why not? Here's another example: the Jewels in the Trashcan. There happens to be a fortune in jewelry discarded in the trashcan on the sidewalk that you stroll by one night. It might seem that you have a golden opportunity to become rich, except it isn't golden at all because it is a *bare* opportunity, one that you would be extremely unlikely to recognize and hence act on—or even consider. These two simple scenarios pump intuitions that might not otherwise be obvious: the importance of getting timely information about genuine opportunities, soon enough for the information to cause us to consider it in time to do something about it. In our eagerness to make "free" choices, uncaused—we like to think—by "external forces," we tend to forget that we shouldn't want to be cut off from all such forces; free will does not *abhor* our embedding in a rich causal context; it actually *requires* it.

I hope you feel that there is more to be said on that topic! These tiny intuition pumps raise an issue vividly, but they don't settle anything—yet. (A whole section will concentrate on free will later.) We need to become practiced in the art of treating such tools warily, watching where we step, and checking for pitfalls. If we think of an intuition pump as a carefully designed persuasion tool, we can see that it might repay us to *reverse engineer* the tool, checking out all the moving parts to see what they are doing.

When Doug Hofstadter and I composed *The Mind's I* back in 1982, he came up with just the right advice on this score: consider the intuition pump to be a tool with many settings, and "turn all the knobs" to see if the same intuitions still get pumped when you consider variations.

So let's identify, and turn, the knobs on the Whimsical Jailer. Assume—until proved otherwise—that every part has a function, and see what that function is by replacing it with another part, or transforming it slightly.

1. Every night
2. he waits
3. until all the prisoners
4. are sound asleep
5. and then he goes around unlocking
6. all the doors,
7. leaving them open for hours on end.

Here is one of many variations we could consider:

One night he ordered his guards to drug one of the prisoners and after they had done this they accidentally left the door of that prisoner's cell unlocked for an hour.

It changes the flavor of the scenario quite a lot, doesn't it? How? It still makes the main point (doesn't it?) but not as effectively. The big difference seems to be between being naturally asleep—you *might* wake up any minute—and being drugged or comatose. Another difference—"accidentally"—highlights the role of the intention or inadvertence on the part of the jailor or the guards. The repetition ("every night") seems to change the odds, in favor of the prisoners. When and why do the odds matter? How much would you pay *not* to have to participate in a lottery in which a million people have tickets and the "winner" is shot? How much would you pay *not* to have to play Russian roulette with a six-shooter? (Here we use one intuition pump to illuminate another, a trick to remember.)

Other knobs to turn are less obvious: The Diabolical Host secretly locks the bedroom doors of his houseguests while they sleep. The Hospital Manager, worried about the prospect of a fire, keeps the doors of all the rooms and wards unlocked at night, but she doesn't inform the patients, thinking they will sleep more soundly if they don't know. Or what if the prison is somewhat larger than usual, say, the size of Australia? You can't lock or unlock all the doors to Australia. What difference does that make?

This self-conscious wariness with which we should approach any intuition pump is itself an important tool for thinking, the philosophers' favorite tactic: *"going meta"*—thinking about thinking, talking about talking, reasoning about reasoning. Meta-language is the language we use to talk about another language, and meta-ethics is a bird's-eye view examination of ethical theories. As I once said to Doug, "Anything you can do I can do meta-." This whole book is, of course, an example of going meta: exploring how to think carefully about methods of thinking carefully (about methods of thinking carefully, etc.).* He recently (2007) offered a list of some of his own favorite small hand tools:

wild goose chases
tackiness
dirty tricks
sour grapes
elbow grease
feet of clay
loose cannons
crackpots
lip service
slam dunks
feedback

---

* The philosopher W. V. O. Quine (1960) called this *semantic ascent*, going *up* from talking about electrons or justice or horses or whatever to talking about *talking about* electrons or justice or horses or whatever. Sometimes people object to this move by philosophers ("With you folks, it's all just semantics!"), and sometimes the move is indeed useless or even bamboozling, but when it's needed, when people are talking past each other, or being fooled by tacit assumptions about what their own words mean, semantic ascent, or going meta, is the key to clarity.

If these expressions are familiar to you, they are not "just words" for you; each is an abstract cognitive tool, in the same way that *long division* or *finding-the-average* is a tool; each has a role to play in a broad spectrum of contexts, making it easier to formulate hypotheses to test, making it easier to recognize unnoticed patterns in the world, helping the user look for important similarities, and so forth. Every word in your vocabulary is a simple thinking tool, but some are more useful than others. If any of these expressions are not in your kit, you might want to acquire them; equipped with such tools you will be able to think thoughts that would otherwise be relatively hard to formulate. Of course, as the old saw has it, when your only tool is a hammer, everything looks like a nail, and each of these tools can be overused.

Let's look at just one of these: sour grapes. It comes from Aesop's fable "The Fox and the Grapes" and draws attention to how sometimes people pretend not to care about something they can't have by disparaging it. Look how much you can say about what somebody has just said by asking, simply, "Sour grapes?" It gets her to consider a possibility that might otherwise have gone unnoticed, and this might very effectively inspire her to revise her thinking, or reflect on the issue from a wider perspective—or it might very effectively insult her. (Tools can be used as weapons too.) So familiar is the moral of the story that you may have forgotten the tale leading up to it, and may have lost touch with the subtleties—if they matter, and sometimes they don't.

Acquiring tools and using them wisely are distinct skills, but you have to start by acquiring the tools, or making them yourself. Many of the thinking tools I will present here are my own inventions, but others I have acquired from others, and I will acknowledge their inventors in due course.* None of the tools on Doug's list are his

---

* Many of the passages in this book have been drawn from books and articles I have previously published, revised to make them more portable and versatile, fit for use in contexts other than the original—a feature of most good tools. For instance, the opening story about von Neumann appeared in my 1995 book *Darwin's Dangerous Idea*, and this discussion of Hofstadter's hand tools appeared in my 2009 *PNAS* paper, "Darwin's 'Strange Inversion of Reasoning.'" Instead of footnoting all of these, I provide a list of sources at the end of the book.

inventions, but he has contributed some fine specimens to my kit, such as **jootsing** and **sphexishness**.

Some of the most powerful thinking tools are mathematical, but aside from mentioning them, I will not devote much space to them because this is a book celebrating the power of *non*-mathematical tools, *informal* tools, the tools of prose and poetry, if you like, a power that scientists often underestimate. You can see why. First, there is a culture of scientific writing in research journals that favors—indeed insists on—an impersonal, stripped-down presentation of the issues with a minimum of flourish, rhetoric, and allusion. There is a good reason for the relentless drabness in the pages of our most serious scientific journals. As one of my doctoral examiners, the neuroanatomist J. Z. Young, wrote to me in 1965, in objecting to the somewhat fanciful prose in my dissertation at Oxford (in philosophy, not neuroanatomy), English was becoming the international language of science, and it behooves us native English-speakers to write works that can be read by "a patient Chinee [*sic*] with a good dictionary." The results of this self-imposed discipline speak for themselves: whether you are a Chinese, German, Brazilian—or even a French—scientist, you insist on publishing your most important work in English, bare-bones English, translatable with minimal difficulty, relying as little as possible on cultural allusions, nuances, word-play, and even metaphor. The level of mutual understanding achieved by this international system is invaluable, but there is a price to be paid: some of the thinking that has to be done apparently *requires* informal metaphor-mongering and imagination-tweaking, assaulting the barricades of closed minds with every trick in the book, and if some of this cannot be easily translated, then I will just have to hope for virtuoso translators on the one hand, and the growing fluency in English of the world's scientists on the other.

Another reason why scientists are often suspicious of theoretical discussions conducted in "mere words" is that they recognize that the task of criticizing an argument not formulated in mathematical equations is much trickier, and typically less conclusive. The language of mathematics is a reliable enforcer of cogency. It's like the net on the basketball hoop: it removes sources of disagreement and judgment about whether the ball went in. (Anyone who has played basketball on a playground court with a bare hoop knows how hard it can be to tell an air ball from a basket.) But sometimes the issues are just too slippery and baffling to be tamed by mathematics.

I have always figured that if I can't explain something I'm doing to a group of bright undergraduates, I don't really understand it myself, and that challenge has shaped everything I have written. Some philosophy professors yearn to teach advanced seminars only to graduate students. Not me. Graduate students are often too eager to prove to each other and to themselves that they are savvy operators, wielding the jargon of their trade with deft assurance, baffling outsiders (that's how they assure themselves that what they are doing requires expertise), and showing off their ability to pick their way through the most tortuous (and torturous) technical arguments without getting lost. Philosophy written for one's advanced graduate students and fellow experts is typically all but unreadable—and hence largely unread.

A curious side effect of my policy of trying to write arguments and explanations that can be readily understood by people outside philosophy departments is that there are philosophers who as a matter of "principle" won't take my arguments seriously! When I gave the John Locke Lectures at Oxford many years ago to a standing-room-only audience, a distinguished philosopher was heard to grumble as he left one of them that he was damned if he would learn anything from somebody who could attract non-philosophers to the Locke Lectures! True to his word, he never learned anything from me, so far as I can tell. I did not adjust my style and have never regretted paying the price. There is a time and a place in philosophy for rigorous arguments, with all the premises numbered and the inference rules named, but these do not often need to be paraded in public. We ask our graduate students to prove they can do it in their dissertations, and some never outgrow the habit, unfortunately. And to be fair, the opposite sin of high-flown

Continental rhetoric, larded with literary ornament and intimations of profundity, does philosophy no favors either. If I had to choose, I'd take the hard-bitten analytic logic-chopper over the deep purple sage every time. At least you can usually figure out what the logic-chopper is talking about and what would count as being wrong.

The middle ground, roughly halfway between poetry and mathematics, is where philosophers can make their best contributions, I believe, yielding genuine clarifications of deeply puzzling problems. There are no feasible algorithms for doing this kind of work. Since *everything* is up for grabs, one chooses one's fixed points with due caution. As often as not, an "innocent" assumption accepted without notice on all sides turns out to be the culprit. Exploring such treacherous conceptual territories is greatly aided by using thinking tools devised on the spot to clarify the alternative paths and shed light on their prospects.

These thinking tools seldom establish a *fixed* fixed point—a solid "axiom" for all future inquiry—but rather introduce a worthy *candidate* for a fixed point, a likely constraint on future inquiry, but itself subject to revision or jettisoning altogether if somebody can figure out why. No wonder many scientists have no taste at all for philosophy; everything is up for grabs, nothing is take-it-to-the-bank secure, and the intricate webs of argument constructed to connect these "fixed" points hang provisionally in the air, untethered to clear foundations of empirical proof or falsification. So these scientists turn their backs on philosophy and get on with their work, but at the cost of leaving some of the most important and fascinating questions unconsidered. "Don't ask! Don't tell! It's premature to tackle the problem of consciousness, of free will, of morality, of meaning and creativity!" But few can live with such abstemiousness, and in recent years scientists have set out on a gold rush of sorts into these shunned regions. Seduced by sheer curiosity (or, sometimes, perhaps, a yearning for celebrity), they embark on the big questions and soon discover how hard it is to make progress on them. I must confess that one of the delicious, if guilty, pleasures I enjoy is watching eminent scientists, who only a few years ago expressed withering contempt for philosophy,* stumble embarrassingly in their own efforts to set the world straight on these matters with a few briskly argued extrapolations from their own scientific research. Even better is when they request, and acknowledge, a little help from us philosophers.

In the first section that follows, I present a dozen general, all-purpose tools, and then in subsequent sections I group the rest of the entries not by the type of tool but by the topic where the tool works best, turning first to the most fundamental philosophical topic—meaning, or content—followed by evolution, consciousness, and free will. A few of the tools I present are actual software, friendly devices that can do for your naked imagination what telescopes and microscopes can do for your naked eye.

Along the way, I will also introduce some false friends, tools that blow smoke instead of shining light. I needed a term for these hazardous devices, and found *le mot juste* in my sailing experience. Many sailors enjoy the nautical terms that baffle landlubbers: port and starboard, gudgeon and pintle, shrouds and spreaders, cringles and fairleads, and all the rest. A running joke on a boat I once sailed on involved making up false definitions for these terms. So a *binnacle* was a marine growth on compasses, and a *mast tang* was a citrus beverage enjoyed aloft; a *snatch block* was a female defensive maneuver, and a *boom crutch* was an explosive orthopedic device. I've never since been able to think of a boom crutch—a removable wooden stand on which the boom rests when the sail is lowered—without a momentary image of *kapow!* in some poor fellow's armpit. So I chose the term as my name for thinking tools that backfire, the ones that only *seem* to aid in understanding but that actually spread darkness and confusion instead of light. Scattered through these chapters are a variety of boom crutches with suitable warning labels, and examples

---

* Two of the best: "Philosophy is to science what pigeons are to statues," and "Philosophy is to science as pornography is to sex: it is cheaper, easier and some people prefer it." (I'll leave these unattributed, but their authors can choose to claim them if they wish.)

to deplore. And I close with some further reflections on what it is like to be a philosopher, in case anybody wants to know, including some advice from Uncle Dan to any of you who might have discovered a taste for this way of investigating the world and wonder whether you are cut out for a career in the field.

II.
A DOZEN GENERAL
THINKING TOOLS

M ost of the thinking tools in this book are quite specialized, made
to order for application to a particular topic and even a particular controversy within the topic. But before we turn to these intuition
pumps, here are a few general-purpose thinking tools, ideas and
practices that have proved themselves in a wide variety of contexts.

1. MAKING MISTAKES

> He who says "Better to go without belief forever than believe
> a lie!" merely shows his own preponderant private horror of
> becoming a dupe. . . . It is like a general informing his soldiers
> that it is better to keep out of battle forever than to risk a
> single wound. Not so are victories either over enemies or over
> nature gained. Our errors are surely not such awfully solemn
> things. In a world where we are so certain to incur them in
> spite of all our caution, a certain lightness of heart seems
> healthier than this excessive nervousness on their behalf.
>
> —WILLIAM JAMES, "The Will to Believe"

> If you've made up your mind to test a theory, or you want
> to explain some idea, you should always decide to publish it
> whichever way it comes out. If we only publish results of a
> certain kind, we can make the argument look good. We must
> publish both kinds of results.
>
> —RICHARD FEYNMAN, *"Surely You're Joking, Mr. Feynman!"*

Scientists often ask me why philosophers devote so much of their effort to teaching and learning the history of their field. Chemists typically get by with only a rudimentary knowledge of the history of chemistry, picked up along the way, and many molecular biologists, it seems, are not even curious about what happened in biology before about 1950. My answer is that the history of philosophy is in large measure the history of very smart people making very tempting mistakes, and if you don't know the history, you are doomed to making the same darn mistakes all over again. That's why we teach the history of the field to our students, and scientists who blithely ignore philosophy do so at their own risk. There is no such thing as philosophy-free science, just science that has been conducted without any consideration of its underlying philosophical assumptions. The smartest or luckiest of the scientists sometimes manage to avoid the pitfalls quite adroitly (perhaps they are "natural born philosophers"—or are as smart as they think they are), but they are the rare exceptions. Not that professional philosophers don't make—and even defend—the old mistakes too. If the questions weren't hard, they wouldn't be worth working on.

Sometimes you don't just want to *risk* making mistakes; you actually want to make them—if only to give you something clear and detailed to fix. Making mistakes is the key to making progress. Of course there are times when it is really important not to make any mistakes—ask any surgeon or airline pilot. But it is less widely appreciated that there are also times when making mistakes is the only way to go. Many of the students who arrive at very competitive universities pride themselves in not making mistakes—after all, that's how they've come so much farther than their classmates, or so they have been led to believe. I often find that I have to encourage them to *cultivate the habit* of making mistakes, the best learning opportunities of all. They get "writer's block" and waste hours forlornly wandering back and forth on the starting line. "Blurt it out!" I urge them. Then they have something on the page to work with.

We philosophers are mistake specialists. (I know, it sounds like a bad joke, but hear me out.) While other disciplines specialize in getting the right answers to their defining questions, we philosophers specialize in all the ways there are of getting things so mixed up, so deeply wrong, that nobody is even sure what the right *questions* are, let alone the answers. Asking the wrongs questions risks setting any inquiry off on the wrong foot. Whenever that happens, this is a job for philosophers! Philosophy—in every field of inquiry—is what you have to do until you figure out what questions you should have been asking in the first place. Some people hate it when that happens. They would rather take their questions off the rack, all nicely tailored and pressed and cleaned and ready to answer. Those who feel that way can do physics or mathematics or history or biology. There's plenty of work for everybody. We philosophers have a taste for working on the questions that need to be straightened out before they can be answered. It's not for everyone. But try it, you might like it.

In the course of this book I am going to jump vigorously on what I claim are other people's mistakes, but I want to assure you that I am an experienced mistake-maker myself. I've made some dillies, and hope to make a lot more. One of my goals in this book is to help you make *good* mistakes, the kind that light the way for everybody.

First the theory, and then the practice. Mistakes are not just opportunities for learning; they are, in an important sense, the *only* opportunity for learning or making something truly new. Before there can be learning, there must be learners. There are only two non-miraculous ways for learners to come into existence: they must either evolve or be designed and built by learners that evolved. Biological evolution proceeds by a grand, inexorable process of trial and error—and without the *errors* the trials wouldn't accomplish anything. As Gore Vidal once said, "It is not enough to succeed. Others must fail." Trials can be either *blind* or *foresighted*. You, who know a lot, but not the answer to the question at hand, can take leaps—foresighted leaps. You can look before you leap, and hence be *somewhat* guided from the outset by what you already know. *You* need not be guessing at random, but don't look down your nose at random guesses; among its wonderful products is . . . you!

Evolution is one of the central themes of this book, as of all my books, for the simple reason that it is the central, enabling process not only of life but also of knowledge and learning and understanding. If you attempt to make sense of the world of ideas and meanings, free will and morality, art and science and even philosophy itself without a sound and quite detailed knowledge of evolution, you have one hand tied behind your back. Later, we will look at some tools designed to help you think about some of the more challenging questions of evolution, but here we need to lay a foundation. For evolution, which knows nothing, the steps into novelty are blindly taken by mutations, which are random copying "errors" in DNA. Most of these typographical errors are of no consequence, since nothing reads them! They are as inconsequential as the rough drafts you didn't, or don't, hand in to the teacher for grading. The DNA of a species is rather like a recipe for building a new body, and most of the DNA is never actually consulted in the building process. (It is often called "junk DNA" for just that reason.) In the DNA sequences that do get read and acted upon during development, the vast majority of mutations are harmful; many, in fact, are swiftly fatal. Since the majority of "expressed" mutations are deleterious, the process of natural selection actually works to keep the mutation rate very low. Each of you has very, very good copying machinery in your cells. For instance, you have roughly a trillion cells in your body, and each cell has either a perfect or an *almost* perfect copy of your genome, over three billion symbols long, the recipe for you that first came into existence when your parents' egg and sperm joined forces. Fortunately, the copying machinery does not achieve perfect success, for if it did, evolution would eventually grind to a halt, its sources of novelty dried up. Those tiny blemishes, those "imperfections" in the process, are the source of all the wonderful design and complexity in the living world. (I can't resist adding: if anything deserves to be called Original Sin, these copying mistakes do.)

The chief trick to making good mistakes is not to hide them—especially not from yourself. Instead of turning away in denial when you make a mistake, you should become a connoisseur of your own mistakes, turning them over in your mind as if they were works of art, which in a way they are. The fundamental reaction to any mistake ought to be this: "Well, I won't do *that* again!" Natural selection doesn't actually think the thought; it just wipes out the goofers before they can reproduce; natural selection won't do *that* again, at least not as often. Animals that can learn—learn not to make that noise, touch that wire, eat that food—have *something* with a similar selective force in their brains. (B. F. Skinner and the behaviorists understood the need for this and called it "reinforcement" learning; *that* response is not reinforced and suffers "extinction.") We human beings carry matters to a much more swift and efficient level. We can actually *think the thought*, reflecting on what we have just done: "Well, I won't do *that* again!" And when we reflect, we confront directly the problem that must be solved by any mistake-maker: what, exactly, is *that*? What was it about what I just did that got me into all this trouble? The trick is to take advantage of the particular details of the mess you've made, so that your next attempt will be informed by it and not just another blind stab in the dark.

We have all heard the forlorn refrain "Well, it seemed like a good idea at the time!" This phrase has come to stand for the rueful reflection of an idiot, a sign of stupidity, but in fact we should appreciate it as a pillar of wisdom. Any being, any agent, who can truly say, "Well, it seemed like a good idea at the time!" is standing on the threshold of brilliance. We human beings pride ourselves on our intelligence, and one of its hallmarks is that we can *remember our previous thinking*, and reflect on it—on how it seemed, on why it was tempting in the first place, and then about what went wrong. I know of no evidence to suggest that any other species on the planet can actually think this thought. If they could, they would be almost as smart as we are.

So when you make a mistake, you should learn to take a deep breath, grit your teeth, and then *examine* your own recollections of the mistake as ruthlessly and as dispassionately as you can manage. It's not easy. The natural human reaction to making a mistake is embarrassment and anger (we are never angrier than when we are angry at ourselves), and you have to work hard to overcome these emotional reactions. Try to acquire the weird practice of savoring your mistakes, delighting in uncovering the strange quirks that led you astray. Then, once you have sucked out all the goodness to be gained from having made them, you can cheerfully set them behind you, and go on to the next big opportunity. But that is not enough: you should actively seek out opportunities to make grand mistakes, just so you can then recover from them.

At its simplest, this is a technique we all learned in grade school. Recall how strange and forbidding long division seemed at first: You were confronted by two imponderably large numbers, and you had to figure out how to start. Does the divisor go into the dividend six or seven or eight times? Who knew? You didn't have to know; you just had to take a stab at it, whichever number you liked, and check out the result. I remember being almost shocked when I was told I should start by just "making a guess." Wasn't this *mathematics*? You weren't supposed to play guessing games in such a serious business, were you? But eventually I appreciated, as we all do, the beauty of the tactic. If the chosen number turned out to be too small, you increased it and started over; if too large, you decreased it. The good thing about long division was that it always worked, even if you were maximally stupid in making your first choice, in which case it just took a little longer.

This general technique of making a more-or-less educated guess, working out its implications, and using the result to make a correction for the next phase has found many applications. A key element of this tactic is making a mistake that is clear and precise enough to have definite implications. Before GPS came along, navigators used to determine their position at sea by first making a guess about where they were (they made a guess about *exactly* what their latitude and longitude were), and then calculating exactly how high in the sky the sun would appear to be if that were—by an incredible coincidence—their actual position. When they used this method, they didn't expect to hit the nail on the head. They didn't have to. Instead they then measured the actual elevation angle of the sun (exactly) and compared the two values. With a little more trivial calculation, this told them how big a correction, and in what direction, to make to their initial guess.* In

---

* This doesn't give navigators their actual position, a point on the globe, but it does give them a *line*. They are somewhere on that *line of position* (LOP). Wait a few hours until the sun has moved on quite a bit. Then choose a point on your LOP, any point, and calculate how high the sun would be now if that point were exactly the right choice. Make the observation, compare the results, apply the correction, and get another LOP. Where it crosses your first LOP is the point where you are. The sun will have changed not only its height but also its compass bearing during those hours so the lines will cross at a pretty good angle. In practice, you are usually moving during those few hours, so you advance your first LOP in the direction you are moving by calculating your speed and drawing an advanced LOP parallel to the original LOP. In real life everything has a bit of slop in it, so you try to get three different

such a method it is useful to make a pretty good guess the first time, but it doesn't matter that it is bound to be mistaken; the important thing is to make the mistake, in glorious detail, so there is something serious to correct. (A GPS device uses the same guess-and-fix-it strategy to locate itself relative to the overhead satellites.)

The more complex a problem you're facing, of course, the more difficult the analysis is. This is known to researchers in artificial intelligence (AI) as the problem of "credit assignment" (it could as well be called blame assignment). Figuring out what to credit and what to blame is one of the knottiest problems in AI, and it is also a problem faced by natural selection. Every organism on the earth dies sooner or later after one complicated life story or another. How on earth could natural selection *see through* the fog of all these details in order to figure out what positive factors to "reward" with offspring and what negative factors to "punish" with childless death? Can it really be that some of our ancestors' siblings died childless *because their eyelids were the wrong shape*? If not, how could the process of natural selection explain why our eyelids came to have the excellent shapes they have? Part of the answer is familiar: following the old adage "If it ain't broke, don't fix it," leave almost all your old, conservative design solutions in place and take your risks with a safety net in place. Natural selection automatically conserves *whatever has worked up to now*, and fearlessly explores innovations large and small; the large ones almost always lead immediately to death. A terrible waste, but nobody's counting. Our eyelids were mostly designed by natural selection long before there were human beings or even primates or even mammals. They've had more than a hundred million years to reach the shape they are today, with only a few minor touch-ups in the last six million years, since we shared a common ancestor with the chimpanzees and the bonobos. Another part of the answer is that natural selection works

LOPs. If they all intersect in exactly the same point, you're either incredibly good or incredibly lucky, but more commonly they form a small triangle, called a *cocked hat*. You consider yourself in the middle of the cocked hat, and that's your new calculated position.

with large numbers of cases, where even minuscule advantages show up statistically and can be automatically accumulated. (Other parts of the answer are technicalities beyond this elementary discussion.)

Here is a technique that card magicians—at least the best of them—exploit with amazing results. (I don't expect to incur the wrath of the magicians for revealing this trick to you, since this is not a *particular* trick but a deep general principle.) A good card magician knows many tricks that depend on luck—they don't always work, or even often work. There are some effects—they can hardly be called tricks—that might work only once in a thousand times! Here is what you do: You start by telling the audience you are going to perform *a* trick, and without telling them what trick you are doing, you go for the one-in-a-thousand effect. It almost never works, of course, so you glide seamlessly into a second try—for an effect that works about one time in a hundred, perhaps—and when it too fails (as it almost always will), you slide gracefully into effect number 3, which works only about one time in ten, so you'd better be ready with effect number 4, which works half the time (let's say). If all else fails (and by this time, *usually* one of the earlier safety nets will have kept you out of this worst case), you have a failsafe effect, which won't impress the crowd very much but at least it's a surefire trick. In the course of a whole performance, you will be very unlucky indeed if you always have to rely on your final safety net, and whenever you achieve one of the higher-flying effects, the audience will be stupefied. "Impossible! How on earth could you have known which was my card?" *Aha!* You didn't know, but you had a cute way of taking a hopeful stab in the dark that paid off. By hiding all the "mistake" cases from view—the trials that didn't pan out—you create a "miracle."

Evolution works the same way: all the dumb mistakes tend to be invisible, so all we see is a stupendous string of triumphs. For instance, the vast majority—way over 90 percent—of all the creatures that have ever lived died childless, but *not a single one of your ancestors* suffered that fate. Talk about a line of charmed lives!

One big difference between the discipline of science and the discipline of stage magic is that while magicians conceal their false starts from the audience as best they can, in science you make your mistakes in public. You show them off so that everybody can learn from them. This way, you get the benefit of everybody else's experience, and not just your own idiosyncratic path through the space of mistakes. (The physicist Wolfgang Pauli famously expressed his contempt for the work of a colleague as "not even wrong." A clear falsehood shared with critics is better than vague mush.) This, by the way, is another reason why we humans are so much smarter than every other species. It is not so much that our brains are bigger or more powerful, or even that we have the knack of reflecting on our own past errors, but that we *share the benefits* that our individual brains have won by their individual histories of trial and error.*

I am amazed at how many really smart people don't understand that you can make big mistakes in public and emerge none the worse for it. I know distinguished researchers who will go to preposterous lengths to avoid having to acknowledge that they were wrong about something. They have never noticed, apparently, that the earth does not swallow people up when they say, "Oops, you're right. I guess I made a mistake." Actually, people love it when somebody admits to making a mistake. All kinds of people love pointing out mistakes. Generous-spirited people appreciate your giving them the opportunity to help, and acknowledging it when they succeed in helping you; mean-spirited people enjoy showing you up. Let them! Either way we all win.

Of course, in general, people do not enjoy correcting the *stupid* mistakes of others. You have to have something *worth* correcting, something original to be right or wrong about, something that

---

* That is the ideal, but we don't always live up to it, human nature being what it is. One of the recognized but unsolved problems with current scientific practice is that negative results—experiments that didn't uncover what they were designed to uncover—are not published often enough. This flaw in the system is famously explored and deplored in Feynman's "Cargo Cult Lecture," a commencement address he gave at Caltech in 1974, reprinted in Feynman, 1985.

requires constructing the sort of pyramid of risky thinking we saw in the card magician's tricks. Carefully building on the works of others, you can get yourself cantilevered out on a limb of your own. And then there's a surprise bonus: if you are one of the big risk-takers, people will get a kick out of correcting your occasional stupid mistakes, which show that you're not so special, you're a regular bungler like the rest of us. I know extremely careful philosophers who have never—apparently—made a mistake in their work. They tend not to get a whole lot accomplished, but what little they produce is pristine, if not venturesome. Their specialty is pointing out the mistakes of others, and this can be a valuable service, but nobody excuses *their* minor errors with a friendly chuckle. It is fair to say, unfortunately, that their best work often gets overshadowed and neglected, drowned out by the passing bandwagons driven by bolder thinkers. In chapter 76 we'll see that the generally good practice of making bold mistakes has other unfortunate side effects as well. Meta-advice: don't take *any* advice too seriously!

2. "BY PARODY OF REASONING": USING *REDUCTIO AD ABSURDUM*

The crowbar of rational inquiry, the great lever that enforces consistency, is *reductio ad absurdum*—literally, reduction (of the argument) to absurdity. You take the assertion or conjecture at issue and see if you can pry any contradictions (or just preposterous implications) out of it. If you can, that proposition has to be discarded or sent back to the shop for retooling. We do this all the time without bothering to display the underlying logic: "If that's a bear, then bears have antlers!" or "He won't get here in time for supper unless he can fly like Superman." When the issue is a tricky theoretical controversy, the crowbar gets energetically wielded, but here the distinction between fair criticism and refutation by caricature is hard to draw. Can your opponent really be so stupid as to believe the proposition you have just reduced to absurdity with a few deft moves? I once graded a student paper that had a serendipitous misspelling, replacing "parity" with "parody," creating the delicious phrase "by parody of reasoning," a handy name, I think, for misbegotten *reductio ad absurdum* arguments, which are all too common in the rough-and-tumble of scientific and philosophical controversy.

I recall attending a seminar on cognitive science at MIT some years ago, conducted by the linguist Noam Chomsky and the philosopher Jerry Fodor, in which the audience was regularly regaled with hilarious refutations of cognitive scientists from elsewhere who did not meet with their approval. On this day, Roger Schank, the director of Yale University's artificial intelligence laboratory, was the *bête noir*, and if you went by Chomsky's version, Schank had to be some kind of flaming idiot. I knew Roger and his work pretty well, and though I had disagreements of my own with it, I thought that Noam's version was hardly recognizable, so I raised my hand and suggested that perhaps he didn't appreciate some of the subtleties of Roger's position. "Oh no," Noam insisted, chuckling. "This is what he holds!" And he went back to his demolition job, to the great amusement of those in the room. After a few more minutes of this I intervened again. "I have to admit," I said, "that the views you are criticizing are simply preposterous," and Noam grinned affirmatively, "but then what I want to know is why you're wasting your time and ours criticizing such junk." It was a pretty effective pail of cold water.

What about my own *reductios* of the views of others? Have they been any fairer? Here are a few to consider. You decide. The French neuroscientist Jean-Pierre Changeux and I once debated neuroscientist Sir John Eccles and philosopher Sir Karl Popper about consciousness and the brain at a conference in Venice. Changeux and I were the materialists (who maintain that the mind *is* the brain), and Popper and Eccles the dualists (who claim that a mind is not a material thing like a brain, but some other, second kind of entity that interacts with the brain). Eccles had won the Nobel Prize many years earlier for the discovery of the synapse, the microscopic gap between neurons that glutamate molecules and other neurotransmitters and neuromodulators cross trillions of times a day. According to Eccles, the brain was like a mighty pipe organ and the trillions of synapses composed the keyboards. The immaterial mind—the immortal soul, according to Eccles, a devout Catholic—played the synapses by somehow encouraging quantum-level nudges of the glutamate molecules. "Forget all that theoretical discussion of neural networks and the like; it's irrelevant rubbish," he said. "The mind is in the glutamate!" When it was my turn to speak, I said I wanted to be sure I had understood his position. If the mind was in the glutamate and I poured a bowl of glutamate down the drain, would that not be murder? "Well," he replied, somewhat taken aback, "it would be very hard to tell, wouldn't it?"*

---

* My other indelible memory of that conference was of Popper's dip in the Grand Canal. He slipped getting out of the motorboat at the boathouse of the Isola di San Giorgio and fell

You would think that Sir John Eccles, the Catholic dualist, and Francis Crick, the atheist materialist, would have very little in common, aside from their Nobel Prizes. But at least for a while their respective views of consciousness shared a dubious oversimplification. Many nonscientists don't appreciate how wonderful oversimplifications can be in science; they can cut through the hideous complexity with a working model that is *almost* right, postponing the messy details until later. Arguably the best use of "over"-simplification in the history of science was the end run by Crick and James Watson to find the structure of DNA while Linus Pauling and others were trudging along trying to make sense of all the details. Crick was all for trying the bold stroke just in case it solved the problem in one fell swoop, but of course that doesn't always work. I was once given the opportunity to demonstrate this at one of Crick's famous teas at La Jolla. These afternoon sessions were informal lab meetings where visitors could raise issues and participate in the general discussion. On this particular occasion Crick made a bold pronouncement: it had recently been shown that neurons in cortical area V4 "cared about" (responded differentially to) color. And then he proposed a strikingly simple hypothesis: the conscious experience of red, for instance, *was* activity in the relevant red-sensitive neurons of that retinal area. *Hmm*, I wondered. "Are you saying, then, that if we were to remove some of those red-sensitive neurons and keep them alive in a petri dish, and stimulate them with a microelectrode, there would be *consciousness of red* in the petri dish?" One way of responding to a

---

feet first into the canal, submerged up to his knees before being plucked out and set on the pier by two nimble boatmen. The hosts were mortified and ready to rush back to the hotel to get nonagenarian Sir Karl a dry pair of trousers, but the pants he was wearing was the only pair he'd brought—and he was scheduled to lead off the conference in less than half an hour! Italian ingenuity took over, and within about five minutes I enjoyed an unforgettable sight: Sir Karl, sitting regally on a small chair in the exact middle of a marble-floored, domed room (Palladio designed it) surrounded by at least half a dozen young women in miniskirts, on their knees, plying his trouser legs with their hairdryers. The extension cords stretched radially to the walls, making of the tableau a sort of multicolored human daisy, with Sir Karl, unperturbed but unsmiling, in the center. Fifteen minutes later he was dry and pounding his fist on the podium to add emphasis to his dualistic vision.

proffered *reductio* is to grasp the nettle and endorse the conclusion, a move I once dubbed *outsmarting*, since the Australian philosopher J. J. C. Smart was famous for saying that yes, according to his theory of ethics, it *was* sometimes right to frame and hang an innocent man! Crick decided to outsmart me. "Yes! It would be an isolated instance of consciousness of red!" Whose consciousness of red? He didn't say. He later refined his thinking on this score, but still, he and neuroscientist Christof Koch, in their quest for what they called the NCC (the neural correlates of consciousness), never quite abandoned their allegiance to this idea.

Perhaps yet another encounter will bring out better what is problematic about the idea of a smidgen of consciousness in a dish. The physicist and mathematician Roger Penrose and the anesthesiologist Stuart Hameroff teamed up to produce a theory of consciousness that depended, not on glutamate, but on quantum effects in the microtubules of neurons. (Microtubules are tubular protein chains that serve as girders and highways inside the cytoplasm of all cells, not just neurons.) At Tucson II, the second international conference on the science of consciousness, after Hameroff's exposition of this view, I asked from the audience, "Stuart, you're an anesthesiologist; have you ever assisted in one of those dramatic surgeries that replaces a severed hand or arm?" No, he had not, but he knew about them. "Tell me if I'm missing something, Stuart, but given your theory, if you were the anesthesiologist in such an operation you would feel morally obliged to anesthetize the severed hand as it lay on its bed of ice, right? After all, the microtubules in the nerves of the hand would be doing their thing, just like the microtubules in the rest of the nervous system, and that hand would be in great pain, would it not?" The look on Stuart's face suggested that this had never occurred to him. The idea that consciousness (of red, of pain, of anything) is some sort of network property, something that involves coordinated activities in myriads of neurons, initially may not be very attractive, but these attempts at *reductios* may help people see why it should be taken seriously.

3. RAPOPORT'S RULES

Just how charitable are you supposed to be when criticizing the views of an opponent? If there are *obvious* contradictions in the opponent's case, then of course you should point them out, forcefully. If there are somewhat hidden contradictions, you should carefully expose them to view—and then dump on them. But the search for hidden contradictions often crosses the line into nitpicking, sea-lawyering,[*] and—as we have seen—outright parody. The thrill of the chase and the conviction that your opponent *has* to be harboring a confusion somewhere encourages uncharitable interpretation, which gives you an easy target to attack. But such easy targets are typically irrelevant to the real issues at stake and simply waste everybody's time and patience, even if they give amusement to your supporters. The best antidote I know for this tendency to caricature one's opponent is a list of rules promulgated many years ago by the social psychologist and game theorist Anatol Rapoport (creator of the winning Tit-for-Tat strategy in Robert Axelrod's legendary prisoner's dilemma tournament).[†]

How to compose a successful critical commentary:

1. You should attempt to re-express your target's position so clearly, vividly, and fairly that your target says, "Thanks, I wish I'd thought of putting it that way."

---

[*] Maritime law is notoriously complicated, strewn with hidden traps and escape clauses that only an expert, a *sea lawyer*, can keep track of, so *sea-lawyering* is using technicalities to evade responsibility or assign blame to others.
[†] The Axelrod tournament (Axelrod and Hamilton, 1981; Axelrod, 1984) opened up the blossoming field of theoretical research on the evolution of altruism. I give an introductory account in *Darwin's Dangerous Idea* (Dennett, 1995, pp. 479–480), and in more recent times there has been an explosion of variations, both simulations and experiments, in laboratories around the world. Rapoport's wonderfully simple implementation of the idea "I won't hit you if you don't hit me" is the seed from which all the later studies and models have grown.

2. You should list any points of agreement (especially if they are not matters of general or widespread agreement).
3. You should mention anything you have learned from your target.
4. Only then are you permitted to say so much as a word of rebuttal or criticism.

One immediate effect of following these rules is that your targets will be a receptive audience for your criticism: you have already shown that you understand their positions as well as they do, and have demonstrated good judgment (you agree with them on some important matters and have even been persuaded by something they said).[*]

Following Rapoport's Rules is always, for me at least, something of a struggle. Some targets, quite frankly, don't deserve such respectful attention, and—I admit—it can be sheer joy to skewer and roast them. But when it is called for, and it works, the results are gratifying. I was particularly diligent in my attempt to do justice to Robert Kane's (1996) brand of incompatibilism (a view about free will with which I profoundly disagree) in my book *Freedom Evolves* (2003), and I treasure the response he wrote to me after I had sent him the draft chapter:

> . . . In fact, I like it a lot, our differences notwithstanding. The treatment of my view is extensive and generally fair, far more so than one usually gets from critics. You convey the complexity of my view and the seriousness of my efforts to address difficult questions rather than merely sweeping them

---

[*] The formulation of Rapoport's Rules here is my own, done from memory of correspondence with Rapoport many years ago, now apparently lost. Samuel Ruth recently pointed out to me that the original source of Rapoport's Rules is in his book *Fights, Games, and Debates* (1960) and his paper "Three Modes of Conflict" (1961), which articulates rule 1, attributing it to Carl Rogers, and variations on the rest of the rules. My version is somewhat more portable and versatile.

under the rug. And for this, as well as the extended treatment, I am grateful.

Other recipients of my Rapoport-driven attention have been less cordial. The fairer the criticism seems, the harder to bear in some cases. It is worth reminding yourself that a heroic attempt to find a defensible interpretation of an author, if it comes up empty, can be even more devastating than an angry hatchet job. I recommend it.

4. STURGEON'S LAW

The science-fiction author Ted Sturgeon, speaking at the World Science Fiction Convention in Philadelphia in September 1953, said,

> When people talk about the mystery novel, they mention *The Maltese Falcon* and *The Big Sleep*. When they talk about the western, they say there's *The Way West* and *Shane*. But when they talk about science fiction, they call it "that Buck Rogers stuff," and they say "ninety percent of science fiction is crud." Well, they're right. Ninety percent of science fiction is crud. But then ninety percent of everything is crud, and it's the ten percent that isn't crud that is important, and the ten percent of science fiction that isn't crud is as good as or better than anything being written anywhere.

Sturgeon's Law is usually put a little less decorously: *Ninety percent of everything is crap.* Ninety percent of experiments in molecular biology, 90 percent of poetry, 90 percent of philosophy books, 90 percent of peer-reviewed articles in mathematics—and so forth—is crap. Is that true? Well, maybe it's an exaggeration, but let's agree that there is a lot of mediocre work done in every field. (Some curmudgeons say it's more like 99 percent, but let's not get into that game.) A good moral to draw from this observation is that when you want to criticize a field, a genre, a discipline, an art form, . . . *don't waste your time and ours hooting at the crap!* Go after the good stuff, or leave it alone. This advice is often ignored by ideologues intent on destroying the reputation of analytic philosophy, evolutionary psychology, sociology, cultural anthropology, macroeconomics, plastic surgery, improvisational theater, television sitcoms, philosophical theology, massage therapy, you name it. Let's stipulate at the outset that there is a great deal of deplorable, stupid, second-rate stuff out there, of all sorts. Now, in order not to waste your time and try our patience, make sure you concentrate on the best stuff you can find, the flagship examples extolled by the leaders of the field, the prize-winning entries, not the dregs. Notice that this is closely related to Rapoport's Rules: unless you are a comedian whose main purpose is to make people laugh at ludicrous buffoonery, spare us the caricature. This is particularly true, I find, when the target is philosophers. The very best theories and analyses of *any* philosopher, from the greatest, most perceptive sages of ancient Greece to the intellectual heroes of the recent past (Bertrand Russell, Ludwig Wittgenstein, John Dewey, Jean Paul Sartre—to name four very different thinkers), can be made to look like utter idiocy—or tedious nitpicking—with a few deft tweaks. Yuck, yuck. Don't do it. The only one you'll discredit is yourself.

5. OCCAM'S RAZOR

Attributed to William of Ockham (or Occam), the fourteenth-century logician and philosopher, this thinking tool is actually a much older rule of thumb. A Latin name for it is *lex parsimoniae*, the law of parsimony. It is usually put into English as the maxim "Do not multiply entities beyond necessity." The idea is straightforward: don't concoct a complicated, extravagant theory if you've got a simpler one (containing fewer ingredients, fewer entities) that handles the phenomenon just as well. If exposure to extremely cold air can account for all the symptoms of frostbite, don't postulate unobserved "snow germs" or "arctic microbes." Kepler's laws explain the orbits of the planets; we have no need to hypothesize pilots guiding the planets from control panels hidden under the surface. This much is uncontroversial, but extensions of the principle have not always met with agreement.

Conwy Lloyd Morgan, a nineteenth-century British psychologist, extended the idea to cover attributions of mentality to animals. Lloyd Morgan's Canon of Parsimony advises us not to attribute fancy minds to insects, fish, and even dolphins, dogs, and cats if their behavior can be explained in simpler terms:

> In no case is an animal activity to be interpreted in terms of higher psychological processes, if it can be fairly interpreted in terms of processes which stand lower in the scale of psychological evolution and development. [1894, p. 128]

Overused, this can be seen as enjoining us to treat all animals and even human beings as having brains but no minds. As we shall see, the tensions that arise when minds are the topic are not well settled by absolute prohibitions.

One of the least impressive attempts to apply Occam's Razor to a gnarly problem is the claim (and provoked counterclaims) that postulating a God as creator of the universe is simpler, more parsimonious, than the alternatives. How could postulating something supernatural and incomprehensible be parsimonious? It strikes me as the height of extravagance, but perhaps there are clever ways of rebutting that suggestion. I don't want to argue about it; Occam's Razor is, after all, just a rule of thumb, a frequently useful suggestion. The prospect of turning it into a Metaphysical Principle or Fundamental Requirement of Rationality that could bear the weight of proving or disproving the existence of God in one fell swoop is simply ludicrous. It would be like trying to disprove a theorem of quantum mechanics by showing that it contradicted the axiom "Don't put all your eggs in one basket."

Some thinkers have carried Occam's Razor to drastic extremes, using it to deny the existence of time, matter, numbers, holes, dollars, software, and so on. One of the earliest ultra-stingy thinkers was the ancient Greek philosopher Parmenides, whose catalogue of existing things was minimal indeed. As a student of mine memorably wrote on an exam, "Parmenides is the one who said, 'There's just one thing—and I'm not it.'" I hate to say it, but that does seem to be what Parmenides was trying to tell us. No doubt it loses something in translation. We philosophers get used to taking such ideas seriously if only because we never can tell when a "crazy" idea is going to turn out to be unfairly and unwisely judged, a victim of failure of imagination.

6. OCCAM'S BROOM

The molecular biologist Sidney Brenner recently invented a delicious play on Occam's Razor, introducing the new term *Occam's Broom*, to describe the process in which inconvenient facts are whisked under the rug by intellectually dishonest champions of one theory or another. This is our first boom crutch, an *anti-thinking* tool, and you should keep your eyes peeled for it. The practice is particularly insidious when used by propagandists who direct their efforts at the lay public, because like Sherlock Holmes's famous clue about the dog that *didn't* bark in the night, the *absence* of a fact that has been swept off the scene by Occam's Broom is unnoticeable except by experts. For instance, creationists invariably leave out the wealth of embarrassing evidence that their "theories" can't handle, and to a nonbiologist their carefully crafted accounts can be quite convincing simply because the lay reader can't see what *isn't there*.

How on earth can you keep on the lookout for something invisible? Get some help from the experts. Stephen C. Meyer's *Signature in the Cell* (2009) purports to expose the systematic impossibility of life having a natural (nonsupernatural) origin, and gives what seems—even to a relatively well-informed reader—to be a fair and exhaustive survey of the theories and models being worked on around the world, showing how irredeemably hopeless they all are. So persuasive is Meyer's case that in November 2009 the eminent philosopher Thomas Nagel declared it his Best Book of the Year in London's *Times Literary Supplement*, one of the world's most influential publications of book reviews! In a spirited correspondence I had with him after his rave appeared, he demonstrated that he knew quite a lot about the history of work on the origin of life, enough to think he could trust his own judgment. And as he noted in a letter to the *Times Literary Supplement* (January 1, 2010), "Meyer's book seems to me to be written in good faith." Had Nagel consulted with scientists working in the field, he would have been able to see Meyer's exploitation of Occam's Broom, whisking inconvenient facts out of view, and he might also have been dismayed to learn that the experts hadn't been sent an early copy of Meyer's book, as he had, or been asked to referee it before publication. Learning that the book he admired was a stealth operation might have shaken his confidence in his judgment, or it might not have. The scientific establishment has been known to squelch renegade critics unjustly on occasion, and perhaps—perhaps—Meyer had no choice but to launch a sneak attack. But Nagel would have been wise to explore this prospect warily before committing himself. It is fair to say that the scientists working on the origin of life do not yet have a secure and agreed-upon theory, but there is no dearth of candidates, an embarrassment of riches rather than an almost empty arena.

Conspiracy theorists are masters of Occam's Broom, and an instructive exercise on the Internet is to look up a new conspiracy theory, to see if you (a nonexpert on the topic) can find the flaws, before looking elsewhere on the web for the expert rebuttals. When Brenner coined the term, he wasn't talking about creationism and conspiracy theories; he was pointing out that in the heat of battle, even serious scientists sometimes cannot resist "overlooking" some data that seriously undermine their pet theory. It's a temptation to be resisted, no matter what.

7. USING LAY AUDIENCES AS DECOYS

One good way of preventing people from *inadvertently* wielding Occam's Broom is a technique that I have been recommending for years, and have several times put to the test—but never as ambitiously as I would like to do. Unlike the other practices I have been describing, this one takes time and money to do properly. I hope others will pursue this technique vigorously and report the results. I have decided to put it here because it addresses some of the same problems of communication that the other general tools confront.

In many fields—not just philosophy—there are controversies that seem never-ending and partly artifactual: people are talking past one another and not making the necessary effort to communicate effectively. Tempers flare, and disrespect and derision start creeping in. People on the sidelines take sides, even when they don't fully understand the issues.

It can get ugly, and it *can* have a very straightforward cause. When experts talk to experts, whether they are in the same discipline or not, they always err on the side of *under-explaining*. The reason is not far to seek: to overexplain something to a fellow expert is a very serious insult—"Do I have to spell it out for you?"—and nobody wants to insult a fellow expert. So just to be safe, people err on the side of under-explaining. It is not done deliberately, for the most part, and it is almost impossible to keep from doing—which is actually a good thing, since being polite in an unstudied way is a nice character trait in anyone. But this gracious disposition to assume more understanding than is apt to be present in one's distinguished audience has an unfortunate by-product: experts often talk past each other.

There is no *direct* cure: entreating all the experts present at a workshop or conference not to under-explain their positions may be met by earnest promises, but it won't work. If anything it will make matters worse since now people will be particularly sensitive to the issue of inadvertently insulting somebody. But there is an indirect and quite effective cure: have all experts present their views to a small audience of curious nonexperts (here at Tufts I have the advantage of bright undergraduates) while the other experts listen in from the sidelines. They don't have to eavesdrop; this isn't a *devious* suggestion. On the contrary, everybody can and should be fully informed that the point of the exercise is to make it comfortable for participants to speak in terms that *everybody* will understand. By addressing their remarks to the undergraduates (the decoy audience), speakers need not worry *at all* about insulting the experts because they are not addressing the experts. (I suppose they might worry about insulting the undergraduates, but that's another matter.) When all goes well, expert A explains the issues of the controversy to the undergraduates while expert B listens. At some point B's face may light up. "So *that's* what you've been trying to say! Now I get it." Or maybe the good effects will have to wait until it is B's turn to explain to the same undergraduates what the issues are, and provoking just such a welcome reaction in A. It may not go perfectly, but it usually goes well and everybody benefits. The experts dissolve some of the artifactual misunderstandings between their positions, and the undergraduates get a first-rate educational experience.

Several times I have set up such exercises at Tufts, thanks to generous support from the administration. I handpick a small group of undergraduates (less than a dozen) and brief them on their role: they are not to accept anything they don't understand. They will be expected to raise their hands, to interrupt, to alert the experts to anything they find confusing or vague. (They do get required reading to pore over beforehand so that they are not utter novices on the topic; they are interested amateurs.) They love the role, and so they should; they are being given made-to-order tutorials from some big guns. The experts, meanwhile, often find that being set the task (well in advance) to explain their position under these conditions helps them find better ways of making their points than they had ever found before. Sometimes these experts have been "protected" for years by layers of fellow experts, postdocs, and advanced graduate students, and they really need the challenge.

8. JOOTSING

It is hard to *find* an application of Occam's Broom, since it operates by whisking inconvenient facts out of sight, and it is even harder to achieve what Doug Hofstadter (1979, 1985) calls *jootsing*, which stands for "*j*umping *o*ut *o*f *t*he *s*ystem." This is an important tactic not just in science and philosophy, but also in the arts. Creativity, that ardently sought but only rarely found virtue, often is a heretofore unimagined violation of the rules of the system from which it springs. It might be the system of classical harmony in music, the rules for meter and rhyme in sonnets (or limericks, even), or the "canons" of taste or good form in some genre of art. Or it might be the assumptions and principles of some theory or research program. Being creative is not just a matter of casting about for something novel—anybody can do that, since novelty can be found in any random juxtaposition of stuff—but of making the novelty *jump* out of some *system*, a system that has become somewhat established, for good reasons. When an artistic tradition reaches the point where literally "anything goes," those who want to be creative have a problem: there are no fixed rules to rebel against, no complacent expectations to shatter, nothing to subvert, no background against which to create something that is both surprising and yet meaningful. It helps to *know* the tradition if you want to subvert it. That's why so few dabblers or novices succeed in coming up with anything truly creative.

Sit down at a piano and try to come up with a good new melody and you soon discover how hard it is. All the keys are available, in any combination you choose, but until you can find something to lean on, some style or genre or pattern to lay down and exploit a bit, or allude to, before you twist it, you will come up with nothing but noise. And not just any violation of the rules will do the trick. I know there are at least two flourishing—well, surviving—jazz harpists, but setting out to make your name playing Beethoven on tuned bongo drums is probably not a good plan. Here is where art shares a feature with science: there are always scads of unexamined presuppositions of any theoretical set-to, but trying to negate them one at a time until you find a vulnerable one is not a good recipe for success in science or philosophy. (It would be like taking a Gershwin melody and altering it, one note at a time, looking for a worthy descendant. Good luck! Almost always, mutations are deleterious.) It's harder than that, but sometimes you get lucky.

Advising somebody to make progress by jootsing is rather like advising an investor to buy low and sell high. Yes, of course, that's the idea, but how do you manage to do it? Notice that the investment advice is not *entirely* vacuous or unusable, and the call for jootsing is even more helpful, because it clarifies what your target looks like if you ever catch a glimpse of it. (Everybody knows what *more money* looks like.) When you are confronting a scientific or philosophical problem, the system you need to jump out of is typically so entrenched that it is as invisible as the air you breathe. As a general rule, when a long-standing controversy seems to be getting nowhere, with both "sides" stubbornly insisting they are right, as often as not the trouble is that there is something they both agree on that is just not so. Both sides consider it so obvious, in fact, that it goes without saying. Finding these invisible problem-poisoners is not an easy task, because whatever seems obvious to these warring experts is apt to seem obvious, on reflection, to just about everybody. So the recommendation that you keep an eye out for a tacit shared false assumption is not all that likely to bear fruit, but at least you're more likely to find one if you're hoping to find one and have some idea of what one would look like.

Sometimes there are clues. Several of the great instances of jootsing have involved abandoning some well-regarded *thing* that turned out not to exist after all. *Phlogiston* was supposed to be an element in fire, and *caloric* was the invisible, self-repellent fluid or gas that was supposed to be the chief *ingredient* in heat, but these were dropped, and so was the *ether* as a medium in which light traveled the way sound travels through air and water. But other admirable jootsings are additions, not subtractions: germs and electrons and—maybe even—the many-worlds interpretation of quantum mechanics! It's never obvious from the outset whether we should joots or not. Ray Jackendoff and I have argued that we must drop the almost always tacit assumption that consciousness is the "highest" or "most central" of all mental phenomena, and I have argued that thinking of consciousness as a special *medium* (rather like the ether) into which contents get transduced or translated is a widespread and unexamined habit of thought that should be broken. Along with many others, I have also argued that if you think it is simply obvious that free will and determinism are incompatible, you're making a big mistake. More about those ideas later.

Another clue: sometimes a problem gets started when somebody way back when said, "Suppose, for the sake of argument, that . . . ," and folks agreed, for the sake of argument, and then in the subsequent parry and thrust everybody forgot how the problem started! I think that occasionally, at least in my field of philosophy, the opponents are enjoying the tussle so much that neither side wants to risk extinguishing the whole exercise by examining the enabling premises. Here are two ancient examples, which of course are controversial: (1) "Why is there something rather than nothing?" is a deep question in need of an answer. (2) "Does God command something because it is good, or is something good because God commands it?" is another important question. I guess it would be wonderful if somebody came up with a *good* answer to either of these questions, so I admit that my calling them pseudo-problems not worth anybody's attention is not very satisfying, but that doesn't show that I'm wrong. Nobody said the truth had to be fun.

9. THREE SPECIES OF *GOULDING*: RATHERING, PILING ON, AND THE GOULD TWO-STEP

The late biologist Stephen Jay Gould was a virtuoso designer and exploiter of boom crutches. Here are three related species, of the genus *Goulding*, named by me in honor of their most effective wielder.

Rathering is a way of sliding you swiftly and gently past a *false dichotomy*. The general form of a rathering is "It is not the case that *blahblahblah*, as orthodoxy would have you believe; it is *rather* that *suchandsuchandsuch*—which is radically different." Some ratherings are just fine; you really must choose between the two alternatives on offer; in these cases, you are not being offered a false, but rather a genuine, inescapable dichotomy. But some ratherings are little more than sleight of hand, due to the fact that the word "rather" implies—without argument—that there is an important incompatibility between the claims flanking it.

Here is a fine example of rathering by Gould in the course of his account of punctuated equilibrium:

> Change does not usually occur by imperceptibly gradual
> alteration of entire species but *rather* [my italics] by isolation
> of small populations and their geologically instantaneous
> transformation into new species. [1992b, p. 12]

This passage invites us to believe that evolutionary change could not be both "geologically instantaneous" and "imperceptibly gradual" at the same time. But of course it can be. In fact, that is just what evolutionary change must be, unless Gould is saying that evolution tends to proceed by saltations (giant leaps in **Design Space**)—but elsewhere he has insisted that he never ever endorsed saltationism. "Geologically instantaneous" speciation can happen over a "short" period of time—let's say fifty thousand years, an elapse of time barely detectable in most geological strata. During that brief moment a typical member of a species might increase in height from, say, half a meter to one meter, a 100 percent increase, but at a rate of a millimeter every century, which strikes me as an imperceptibly gradual change.

Let's make up some other examples of rathering, to make sure the nature of the trick is clear.

> It is not that people are mere "moist robots" (as Dilbert says, with the concurrence of most researchers in cognitive science); it is *rather* that people have free will, and are morally responsible for their good and bad deeds.

Again, why not both? What is missing is an argument to the effect that "moist robots" cannot also be people with free will who are morally responsible. This example plays on a common—but controversial—assumption. Here's another:

> Religion is not the opiate of the masses, as Marx said; it is *rather* a deep and consoling sign of humanity's recognition of the inevitability of death.

Yet again, why can't it be both the opiate and a consoling sign? I think you get the point by now, and you can hunt for ratherings in a document more easily than you can hunt for false dichotomies, which never get announced as such; just type "rather" in your search box and see what comes up. Remember: not all "rather"s are ratherings; some are legitimate. And some ratherings don't use the word "rather." Here is one that uses the terser for "_____, not _____"; I made it up from elements in the work of several ideologues of cognitive science.

> Nervous systems need to be seen as actively generating probes of their environment, not as mere computers acting passively on inputs fed to them by sense organs.

Who says computers acting on inputs fed to them can't actively generate probes? This familiar contrast between drearily "passive" computers and wonderfully "active" organisms has never been properly defended, and is one of the most ubiquitous imagination-blockers I know.

A variation on rathering used frequently by Gould may be called *piling on*:

> We talk about the "march from monad to man" (old-style language again) as though evolution followed continuous pathways of progress along unbroken lineages. Nothing could be further from reality. [1989a, p. 14]

What could not be further from reality? At first it might appear as if Gould was saying that there is no continuous, unbroken lineage between the "monads" (single-celled organisms) and us, but of course there is. There is no more secure implication of Darwin's great idea than that. So what can Gould be saying here? Presumably we are meant to put the emphasis on "pathways of *progress*"—it is (only) the belief in progress that is "far from reality." The pathways are continuous, unbroken lineages all right, but not lineages of (global) progress. This is true: they are (unbroken) continuous lineages of (mainly) local progress. We come away from this passage from Gould—unless we are wary—with the sense that he has shown us something seriously wrong with the standard proposition of evolutionary theory that there are continuous pathways (unbroken lineages) from monads to man. But, to use Gould's own phrase, "Nothing could be further from reality."

Yet another trick of his is the *Gould Two-Step*, a device I described in print some years ago, which was then named by the evolutionary theorist Robert Trivers (personal correspondence, 1993), in honor of its inventor:

> In the first stage, you create the strawperson, and "refute" it (everybody knows that trick). Second (this is the stroke of

genius), you yourself draw attention to the evidence that you have taken the first step—the evidence that your opponents don't in fact hold the view you have attributed to them—but interpret these citations as their grudging concessions to your attack! [Dennett, 1993, p. 43]

In my essay, a letter to the editor of the *New York Review of Books* (1993), where Gould had two months earlier savagely criticized Helena Cronin's fine book *The Ant and the Peacock* (November 19, 1992), I presented three examples of the Gould Two-Step. Here is the most portable of those examples:

The most transparent case is Gould's invention of "extrapolationism," described as a logical extension of "Cronin's adaptationism." This is a doctrine of pan-continuity and pan-gradualism that is conveniently—indeed trivially—refuted by the fact of mass extinction. "But if mass extinctions are true breaks in continuity, if the slow building of adaptation in normal times does not extend into predicted success across mass extinction boundaries, then extrapolationism fails and adaptationism succumbs." I cannot see why any adaptationist would be so foolish as to endorse anything like "extrapolationism" in a form so "pure" as to deny the possibility or even likelihood that mass extinction would play a major role in pruning the tree of life, as Gould puts it. It has always been obvious that the most perfect dinosaur will succumb if a comet strikes its homeland with a force hundreds of times greater than all the hydrogen bombs ever made. There is not a word in Cronin's book that supports his contention that she has made this error. If Gould thinks the role of mass extinctions in evolution is relevant to either of the central problems Cronin addresses, sexual selection and altruism, he does not say how or why. When Cronin turns, in her last chapter, to a fine discussion of the central question in evolutionary theory she has *not* concentrated on, the origin of species, and points out that it is still an outstanding problem, Gould pounces on this as a last minute epiphany, an ironic admission of defeat for her "panadaptationism." Preposterous! [p. 44]

There is a good project for a student of rhetoric: combing through Gould's huge body of publications and cataloguing the different species of boom crutch he exploited, beginning with rathering, piling on, and the Gould Two-Step.

10. THE "SURELY" OPERATOR: A MENTAL BLOCK

When you're reading or skimming argumentative essays, especially by philosophers, here is a quick trick that may save you much time and effort, especially in this age of simple searching by computer: look for "surely" in the document, and check each occurrence. Not always, not even most of the time, but often the word "surely" is as good as a blinking light locating a weak point in the argument, a warning label about a likely **boom crutch**. Why? Because it marks the very edge of what the author is actually sure about and hopes readers will also be sure about. (If the author were really sure all the readers would agree, it wouldn't be worth mentioning.) Being at the edge, the author has had to make a judgment call about whether or not to attempt to demonstrate the point at issue, or provide evidence for it, and—because life is short—has decided in favor of bald assertion, with the presumably well-grounded anticipation of agreement. Just the sort of place to find an ill-examined "truism" that isn't true!

I first noticed this useful role of "surely" when commenting on an essay by Ned Block (1994), which included several prime examples directed against my theory of consciousness. Here's one, conveniently italicized* by Block to emphasize its obviousness typographically:

But surely it is nothing other than a biological fact about people— not a cultural construction—that some brain representations persevere enough to affect memory, control behavior, etc. [p. 27]

---

* Not to be outdone, the philosopher Jerry Fodor (2008) has adopted the practice of putting his "surely"s in italics—and repeating them (e.g., p. 38), as if to say, *Take that, doubters! Take that, doubters!*

This is meant to dismiss—without argument—my theory of human consciousness as something that must, in effect, be learned, a set of cognitive micro-habits that are not guaranteed to be present at birth. "Wherever Block says 'Surely,'" I said, "look for what we might call a mental block" (Dennett, 1994a, p. 549). Block is one of the most profligate abusers of the "surely" operator among philosophers, but others routinely rely on it, and every time they do, a little alarm bell should ring. "Here is where the unintended sleight-of-hand happens, whisking the false premise by the censors with a nudge and a wink" (Dennett, 2007b, p. 252).

I decided recently to test my hunch about "surely" a bit more systematically. I went through dozens of papers—about sixty—on the philosophy of mind at philpapers.org/ and checked for occurrences of "surely." Most papers did not use the word at all. In those that did use it (between one and five times in the sample I checked), most instances were clearly innocent; a few were, well, arguable; and there were six instances where the alarm bell sounded loud and clear (for me). Of course others might have a very different threshold for obviousness, which is why I didn't bother tabulating my "data" in this informal experiment. I encourage doubters to conduct their own surveys and see what they find. A particularly egregious example of the "surely" operator will be dismantled in detail later, in chapter 64.

11. RHETORICAL QUESTIONS

Just as you should keep a sharp eye out for "surely," you should develop a sensitivity for rhetorical questions in any argument or polemic. Why? Because, like the use of "surely," they represent an author's eagerness to take a short cut. A rhetorical question has a question mark at the end, but it is not meant to be answered. That is, the author doesn't bother waiting for you to answer since the answer is so flipping obvious that you'd be embarrassed to say it! In other words, most rhetorical questions are telescoped *reductio ad absurdum* arguments, too obvious to need spelling out. Here is a good habit to develop: Whenever you see a rhetorical question, try—silently, to yourself—to give it an unobvious answer. If you find a good one, surprise your interlocutor by answering the question. I remember a *Peanuts* cartoon from years ago that nicely illustrates the tactic. Charlie Brown had just asked, rhetorically, "Who's to say what is right and wrong here?" and Lucy responded, in the next panel, "I will."

12. WHAT IS A DEEPITY?

My late friend, the computer scientist Joseph Weizenbaum had a yearning to be a philosopher and tried late in his career to gravitate from technicalities to profundities. He once told me that one evening, after holding forth with high purpose and furrowed brow at the dinner table, his young daughter Miriam said, "Wow! Dad just said a deepity!" What a wonderful impromptu coinage!* I decided to adopt it and put it to somewhat more analytic use.

A deepity is a proposition that *seems* both important and true—and profound—but that achieves this effect by being ambiguous. On one reading it is manifestly false, but it would be earth-shaking if it were true; on the other reading it is true but trivial. The unwary listener picks up the glimmer of truth from the second reading, and the devastating importance from the first reading, and thinks, Wow! That's a deepity.

Here is an example. (Better sit down: this is heavy stuff.)

Love is just a word.

Oh wow! Cosmic. Mind-blowing, right? Wrong. On one reading, it is manifestly false. I'm not sure what love is—maybe an emotion or emotional attachment, maybe an interpersonal relationship, maybe the highest state a human mind can achieve—but we all know it isn't a word. You can't find love in the dictionary!

We can bring out the other reading by availing ourselves of a

_____

* Miriam encountered my use of her term on the Internet recently and got in touch with me. Her own version of its coining is somewhat different, but in the same spirit: "In my family it carries a bit of scorn—an idea masquerading as Truth in order to elevate the speaker." She has graciously consented to my use of the version her father told me (as I recall it), and to my rather narrower redefinition of her brilliant neologism.

convention philosophers care mightily about: when we *talk about* a word, we put it in quotation marks, thus:

"Love" is just a word.

This is true; "love" is an English word, but just a word, not a sentence, for example. It begins with "L" and has four letters and appears in the dictionary between "lousy" and "low-browed," which are also just words. "Cheeseburger" is just a word. "Word" is just a word.

But this isn't fair, you say. Whoever said that love is just a word meant something else, surely. No doubt, but they didn't say it. Maybe they meant that "love" is a word that misleads people into thinking that it is the term for something wonderful that doesn't really exist at all, like "unicorn," or maybe they meant that the word was so vague that nobody could ever know whether it referred to any particular thing or relation or event. But neither of these claims is actually very plausible. "Love" may be a troublesome, hard-to-define word, and love may be a hard-to-be-sure-about state, but those claims are obvious, not particularly informative or profound.

Not all deepities are quite so easily analyzed. Richard Dawkins recently alerted me to a fine deepity by Rowan Williams, the Archbishop of Canterbury, who described his faith as a

silent waiting on the truth, pure sitting and breathing in the presence of the question mark.

I leave the analysis of this as an exercise for you.

SUMMARY

A tool wielded well becomes almost as much a part of you as your hands and feet, and this is especially true of tools for thinking. Equipped with these simple all-purpose thinking tools, you can approach the difficult explorations ahead with sharper senses: you can see an opening, hear a warning bell, smell a rat, or feel a misstep that you might well miss without their help. You also have some maxims to bear in mind—Rapoport's Rules and Sturgeon's Law, for instance—that can whisper advice in your ear like Jiminy Cricket, reminding you to control your aggression as you plunge boldly into the thicket swinging your weapons. Yes, thinking tools are also weapons, and the imagery of combat is appropriate. Competitiveness is, apparently, a natural by-product of the intellectual ambition and boldness required to tackle the toughest problems. We've seen that in the heat of battle even great thinkers can resort to dirty tricks in their eagerness to get you to see things their way, and constructive criticism can quickly shade into ridicule when an opportunity to launch a zinger arises.

The problems we will be confronting are all hot-button issues: meaning, evolution, consciousness, and especially free will. You will feel dread or repugnance welling up as you approach some of the prospects, and rest assured that you are not alone in this; even the most vaunted experts are susceptible to wishful thinking and can be blinded to a truth by a conviction that is supported more by emotional attachment than reason. People really care about whether they have free will or not, about how their minds can reside in their bodies, and about how—and even whether—there can be meaning in a world composed of nothing but atoms and molecules, photons and Higgs bosons. People *should* care. What could be more important, in the end, than these questions: What in the world are we, and what should we do about it? So watch your step. There is treacherous footing ahead, and the maps are unreliable.

III:
TOOLS FOR THINKING ABOUT MEANING OR CONTENT

Why begin with meaning? I am starting with meaning because it is at the heart of all the tough problems, for a simple reason: these problems don't arise until we start talking about them, to ourselves and others. Badgers don't worry about free will, and even dolphins can't be nagged by the problem of consciousness, because *asking questions* is not part of their repertoire. Curiosity may have killed the cat, but it drives us reflective human beings into thickets of bafflement. Now, maybe this is the down side of language, and we'd be better off—happier, healthier mammals—if we were as oblivious to these issues as our great ape kin are. But since we have language, we're stuck with the Big Questions, and for better or worse, they don't strike us as trivial.

The first step in any effective exploration is to get as clear as we can about our starting point and our equipment. Words have meanings. How is this possible? We word-users mean things by saying things. How is this possible? How can we understand each other? Our dogs seem to be able to "understand" (sort of) a few words, even a few hundred words, but aside from such domesticated stunts, and the rudimentary signaling systems found in nature (in primates, in birds, . . . in cuttlefish!), words are what distinguish our minds from all other animal minds. That is a striking difference, but it still seems that nonhuman animals—"higher" animals—have minds, and hence in some perhaps limited way deal with meanings: the meanings of their perceptual states, their urges and desires, and even their dreams.

Sometimes animals strike us as very much like us, as people dressed up in cat costumes, bearskins, and dolphin suits. This is true in every human culture: animals are seen as seeing, knowing, wanting, trying, fearing, deciding, lusting, remembering, and so forth. In short, they are seen as like us in having *minds* filled with *meaningful* . . . something-or-others (ideas? beliefs? mental representations?). How can there be meanings in brains? A perennially tempting idea is that since words have meanings, maybe the meaningful things in our brains—and in animal brains—are like words, composed into mental sentences, expressing beliefs, and so on. But if words get their meanings from the minds that utter them, from where do mindwords get their meanings? Do animal brains store both the mindwords and their definitions, in a sort of cerebral dictionary? And if animals—at least "higher" animals—have always had brains full of mindwords, why can't they talk?* The idea of a language of thought is deeply problematic, but our thoughts and beliefs must be composed of something. What else could it be?†

---

* They can, some enthusiasts will say, in languages we haven't discovered or translated yet. This is a perennially attractive idea, but the exhaustive studies of ape, bird, and dolphin communication conducted in recent years show that animals' ability to "share their thoughts" is very limited. If that's language, then termites are engineers, praying mantises have religion, and wolves have parliaments.

† Jerry Fodor (1975) brandished this rhetorical question very effectively in his pioneering book, *The Language of Thought*, and emphasized its implied answer by citing Lyndon Johnson's defiant observation "I'm the only President you've got" (p. 27).

13. MURDER IN TRAFALGAR SQUARE

Here is our first intuition pump. Jacques shoots his uncle dead in Trafalgar Square and is apprehended on the spot by Sherlock; Tom reads about it in the *Guardian*, and Boris learns of it in *Pravda*. Now Jacques, Sherlock, Tom, and Boris have had remarkably different experiences—to say nothing of their earlier biographies and future prospects—but there is one thing they share: they all believe that a Frenchman has committed murder in Trafalgar Square. They did not all *say* this, not even "to themselves"; *that proposition* did not, we can suppose, "occur to" any of them, and even if it had, it would have had very different import for Jacques, Sherlock, Tom, and Boris. Yet they all believe that a Frenchman committed murder in Trafalgar Square. This is a shared property that is visible, in effect, only from one very limited point of view—the point of view of **folk psychology**. Ordinary folk psychologists—all of us—have no difficulty imputing such useful commonalities to people. We do it without knowing much of anything about what lies between the ears of those to whom we attribute those beliefs. We may think that these four fellows must also have something *else* in common—a similarly shaped something-or-other in their brains that somehow registers their shared belief—but if so, we are lapsing into dubious theorizing. There *may* in fact be some such neural structures in common—if all four brains happen to "spell" the belief that a Frenchman has committed murder in Trafalgar Square the same way—but this is not at all necessary, and is in fact very unlikely, for reasons we will briefly explore here.

The two sentences "I'm hungry" and "*J'ai faim*" share a property, in spite of being composed of differently shaped letters (or different phonemes when uttered aloud), in different languages, and having different grammatical structures: they *mean*, or are *about*, the same thing: the speaker's hunger. This shared property, the *meaning* (of the two sentences in their respective languages), or the *content* (of the beliefs they express), is a central topic in philosophy and cognitive science. This *aboutness* that, for example, sentences, pictures, beliefs, and (no doubt) some brain states exhibit, is known in philosophical jargon as *intentionality*, an unfortunate choice as a technical term, since outsiders routinely confuse it with the everyday idea of doing something intentionally (as in "Are your intentions honorable?"). Here is a sentence to remind you of the differences: A cigarette is not *about* smoking, or about anything else, in spite of the fact that it is *intended* to be smoked; a "NO SMOKING" sign *is* about smoking and hence exhibits intentionality; the belief that there's a mugger behind that tree exhibits intentionality (it's about a—possibly nonexistent—mugger), but it is surely not intentional in the ordinary sense (you don't "believe it on purpose"; it just comes to you); running away from the tree is intentional in the ordinary sense, but isn't about anything. If you simply make a habit of substituting the awkward word "aboutness" whenever you encounter the philosophical term "intentionality," you will seldom go wrong. Aside from the agreement that meaning and content are intimately related and mutually dependent phenomena, or even a single phenomenon (intentionality), there is still precious little consensus about what content (or meaning) is and how best to capture it. That's why we have to approach this topic gingerly. It's a feast of problems, but we can sneak up on the questions, taking small bites.

This example of the four different believers is meant to demonstrate how brains could have little in common while still sharing an "intentional" property: believing "the same thing." Jacques was an eyewitness—indeed, the perpetrator—of the murder, Sherlock's experiential intimacy with the event is only slightly less direct, but Tom and Boris learned this fact in strikingly different terms. There are indefinitely many different ways of acquiring the information that a Frenchman committed murder in Trafalgar Square and indefinitely many different ways of using that information to further one's projects (answering questions on quiz shows, winning bets, titillating French tourists in London, etc.). If there is a good reason to think that all these sources and outcomes must funnel through some common structure in the brain, we'll discover it eventually, but in the meantime we shouldn't jump to conclusions.

Before leaving this intuition pump we should follow Doug Hofstadter's advice and *turn the knobs* to see what its parts are doing. Why did I choose the particular proposition I did? Because I needed something memorable and striking enough to get reported in different languages many miles away from the scene. Most of our belief acquisition isn't like that at all, and it is worth noting this. For instance, Jacques, Sherlock, Tom, and Boris share indefinitely many other beliefs that did not arise so dramatically: the beliefs that, for instance, chairs are larger than shoes, that soup is liquid, that elephants don't fly. If I try to inform you that salmon in the wild don't wear hearing aids, you will tell me that this is not news to you, but when did you learn it? You weren't born knowing it, it was not part of any curriculum at school, and it is extremely unlikely that you ever framed a sentence in your mind to this effect. So while it might seem obvious that Boris must have learned about the Frenchman by "simply uploading" the relevant Russian sentence in *Pravda* into his brain, and then "translating" it into, oh, Brainish, there is nothing obvious about the supposition that Boris's brain performed a similar clerical job (from *what* into Brainish?) for the fact about salmon.

Here's another knob: suppose Fido, a dog, and Clyde, a pigeon, are also eyewitnesses of the murder; they may carry away *something* about the event, an adjustment in their brains that could influence later behavior, but it wouldn't be the fact that a Frenchman committed murder in Trafalgar Square, even though the information sustaining that fact might be present in the light and sound that impinged on their sense organs. (A videotape of the event might provide legal evidence of this, for instance, but it would be lost on Fido and Clyde.) So this intuition pump risks carrying a seriously anthropocentric bias into our exploration of meaning. Words and sentences are exemplary vehicles of meaning, but for animals that don't use them, the idea that their *brains* nevertheless use them is at least far-fetched—which doesn't make it false. If it turns out to be true, it will be a most eye-opening discovery, but we've had those before.

The phenomena of intentionality are both utterly familiar—as salient in our daily lives as our food, furniture, and clothes—and systematically elusive from scientific perspectives. You and I seldom have difficulty distinguishing a birthday greeting from a death threat from a promise, but consider the engineering task of making a reliable death-threat-detector. What do all death threats have in common? Only their meaning, it seems. And meaning is *not* like radioactivity or acidity, a property readily discriminated by a well-tuned detector. The closest we have come yet to creating a general-purpose meaning-detector is IBM's Watson, which is much better at sorting by meanings than any earlier artificial intelligence system, but notice that it is not at all simple, and would still (probably) misidentify some candidates for death threats that a child would readily get. Even small children recognize that when one laughing kid yells to another, "So help me, I'll kill you if you do that again!" this is not really a death threat. The sheer size and sophistication of Watson are at least indirect measures of how elusive the familiar property of meaning is.

14. AN OLDER BROTHER LIVING IN CLEVELAND

Still, meaning is not an utterly mysterious property. One way or another, structures in our brains somehow "store" our beliefs. When you learn that pudus are mammals, *something* has to change in your brain; something has to become relatively fixed in a way it wasn't fixed before you learned this, and whatever it is must have enough *aboutness*, one way or another, to account for your newfound ability to identify pudus as closer kin to buffalos than to barracudas. So it is indeed tempting to imagine that beliefs are "stored in the brain" rather the way data files are stored on your hard disk, in some systematic code—which might be different in each individual, as different as fingerprints. Jacques's beliefs would be written in his brain in Jacquish, and Sherlock's in Sherlockish. But there are problems with this attractive idea.

Suppose we have entered the golden age of neurocryptography, and it becomes possible for a "cognitive micro-neurosurgeon" to do a bit of tinkering and *insert* a belief into a person's brain, writing the relevant proposition in the person's neurons, using the local brain language, of course. (If we can learn to *read* brain-writing, presumably we can *write* brain-writing, if our tools are delicate enough.) Let us suppose we are going to insert into Tom's brain the following false belief: *I have an older brother living in Cleveland.* Let us suppose the cognitive micro-neurosurgeon can do the requisite rewiring, as much and as delicate as you please. This rewiring will either impair Tom's basic rationality or not. Consider the two outcomes. Tom is sitting in a bar and a friend asks, "Do you have any brothers or sisters?" Tom says, "Yes, I have an older brother living in Cleveland." "What's his name?" Now what is going to happen? Tom may reply, "Name? Whose name? Oh my gosh, what was I saying? I don't have an older brother! For a moment, there, it seemed to me that I had an older brother living in Cleveland!" Alternatively, he may say, "I don't know his name," and when pressed he will deny all knowledge of this brother and assert things like "I am an only child and have an older brother living in Cleveland." In neither case has our cognitive micro-neurosurgeon succeeded in wiring in a new belief. In the first case, Tom's intact rationality wipes out the (lone, unsupported) intruder as soon as it makes an appearance. An evanescent disposition to say, "I have an older brother living in Cleveland" isn't really a belief—it's more in the nature of a tic, like a manifestation of Tourette's syndrome. And if poor Tom persists with this pathology, as in the second alternative, his frank irrationality on the topic of older brothers disqualifies him as a believer. Anybody who doesn't understand that you can't be an only child and have an older brother living in Cleveland really doesn't understand the sentence he asserted, and what you really don't understand you may "parrot" but you can't believe.

This science-fiction example highlights the tacit presumption of mental competence that underlies all belief attributions; unless you have an indefinitely extensible repertoire of ways to *use* your candidate belief (if that is what it is) in different contexts, it is not a belief in any remotely recognizable sense. If the surgeon has done the work delicately, preserving the competence of the brain, that brain will undo this handiwork as soon as the issue arises—or else, pathologically, the brain will surround the handiwork with layers of pearly confabulation ("His name is Sebastian, and he's a circus acrobat who lives in a balloon"). Such confabulation is not unknown; people suffering from Korsakoff's syndrome (the amnesia that often afflicts alcoholics) can be astonishingly convincing in spinning tales of their "remembered" pasts that have not a shred of truth in them. But this very elaboration is clear evidence that the person doesn't *just* have an isolated "proposition" stored in her brain; even a delusional belief *requires* the support of a host of non-delusional beliefs and the ability to acknowledge the implications of all this. If she doesn't believe her older brother also is male, breathing, west of Boston, north of Panama, and so on and so forth, then it would be worse than misleading to say that the surgeon's feat was inserting a *belief.*

What this intuition pump shows is that nobody can have just one belief. (You can't believe a dog has four legs without believing that legs are limbs and four is greater than three, etc.)* It shows other things as well, but I won't pause to enumerate them. Nor will I try to say now how one might use a variation on this very specific thinking tool for other purposes—though you are invited to turn the knobs yourself, to see what you come up with. I want to get a varied assortment of such thinking tools on display before we reflect more on their features.

---

* This conclusion is often called the *holism* of the mental (or the intentional); holism has been staunchly denied by Jerry Fodor, who claims to have no trouble imagining a creature with exactly one belief (Fodor and Lepore, 1992).

15. "DADDY IS A DOCTOR"

A young child is asked what her father does, and she answers, "Daddy is a doctor." Does she believe what she says? In one sense, of course, but what would she have to know to *really* believe it? (What if she'd said, "Daddy is an arbitrager" or "Daddy is an actuary"?) Suppose we suspected that she was speaking without understanding, and decided to test her. Must she be able to produce paraphrases or to expand on her claim by saying her father cures sick people? Is it enough if she knows that Daddy's being a doctor precludes his being a butcher, a baker, a candlestick maker? Does she know what a doctor is if she lacks the concept of a fake doctor, a quack, an unlicensed practitioner? For that matter, how much does she need to understand to know that Daddy is her father? (Her adoptive father? Her "biological" father?) Clearly her understanding of what it is to be a doctor, as well as what it is to be a father, will grow over the years, and hence her understanding of her own sentence, "Daddy is a doctor," will grow. Can we specify—in any nonarbitrary way—how much she must know in order to understand this proposition "completely"? If understanding comes in degrees, as this example shows, then belief, which depends on understanding, must come in degrees as well, even for such mundane propositions as this. She "**sorta**" believes her father is a doctor—which is not to say she has reservations or doubts, but that she falls short of the understanding that is an important precondition for any useful concept of belief.

16. MANIFEST IMAGE AND SCIENTIFIC IMAGE

It's time to erect some staging before proceeding in our quest to understand what meanings are. Here is a thinking tool that provides a valuable perspective on so many issues that it should be in everybody's kit, but so far it hasn't spread far from its home in philosophy. The philosopher Wilfrid Sellars devised it in 1962 to clarify thinking on what science shows us about the world we live in. The *manifest* image is the world as it seems to us in everyday life, full of solid objects, colors and smells and tastes, voices and shadows, plants and animals, and people and all their stuff: not only tables and chairs, bridges and churches, dollars and contracts, but also such intangible things as songs, poems, opportunities, and free will. Think of all the puzzling questions that arise when we try to line up all those things with the things in the *scientific* image: molecules, atoms, electrons, and quarks and their ilk. Is anything *really* solid? The physicist Sir Arthur Eddington wrote, early in the twentieth century, about the "two tables," the solid one of everyday experience and the one composed of atoms, widely separated in mainly empty space, more like a galaxy than a piece of wood. Some people said that what science showed was that *nothing was really solid*, solidity was an illusion, but Eddington knew better than to go that far. Some people have said that color is an illusion. Is it? Electromagnetic radiation in the narrow range that accounts for human vision (the range in between infrared and ultraviolet) is not made of little colored things, and atoms, even gold atoms, aren't colored. But still, color is not an illusion in the sense that matters: nobody thinks Sony is lying when it says that its color televisions really show the world of color, or that Sherwin-Williams should be sued for fraud for selling us many different colors in the form of paint. How about dollars? These days the vast majority of them aren't made of silver or even paper. They are *virtual*, made of information, not material, just like poems and promises. Does that mean that they are an illusion? No, but don't hunt for them among the molecules.

Sellars (1962, p. 1) famously said, "The aim of philosophy, abstractly formulated, is to understand how things in the broadest possible sense of the term hang together in the broadest possible sense of the term." That is the best definition of philosophy I have encountered. The task of figuring out how to put all the familiar *things* in our manifest image into registration with all the relatively unfamiliar *things* of the scientific image is not a job that scientists are especially well equipped to do. Please tell me, Dr. Physicist, just what a *color* is. Are there any colors according to your theory? Dr. Chemist, can you provide the chemical formula for a *bargain*? Surely (ding!) there are bargains. What are they made of? Hmm. Maybe there aren't any bargains, not really! But then what's the difference—the *chemical* difference?—between something that is a bargain and something that only seems to be a bargain? We could go on in this vein, looking at a host of puzzlers that only philosophers have tried hard to resolve, but instead, let's step back, as Sellars invites us to do, and look at the fact that there are these two remarkably different perspectives on the world. Why are there two? Or are there many? Let's try to answer this question by starting in the scientific image and seeing if we can spot the emergence of the manifest image from that vantage point.

Every organism, whether a bacterium or a member of *Homo sapiens*, has a set of things in the world that matter to it and which it therefore needs to discriminate and anticipate as best it can. Philosophers call a list of things deemed to exist an *ontology* (from the Greek word for "thing," surprise, surprise). Every organism thus has an ontology. Another name for it is the organism's *Umwelt* (von Uexküll, 1957; *Umwelt* is the German word for "environment," surprise, surprise). An animal's *Umwelt* consists in the first place of *affordances* (Gibson, 1979), things to eat or mate with, or shun, openings to walk through or look out of, holes to hide in, things to stand on, and so forth. An organism's *Umwelt* is in one sense an *inner* environment, a "subjective" and even "narcissistic" ontology, composed of only the things that most matter to *it*, but its *Umwelt* is not necessarily inner or subjective in the sense of being conscious. *Umwelt* is really an engineering concept; consider the ontology of a computer-controlled elevator, the set of all the things it needs to keep track of in order to do its job.* One of von Uexküll's studies was of the *Umwelt* of a tick. We may suppose that the *Umwelt* of a starfish or worm or daisy is more like the ontology of the elevator than like *our Umwelt*, which is, in fact, our manifest image.

Our manifest image, unlike the daisy's ontology or *Umwelt*, really is manifest, really is subjective in a strong sense. It's the world we live in, the world according to us.† Like the daisy's ontology, however, much of our manifest image has been shaped by natural selection over eons, and is part of our genetic heritage. One of my favorite examples of how different an *Umwelt* can be compares an anteater to an insectivorous bird (Wimsatt, 1980). The bird tracks individual insects and must deal with their erratic flight patterns by having a high flicker-fusion rate (in effect it sees more "frames per second" than we do, and hence a movie would be like a slide show to it). The anteater just averages over the whole ant-infested area and lets its big tongue take up the slack. A philosopher might say that "ant" for an anteater is a *mass term*, like "water" and "ice" and "furniture," not a *sortal* (you can count them) like "olives" and "raindrops" and "chairs." When an anteater sees a nice blob of *ant*, it slurps it up with its tongue, as oblivious to the individuals as we are to the individual glucose molecules we slurp up when we eat a sweet.

Most of our manifest image is not genetically inherited; it is somehow inculcated in our early childhood experience. Words are a very important category of thing for us, and are the medium through which much of our manifest image is transmitted, but the capacity to

---

* We will consider the important details of this example in chapter 27.
† I apologize to those of you who like to fantasize about what it's like to be a daisy, and I offer the concept of the *Umwelt* as a consolation: it lets you do justice to the very real discriminatory prowess of a daisy without going overboard.

categorize some events in the world as words, and our desire to speak, may well be at least partly a genetically inherited talent—like the bird's capacity to make out individual flying insects, or a wasp's desire to dig a nest. Even without grammar to knit them together into sentences, words as mere labels can help bring important categories into sharply focused existence in our manifest image: Mommy, doggie, cookie. Could you ever frame a clear concept of a bargain, or a mistake, or a promise—let alone a home run or a bachelor—without the help of the words I've just used to mention them? Our consideration of Doug Hofstadter's list of favorite thinking tools has already shown us how terms can structure and flavor our minds, enriching our personal manifest images with *things*—loose cannons and lip service and feedback—that are otherwise almost invisible.

17. FOLK PSYCHOLOGY

Probably the most important pattern in our manifest image, because it anchors so many other categories that matter to us, is the pattern I call *folk psychology*. I coined the term in its current meaning in 1981, but it apparently had an earlier incarnation in the writings of Wilhelm Wundt and Sigmund Freud and others (*Volkpsychologie*), where it meant something about national character (the *Geist* of the German *Volk*—you don't want to know). This was an antecedent I had missed, as did many others who adopted the term. I proposed *folk psychology* as a term for the *talent* we all have for interpreting the people around us—and the animals and the robots and even the lowly thermostats—as *agents* with information about the world they act in (*beliefs*) and the goals (*desires*) they strive to achieve, choosing the most *reasonable* course of action, given their beliefs and desires.

Some researchers like to call folk psychology "theory of mind" (or just TOM), but this strikes me as misleading, since it tends to prejudge the question of how we manage to have such a talent, suggesting that we have, and apply, a theory. In a similar spirit, we would have to say that you have a *bicycle theory* if you know how to ride a bicycle, and it's your *nutrition theory* that accounts for your ability to avoid starving to death and refrain from eating sand. This doesn't strike me as a useful way of thinking about these competences. Since everybody agrees that we have the interpretive talent, and everybody does not agree about how we manage to be so competent, I think it's best to keep "theory" out of it and to use a somewhat more neutral term for the time being. Academic or scientific psychology is also in the business of explaining and predicting the minds of others, and it really does have theories: behaviorism, cognitivism, neurocomputational models, Gestalt psychology, and a host of others. Folk psychology is a talent we excel in without formal education. *Folk physics* then, in parallel fashion, is the *talent* we have for expecting liquids to flow, unsupported things to drop, hot substances to burn us, water to quench our thirst, and rolling stones to gather no moss. It's another interesting question, how our brains manage to generate *these* almost always correct expectations so effortlessly, even if we've never taken a physics course.

Folk psychology is "what everyone knows" about their minds and the minds of others: people can feel pain or be hungry or thirsty and know the difference, they can remember events from their past, anticipate lots of things, see what is in front of their open eyes, hear what is said within earshot, deceive and be deceived, know where they are, recognize others, and so forth. The confidence with which we make these assumptions is breathtaking, given how little we know about what is actually going on inside the heads of these people (to say nothing of other animals). So sure are we about all this that it takes some strenuous distancing even to notice that we're doing it.

Artists and philosophers agree on one thing: one of their self-appointed tasks is to "make the familiar strange."* Some of the great strokes of creative genius get us to break through the crust of excessive familiarity, **jootsing** into the new perspective where we can look at ordinary, obvious things with fresh eyes. Scientists couldn't agree more. Newton's mythic moment was asking himself the weird question about why the apple fell *down* from the tree. ("Well, why *wouldn't* it?" asks the everyday non-genius. "It's *heavy!*"—as if this were a satisfactory explanation.) If you are not blind and have blind friends, you will probably confirm my hunch that no matter how much time you've spent in their company, you *still* find yourself occasionally using your hands to point to things or draw explanatory shapes in front of their unseeing eyes, in order to get them to believe and understand what

---

* Among those credited with this aphorism are the philosopher Ludwig Wittgenstein, the artist Paul Klee, and the critic Viktor Shklovsky.

you believe and understand. The "default" expectation when you are in the presence of another awake human being is that both of you can see the same things, hear the same things, smell the same things. You drive down the highway at sixty miles per hour, unperturbed by the fact that another car is coming your way in the opposite lane at the same speed. How do you know there won't be a terrible collision? You unthinkingly assume that the driver (whom you can't even see, and almost certainly don't know) *wants* to stay alive and *knows* that the best way of doing that is staying on the right side of the road. Notice that all it would take to put you in a more anxious frame of mind would be a radio news report informing the world that a new robotic car-driving system was being tested on your route today. Yes, it's *designed* to be safe, and after all, Google created it, but your confidence in the rationality and knowledge of the average oncoming human driver exceeds that of the vaunted robot (except perhaps late on Saturday night).

How come "everybody knows" folk psychology? Is it, after all, TOM, a sort of theory that you learn as a child? Is any of it innate, or if we learn it all, how do we do that and when? There has been a flood of research on these questions in the last thirty years. My answer (still, after all these years of research) is that it is not so much a theory as a practice, a way of investigating the world that comes so naturally it must have some genetic basis in our brains. You do have to learn some of this "at mother's knee," and if you were somehow deprived of all contact with other human beings as you grew up, you would probably be strikingly inept in folk psychology (along with your other serious disabilities), but the urge is very strong to interpret things that move in irregular ways (unlike a pendulum or a ball rolling down a hill) as agents. A favorite demonstration of this in introductory psychology courses is a brief animation made (using stop-action cinematography) by Fritz Heider and Mary-Ann Simmel in 1944. It shows two triangles and a circle moving around, in and out of a box. The geometric shapes couldn't look less like people (or animals), but it is almost irresistible to see their interactions as purposeful, driven by lust, fear, courage, and anger. This antique demo can be found on many websites, such as www.psychexchange.co.uk/videos/view/20452/.

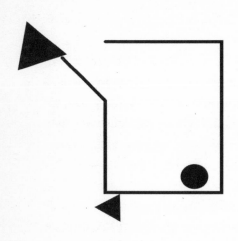

We are born with an "agent detection device" (Barrett, 2000; see also Dennett, 1983), and it is on a hair trigger. When it misfires, as it often does in stressful circumstances, we tend to see ghosts, goblins, imps, leprechauns, fairies, gnomes, demons, and the like where all that is really there are waving branches, toppling stone walls, or creaking doors (Dennett, 2006a). From an early age we effortlessly and involuntarily see others as agents, and not just happy or angry or baffled or afraid, but as *in on the secret* or *wondering which way to turn* or even *unwilling to accept the deal offered*. It isn't brain surgery, or rocket science; it's easy. The power and ease of use of folk psychology is due, I have argued, to the simplifying assumptions that enable it. It is *like* an idealized model in science—maximally abstract and stripped down to the essentials. I call this the *intentional stance*.

18. THE INTENTIONAL STANCE

So far, so good. Almost all of us are good at folk psychology.* We have a talent for thinking of others (and ourselves) as having minds, a practice as effortless as breathing, most of the time. We depend on it without a qualm or a second thought, and it is stupendously reliable. Why is it so easy and how does it work? Here we need to pause and erect some more staging, which will make life much easier for us as we proceed with our explorations.

How does folk psychology work? We can get a good glimpse of the answer by noting how it works when we apply it to things that *aren't* other people. Suppose you are playing chess against a computer. You want to win, and the only good way of working toward that goal is to try to anticipate the computer's responses to your moves: "if I moved my bishop there, the computer would take it; if I moved the pawn instead, the computer would have to move its queen; . . ." How do you know what the computer would do? Have you looked inside? Have you studied its chess-playing program? Of course not. You don't have to. You make your confident predictions on the quite obvious assumptions that the computer

---

* The exceptions help us see the contrast. One of the clearest symptoms of autism, severe and mild, in its various forms, is difficulty with folk psychology. Those with autism who manage to interpret other people at all, such as Temple Grandin, really *do* seem to rely on a hard-won theory. Where we view others effortlessly and, indeed, involuntarily understand the meanings of gestures and smiles and circumstances, she has to deduce these implications of what she observes. She has resourcefully gathered evidence so that she can identify the hallmarks of a friendly greeting as opposed to a threat, and tell when people are agreeing on something. She has taught herself to identify promises and purchases, telling jokes and telling lies. The character Sheldon Cooper in *The Big Bang Theory* is a well-known fictional example of somebody with Asperger's syndrome, a mild form of autism, and we see and hear his brilliant scientific mind churning away, inferring the details of the situations he is confronted with as if he were analyzing the effects of catalysts in chemical reactions in a test tube. Temple Grandin, and the fictional Sheldon Cooper, clearly have a theory of mind. If we others do as well, it is not much like their theories.

1. "knows" the rules and "knows how" to play chess,
2. "wants" to win, and
3. will "see" these possibilities and opportunities for what they are, and act accordingly (that is, rationally).

In other words, you assume the computer is a *good* chess player, or at least not an idiotic, self-destructive chess player. You treat it, in *other* other words, as if it were a human being with a mind. In still further other words, when you use folk psychology to anticipate and understand its moves, you have *adopted the intentional stance.*

The intentional stance is the strategy of interpreting the behavior of an entity (person, animal, artifact, or whatever) by treating it *as if* it were a rational agent who governed its "choice" of "action" by a "consideration" of its "beliefs" and "desires."* The scare quotes around all these terms draw attention to the fact that some of their standard connotations may be set aside in the interests of exploiting their central features: their role in practical reasoning, and hence in the prediction of the behavior of practical reasoners. Anything that is usefully and voluminously predictable from the intentional stance is, by definition, an *intentional system*, and as we shall see, many fascinating and complicated things that don't have brains or eyes or ears or hands, and hence really don't have minds, are nevertheless intentional systems. Folk psychology's basic trick, that is to say, has some bonus applications outside the world of human interactions. (We will see applications not just in computer technology and cognitive neuroscience, but also in evolutionary and developmental biology, to name the most important areas.)

---

* I called it the "intentional" stance instead of, say, the "rational agent" stance or the "belief-desire" stance because at the time (1971) much of the work by philosophers on *intentionality* involved the logic of the "intentional idioms" that serve to report on the *propositional attitudes* of belief, desire, expectation. It is the aboutness alluded to in these idioms that not only raise logical problems but also point to solutions. A belief or a sentence can be about something that does not exist, such as Santa Claus, and a desire can be for something that doesn't exist: the Fountain of Youth or just a cold glass of water in the middle of a desert. The intentional stance is *about* what agents are thinking *about*. It is *not* something that we *intentionally* adopt in the normal course of things; it is typically involuntary and seldom noticed.

I propose we simply postpone the worrisome question of what *really* has a mind, about what the *proper* domain of the intentional stance is. Whatever the right answer to that question is—if it has a right answer—this will not jeopardize the plain fact that the intentional stance *works* remarkably well as a prediction method in these other areas, almost as well as it works in our daily lives as folk psychologists dealing with other people. This move of mine annoys and frustrates some philosophers, who want to blow the whistle and insist on properly settling the issue of what a mind, a belief, a desire *is* before taking another step. *Define your terms, sir!* No, I won't. That would be premature. I want to explore first the power and the extent of application of this good trick, the intentional stance. Once we see what it is good for, and why, we can come back and ask ourselves if we still feel the need for formal, watertight definitions. My move is an instance of *nibbling* on a tough problem instead of trying to eat (and digest) the whole thing from the outset. Many of the thinking tools I will be demonstrating are good at nibbling, at roughly locating a few "fixed" points that will help us see the general shape of the problem. In *Elbow Room* (1984a), I compared my method to the sculptor's method of roughing out the form in a block of marble, approaching the final surfaces cautiously, modestly, working by successive approximation. Many philosophers apparently cannot work that way and have to secure (or so they think) the utterly fixed boundaries of their problems and possible solutions before they can venture any hypotheses.

The three stances

So let's see where the power of the intentional stance comes from, by comparing it with other tactics of anticipation. Let's begin by identifying three main stances (which could be subdivided further for some purposes, but not ours here): the physical stance, the design stance, and the intentional stance.

The *physical stance* is simply the standard laborious method of the physical sciences, in which we use whatever we know about the laws of physics and the physical constitution of the things in question to devise our predictions. When I predict that a stone released from my hand will fall to the ground, I am using the physical stance. In general, for things that are neither alive nor artifacts, the physical stance is the only available strategy, though there are important exceptions, as we shall see. Every physical thing, whether designed or alive or not, is subject to the laws of physics and hence behaves in ways that *in principle* can be explained and predicted from the physical stance. If the thing I release from my hand is an alarm clock or a goldfish, I make the same prediction about its downward trajectory, on the same basis. Predicting the more interesting behaviors of alarm clocks and goldfish from the physical stance is seldom practical.

Alarm clocks, being designed objects (unlike a stone), are also amenable to a fancier style of prediction—prediction from the *design stance*. Suppose I categorize a novel object as an alarm clock: I can quickly reason that *if* I depress a few buttons just so, *then* some time later the alarm clock will make a loud noise. I don't need to work out the specific physical laws that explain this marvelous regularity; I simply *assume* that it has a particular design—the design we call an alarm clock—and that it will function properly, as designed. Design-stance predictions are riskier than physical-stance predictions because of the extra assumptions I have to take into account:

1. that an entity *is* designed as I suppose it to be, and
2. that it will operate according to that design—that is, it will not malfunction.

Designed things are occasionally misdesigned, and sometimes they break. Nothing that happens to, or in, a stone counts as its malfunctioning, since it has no function in the first place, and if it breaks in two, the result is two stones, not a single broken stone. When a designed thing is fairly complicated (a chainsaw in contrast to an ax, for instance), the moderate price one pays in riskiness is more than compensated for by the tremendous ease of prediction. Nobody would prefer to fall back on the fundamental laws of physics to predict the behavior of a chain saw when there is a handy diagram of its moving parts available to consult instead.

An even riskier and swifter stance is our main topic, the *intentional stance*, a subspecies of the design stance in which the designed thing is treated as an agent of sorts, with beliefs and desires and enough rationality to do what it ought to do given those beliefs and desires. An alarm clock is so simple that this fanciful anthropomorphism is, strictly speaking, unnecessary for our understanding of why it does what it does, but adoption of the intentional stance is more useful—indeed, well-nigh obligatory—when the artifact in question is much more complicated than an alarm clock. Let's slowly spell out the practice of adopting the intentional stance, focusing on our example of a chess-playing computer, to make sure we aren't overlooking anything important:

> First, list the legal moves available to the computer when its turn to play comes up (usually there will be several-dozen candidates).

> Now rank the legal moves from best (wisest, most rational) to worst (stupidest, most self-defeating).

> Finally, make your prediction: the computer will make the best move.

You may well not be sure what the best move is (the computer may "appreciate" the situation better than you do!), but you can almost always eliminate all but four or five candidate moves, which still gives you tremendous predictive leverage. You *could* improve on this leverage and predict in advance exactly which move the computer will make—at a tremendous cost of time and effort—by falling back to the design stance. Get the "source code" (see chapter 27) of the program and then "hand simulate" it, running through the millions or billions of tiny steps the computer will take in the course of finding its response to the move you are thinking of making. This will definitely tell you what the computer would do if you made your move, but the time clock would run out—indeed your life would be over—long before you reached the conclusion. Too much information! But still, using the design stance is *much* easier than falling all the way back to the physical stance and trying to calculate the flow of electrons that results from pressing the computer's keys. So the physical stance is utterly impractical when trying to predict and explain the moves of the computer, and even the design stance is too much work, unless you get another computer to do it for you (which is cheating). The intentional stance finesses all that laborious information-gathering and computation and riskily settles on a pretty good bet: the computer will be "rational" enough to find and make the best move (given what it wants—to win—and what it knows—the positions and powers of all the pieces on the board). In many situations, especially when the best move for the computer to make is so obvious it counts as a "forced move," or a "no brainer," the intentional stance can predict its move with well-nigh perfect accuracy without much effort.

It is obvious that the intentional stance works effectively when the goal is predicting a chess-playing computer, since *its* designed purpose is to "reason" about the best move to make in the highly rationalistic setting of chess. If a computer program is running an oil refinery, it is almost equally obvious that its various moves will be made in response to its detection of conditions that more or less dictate what it should do, given its larger designed purposes. Here the presumption of *excellence or rationality of design* stands out vividly, since an incompetent programmer's effort might yield a program that seldom did what the experts said it ought to do in the circumstances. When information systems (or control systems) are well designed, the rationales for their actions will be readily discernible, and highly predictive—whether or not the engineers who wrote the programs attached "comments" to the source code explaining these rationales to onlookers, as good practice dictates. (More on this computer talk later.) We needn't know anything about computer programming to predict the behavior of the system; we need to know about the rational demands of running an oil refinery.

And now we can see why and how the intentional stance works to predict *us*. When we treat *each other* as intentional systems, we are similarly finessing our ignorance of the details of the processes going on in each other's skulls (and in our own!) and relying, unconsciously, on the fact that to a remarkably good first approximation, people are rational. If we are suddenly thrust into a novel human scenario, we can usually make sense of it effortlessly, indeed involuntarily, thanks to our innate ability to see what people ought to believe (the truth about what's put before them) and ought to desire (what's good for them).

There is no controversy about the fecundity of our folk-psychological anticipations, but much disagreement over how to explain this bounty. Do we learn dozens or hundreds or thousands of "laws of nature" along the lines of

"If a person is awake with eyes open and facing a bus, he will tend to believe there is a bus in front of him," and

"Whenever people believe they can win favor at low cost to themselves, they will tend to cooperate with others, even strangers,"

or are all these rough-cast laws generated on demand by an implicit sense that these are the rational responses under the circumstances? The latter, I claim. Whereas there are indeed plenty of stereotypic behavior patterns that can be encapsulated by such generalizations (which might, in principle, be learned one at a time as we go through life), it is actually hard to generate a science-fictional scenario so novel, so unlike all other human predicaments, that people are simply unable to imagine how people might behave under those circumstances. "What would *you* do if that happened to you?" is the natural question to ask, and along with such unhelpful responses as "I'd probably faint dead away" comes the tellingly *rational* answer: "Well, I hope I'd be clever enough to see that I should do X." And when we see characters behaving oh so cleverly in these remarkably non-stereotypical settings, we have no difficulty understanding what they are doing and why. Like our capacity to understand entirely novel sentences of our natural languages, sentences we have never before heard in our lives, our ability to make sense of the vast array of human interactions bespeaks a generative capacity that is to some degree innate in normal people.

We just as naturally and unthinkingly extend the intentional stance to animals, a non-optional tactic if we are trying to catch a wily beast, and a useful tactic if we are trying to organize our understanding of the behaviors of simpler animals, and even plants. The clam has its behaviors, and they are rational, given its limited outlook on the world. We are not surprised to learn that trees that are able to sense the slow encroachment of rivals (because more of the sunlight now falling on them is reflected off tall green things in the vicinity) shift resources into growing taller faster. After all, that's the smart thing for a plant to do under those circumstances. Among artifacts, even the lowly thermostat can sustain a rudimentary intentional-stance interpretation: it wants to keep the temperature at the level you asked it to, samples the temperature frequently to arrive at an up-to-date belief about the actual temperature, compares that to the desired temperature, and acts accordingly. This is what you might tell a young child, to explain the point of the thermostat without getting technical.

This simple theory of intentional systems is a theory about how and why we are able to make sense of the behaviors of so many complicated things by considering them as *agents*. It is *not* directly a theory of the internal mechanisms that somehow achieve the rational guidance thereby predicted. The intentional stance gives you the "specs," the job description, of an intentional system—what it should discriminate, remember, and do, for instance—and leaves the implementation of those specs to the engineers (or evolution and development, in the case of an intentional system that is an organism). Give me an agent that knows the difference between dollar bills and ten-dollar bills, can make change, detect counterfeits, and is willing and able to deliver the product the customer wants twenty-four hours a day. This intentional-stance characterization is either the specs for a vending machine or a rudimentary job description of a convenience store clerk, entirely noncommittal about what kind of innards or further talents the entity might have.

This equivalence, or neutrality, is not a bug but a feature, as the software engineers like to say. It permits intentional-systems theory to play the chief organizing role in bridging the chasm of confusion between our minds and our brains, as we shall see in the next three chapters. Briefly, it allows us to see *what is in common* between "real" beliefs (the beliefs of *persons*) and "mere" belief-like states (of vending machines, animals, young children, and, most usefully, sub-personal *parts* of persons). To anticipate, we can use the intentional stance to give the specs of the *competences* of subsystems in the brain in advance of any detailed knowledge of how those competences are implemented. We analyze the big, fancy "real" person into sub-personal agents, with their own agendas and methods, and then analyze these in turn into yet simpler, stupider agents. Eventually, we arrive at intentional systems that are simple enough to describe without further help from the intentional stance. Bridging the chasm between **personal-level folk psychology** and the **sub-personal** activities of neural circuits is a staggering task of imagination that benefits from this principled relaxation of the conditions that philosophers have tried to impose on (genuine, adult) human belief and desire. Where on the downward slope to insensate thinghood does "real" believing and desiring stop and mere "as if" believing and desiring take over? This demand for a bright line is ill motivated, as we have already seen in chapter 15 and will see again with the help of several other thinking tools.

The use of the intentional stance in both computer science and animal psychology is ubiquitous, and intentional-systems theory explains why this is so. Some theorists in evolutionary biology claim to do without it, but they are fooling themselves, as we shall see in the section on evolution.*

---

* My 1983 target article in *Behavioral and Brain Sciences*, "Intentional Systems in Cognitive Ethology: The 'Panglossian Paradigm' Defended," provides the details, accompanied by a fascinating chorus of objections and rebuttals. For a more recent elaboration of the intentional stance and a further rebuttal to the common objections, see my essay "Intentional Systems Theory" (2009c), from which portions of this section are derived.

19. THE PERSONAL/SUB-PERSONAL DISTINCTION

Your eyes don't see; you do. Your mouth doesn't enjoy chocolate cake; you do. Your brain doesn't abhor the stinging pain in your shoulder; you do. Your hand doesn't sign a contract; you do. Your body may be aroused, but you fall in love. This is not just a "grammatical" point, like the fact that we say, "It's raining," when there is a thunderstorm, not "the thunderstorm is raining." Nor is it *just* a matter of definitional convention. People sometimes ask, dismissively, "Isn't this just semantics?" which is taken to mean that nothing much hangs on how we "define our terms." But how we define our terms often does make a big difference, and this is one of those times. Our way of speaking about *persons* and what they can do and suffer is grounded in some important facts.

At first blush it seems that there are things a whole person can do that none of a person's proper parts can do, and this is almost right, but a ghoulish exercise of imagination suggests that if this is so, then a person is (roughly) a proper part of a human body, namely, an intact and functioning brain. (Do you *have* a brain, or *are* you a brain? Not a straightforward question to answer.) If you cut off my arms, I can still sign a contract (with a pen in my toes or a vocal directive), but if you shut down my brain, nothing my arms and hands could do counts as signing a contract. Pluck out my eyes and I cannot see, unless I get fitted with prosthetic eyeballs, which are not such a distant science-fiction fantasy. What if you start "amputating" parts of my brain? If you were to remove the occipital cortex while leaving my eyes and optic nerve intact, I would be "cortically blind" but might still have some residual visual competence (for instance, the famous condition known as blindsight). No doubt we could amputate a bit more brain and wipe out the blindsight, while still leaving *you* a life to lead. The tempting idea is that such a process of elimination, removing hearing, touch, taste, and smell, could pare down the brain to the ultimate headquarters of *you*—and that is where, and what, a person would be. Tempting but wrong. The brain's multitudinous competences are so intertwined and interacting that there simply is no central place in the brain "where it all comes together" for consciousness.* For that matter, many of the competences, dispositions, preferences, and quirks that make you *you* depend on paths through your body outside your brain; the always popular philosophical thought experiment of the brain transplant (which would you rather be: the brain "donor" or the brain "recipient"?) is enabled by a very distorting idealization. As I once put it, "One cannot tear me from my body, leaving a nice clean edge" (1996a, p. 77).

Probably the most important property of the Internet is its decentralization; it has no hub or headquarters anywhere in the world where dropping a well-placed bomb would kill it. Its proper parts have a high degree of redundancy and versatility, so it "degrades gracefully" if it degrades at all when any proper part of it is disabled. Hal, the intelligent computer in *2001: A Space Odyssey*, has a "Logic Memory Center," a room full of memory cassettes that Dave can detach one by one, shutting Hal down for good. The Internet has no such center, and while nature has not equipped us with quite such a fine level of distributed invulnerability, there is still considerable decentralization of *you* in your body, and considerable versatility in your parts. The organization of your brain proves to be remarkably *plastic* (able to morph into new configurations) so that you can go on being you, pursuing your dreams, confounding your enemies, concocting your stratagems, reliving your trials and triumphs, in spite of the removal

---

* This is the central claim argued in my book *Consciousness Explained* (1991a); the idea of such a special place—I call it the Cartesian Theater—is apparently indomitably tempting, for many thinkers still don't get it, in spite of all the reasons advanced by me and others.

of important but not quite "vital" bodily parts. That is one reason why *you* can have competences that none of your parts have. Or we can turn the point inside out: the only way to understand or make sense of the powers of the *parts* of a whole live body is to consider how they contribute to the coordination of the whole magnificent system.

Consider a few more instances: Your brain doesn't understand English; you do. Your brain doesn't find the joke hilarious; you do. Even if the activities of competent structures in your brain play the major causal roles in your understanding and appreciation, they couldn't do their work without the training and support provided, over the years, by all your sense organs and limbs and other effectors.*

So it is not just conventional when we posit a *person*, the enduring, conscious, rational agent whose live body this is, as the *subject of record* for most of our everyday attributions: it is *you* who made the mistake, won the race, had a crush on Leslie, speak passable French, want to go to Brazil, prefer blondes, committed the libel. (See also chapter 62.) You are hungry, tired, and peevish, all thanks to your sub-personal parts—and nothing else.

But then what about those proper parts? Are they just like bricks stacked up into a living human body? The answer is yes, if we look at the smallest parts: atoms. But it is no at every other level, from the molecular to the cellular and higher. The proteins that are the workhorses inside your cells are amazingly competent and discriminating little robots—nanobots, we might call them. The neurons that do most of the transmission and switching and adjusting work in your brain are more versatile and competent robots—microbots, we might call them. They form coalitions that compete and cooperate in larger structures, communicating back and forth, suppressing each

---

* It is not often remarked that in that favorite thought experiment of philosophers, *the brain in the vat*, the living brain *has* to have had a life in a body to configure all the hardware with the software of years of experience. If you were "just" to build a brain from scratch, letting the connections between elements be whatever they happened to be (wiring up the brand-new brain at random, in other words), the probability of the brain having any competence, harboring any coherent ideas or intentions or projects, or any (apparent) memories would be **Vanishing** (see chapter 35). See also chapter 32.

other, analyzing the flood of information from the senses, waking up dormant information structures "in memory" (which is not a separate place in the brain), and orchestrating the subtle cascades of signals that move your muscles when you act.

All these levels higher than the basic atomic building blocks exhibit a degree of *agency*. In other words, they are interpretable as *intentional systems*. At the molecular level (motor proteins, DNA proofreading enzymes, gatekeepers at trillions of portals in the membranes of your cells, and the like), their competences are very "robotic" but still impressive, like the armies of marching brooms in *The Sorcerer's Apprentice*, or Maxwell's Demon, to take two fictional examples. At the cell level, the individual neurons are more exploratory in their behavior, poking around in search of better connections, changing their patterns of firing as a function of their recent experience. They are like prisoners or slaves rather than mere machines (like the protein nanobots); you might think of them as nerve cells in jail cells, myopically engaged in mass projects of which they have no inkling, but ever eager to improve their lot by changing their policies. At higher levels, the myopia begins to dissipate, as groups of cells—tracts, columns, ganglia, "nuclei"—take on specialized roles that are sensitive to ever-wider conditions, including conditions in the external world. The sense of agency here is even stronger, because the "jobs done" require considerable *discernment* and even *decision-making*.

These agents are like white-collar workers, analysts and executives with particular responsibilities, but also, like white-collar workers everywhere, they have a healthy dose of competitive zeal and a willingness to appropriate any power they encounter in the course of their activities, or even usurp control of any ill-defended activities engaged in by their neighbors or others in communication with them. When we reach agents at this level of competence, the sub-personal parts are intelligent bricks indeed, and we can begin to see, at least in sketchy outline, how we might fashion a whole comprehending person out of them. ("Some assembly required," as it says on the carton containing all the bicycle parts, but at least we don't have to cut and bend the metal, and make the nuts and bolts.)

This idea, that we can divide and conquer the daunting problem of imagining how a person could be composed of (nothing but) mindless molecules, can be looked at bottom-up, as we have just done, or top-down, starting with the whole person and asking what smallish collection of very smart homunculi could conspire to do all the jobs that have to be done to keep a person going. Plato pioneered the top-down approach. His analysis of the soul into three agent-like parts, analogized to the Guardians, the Auxiliaries, and the Workers, or the rational, the spirited, and the appetitive, was not a very good start, for reasons well analyzed over the last two millennia. Freud's id, ego, and superego of the last century was something of an improvement, but the enterprise of breaking down a whole mind into sub-minds really began to take shape with the invention of the computer and the birth of the field of artificial intelligence (AI), which at the outset had the explicit goal of analyzing the cognitive competences of a whole (adult, conscious, language-using) person into a vast network of sub-personal specialists, such as the goal-generator, the memory-searcher, the plan-evaluator, the perception-analyzer, the sentence-parser, and so on.

20. A CASCADE OF HOMUNCULI

In the millennia-old quest to understand the mind, theorists have often succumbed to the temptation to imagine an inner agent, a little man—*homunculus*, in Latin—who sits in the control room in the brain and does all the clever work. If you think of the human nervous system as, say, a huge telephone switchboard network (as thinkers liked to do as recently as the 1950s and 1960s), you have the problem of the telephone operator at the center: Is his or her mind composed of a smaller telephone network with its own central operator, whose mind in turn is composed of . . . ? Any theory that posits such a central homunculus is doomed by the prospect of an infinite regress.

But maybe the mistake isn't postulating a homunculus, but postulating a *central* homunculus. In my first book, *Content and Consciousness* (1969), I made a big blunder, tempted by a wisecrack I couldn't resist. I wrote,

> The "little man in the brain", Ryle's "ghost in the machine",
> is a notorious non-solution to the problems of mind, and
> although it is not entirely out of the question that the "brain
> writing" analogy will have some useful application, it does
> appear merely to replace the little man in the brain with a
> committee. [p. 87]

And what, exactly, is wrong with a committee? (*Aha*—my implied *reductio* is called out!) I eventually came to realize (in *Brainstorms*, 1978a) that the idea of replacing the little man in the brain with a committee is not such a bad one; it is, I think, one of the fundamental good ideas of cognitive science. This was the classic strategy of GOFAI (*good old-fashioned artificial intelligence*; Haugeland, 1985) that came to be known as *homuncular functionalism*:

The AI programmer begins with an intentionally characterized problem, and thus frankly views the computer
anthropomorphically: if he *solves* the problem he will say he
has designed a computer that can [e.g.,] understand questions in English. His first and highest level of design breaks
the computer down into subsystems, each of which is given
intentionally characterized tasks; he composes a flow chart
of evaluators, rememberers, discriminators, overseers and
the like. These are *homunculi* with a vengeance. . . . Each
homunculus in turn is analyzed into *smaller* homunculi, but,
more important, into *less clever* homunculi. When the level is
reached where the homunculi are no more than adders and
subtractors, by the time they need only the intelligence to
pick the larger of two numbers when directed to, they have
been reduced to functionaries *who can be replaced by a machine.*
[p. 80]

The particular virtue of this strategy is that it pulled the rug out
from under the *infinite regress* objection. According to homuncular functionalism the ominous infinite regress can be sidestepped,
replaced by a *finite* regress that terminates, as just noted, in operators whose task is so dull they can be replaced by machines. The key
insight was breaking up all the work we imagined being done by a
central operator and distributing it around to lesser, stupider agents
whose work was distributed in turn, and so forth.

This was a fine advance, but an unwanted artifact of the top-down
approach of classic GOFAI was its rigid bureaucratic efficiency! We
may have been able to imagine getting rid of the central king or the
CEO, but we still had an army of midlevel executives reporting to an
array of vice presidents (whose interactions constituted the highest
level of the system) and ordering their subordinates into action, who
in turn would call up more menial clerical workers, and so forth.
This hyper-efficient organization, with no wasted motion, no feather-
bedding, no insubordination, was largely dictated by the fact that the

large computers on which the early AI models were developed were tiny and slow by today's standards, and people wanted results fast. If you needed to impress the funding agency, your AI had better not take hours to answer a simple question. It should be businesslike in its execution. Besides, writing thousands of lines of code is a lot of work, and if you have succeeded in breaking down the target task— answering questions about moon rocks or diagnosing kidney diseases or playing chess, for instance—into a manageable set of subtasks that you can see how to program and then integrate into a workable system, you can have your "proof of concept"* at a feasibly low cost in terms of time and money.

Notice that computers have always been designed to keep needs and job performance almost entirely independent. Down in the hardware, the electric power is doled out evenhandedly and abundantly; no circuit risks starving. At the software level, a benevolent scheduler system doles out machine cycles to whatever process has the highest priority, and although there may be a bidding mechanism of one sort or another that determines which processes get priority, this is an orderly queue, not a struggle for life. As Marx would have it, "From each according to his abilities, to each according to his needs." The computer scientist Eric Baum has aptly dubbed this hierarchy *"politburo"* control. Probably a dim appreciation of this fact underlies the common folk intuition that a computer could never *care* about anything. Not because it is made out of the wrong materials—why should silicon be any less suitable a substrate for caring than carbon?—but because its internal economy has no built-in risks or opportunities, so it doesn't *have* to care.

Neurons are not like this. The general run of the cells that com-

---

* *Proof of concept* is a useful but dangerous bit of engineering jargon: asked to design a very sophisticated and complicated widget, you design a very simple widget—you solve what is nicely called a *toy problem*—and when it works on its stripped-down task, you declare that you have "proof of concept" and now it's "just" a matter of *scaling up* to the fully competent widget that was requested, which will require only more time and money; the hard, conceptual problem has been "solved." Sometimes this works just as advertised.

prise our bodies are probably just willing slaves—rather like the self-less, sterile worker ants in a colony, doing stereotypic jobs and living out their lives in a relatively noncompetitive (Marxist) environment. But brain cells—I now think—must compete vigorously in a marketplace. For what? What could a neuron *want*? The energy and raw materials to continue to thrive—just like its unicellular eukaryote ancestors and more distant cousins, the bacteria and archaea. Neurons are biological robots of sorts; they are certainly not conscious in any rich sense. Remember, they are eukaryotic cells, akin to yeast cells or fungi. If individual neurons are conscious, then so is athlete's foot! But neurons, like their mindless unicellular cousins, are highly competent agents in a life-or-death struggle, not in the environment between your toes, but in the demanding environment of the brain, where the victories go to the cells that can network more effectively, contribute to more influential trends at the **virtual machine** levels where large-scale human purposes and urges are discernible. Many of the subsystems in the nervous system are organized as *opponent processes*, engaged in a tug-of-war between two sub-subsystems, each trying to have its own way. (Our emotions, for instance, are well seen as rival storms displacing each other as best they can, thwarting each other or collaborating against yet another storm.) I now think, then, that the opponent-process dynamics of emotions, and the roles they play in controlling our minds, are underpinned by an *economy* of neurochemistry that harnesses the competitive talents of individual neurons. (Note that the claim is that neurons are still good team-players within the larger economy, unlike the more radically selfish agents, cancer cells. I recall Nobel laureate biologist François Jacob's dictum that the dream of every cell is to become two cells; neurons vie to stay active and to be influential, but do not dream of multiplying.) In this view, intelligent control of an animal's behavior is still a computational process—in the same way that a transaction in the stock market is a computational process—but the neurons are *selfish neurons*, as neuroscientist Sebastian Seung (2007) has said, striving to maximize their intake of the different currencies of reward we have found in the brain. And what do neurons *buy* with their dopamine, serotonin, or oxytocin? They are purchasing greater influence in the networks in which they participate, and hence greater security. (The fact that mules are sterile doesn't stop them from fending for themselves, and neurons can similarly be moved by self-protective instincts they inherited ultimately from their reproducing ancestors.)

So bottom-up, neuroscientifically inspired, homuncular functionalism is looking better and better as a model of how the brain works, since the more chaotic and competitive "computational architectures" it generates are more plausible from a biological point of view: we can begin to discern the developmental processes that could build and revise these architectures, starting in the embryo and continuing into adulthood, and also see how they could have evolved from simpler nervous systems, themselves teams of less accomplished homunculi, which **sorta** perceive, signal, and remember.*

---

* Not everybody likes this idea. A recent book, *Philosophical Foundations of Neuroscience* (2003), the collaborative effort of a neuroscientist, Max Bennett, and a philosopher, P. M. S. Hacker, heaps scorn on it. For a detailed rebuttal (and their rebuttal to my rebuttal), see Bennett et al., 2009.

21. THE *SORTA* OPERATOR

Why indulge in this "*sorta*" talk? Because when we analyze—or synthesize—this stack of ever-more competent levels, we need to keep track of two facts about each level: what it *is* and what it *does*. What it *is* can be described in terms of the structural organization of the parts from which it is made—so long as we can assume that the parts function as they are supposed to function. What it *does* is some (cognitive) function that it (sorta) performs—well enough so that at the next level up, we can make the assumption that we have in our inventory a competent building block that performs just that function—sorta, good enough to use. This is the key to breaking the back of the mind-bogglingly complex question of how a mind could ever be composed of material mechanisms. At the dawn of the computer age, Alan Turing, who deserves credit as the inventor of the computer if anybody does, saw this prospect. He could start with mindless bits of mechanism, without a shred of mentality in them, and organize them into more competent mechanisms, which in turn could be organized into still more competent mechanisms, and so forth without apparent limit. What we might call the *sorta* operator is, in cognitive science, the parallel of Darwin's gradualism in evolutionary processes (more on this in part VI). Before there were bacteria, there were sorta bacteria, and before there were mammals, there were sorta mammals, and before there were dogs, there were sorta dogs, and so on.

We need Darwin's gradualism to explain the huge difference between an ape and an apple, and we need Turing's gradualism to explain the huge difference between a humanoid robot and a hand calculator. The ape and the apple are made of the same basic ingredients, differently structured and exploited in a many-level cascade of different functional competences. There is no principled dividing line between a sorta ape and an ape. Both the humanoid robot and the hand calculator are made of the same basic, unthinking, unfeeling Turing-bricks, but as we compose them into larger, more competent structures, which then become the elements of still more competent structures at higher levels, we eventually arrive at parts so (sorta) intelligent that they can be assembled into competences that deserve to be called comprehending. We use the **intentional stance** to keep track of the beliefs and desires (or "beliefs" and "desires" or sorta beliefs and sorta desires) of the (sorta-) rational agents at every level from the simplest bacterium through all the discriminating, signaling, comparing, remembering circuits that comprise the brains of animals from starfish to astronomers. There is no principled line above which true comprehension is to be found—even in our own case. The small child sorta understands her own sentence "Daddy is a doctor," and I sorta understand "E = mc²." Some philosophers resist this *anti-essentialism* (see chapter 43): either you believe that snow is white or you don't; either you are conscious or you aren't; nothing counts as an approximation of any mental phenomenon; it's all or nothing. And to such thinkers, the powers of minds are insoluble mysteries because minds are "perfect," and perfectly unlike anything to be found in mere material mechanisms.

22. WONDER TISSUE

In his excellent book on Indian street magic, *Net of Magic: Wonders and Deceptions in India*, Lee Siegel (1991) writes,

> "I'm writing a book on magic," I explain, and I'm asked, "Real magic?" By *real magic* people mean miracles, thaumaturgical acts, and supernatural powers. "No," I answer: "Conjuring tricks, not real magic." *Real magic*, in other words, refers to the magic that is not real, while the magic that is real, that can actually be done, is *not real magic*. [p. 425]

"Real magic" is—by definition, you might say—miraculous, a violation of the laws of nature. Many people want to believe in real magic. When the Amazing Randi, magician, skeptic, and ghostbuster supreme, duplicates the tricks of self-styled psychics such as Uri Geller, he is showing that the startling effects are not real magic; they are conjuring. But this doesn't convince some people. At the question-and-answer session following a performance in Winnipeg many years ago, a member of the audience charged Randi with a double deception: he was just as much a real psychic as Geller—he just pretended to be a mere conjurer exposing Geller's duplicity so he could ride Geller's more famous coattails to fame and fortune! It's hard to rebut that weird challenge, except by teaching everybody in the audience exactly how the tricks are done, which Randi, honoring the tradition of magicians around the world, is reluctant to do. (Penn and Teller have pioneered routines that do expose the secret mechanics of magic tricks, and after enduring condemnation by some of their fellow magicians, they have shown how the traditional taboo can be violated without spoiling the magic show.)

A similar eagerness to believe in real magic afflicts many people when the topic is the relationship between the mind and the brain. Some people, including not a few neuroscientists and psychologists— and philosophers—are at least subliminally attracted to the idea that somehow or other the dynamic properties of neural tissue can do something you might call miraculous, something that harnesses hidden forces undreamed of by science. Maybe they are right, but we mustn't assume that they are from the outset. The rule has to be: *no wonder tissue!*

Here is something we know with well-nigh perfect certainty: nothing physically inexplicable plays a role in any computer program, no heretofore unimagined force fields, no mysterious quantum shenanigans, no *élan vital*. There is certainly no wonder tissue in any computer. We know exactly how the basic tasks are accomplished in computers, and how they can be composed into more and more complex tasks, and we can explain these constructed competences with no residual mystery. So although the virtuosity of today's computers continues to amaze us, the computers themselves, as machines, are as mundane as can-openers. Lots of prestidigitation, but no "real magic."

This is a valuable fact, so valuable that it will get a detailed demonstration in the next section. Its value lies in the fact that any time we can make a computer do something that has *seemed* miraculous, we have a proof that it *can* be done without wonder tissue. *Maybe* the brain does it another way, maybe even with wonder tissue (*maybe* Randi is a real psychic, just like Geller!), but we have no good reason to believe it. Computers thus play an important role as demystifiers, and that is a good reason to insist on developing computer models of anything we are trying to understand, whether it be hurricanes or housing bubbles or HIV or human consciousness.

The term *wonder tissue* is a thinking tool along the lines of a policeman's billy club: you use it to chastise, to persuade others not to engage in illicit theorizing. And, like a billy club, it can be abused. It is a special attachment for the thinking tool **Occam's Razor** and thus enforces a certain scientific conservatism, which can be myopic.

I owe my favorite example of this to William Bateson, one of the fathers of modern genetics, and here's what he had to say not *so* long ago, in 1916:

> The properties of living things are in some way attached to a material basis, perhaps in some special degree to nuclear chromatin [chromosomes]; and yet it is inconceivable that particles of chromatin or of any other substance, however complex, can possess those powers which must be assigned to our factors or gens [genes]. The supposition that particles of chromatin, indistinguishable from each other and indeed almost homogeneous under any known test, can by their material nature confer all the properties of life surpasses the range of even the most convinced materialism. [p. 91]

He just could not imagine DNA. The idea that there might be three billion base-pairs in a double helix inside every human cell was simply not within the scope of his imagination. Fortunately, other biologists didn't share Bateson's pessimism, and they went on to discover just how the apparently miraculous feat of transmitting genetic information from generation to generation is achieved by some pretty fantastic molecules. But along that path of discovery, they held themselves to the rule: no wonder tissue. They knew—from genetics—a lot about the competences their quarry had to possess, and they set their task as the construction of a physically possible model of something that would have those competences.

We face a similar task today. Experimental psychology is giving us an ever-more detailed catalogue of the competences and frailties of the mind—the triumphs of perception and the embarrassments of illusion, the pace of language learning and the conditions of distraction, lust, fear, and mirth—and now, as "convinced materialists," we need to figure out how on earth the brain does it all, without postulating wonder tissue.

As our understanding grows, what counts as wonder tissue shifts.

When "connectionist" and other "neural network" models burst on the scene in the mid-1980s,* they demonstrated learning capabilities and pattern-recognition powers that nobody would have dared postulate in small tracts of neurons a few years earlier. We still don't know exactly how—or even if—the brain exploits the computational powers exhibited by these semi-realistic models, but it is now okay to postulate a connectionist competence for some neural network that you can't *yet* explain as long as you are up-front about it and the competence is not clearly beyond the demonstrated range of feats. (Randi may not do the trick the very same way Geller does, but we are safe in concluding that there is some variation of Randi's method that explains Geller's ability, which gives us guidance in inquiring further into the processes that are actually involved.) The main objection to wonder tissue is that it does not give us a way of solving the problem, but a way of giving up, of assuming that it is a mystery that can never be solved.

---

* For an overview and introduction, see my "Logical Geography of Computational Approaches: A View from the East Pole" (1986). For the definitive first anthology, see McClelland, Rumelhart, and PDP Research Group (1986).

23. TRAPPED IN THE ROBOT CONTROL ROOM

Robots have no **wonder tissue** in them (by definition, in effect), so they provide an antiseptically clean platform for thought experiments, such as this one:

You wake up one morning to find yourself in an unfamiliar bed in a strange windowless room; two of its walls are covered with tiny blinking lights of various colors, and the other two are covered with thousands of pushbuttons. There are numbers on the lights and buttons, but no labels. Somebody has left you a note on the bedside table.

> Good morning! You were drugged and kidnapped while you slept and brought here to your new home. There is food in the fridge and a bathroom in the corner, so your local bodily needs will all be met. You are imprisoned in the control room of a giant robot. Each light, when it turns on, provides rich and relevant information about the robot's circumstances; these lights are all outputs from highly sophisticated neural net analyzers of the raw inputs streaming from the robot's high-definition video eyes and microphone ears, touch sensors, and olfactory sensors. The buttons initiate robotic actions, all coordinated and ready to execute.
>
> The robot inhabits a dangerous world, with many risks and opportunities. Its future lies in your hands, and so, of course, your own future as well depends on how successful you are in piloting your robot through the world. If it is destroyed, the electricity in this room will go out, there will be no more food in the fridge, and you will die. Good luck!

This is a nasty predicament. With your heart in your mouth, you start experimenting, pushing buttons to see what happens. You push the yellow button numbered 4328 and notice that when you do, the blue light numbered 496 flickers out. Were you scratching the robot's itch or closing the robot's eyes or maybe "eating" something, thereby satisfying the robot's pressing metabolic needs? You push button 4328 a second time, and a different scattering of lights turn on. What has changed in the world? What does this *mean*? This is tantalizing because you have been told that there is a tremendous amount of *information* in those lights, but which light signals which information, and which button orders which robotic action?

If only the lights and buttons were labeled! Then—if the labels were in a language you understood—you might be able to solve the problem. Or if only there were a window in the room that you could open, so you could look out and see what moved when you pushed a button! Does the robot have arms and legs? With a window, you could try to correlate events in the outside world with the flashing lights on the walls. Without a window, you have all this information ready at hand, but no way to interpret it. You have hundreds of robotic actions to set into motion, but no way of figuring out what effects they can achieve in the world.

It appears that you are in an impossible situation. However clever and imaginative you are, you won't be able to figure out the meanings of the events occurring on the walls of your room, given all the data at your disposal. But if you can't solve this problem, we have something approaching a paradox, because your predicament here is none other than your brain's predicament! It is trapped in a windowless room—your skull—with millions of input lines positively humming with information about the external world and your bodily circumstances, and millions of output lines poised to stimulate muscles into contraction or relaxation. And your brain can't open a window in your skull and look out to see what's happening that might be causing the patterns of signals streaming into your visual cortex. (What good would such a window be for your brain in any case? Unlike you, it has no eyes in addition to the eyes whose signals it is receiving and trying to interpret, and no prior memories of what things in the world look like.)

Perhaps, you may think, the brain's task is made easier by the fact that the pattern of excitation—the blinking lights—on the surface of the visual cortex when you're looking at a duck, for example, is actually shaped like a duck!* This would be fine, if we could suppose your brain had learned, as you have, what a duck looks like, but how is your brain ever going to learn that?

How can your brain learn anything if it first has to "decode" all its signals? And decode those signals into what? Turkish? Printed labels in Turkish mean nothing to you unless you understand Turkish. Does your brain have to understand a language before it can derive any value from its input? As we have already seen, this idea, that brains come equipped with an internal language that they never have to learn—Mentalese, or the Language of Thought (Fodor, 1975, 2008)—is tantalizing. It seems to be a step in the right direction, but until the details are provided about how it works, and how it evolved in the first place, declaring that there is such a language of thought is just renaming the problem without solving it. We know that the brain solves the problem *somehow*; our brains do manage quite reliably to find the appropriate outputs to cope with the predicaments and opportunities the input information heralds. And we know that the brain's solution—whatever it is—can't be *just* like a language (like English or Turkish) since it isn't acquired in childhood the way we acquire our native tongues. Would it be more like a written language (with memories duly inscribed in the brain's archives) or a purely spoken language? Does it have a vocabulary of thousands or millions or billions of "words"? Does word order matter? Is there a grammar? Can one part of the brain misunderstand another part's message?

If the language-of-thought hypothesis postulates a homunculus in the control room who understands the language (like you in the giant robot, reading the labels on the lights and buttons), it merely

---

* Yes, the patterns of excitation in the occipital (visual) cortex (and other regions) actually do take on the (distorted) shapes of the objects in the world in front of your eyes, but is anything in your brain *looking at* those shapes? Maybe something is **sorta** looking at those shapes. This is an idea to approach with caution.

postpones the task of figuring out how learning and comprehension can be composed out of machinery consisting of uncomprehending parts. And if it *doesn't* postulate a homunculus who decodes the messages, then the system, whatever it is, isn't much like a language after all. And since nobody has yet come up with the details of how such a language of thought would work, or get installed during development and experience, it is probably better not to kid ourselves, not to lull ourselves into thinking we are making progress when we probably aren't.

This intuition pump shows us that your brain is importantly *not* in the same predicament you would be in, trapped in the control room. Its task is—must be—partly solved in advance by the way some inputs are "wired up" to some outputs so that there is some leverage in the brain with which to learn and refine further appropriate relationships. This is another way of dramatizing the widely recognized claim that our brains are not "blank slates" at birth (Pinker, 2002), but are already designed by natural selection to embody various preferences, anticipations, and associations. And as long as some of the appropriate connections are built in, they don't have to be labeled.

Before there can be comprehension, there has to be **competence without comprehension.** This is nature's way. Bacteria have all sorts of remarkable competences that they need not understand at all; their competences serve them well, but they themselves are clueless. Trees have competences whose exercise provides benefits to them, but they don't need to know why. The process of natural selection itself is famously competent, a generator of designs of outstanding ingenuity and efficacy, without a shred of comprehension.

Comprehension of the kind we human adults enjoy is a very recent phenomenon on the evolutionary scene, and it has to be composed of structures whose competence is accompanied by, enabled by, a minimal sort of semi-comprehension, or pseudo-comprehension—the kind of (hemi-semi-demi-)comprehension enjoyed by fish or worms. These structures are designed to behave appropriately most of the time, without having to know why their behavior is appropriate.

The alternative, putting a full-fledged Comprehender in the control room, confronted by all the inputs and outputs, is a guaranteed dead end. Why? Because if this power of comprehension is inexplicable, you have installed wonder tissue, a miracle, at the base of your theory, and if it is explicable—in terms of processes and activities and powers that do not themselves have the power of comprehension—you have wasted your turn and are right back at the beginning with those of us who are trying to explain how comprehension grows out of competence.

IV.
AN INTERLUDE ABOUT COMPUTERS

Time out. As you have probably noticed, I have mentioned computers quite a bit already, and there is much more computer lore to come in the pages ahead. Computers are without a doubt the most potent thinking tools we have, not just because they take the drudgery out of many intellectual tasks, but also because many of the concepts computer scientists have invented are excellent thinking tools in their own right. We are all swimming in the flood of computer jargon these days—software and hardware, bandwidth and gigahertz—and surely most of you have absorbed fairly accurate impressions about what the new buzzwords mean. I have discovered, however, that although my students nod knowingly when I deploy such terms in my classes, their comprehension is uneven, and they sometimes confound me by arriving at weird misunderstandings of what I was trying to convey to them. So I am going to teach you how to write programs for the world's simplest computer.

If you take the time and effort now to master a few basic skills, it will pay off handsomely in deepening your understanding of what follows. (And if you are already a seasoned computer professional, you might find some of my ways of explaining the issues useful when talking to nonexperts, or you can skip ahead.) I have test-flown what follows on hundreds of computer-phobic undergraduates, with happy results: even those who would rather memorize a page of the phone book than solve a puzzle acknowledge the pleasure, the tingle of satisfaction, in making this idiotically simple computer do its stuff. And when you complete the exercise, you will have been initiated into the Seven Secrets of Computer Power.

24. THE SEVEN SECRETS OF COMPUTER POWER REVEALED

Computers have powers that in earlier centuries would have seemed miraculous—"real magic"—but although many computer programs are dauntingly complicated, all of them are composed of steps that are completely explainable in very simple terms. There is no room for mysteries in what computers do. That very fact is part of the value of computers as thinking tools, and explaining—in outline—how this works is philosophically interesting in its own right. How computers do their "magic" is well worth understanding at an elementary level. This chapter provides that demystification.

We start by considering what is probably the simplest imaginable computer, a *register machine*, to see just what its powers are and why. We will then go on to see how a *Turing machine*, and a *Von Neumann machine* (such as your laptop) are just like register machines, only more efficient. (Anything your laptop can do, a register machine can do, but don't hold your breath; it might take centuries.) Then we can understand how other computer "architectures" could further multiply the speed and capacity of our basic machine, the register machine. The architecture of the human brain is, of course, one of the most interesting and important architectures to consider.

Hang on. Am I claiming that your brain is just a gigantic computer? No—not yet in any case. I am pointing out that *if* your brain is a gigantic computer, then there *will be a way* of understanding all its activities with no residual mysteries—if only we can find it. Our method will be *reverse engineering*: studying a complicated system to uncover how it does what it does. Reverse engineering tells us how the heart executes its duties as a pump and how the lungs gather oxygen and expel carbon dioxide. Neuroscience is the attempt to reverse engineer the brain. We know what brains are *for*—for anticipating and guiding and remembering and learning— but now we need to figure out how they accomplish all this.

This is a topic of passionate controversy. The novelist Tom Wolfe (2000) pinpointed the tender spot around which the battles rage with the title of his essay "Sorry, But Your Soul Just Died." If we are to explore this dangerous territory—and not just waste every- body's time with declamations and denunciations—we need some sharper tools. We need to know what computers can do *and how they do it* before we can responsibly address the question of whether or not our brains harbor and exploit incomprehensible or miraculous phenomena beyond the reach of all possible computers. The only sat- isfactory way of *demonstrating* that your brain isn't—couldn't be—a computer would be to show either (1) that some of its "moving parts" engage in sorts of information-handling activities that no computers can engage in, or (2) that the simple activities its parts do engage in cannot be composed, aggregated, orchestrated, computer-fashion, into the mental feats we know and love.

Some experts—not just philosophers, but neuroscientists, psy- chologists, linguists, and even physicists—have argued that "the computer metaphor" for the human brain/mind is deeply misleading, and, more dramatically, that brains can do things that computers can't do. Usually, but not always, these criticisms presuppose a very naïve view of what a computer is or must be, and end up proving only the obvious (and irrelevant) truth, that brains can do lots of things that your laptop can't do (given its meager supply of transducers and effectors, its paltry memory, its speed limit). If we are to evaluate these strong skeptical claims about the powers of computers *in gen- eral*, we need to understand where computer power *in general* comes from and how it is, or can be, exercised.

The brilliant idea of a register machine was introduced at the dawn of the computer age by the logician Hao Wang (1957), a student of Kurt Gödel's, by the way, and a philosopher. It is an elegant tool for thinking, and you should have this tool in your own kit. It is not anywhere near as well known as it should be.* A register machine is an idealized, imaginary (and perfectly possible) computer that consists of nothing but some (finite number of) *registers* and a *processing unit*.

The *registers* are memory locations, each with a unique address (register 1, register 2, register 3, and so on) and each able to have, as *contents*, a single integer (0, 1, 2, 3, . . .). You can think of each register as a large box that can contain any number of beans, from 0 to . . . , however large the box is. We usually consider the boxes to be capable of holding *any* integer as contents, which would require infinitely large boxes, of course. Very large boxes will do for our purposes.

The *processing unit* is equipped with just three simple competences, three "instructions" it can "follow," in stepwise, one-at-a-time fashion. Any sequence of these instructions is a program, and each instruction is given a number to identify it. The three instructions are:

End. That is, it can stop or shut itself down.

Increment register n (add 1 to the contents of register n; put a bean in box n) and go to another step, step m.

Decrement register n (subtract 1 from the contents of register n; remove one bean from box n) and go to another step, step m.

The *Decrement* instruction works just like the *Increment* instruction, except for a single all-important complication: What should it do if the number in register n is 0? It cannot subtract 1 from this (registers cannot hold negative integers as contents; you can't take a bean out of an empty box), so, stymied, it must *Branch*. That is, it must go to some other place in the program to get its next instruction. This requires every *Decrement* instruction to list the place in the program to go to

* I am grateful to my colleague George Smith for introducing me to register machines, in an introductory course on computers we co-taught at Tufts in the mid-1980s. He recognized the tremendous pedagogical potential of register machines, and developed the expository structure I adapt here for a slightly different audience. The Curricular Software Studio that George and I founded at Tufts grew out of that course.

next if the current register has content o. So the full definition of *Decrement* is:

> *Decrement* register *n* (subtract 1 from the contents of register *n*) if you can and go to step *m* **OR** if you can't decrement register *n*, *Branch* to step *p*.

Here, then, is our inventory of everything a register machine can do, with handy short names: *End, Inc,* and *Deb* (for *Decrement-or-Branch*).

At first glance, you might not think such a simple machine could do anything very interesting; all it can do is *put a bean in the box* or *take a bean out of the box* (if it can find one, and branch to another instruction if it can't). In fact, however, it can compute anything any computer can compute.

Let's start with simple addition. Suppose you wanted the register machine to *add* the contents of one register (let's say, register 1) to the contents of another register (register 2). So, if register 1 has contents [3] and register 2 has contents [4], we want the program to end up with register 2 having contents [7] since 3 + 4 = 7. Here is a program that will do the job, written in a simple language we can call RAP, for Register Assembly Programing:

program 1: ADD [1,2]

STEP	INSTRUCTION	REGISTER	GO TO STEP	[BRANCH TO STEP]
1.	*Deb*	1	2	3
2.	*Inc*	2	1	
3.	*End*			

The first two instructions form a simple *loop*, decrementing register 1 and incrementing register 2, over and over, *until register 1 is empty*, which the processing unit "notices" and thereupon *branches* to step 3, which tells it to halt. The processing unit cannot tell what the content of a register is except in the case where the content is o. In terms of the beans-in-boxes image, you can think of the processing unit as blind, unable to see what is in a register until it is empty, something it can detect by groping. But in spite of the fact that it cannot tell, in general, what the contents of its registers are, if it is given program 1 to run, it will *always* add the content of register 1 (whatever number is in register 1) to the content of register 2 (whatever number is in register 2) and then stop. (Can you see why this must always work? Go through a few cases to make sure.) Here is a striking way of looking at it: the register machine can add two numbers together perfectly without knowing which numbers it is adding (or what numbers are or what addition is)!

Exercise 1

> *a. How many steps will it take the register machine to add 2 + 5 and get 7, running program 1 (counting End as a step)?*
> *b. How many steps will it take to add 5 + 2?*
> *(What conclusion do you draw from this?)**

There is a nice way to diagram this process, in what is known as a *flow graph*. Each circle stands for an instruction. The number inside the circle stands for the *address* of the register to be manipulated (not the content of a register) and "+" stands for *Inc* and "−" stands for *Deb*. The program always starts at α, alpha, and stops when it arrives at Ω, omega. The arrows lead to the next instruction. Note that every *Deb* instruction has two outbound arrows, one for where to go when it can decrement, and one for where to go when it can't decrement, because the contents of the register is 0 (*branching on zero*).

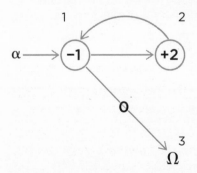

---

* Solutions to the problems in the exercises can be found in the appendix.

Now let's write a program that simply *moves* the contents of one register to another register:

program 2: MOVE [4,5]

STEP	INSTRUCTION	REGISTER	GO TO STEP	[BRANCH TO STEP]
1.	Deb	5	1	2
2.	Deb	4	3	4
3.	Inc	5	2	
4.	End			

Here is the flow graph:

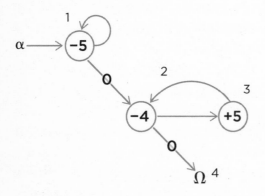

Notice that the first loop in this program cleans out register 5, so that whatever it had as content at the beginning won't contaminate what is built up in register 5 by the second loop (which is just our addition loop, adding the content of register 4 to the 0 in register 5). This initializing step is known as *zeroing out* the register, and it is a very useful, standard operation. You will use it constantly to prepare registers for use.

A third simple program *copies* the content of one register to another register, leaving the original content unchanged. Consider the flow graph and then the program:

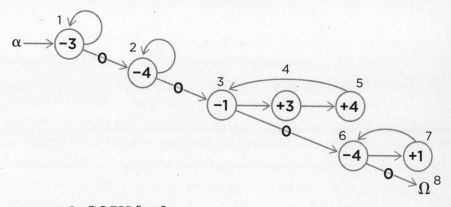

program 3: COPY [1,3]

STEP	INSTRUCTION	REGISTER	GO TO STEP	[BRANCH TO STEP]
1.	*Deb*	3	1	2
2.	*Deb*	4	2	3
3.	*Deb*	1	4	6
4.	*Inc*	3	5	
5.	*Inc*	4	3	
6.	*Deb*	4	7	8
7.	*Inc*	1	6	
8.	*End*			

This is certainly a roundabout way of copying, since we do it by first *moving* the contents of register 1 to register 3 while making a duplicate copy in register 4, and then moving that copy back into register 1. But it works. Always. No matter what the contents of registers 1, 3, and 4 are at the beginning, when the program halts, whatever was in register 1 will still be there and a copy of that content will be in register 3.

If the way this program works isn't dead obvious to you yet, get out some cups for registers (pencil a number on each cup, its address) and a pile of pennies (or beans) and "hand simulate" the whole process. Put a *few* pennies in each register and make a note of how many you put in register 1 and register 3. If you follow the program slavishly, when you finish, the number of pennies in register 1 will be the same as it was at first, and the same number will now be in register 3. *It is very important that you internalize the basic processes of the register machine*, so you don't have to think hard about them, because we're going to be exploiting this new talent in what follows. So take a few minutes to *become* a register machine (the way an actor can become Hamlet).

I find that some of my students lapse into a simple error: they imagine that when they decrement a register, they have to put that penny, the one they just took from register *n*, in some other register. No. Decremented pennies just go back in the big pile, your "infinite" supply of pennies to use in this simple adding-and-subtracting routine.

With *moving*, *copying*, and *zeroing out* in our kit, we are ready to go back to our addition program and improve it. Program 1 puts the right answer to our addition problem in register 2, but in the process it destroys the original contents of registers 1 and 2. We might want to have a fancier addition program that saves these values for some later use, while putting the answer somewhere else. So let's consider the task of adding the content of register 1 to the content of register 2, putting the answer in register 3 and leaving the contents of registers 1 and 2 intact.

Here is a flow graph that will accomplish that:

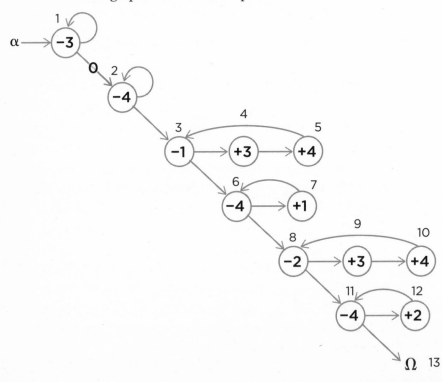

We can analyze the loops, to see what each does. First we zero out the *answer register*, register 3, and then we zero out a spare register (register 4) to use as a temporary holding tank or *buffer*. Then we copy the content of register 1 to both registers 3 and 4, and move that content back from the buffer to 1, restoring it (and in the process, zeroing out register 4 for use again as a buffer). Then we repeat this operation using register 2, having the effect of adding the content of register 2 to the content we'd already moved to register 3. When the program halts, buffer 4 is empty again, the answer is in register 3, and the two numbers we added are back in their original places, registers 1 and 2.

This thirteen-step RAP program puts all the information in the flow graph in the form that the processing unit can read:

program 4: Non-destructive ADD [1,2,3]

STEP	INSTRUCTION	REGISTER	GO TO STEP	[BRANCH TO STEP]
1.	*Deb*	3	1	2
2.	*Deb*	4	2	3
3.	*Deb*	1	4	6
4.	*Inc*	3	5	
5.	*Inc*	4	3	
6.	*Deb*	4	7	8
7.	*Inc*	1	6	
8.	*Deb*	2	9	11
9.	*Inc*	3	10	
10.	*Inc*	4	11	
11.	*Deb*	4	12	13
12.	*Inc*	2	11	
13.	*End*			

I am not going to recommend that you simulate this program by hand with the cups and pennies. Life is short, and *once you have internalized the basic processes in your imagination*, you can now take advantage of a prosthetic device, RodRego, a register machine you can download from http://sites.tufts.edu/rodrego/.

Home screen for the original RodRego register machine, 1986

There are both PC and Mac versions of RodRego available to run on your computer. We developed this thinking tool more than twenty years ago at the Curricular Software Studio, and hundreds of students and others have used it to become fluent register machine thinkers. You can type in your RAP programs and watch them run, with either beans or numbers in the registers. There are also animated PowerPoint demonstrations of the path taken by the processing unit through the flow graph for addition, for instance, so you can see exactly how RAP instructions correspond to the circles in the flow graph.

Now let's turn to subtraction. Here is a first stab at a flow graph for subtracting the content of register 2 from the content of register 1, putting the answer in register 4. Can you see what is wrong with it?

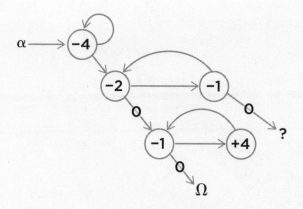

This will work only when the content of register 1 is greater than the content of register 2. But what if this isn't so? Register 1 will "zero out" halfway through one pass in the subtraction loop, before it can finish the subtraction. What should happen then? We can't just ask the computer to end, for this leaves the wrong answer (o) in register 4. We can use this zeroing out to start a new process, which first backs up half a loop and undoes the provisional decrementing from register 2. At this point the content of register 2 (not register 1) gives the right answer if we interpret it as a *negative* number, so you can simply *move* that content to register 4 (which is already zeroed out) and put a sign somewhere indicating that the answer is a negative number. The obvious thing to do is to reserve a register for just this task—let's say, register 3. Zero it out at the beginning, along with register 4, and then have the program put a "flag" in register 3 as the sign of the answer, with o meaning + and 1 meaning −. Following is the flow graph, with comments explaining what each step or loop does. (You can put such comments in your RAP programs, in between # marks. They are for you and other human beings; RodRego will ignore them.)

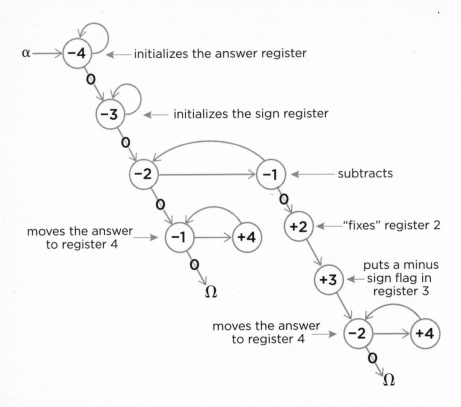

$\alpha \longrightarrow$ **-4** $\longleftarrow$ initializes the answer register

-3 $\longleftarrow$ initializes the sign register

-2 $\longrightarrow$ **-1** $\longleftarrow$ subtracts

moves the answer
to register 4 $\longrightarrow$ **-1** $\longrightarrow$ **+4**   **+2** $\longleftarrow$ "fixes" register 2

Ω

+3 $\longleftarrow$ puts a minus
sign flag in
register 3

moves the answer
to register 4 $\longrightarrow$ **-2** $\longrightarrow$ **+4**

Ω

Exercise 2

   a. *Write the RAP program for this flow graph. (Note that since the pro-gram branches, you can number the steps in several different ways. It doesn't matter which way you choose as long as the "go to" commands point to the right steps.)*

   b. *What happens when the program tries to subtract 3 from 3 or 4 from 4?*

   c. *What possible error is prevented by zeroing out register 3 before trying the subtraction at step 3 instead of after step 4?*

With addition and subtraction under our belts, multiplication and division are easily devised. Multiplying *n* times *m* is just adding *n* to itself *m* times. So we can instruct the computer to do just that, using one register as a *counter*, counting down from *m* to o by decrementing once each time the addition loop is completed.

Exercise 3

    a. *Draw a flow graph (and write the RAP program) for multiplying the content of register 1 by the content of register 3, putting the answer in register 5.*

    b. *(Optional)* By copying and moving, improve the multiplier you created in problem a: when it stops, the original contents of register 1 and register 3 are restored, so that you can easily check the inputs and outputs for correctness after a run.*

    c. *(Optional) Draw a flow graph and write a RAP program that examines the contents of register 1 and register 3 (without destroying them!) and writes the address (1 or 3) of the larger content in register 2, and puts 2 in register 2 if the contents of registers 1 and 3 are equal. (After this program has executed, the contents of register 1 and register 3 should be unchanged, and register 2 should say if their contents are equal, and if not, which of those two registers has the larger content.)*

Division, similarly, can be done by subtracting the divisor over and over again from the dividend and counting up the number of times we can do that. We can leave the remainder, if any, in a special remainder register. But here we must be careful to add one crucial safety measure: we mustn't divide by zero (must we?), so before any division starts, we should run a simple check on the divisor, by trying to decrement it. If we can decrement it, we should increment it just once (restoring it to its proper value) and then proceed with the division. If we hit zero, however, when we try to decrement it, we need to raise an alarm. We can do this by reserving a register for an ERROR

---

* This means the other exercises are compulsory! I mean it. If you want to take advantage of this thinking tool, you have to practice, practice, practice until you become fluent. Working through the simple compulsory exercises may take you an extra hour or two, but it's worth it.

flag: a 1 in register 5 can mean "TILT! I've just been asked to divide by zero!"

Here is the flow graph for dividing the content of register 1 by the content of register 2, putting the answer in register 3, the remainder in register 4, and highlighting register 5 for an "error message" (a 1 means "I was asked to divide by zero").

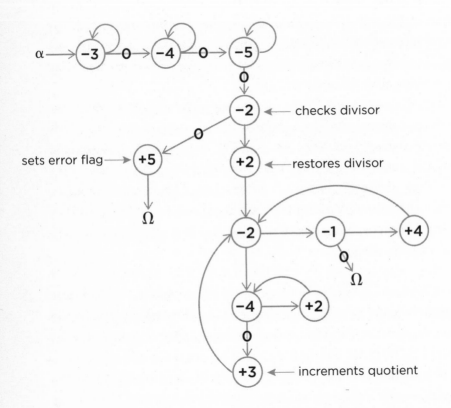

Walk through the flow graph, and notice how zero in the divisor aborts the operation and raises a flag. Notice, too, that register 4 is doing double duty, serving not only as a copy of the divisor, for restoring the divisor for each successive subtraction, but also as a potential remainder register. If register 1 zeros out before register 4 can dump its content back into register 2 for another subtraction, that content is the remainder, right where it belongs.

Secret 1: Competence without Comprehension: Something—
e.g., a register machine—can do perfect arithmetic without
having to comprehend what it is doing.

The register machine isn't a mind; it comprehends nothing; but
it **sorta** comprehends three simple things—*Inc, Deb,* and *End*—in
the sense that it slavishly executes these three "instructions" whenever they occur. They aren't *real* instructions, of course; they are
sorta instructions. They look like instructions to us, and the register
machine executes them as if they were instructions, so it's more than
handy to call them instructions.

As you can now see, *Deb*, Decrement-or-Branch, is the key to the
power of the register machine. It is the only instruction that allows
the computer to "notice" (sorta notice) anything in the world and use
what it notices to guide its next step. And in fact, this *conditional
branching* is the key to the power of all stored-program computers,
a fact that Ada Lovelace recognized back in the nineteenth century
when she wrote her brilliant discussion of Charles Babbage's Analytical Engine, the prototype of all computers.[*]

Assembling these programs out of their parts can become a rather
routine exercise once we get the hang of it. In fact, once we have
composed each of the arithmetic routines, we can use them again
and again. Suppose we numbered them, so that ADD was operation
0 and SUBTRACT was operation 1, MULTIPLY was operation 2,
and so forth. COPY could be operation 5, MOVE could be operation
6, and so on. Then we could use a register to store an instruction, by
number.

---

[*] Ada Lovelace, daughter of the poet Lord Byron, was an amazing mathematician and much
else. In 1843 she published her translation of an Italian commentary on Babbage's Analytical
Engine, together with her own notes, which were longer and deeper than the piece she had
translated: Menabrea (1842). Included in these notes was her carefully worked-out system for
using Babbage's Engine to compute Bernoulli numbers. For this she is often hailed as the
first computer programmer.

Exercise 4 (Optional)

Draw a flow graph, and write a RAP program that turns a register machine into a simple pocket calculator, as follows:

a. *Use register 2 for the operation:*

   0 = *ADD*
   1 = *SUBTRACT*
   2 = *MULTIPLY*
   3 = *DIVIDE*

b. *Put the values to be acted on in registers 1 and 3.*
   (Thus 3 0 6 would mean 3 + 6, and 5 1 3 would mean 5 − 3, and 4 2 5 would mean 4 × 5, and 9 3 3 would mean 9 ÷ 3). Then put the results of the operation in registers 4 through 7, using register 4 for the sign (using 0 for + and 1 for −) and register 5 for the numerical answer, register 6 for any remainder in a case of division, and register 7 as an alarm, signaling a mistake in the input (either divide-by-zero or an undefined operation in register 2).

Notice that in this example, we are using the contents of registers (in each case, a number) to stand for four very different things: a number, an arithmetical operation, the sign of a number, and an error flag.

SECRET 2: What a number in a register stands for depends on the program that we have composed.

Using the building blocks we have already created, we can construct more impressive operations. With enough patience we could draw the flow graph and write the program for SQUARING the number in register 7, or a program to FIND THE AVERAGE of the contents in registers 1 through 20, or FACTOR the content of register 6, putting a 1 in register 5 if 5 is a factor, or COMPARE the contents of register 3 and register 4 and put the larger content in register 5 unless it is exactly twice as large, in which case put a flag in register 7. And so forth.

A particularly useful routine would SEARCH through a hundred registers to see if any of them had a particular content, putting the number of that register's *address* in register 101. (How would it work? Put the TARGET number in register 102, and a copy of the target in register 103; zero out register 101, then, starting at register 1, subtract its contents from the contents of 103 (after incrementing register 101), looking for a zero answer. If you don't get it, go on to register 2, and so forth. If any register has the target number, halt; the address of that register will be in register 101.) Thanks to the basic "sensory" power embodied in *Deb*—its capacity to "notice" a zero when it tries to decrement a register—we can turn the register machine's "eyes" in on itself, so it can examine its own registers, moving contents around and switching operations depending on what it finds where.

SECRET 3: Since a number in a register can stand for anything, this means that the register machine can, in principle, be designed to "notice" anything, to "discriminate" any pattern or feature that can be associated with a number—or a number of numbers.

For instance, a black-and-white picture—*any* black-and-white picture, including a picture of this page—can be represented by a large bank of registers, one register for each pixel, with 0 for a white spot and 1 for a black spot. Now, write the register machine program that can search through thousands of pictures looking for a picture of a straight black horizontal line on a white background. (Don't actually try to do it. Life is short. Just imagine in some detail the difficult and hugely time-consuming process that would accomplish this.) Once you've designed—in your imagination—your horizontal-line-recognizer, and your vertical-line-recognizer, and your semi-circle-recognizer, think about how you might yoke these together with a few (dozen) other useful discriminators and make something that could discriminate a (capital) letter "A"—in hundreds of different fonts! This is one of the rather recent triumphs of computer programming, the *Optical Character Recognition* (OCR) software that can scan a printed page and turn it quite reliably into a computer text file (in which each alphabetic or numerical symbol is represented by a number, in ASCII code, so that text can be searched, and all the other wizardry of word-processing can be accomplished—by nothing but arithmetic). Can an OCR program *read*? Not really; it doesn't understand what is put before it. It **sorta** reads, which is a wonderfully useful competence that can be added to our bountiful kit of moving parts.

SECRET 4: Since a number can stand for anything, a number can stand for an instruction or an address.

We can use a number in a register to stand for an instruction, such as ADD or SUBTRACT or MOVE or SEARCH, and to stand for addresses (registers in the computer), so we can store a whole sequence of instructions in a series of registers. If we then have a main program (program A) that instructs the machine to go from register to register doing whatever that register instructs it to do, then we can store a second program B in those registers. When we start the machine running program A, the first thing it does is to consult the registers that tell it to run program B, which it thereupon does. This means that we could store program A once and for all in the register machine's central processing unit in a reserved set of registers (it could be "firmware" burnt into the ROM—read-only memory), and then use program A to run programs B, C, D, and so on, depending on what numbers we put in the regular registers. By installing program A in our register machine, we turn it into a *stored-program computer*.

Program A gives our register machine the competence to faithfully execute whatever instructions we put (by number) into its registers. Every possible program it can run consists of a series of numbers, in order, that program A will consult, in order, doing whatever each number specifies. And if we devise a system for putting these instructions in unambiguous form (for instance, requiring each instruction name to be the same length—say two digits), we can treat the whole series of numbers that compose the B program, say,

86, 92, 84, 29, 08, 50, 28, 54, 90, 28, 54, 90

as one great big long number:

869284290850285490285490

This number is both the unique "name" of the program, program B, and the program itself, which is executed, one step at a time, by program A. Another program is

28457029759028752907548927490275424850928428540423,

and another is

890829647249028495249885674339043850388245980285454442547 89653985

but most interesting programs would have much, much longer names, millions of digits long. The programs you have stored on your laptop, such as a word processor and a browser, are just such long numbers, many millions of (binary) digits long. A program that is 10 megabytes in size is a string of eighty million 0s and 1s.

SECRET 5: All possible programs can be given a unique number as a name, which can then be treated as a list of instructions to be executed by a Universal machine.

Alan Turing was the brilliant theoretician and philosopher who worked this scheme out, using another simple imaginary computer, one that chugs back and forth along a paper tape divided into squares, making its behavior depend (*aha!*—conditional branching) on whether it reads a zero or a one on the square currently under its reading head. All the Turing machine can do is flip the bit (erasing 0, writing 1, or vice versa) or leave the bit alone, and then move left or right one tape square *and go to its next instruction*. I think you will agree that writing Turing machine programs to ADD and SUBTRACT and perform other functions, using just the binary numbers 0 and 1 instead of all the natural numbers (0, 1, 2, 3, 4, 5, etc.), and moving just one square at a time, is a more daunting exercise than our register machine exercises, but the point Turing made is exactly the same. A Universal Turing machine is a device with a program A (hardwired, if you like) that permits it to "read" its program B off its paper tape and then execute that program using whatever else is on the tape as data or input to program B. Hao Wang's register machine can execute any program that can be reduced to arithmetic and conditional branching, and so can Turing's Turing machine. Both machines have the wonderful power to take the *number* of any other program and execute *it*. Instead of building thousands of different computing machines, each hardwired to execute a particular complicated task, we build a single, general-purpose Universal machine (with program A installed), and then we can get it to do our bidding by feeding it programs—software—that create **virtual machines**.

The Universal Turing machine is a universal mimic, in other words. So is our less well-known Universal register machine. So is your laptop. There is nothing your laptop can do that the Universal register machine can't do, and vice versa. But don't hold your breath. Nobody said that all machines were equal in speed. We've already seen that our register machine is achingly slow at something as laborious as division, which it does by serial subtraction, for heaven's sake! Are there no ways to speed things up? Indeed there are. In fact, the history of computers since Turing's day is precisely the history of ever-faster ways of doing what the register machine does—and nothing else.

SECRET 6: All the improvements in computers since Turing invented his imaginary paper-tape machine are simply ways of making them faster.

For instance, John von Neumann created the architecture for the first serious working computer, and in order to speed it up, he widened the window or reading head of Turing's machine from 1-bit-at-a-time to many-bits-at-a-time. Many early computers read 8-bit "words" or 16-bit "words" or even 12-bit words. Today 32-bit words are widely used. This is still a bottleneck—the von Neumann bottleneck—but it is thirty-two times wider than the Turing machine bottleneck! Simplifying somewhat, we can say that each word is COPIED from memory one at a time, into a special register (the Instruction Register), where it is READ and executed. A word typically has two parts, the Operation Code (e.g., ADD, MULTIPLY, MOVE, COMPARE, JUMP-IF-ZERO) and an Address, which tells the computer which register to go to for the contents to be operated on. So, **10101110** 11101010101 might tell the computer to perform operation **10101110** on the contents of register 11101010101, putting the answer, always, in a special register called the Accumulator. The big difference between the register machine and a Von Neumann machine is that the register machine can operate on any register (*Inc* and *Deb* only, of course), while a Von Neumann machine does all the arithmetic work in the Accumulator, and simply COPIES and MOVES (or STORES) contents to the registers that make up the memory. It pays for all this extra moving and copying by being able to perform many different fundamental operations, each hardwired. That is, there is a special electronic circuit for ADD and another for SUBTRACT and yet another for JUMP-IF-ZERO, and so forth. The Operation Code is rather like an area code in the telephone system or a zip code in the mail: it sends whatever it is working on to the right place for execution. This is how software meets hardware.

How many primitive operations are there in real computers these days? There can be hundreds, or thousands, or in a return to the good old days, a computer can be a RISC (Reduced Instruction Set Computer), which gets by with a few-dozen primitive operations but makes up for it in the blinding speed with which they are executed. (If *Inc* and *Deb* instructions could be carried out a million times faster than a hardwired ADD operation, it would pay to compose ADD by using *Inc* and *Deb*, as we did earlier, and for all additions with less than a million steps, we'd come out ahead.)

How many registers are there in real computers these days? Millions or even billions (but they're each finite, so that really large numbers have to be spread out over large numbers of registers). A byte is 8 bits. If you have 64 megabytes of RAM (random access memory) on your computer, you have sixteen million 32-bit registers, or the equivalent. We saw that numbers in registers can stand for things other than positive integers. *Real* numbers (like π or $\sqrt{2}$ or $\frac{1}{3}$) are stored using a system of "floating point" representations, which breaks the number into two parts, the *base* and the *exponent*, as in scientific notation ("1.495×10^{41}"), which permits computer arithmetic to handle (approximations of) numbers other than the natural numbers. Floating-point operations are just arithmetical operations (particularly multiplications and divisions) using these floating-point numbers as values, and the fastest super-computer you could buy twenty years ago (when I wrote the first version of this chapter) could perform over 4 MEGAFLOPS: over 4 million *fl*oating point *o*perations *per* *s*econd.

If that isn't fast enough for you, it helps to yoke together many such machines in parallel, so they are all working at the same time, not serially, waiting in a queue for results to work on. There is nothing that such a parallel machine can do that a purely serial machine cannot do, slower. In fact, most of the parallel machines that have been actively studied in the last twenty years have been **virtual machines** simulated on standard (nonparallel) Von Neumann machines. Special-purpose parallel hardware has been developed, and computer designers are busily exploring the costs and benefits of widening the von Neumann bottleneck, and speeding up the traffic through it, in all sorts of ways, with co-processors, cache memories, and various other approaches. Today, Japan's Fujitsu K-computer can operate at 10.51 PETAFLOPS—which is over ten thousand *trillion* floating-point operations per second.

That *might* be almost fast enough to simulate the computational activity of your brain in real time. Your brain is a parallel processor par excellence, with something in the neighborhood of a hundred billion neurons, each quite a complicated little agent with an agenda. The optic "nerve," carrying visual information from your eye to your brain, is, all by itself, several million channels (neurons) wide. But neurons operate much, much slower than computer circuits. A neuron can switch state and send a pulse (plausibly, its version of *Inc* or *Deb*) in a few milliseconds—thousandths, not millionths or billionths, of a second. Computers move bits around at near the speed of light, which is why making computers smaller is a key move in making them faster; it takes roughly a billionth of a second for light to travel a foot, so if you want to have two processes communicate faster than that, they have to be closer together than that.

SECRET 7: There are no more secrets!

Perhaps the most wonderful feature of computers is that because they are built up, by simple steps, out of parts (operations) that are also dead simple, there is simply no room for them to have any secrets up their sleeve. No ectoplasm, no "morphic resonances," no invisible force fields, no hitherto unknown physical laws, no **wonder tissue**. You *know* that if you succeed in getting a computer program to model some phenomenon, there are no causes at work in the model other than the causes that are composed of all the arithmetical operations.

Now what about quantum computing, which is all the rage these days? Aren't quantum computers capable of doing things that no ordinary computer can do? Yes and no. What they can do is solve many problems, compute many values simultaneously, thanks to "quantum superposition," the strange and delicate property in which an unobserved entity can be in "all possible" states at once, until observation brings about "collapse of the wave packet." (Consult your favorite popular physics book or website for more on this.) Basically, a quantum computer is just the latest—very impressive—innovation in speed, a quantum leap, one might say, in processing speed. A Turing machine chugging along on its paper tape, or a register machine running around incrementing and decrementing single registers, has a very strict limit on what it can do in practically small chunks of time—minutes or hours or days. A supercomputer like the Fujitsu K-computer can do all the same things trillions of times faster, but that is still not fast enough to solve some problems, especially in cryptography. That is where the speed bonus of quantum computers could pay off—if people can solve the ferociously difficult engineering problems encountered in trying to make a stable, practical quantum computer. It may not be possible, in which case we may have to settle for mere quadrillions of FLOPS.

25. VIRTUAL MACHINES

Real machines are made of moving material parts and are typically named for the jobs they are designed to do. Lawnmowers, can-openers, and coffee grinders each come in a variety of designs, sometimes operating on different physical principles, but they have in common that the machines with the same name *do the same job* at some level of description. Maybe some do it better, but it all depends on what the user wants. A homeowner may prefer a slow lawnmower that is quiet; the owner of a cafe may prefer a coffee grinder that adjusts more accurately for the size of the grind at the cost of being harder to operate. Some machines are versatile: by plugging in a different attachment, you can turn a drill into a saw or a sander. Computers are like that, only instead of having a dozen different things they can be made to do, they can do kazillions of different things. And instead of having to plug in a different attachment for each task, you open a different program—a very long string of zeroes and ones—which changes all the necessary internal switches to just the right settings to accomplish the job. Each of these different systems of settings is a different machine—a different *virtual* machine, a machine "made of instructions," not gears and bearings, wires and pulleys. In computers, instructions can take the place of gears and pulleys because instead of processing bread dough or paper pulp or steel billets, computers process information, and information can always be translated into binary code, zero and one, the only code the computer can—or needs to—"read." Those zeroes and ones are shunted by the trillions through the circuits printed on the silicon chips, temporarily opening and closing gates, moving the streams of information to one circuit or another, thereby controlling what happens to it. The hardware's millions of tiny places that can be in either state 0 or state 1 are the only "moving parts" of the machine, and which machine a computer is at any moment depends on the settings of thousands or millions of little elements.

A virtual machine is what you get when you impose a particular pattern of instructions (more literally, dispositions) on a real machine that has lots of *plasticity*—interacting parts that can be in many different states. Since a virtual machine does informational work, it can *do the same job* as a computer whose "moving parts" are state-changes in hardware by making all those state-changes in *representations* of those moving parts. You can do long division with a pencil on a piece of paper, or if you are really good at long division, you can do it "in your head" by just representing—imagining—the marks on an imaginary page or blackboard. The yield is just as good either way since it's information: an answer. Imagining making a ham sandwich, in contrast, is a poor substitute for making a ham sandwich if you're hungry. So good are computers at doing informational work "in their heads" (by representing the machine that does the work) that it can be next to impossible to tell whether the machine you are using and interacting with is a "dedicated," "hard-wired," special-purpose information-processing machine or a virtual machine running on a general-purpose chip. For instance, most if not all of the tiny, cheap computer chips that are now embedded in elevators and air-conditioners, your car, your refrigerator, and the remote control for your television set are actually general-purpose computers, capable of executing versions of all the programs you run on your laptop, but doomed to spend their entire lives executing a single relatively simple program (the ignition-control program, the defrosting cycle, etc.) "burned" into a ROM that freezes all their magnificent competence into a single trick or two. This is cheaper than making special-purpose chips designed to do only these simple tasks.

The concept of a virtual machine is one of the most useful imagination-stretchers to come out of computer science, and having proved its worth in that domain, it is ripe for importing to other areas. I am using the term in a somewhat extended sense (and will explain why, in due course), so it is worth knowing what the original—and some say proper—meaning of the term is. Computer scientists Gerald Popek and Robert Goldberg (1974) introduced the term. In its original use, it meant "an efficient, isolated duplicate of a real machine"—a duplicate made out of . . . instructions. A real machine, call it A, is actual hardware, made of silicon chips and wires and so forth, and a virtual machine is a computer program (running on some other, *different* real machine, B) that perfectly imitates the A hardware: it may run a bit slower, because it has to compose all of A's most basic operations out of the basic operations available on its own hardware, B, but it runs all the same programs. If you have a program that was written to run on the A hardware, it should run without a hitch on the B hardware as well when the B hardware is running the virtual machine imitation of A.

This is a remarkably useful trick, and not just because of the apparent thrift it suggests: Say you don't have a Mac, but have all this valuable software lying around that only runs on Macs. Well, then, write a virtual machine (VM) imitation of a Mac that runs on your PC, and then your PC can run all the Mac software whenever it runs the Mac VM. Your PC will "pretend" it's a Mac, and the software will be none the wiser! Think of someone who has broken his arm and has it in a plaster cast. The cast severely restricts the movement of his arm, and its weight and shape also call for adjustments in the rest of his bodily movements. Now think of a mime (Marcel Marceau, say) imitating someone with a plaster cast on his arm; if the mime does the trick well, his bodily motions will be restricted in exactly the same ways: he has a *virtual cast* on his arm—and it will be "almost visible." A PC imitating a Mac by running a Mac VM should be indistinguishable—to the software running on it, and to the outside observer—from an actual Mac.

Reality reverses my example, more or less. Although people have developed MAC VMs that run on PCs, to my knowledge these are more stunts than serious, usable software. Macs, on the other hand, do have a reliable, user-friendly VM that runs the PC operating system, Windows, allowing Mac owners to run any PC Windows software they like. Most programs these days are not written to run on particular *hardware*; they are written to run on particular *operating systems* (that in turn run on various hardwares). That's one reason for extending the concept of a virtual machine, to include virtual imitations of operating systems. An operating system is itself a sort of virtual machine, allowing slightly different hardwares to run the same programs, but an operating system is *only* software; it does not imitate any actual hardware but creates, by stipulation in effect, an imaginary machine that obeys certain rules, accepts certain inputs, and so forth.

Another reason for extending the concept is that one of the most popular and ubiquitous virtual machines today is the Java Virtual Machine, or JVM, which, like an operating system, is not an imitation of any actual hardware machine, but rather exists *only* as a software machine. Java is the invention that is most responsible for giving the Internet its versatility; it lets you download little programs—Java applets—from websites that permit you to solve crossword puzzles, play Sudoku, explore maps, enlarge photos, participate in adventure games with other players halfway around the world, and do a lot of "serious" computing too. A website designer can write programs in the Java programming language without having to know whether the computers of the users who go to that website will be Macs or PCs (or Linux machines), because a Java applet always runs on a JVM specifically designed to run on either a Mac or a PC or a Linux machine. The appropriate JVM is automatically downloaded to your computer and installed in a few seconds, and then the Java applet runs on the JVM, like magic. (You may have noticed Java updates being downloaded to your computer—or you may not have noticed! Ideally, you can forget about which JVM is installed on your computer and just expect that any website you go to either will have Java applets that already run on your JVM or will install the appropriate Java update then and there so it will run.)

In my extended sense of the term, then, almost any computer

program can be considered a virtual machine, since it is software—a systematic list of instructions—that, when it runs, turns a general-purpose computer into a special-purpose machine *that could have been designed and wired up as hardware.* One of Alan Turing's most brilliant contributions to science—indeed to human civilization since mid-twentieth century—is the idea of a "Universal" computer (what we call today a Universal Turing machine), which can be *turned into* any other clearly designed computer simply by installing and running a program on it! (In case you decided to skip it, this is explained in detail in chapter 24.) You don't have to build all the different imaginable hardware computers; one hardware computer is all you ever need; software will do all the rest. Ever since Turing's time, we've had the remarkable idea that you can take some complicated hunk of stuff—hardware—with lots of plasticity—adjustable "memory" boxes or registers—and put a set of instructions in those memory boxes, which, when executed, will turn your hunk of stuff into whatever computer you can clearly imagine.

A Turing machine—or a laptop—executes one instruction at a time and moves to the next instruction, but we can generalize the idea to "parallel" computers that can execute many (millions of) instructions at one time. A *register* is any place in the hardware that can hold itself in one state or another (like the zero state and the one state of the bits in your computer, but not necessarily restricted to two different states) until something tells it to change its state. Any system of registers that can perform certain elementary operations on the basis of those states (such as changing a register from one state to another, or using the state of a register to determine what operation to do next) can have its registers set in such a way as to "compute a function" or "run a program." So any such hardware can run a virtual machine designed to exploit these basic steps. And a trick that can be done once can be done two or three or more times, implementing virtual machines in virtual machines in virtual machines in . . . hardware.

Consider a chess-playing program written in Common Lisp (a

high-level computer language) running on Windows 7 (an operating system) running on a PC. This is a PC pretending to be a Windows machine pretending to be a Lisp machine pretending to be a chess-playing machine. If we look at the details of the program at the highest level, they will be more or less comprehensible to a computer-savvy, chess-savvy observer (*"Aha!* This subroutine generates all the legal responses to moving the bishop and then calls the evaluation subroutine which . . ."). In contrast, looking at the actual machine code of the same program, the strings of zeroes and ones that are fed into the hardware instruction register, is a good way to go crazy or blind, so we wisely focus our attention on the higher levels. At each level, we *can* see the woods in spite of all the trees because the lower-level details are conveniently invisible. The parallel between the cascade of virtual machines on a computer and the **cascade of homunculi** in homuncular functionalism about the mind is no mere coincidence. It is the spectacular success of virtual machines in helping us create and comprehend material implementations of hitherto mind-boggling tasks (making airline reservations, playing chess, predicting the weather, taking dictation, etc.) that inspires the hope that we can pull off a similar—only similar—stunt when we reverse engineer the brain.

Perhaps, then, the similarities between human brains whose owners speak French, in spite of all the anatomical differences observable, are best described at the *virtual-machine level:* all of the French-speakers have one version or another of the FVM, the French Virtual Machine, a system made of interlocking dispositions or microhabits stored, somehow, in the brains' billions of registers. Brains of English-speakers will be distinguished by a similar system of reliable patterns, the EVM. If you say to a French-speaker, *"Donnez-moi le sel, s'il vous plaît,"* the FVM will reliably control the same behavior you elicit from an English-speaker by feeding the EVM in her brain the input "Please pass me the salt." Now, how do we build an FVM or EVM that will run in a brain?

We don't yet know how to describe such different levels in the activities of brains of people playing chess or speaking French.* No doubt there will be nothing like the precise mappings that have enabled computer programmers to design their inventions at the highest levels with full confidence that a running program will emerge from the compiler (a program that takes the high-level instructions and translates them into code that can run on the hardware). But we do now have an important proof of concept: we know at least one way to make sense of the high-level competences of a machine with trillions of moving parts—without invoking any **wonder tissue**.

----

* Cognitive neuroscience and computational neuroscience are the research efforts trying to figure out these levels. The difference between the two subfields is mainly a matter of emphasis, with computational neuroscientists more insistent on creating actual working (computer) models of their ideas, while cognitive neuroscientists are often content to sketch higher-level patterns of competence and interaction that must be implemented in any lower-level model. In computer science a similar tug-of-war has existed for years, with, at one pole, AI visionaries who don't bother writing actual programs but settle instead for demonstrating facts about the *specs* for any successful program for one task or another, and at the other pole, hard-bitten engineering types who aren't impressed until they see code that actually runs and does the job. The rest, they sneer, is not software; it is vaporware. Their impatience with their more speculative colleagues is nothing compared to the hostility one can observe between different levels of neuroscientists. As one lab director (whose specialty was the calcium channels in neural axons) once said to me, "In our lab we have a saying; if you work on one neuron, that's neuroscience. If you work on two neurons, that's psychology." And he didn't mean it as a compliment! Since cognitive neuroscience gets the lion's share of media attention (everybody is fascinated by new discoveries about visual illusions, memory, consciousness, speaking, and understanding, but not everybody can get excited about the hundreds of different neuromodulators and their receptors, or astrocyte-neuron interactions, . . . or calcium channels), there is often a high level of professional jealousy infecting the attitudes of computational neuroscientists toward their neighbors in cognitive neuroscience.

26. ALGORITHMS

In *Darwin's Dangerous Idea* (1995a), I introduced this way of seeing what Darwin's great idea comes to:

> Life on Earth has been generated over billions of years in a single branching tree—the Tree of Life—by one algorithmic process or another.

So what, exactly, is an algorithm? There are actually several competing senses of the term, and mine is perhaps the most commodious. What follows is drawn, with revisions, from my book.

Darwin discovered the power of an *algorithm*. An algorithm is a certain sort of formal process that can be counted on—logically—to yield a certain sort of result whenever it is "run" or instantiated. Algorithms are not new, and they were not new in Darwin's day. Many familiar arithmetic procedures, such as performing long division and balancing your checkbook, are algorithms, and so are the decision procedures for playing perfect tic-tac-toe and for putting a list of words into alphabetical order. What is relatively new—and permits us valuable hindsight on Darwin's discovery—is the theoretical reflection by mathematicians and logicians on the nature and power of algorithms in general, a twentieth-century development that led to the birth of the computer, which in turn has led to a much deeper and more lively understanding of the powers of algorithms in general.

The term *algorithm* descends, via Latin (*algorismi*) to early English (*algorism* and, mistakenly therefrom, *algorithm*), from the name of a Persian mathematician, Mûusâ al-Khowârizm, whose book on arithmetical procedures written in the ninth century was translated into Latin in the eleventh century by either Adelard of Bath or Robert of Chester. The idea that an algorithm is a foolproof and somehow "mechanical" procedure has been present for centuries, but it was the pioneering work of Alan Turing, Kurt Gödel, and Alonzo Church in the 1930s that more or less fixed our current understanding of the term. Three key features of algorithms will be important to us, and each is somewhat difficult to define.

(1) *Substrate neutrality*: The procedure for long division works equally well with pencil or pen, paper or parchment, neon lights or skywriting, using any symbol system you like. The power of the procedure is due to its *logical* structure, not the causal powers of the materials used in the instantiation, just so long as those causal powers permit the prescribed steps to be followed exactly.

(2) *Underlying mindlessness*: Although the overall design of the procedure may be brilliant, or yield brilliant results, each constituent step, and the transition between steps, is utterly simple. How simple? Simple enough for a dutiful idiot—or for a straightforward mechanical device—to perform. The standard textbook analogy notes that algorithms are *recipes* of sorts, designed to be followed by *novice* cooks. A recipe book written for great chefs might include the phrase "poach the fish in a suitable wine until almost done," but an algorithm for the same process might begin "choose a white wine that says 'dry' on the label; take a corkscrew and open the bottle; pour an inch of wine in the bottom of a pan; turn the burner under the pan on high; . . ."—a tedious breakdown of the process into dead-simple steps, requiring no wise decisions or delicate judgments or intuitions on the part of the recipe-reader.

(3) *Guaranteed results*: Whatever it is that an algorithm does, it always does it, if it is executed without misstep. An algorithm is a foolproof recipe.

It is easy to see how these features made the computer possible. *Every computer program is an algorithm*, ultimately composed of simple steps that can be executed with stupendous reliability by one simple mechanism or another. Electronic circuits are the usual choice, but the power of computers owes nothing (save speed) to the causal peculiarities of electrons darting about on silicon chips. The very same algorithms can be performed even faster by devices shunting photons in glass fibers, or much, much slower by teams of people using paper and pencil.

What Darwin discovered was not really *one* algorithm, but rather a large class of related algorithms that he had no clear way to distinguish.

27. AUTOMATING THE ELEVATOR

Before leaving our interlude about computers, I want to introduce one more group of useful ideas, about **source code, comments,** and **object code**, which have an important application in our quest to understand how meaning could reside in brains. It is often wise to study a dead-simple example in some detail, to get a secure grip on our concepts before tackling a mind-buster. (In the field of artificial intelligence, these are nicely known as *toy problems*. First you solve the toy problem before tackling the gnarly great real-world problem.) So this is a story—made up, for simplicity's sake, but otherwise realistic—about how human elevator operators got replaced by computer chips.

In my youth there were elevator operators, people whose job was to go up and down in an elevator all day, stopping at the right floors to take on and let off passengers. In the early days they manipulated a curious handle that could be swung clockwise or counterclockwise to make the elevator go up or down, and they needed skill to stop the elevator at just the right height. People often had to step up or down an inch or two upon entering and leaving, and operators always warned people about this. They had lots of rules about what to say when, and which floors to go to first, and how to open the doors, and so forth. Their training consisted in memorizing the rules and then practicing: following the rules until it became second nature. The rules themselves had been hammered out over the years in a design process that made a host of slight revisions and improvements. Let's suppose that this process had more or less settled down, leaving an ideal rulebook as its product. It worked wonderfully. Anybody who followed the rules exactly was an excellent elevator operator.

Now imagine what happened when it became possible for a simple computer program to take over all the control tasks of the operator. (In fact, this happened gradually, with various automatic mechanical devices being introduced to take the more skilled tasks away from the operator, but we'll imagine that elevators went from human operators to completely computer-controlled systems in one leap.)

The elevator manufacturer, let's suppose, calls in a team of software engineers—programmers—and hands them the rulebook that the human elevator operators have been following: "*This* is a specification of the performance we want; make a computer program that follows all the rules in this book as well as the best human operators and we'll be satisfied." As the programmers go through the rulebook, they make a list of all the actions that have to be taken, and the conditions under which they are prescribed or forbidden. In the process they can clean up some of the untidiness in the rulebook. For instance, if they build in sensors to ensure that the elevator always stops at exactly the right level, they can eliminate the loop that requires the operator to say, "Please step up" or "Please step down," but they might leave intact a simple (recorded voice saying), "[*N*]th floor; watch your step." Then they write out a sketch of the program in what is often called pseudo-code, a sort of mongrel language that is halfway between everyday human language and the more demanding system of source code. A line of pseudo-code might look something like this: "if callfloor > currentfloor, then ASCEND until callfloor = currentfloor and STOP; OPENDOOR. WAIT. . . ."

Once the plan is clear in pseudo-code, and seems to be what is wanted, the pseudo-code can be translated into source code, which is a much more rigorous and structured system of operations, including definitions of terms—variables, subroutines, and so forth. Human beings can still quite readily decipher source code—after all, they write it—and hence the rules and terms of the rulebook are still quite explicitly represented there, if you know how to look for them. This is made easier by two features: First, the names for the variables and operations are usually chosen to wear their intended meaning on their sleeves (callfloor, weightsum, TELLFLOOR, etc.). Second, as we saw in chapter 24, programmers can add *comments* to their source code, parenthetical explanations that tell other human readers of the source code what the programmer had in mind, and what the various parts are supposed to do. When you write a program, it is wise to add comments for yourself as you go, since you may easily forget what you thought the line of code was doing. When you go back to correct programming errors, these comments are very useful.

Source code has to be very carefully composed according to a strict syntax, with every element in the right place and all the punctuation in the right order, since it has to be fed to a *compiler* program, which takes the source code and translates *it* into the sequences of fundamental operations (in *object code*) that the actual machine (or virtual machine) can execute. A compiler can't be asked to guess what a programmer means by a line of source code; the source code must tell the compiler exactly what operations to perform—but the compiler program may have lots of different ways of performing those tasks and will be able to figure out an efficient way under the circumstances. Some compilers are better than others; if you feed the same program (written in source code) into two different compilers, the object code that one compiler produces may run significantly faster than the other object code, for instance. Imagine you've written a chess program, and you feed its source code to two different compilers. Then play the two compiled versions against each other on the same computer. Even though the two versions "think all the same thoughts in the same order" (they have to—they have exactly the same source code), one may always beat the other simply because it thinks those thoughts faster, using fewer basic machine cycles, and hence can look farther ahead during the time available!

Back to our elevator. Once the compiler has compiled the object code, it can be *executed* (it's an executable file, and usually has the suffix ".exe" in its name) by the (virtual) machine. It may need rounds of debugging (back to the source code, adjust it, then recompile, etc.), but eventually it's a "finished" product. It can be "burned" into ROM on a tiny chip that contains a Universal machine—and any number of virtual machines on top of it—and installed in the elevator. Installing it involves hooking up the inputs from transducers, such as the signals from the buttons, and from the scale in the floor that measures the combined weight of the passengers, and from other parts, and hooking up the outputs to effectors (running the motors that open and close the door, and raise and lower the car, and updating the displays or playing the recordings). *Tada!* A machine has replaced one actual human being—not a figurative homunculus. And the machine *follows the same rules* as the human operator. Does it really? *Really?* Ok, it doesn't. It **sorta** follows the same rules. This is a nice intermediate case between a human being who memorizes—and hence literally represents in her mind, and consults—the rules that dictate her behavior, and the planets, whose orbits are elegantly described by equations that the planets "obey." We human beings also often occupy an intermediate level, when we have internalized or routinized through practice a set of explicit rules that we may then discard or even forget ("i" before "e" except after "c" or when it sounds like "a" as in "neighbor" and "weigh"). And it is also possible to **sorta** follow rules that have still not been explicit in debugged form: the rules of English grammar, for instance, which continue to challenge linguists. Put in terms of this example, linguists today are still thrashing around trying to write the rulebook for speaking good English, while every ten-year-old native English-speaker has somehow installed and debugged a pretty good version of the object code for the EVM!*

Notice, before we leave this example, that the comments inserted in the source code to help the program designers keep track of the purposes of all the interlocking software parts have no counterpart in the design process that creates all the hardware, firmware, and software that characterize our brains. When natural selection installs various functional structures in our brains, this is like uncommented code—it's there for a reason, but the reason is not represented in the structure by any labeling or explanation, which the brain couldn't

---

* My colleague Ray Jackendoff (1993) calls this the paradox of language learning: children somehow effortlessly absorb, and follow, the rules of grammar that professional linguists are still trying to figure out how to express.

understand anyway. (This will be discussed in more detail in chapter 40.) There are also uncommented, unannounced reasons for the adjustments that occur during development and learning. We, like the linguists, are still struggling to reverse engineer all these "rules" and "procedures." This task is even harder than reverse engineering object code for the purpose of recovering source code (minus the comments), but it can be done in principle.

SUMMARY

For hundreds of years we've had plenty of evidence that the brain is somehow the seat of the soul, but until the middle of the twentieth century it was all but unimaginable how this could possibly be true. The brain could be seen to be composed of lots of different, curiously shaped organs, in left and right pairs, given vivid names by early anatomists—the hippocampus (seahorse), the amygdala (almond), the wrinkly cortex (bark)—but what on earth did these parts do? They didn't digest food or purify the blood, did they? Was the brain just an organ for cooling the blood, a sort of radiator, as Aristotle thought? The parts were connected by nerve fibers, so perhaps they communicated with each other somehow. Descartes suggested that some nerve fibers were like bell-pull wires—when you tugged at one end, something happened at the other end, but what, exactly? A bell ringing wouldn't seem to get you any closer to understanding the brain as the mind, and nobody had any better ideas.*

Then along came Turing, building on a tradition that went back to Babbage and Pascal and Leibniz and others, with the suggestion that a brain could be composed of simple parts that were ultimately just mechanical (like a mousetrap, a ringing bell, a lock and key, a synapse), but if these parts were organized to interact together in clever ways, they might actually be able to do something intelligent on their own, without human intervention, and without any ghosts in the machine to guide them along. They might compute. Before

---

* Actually, Descartes's great imagination got him at least close to some very good ideas. He imagined that the tugging wires might open tiny gates or pores, releasing floods of pent-up "animal spirits" (cerebrospinal fluid) that could then do some kind of hydraulic work; not a bad sketch of an amplifier! Even better, he saw that at least some intelligent (apt, appropriate) work could be done entirely mechanically by such a device: an automatic *reflex*. Pulling your foot from a hot fire when the heat tugged on a wire was his example: all just brain-machinery, no mind required!

Turing hit on his idea, "computer" was a job title; industry and government hired thousands of people to *be* computers, calculating tables for use in business, navigation, gunnery, and banking, for instance. Maybe, he surmised, the brain is itself like a (human) computer; maybe it processes information by slavishly following huge lists of very simple instructions (like *Inc* and *Deb*). Once the early theorists of cognitive science, Alan Turing and John von Neumann, the creator of cybernetics, Norbert Wiener, and the creator of information theory, Claude Shannon, as well as many others, articulated the idea, it could even seem obviously right—how could we not have seen it all along? Brains must take in information from the sense organs and process it, by somehow computing with it, until they have extracted the valuable ore of meaning, which, by further computing, they could then categorize and store for future use in guiding the behavior of the body, which provided the brain with its energy and protective home. The key innovation in Turing's vision was that it eliminated the awkward element that was all too evident in earlier imaginings of information-processing: junctures that required a clerk or translator or librarian, that required, in short, some kind of *understander* to appreciate the import of the signals. Turing saw that in one sense this was inescapable: intelligent processes would always *require* choosing one course or another on the basis of the discrimination of some difference in the signal. But he could reduce this understanding to the barest minimum: conditional branching, the mindless process by which a device decides (sorta decides) to go left rather than right because it senses (sorta senses) 1 rather than 0, A rather than B, x rather than y. That, and arithmetic, were all you needed. You could then build up devices of any level of discernment by piling virtual machines on top of virtual machines on top of virtual machines—to put it anachronistically. This vision has been tempting for more than fifty years, but the details, as we've already begun to see, are not falling into place easily. If brains are computers, they aren't much like the computers we use every day. We need to remind ourselves of the fundamental features of computers so that we can consider more biologically realistic alternatives to the businesslike architectures that are featured in our stereotypes.

The point of this interlude has been to clarify, and add just enough detail to, that vision so that you can *use* it as a thinking tool, an imagination prosthesis to help you understand the issues we are now going to address: first, a bit more on how meanings might reside in brains (and other machines), and then how such clever architectures could get designed by evolution without assistance from any Master Programmer or Intelligent Designer. You will then be in a good position to use the thinking tools you have acquired to think effectively about consciousness and free will, the two most treacherous topics I know.

V

MORE TOOLS
ABOUT MEANING

28. A THING ABOUT REDHEADS

We have already seen some problems with the otherwise tempting idea that all the information we carry around in our brains—our beliefs, perceptions, memories, policies, and so on—is broken into sentence-like pieces that are filed away and ready to be awakened. Brain-writing cannot just *install* a false belief, and people can share a belief (about that murder in London, for instance) without—apparently—having to share a formula in Brainish. But what *else* could store information in the brain? We human beings can learn things "piecemeal," so there must be some way of adding independent facts *roughly* one at a time.

Economists (and others) often like to point out that you cannot do just one thing. Doing "one thing" always has consequences. Similarly, the idea that you can *learn* just one thing is dubious. But to a first approximation you can. You earlier learned in these pages that there is a mammal called a pudu. Unless you paused to check on this, you probably can't affirm anything else about pudus, aside from the fact that they nurse their young, have backbones, and are relatively rare (since otherwise you surely would have heard of them). It's no mystery how you learned this: you read a sentence and believed it. But can animals or small children who do not yet have a language learn *a single fact* (like a fact expressed in a simple sentence) from some interesting bit of experience? The idea that knowledge or belief or learning *has* to be decomposable into sentence-sized gobbets is probably an illusion of anthropomorphism. We human beings encounter lots of declarative sentences, spoken and written, in the course of a day, and we thereby come to know all manner of facts (and believe a smattering of falsehoods). Some we store in libraries and archives, and some we store only in our brains. We seldom memorize the actual sentences, word for word, but when we salt away the gist of an encountered sentence, it must be—mustn't it?—a matter of storing a sentence-like something-or-other, a formula in Brainish. If this isn't so, what are the alternatives?

Suppose Pat says that Mike "has a thing about redheads." What Pat means, roughly, is that Mike has a stereotype of a redhead that is rather derogatory and influences Mike's expectations about, and interactions with, redheads. It's not just that Mike is prejudiced against redheads, but that he has a rather idiosyncratic and *particular* thing about redheads. And Pat might be right—more right than he knew! It could turn out that Mike does have a *thing*, not an *idea* or a *thought* or a *belief* or an *image* or any of the other traditional things that furnish our conscious experience, but a bit of **sub-personal** cognitive machinery in his brain, that is *about redheads* in the sense that it systematically comes into play whenever the topic is redheads or a redhead, and adjusts various parameters of Mike's cognitive machinery, making flattering hypotheses about redheads less likely to be entertained, or confirmed, making relatively aggressive behavior vis-à-vis redheads closer to implementation than otherwise it would be, and so on. Such a *thing about redheads* could be very complex in its operation or quite simple. The contribution of Mike's thing about redheads could be perfectly determinate and also undeniably meaningful, and yet no *expression* of this meaning as a *sentence-believed-true* could be more than a mnemonic label for its role. That is, it might be impossible to characterize the role of this thing as a *belief*, weirdly specific or weirdly vague, that *all redheads are F* . . . (where we cash out "*F*" with whatever content seems to do the most justice to Mike's attitude). Mike certainly has an *attitude* about redheads, but it isn't any particular *propositional* attitude, to use the philosophical jargon. In other words, it defies categorization in the format

Mike believes that: for all *x*, *if x* is a redhead then . . . ,

no matter how deviously we pile on the exclusion clauses, qualifiers, probability operations, and other explicit adjusters of content.

Philosophers (and other theorists) have often tried to "reduce" all cognitive states to information-bearing states—call them beliefs and desires—that can be expressed in such formulas, and while the tactic is a great way of providing a rough sketch of some person's psychology (it's the **intentional stance**, in effect), the idea of making it ultra-precise is hopeless. We can say, if we like, that various beliefs are *implicit* in the system. What this means is that the system is (currently) designed to operate "under the assumption" that the world's redheads have such-and-such features. When computer programmers put a **comment** on the **source code**, telling everyone that this system relies on a defined set of assumptions, they know enough not to devote labor trying to render the propositions precise, because they appreciate that these are mnemonic labels for us observers, not anything the computer has to **sorta** read and **sorta** understand, and even for us observers the comments are not *specifications* of content that can be used the way a chemist uses formulae to describe molecules. Giving an intentional-stance interpretation of some sub-personal brain structure is like putting a comment on a few lines of code; when done well, it provides an illuminating label, not a *translation* into English or other natural language of some formula in Brainish that the brain is using in its information-processing. By missing this trick, some philosophers have created fantasy worlds of internal sentence-manipulating machinery, where it is imagined to make all the difference whether the content of a particular brain event is expressed using a disjunctive predicate (*I see a boy-OR-girl*) or with a predicate lacking logical structure (*I see a child*), for instance.

What is the aim of this intuition pump? It is simply an attempt to suggest that the familiar refrain in support of the language of thought—"What else could it be?"—might have a good answer that would take the wind out of the sails of those who find it obvious. I wish I could provide an ambitious, alternative computational architecture that triumphantly displayed a working alternative, but I can't. Nobody can yet, but then almost nobody is trying, since the conviction is still widespread that the language of thought is "the only straw floating," as somebody put it many years ago. Bear in mind, however, that nobody in cognitive science has developed a working model of the language of thought either, or has even tried very hard. It's a very, very difficult problem.* I would like to encourage an open mind on this score.

---

* An aside for the experts: CYC (Lenat and Guha, 1990) is certainly the most impressive artificial intelligence (AI) implementation of something like a language of thought, an enCYClopedic, largely hand-coded database with a proprietary inference engine presiding over it. CYC has been under development for over a quarter of a century now, the work of many hands, but it achieves its power by being ruthlessly nonbiological and nonpsychological in its design. (See the excellent Wikipedia entry on CYC.) Mike's thing about redheads almost certainly is not an axiomatized redhead-microtheory composed in Brainish and incorporated into a large database rather like CYC. We do not yet know how much can be done by a host of things about things of this ilk because we have not yet studied them directly, except in very simple models (such as the insectoid subsumption architectures of Rodney Brooks and his colleagues—see Brooks, 1987). One of the chief theoretical interests of Brooks's Cog project (a humanoid robot—see Dennett, 1994b) was that it pushed these profoundly nonpropositional models of contentful structures into territory that is recognizable as human psychology.

29. THE WANDERING TWO-BITSER, TWIN EARTH, AND THE GIANT ROBOT

It may seem that by mentioning Mike's thing about redheads and source code in the same paragraph, I am encouraging readers to ignore a crack in the foundation, indeed a yawning chasm in the middle of my discussion of intentionality: the problem of *original intentionality*. John Searle (1980) coined the term, and the sharp distinction he draws between *original* and *derived* intentionality is on the face of it intuitively satisfying and even deeply compelling. The doctrine of original intentionality is the claim that whereas some of our artifacts may have a kind of intentionality derived from us—our books and movies, our computers and signposts, for instance—we have original (or intrinsic) intentionality, utterly underived. For example, the printed words on this page are about philosophy only because we readers and writers of English have thoughts and beliefs about philosophy that we contrive to convey using these trails of ink, which wouldn't be about anything at all without us word-users. Our thoughts and beliefs, in contrast, mean what they mean independently of any ulterior users; they exhibit original intentionality, and are the source ultimately of all the derived intentionality in many of our artifacts. These include not just words and sentences and books, but maps, movies, paintings, signs, symbols, diagrams and other technical representations, and, importantly, computers. Both a shopping list on a scrap of paper and a shopping list on your iPhone are about groceries only in virtue of the use you make of these symbol structures, the interpretation you bestow on them, in aid of your desire to buy groceries and your belief that the supermarket is the place to go, which are about groceries more directly and originally. Aristotle said that God is the Unmoved Mover, and this doctrine announces that we are the Unmeant Meaners.

We can all agree with Searle that nothing has *intrinsic* intentionality just in virtue of its physical shape or other such properties. If, by cosmic coincidence, the shape

FREE BEER

appeared in traces of different minerals in a cliff face on Mars, it would not ("in itself") be an announcement about an alcoholic beverage, no matter how eager earthling readers were to interpret it that way. The shape wouldn't be about anything, in spite of first appearances. If some complicated events and objects in the world are about other things, it must be that they derive their aboutness somehow from being in the service of representing, interpreting intentional systems whose states (beliefs, desires, brain states) already have intentionality somehow.

The question then is whether *anything* has original intentionality! And at first blush it might seem obvious that something has to have original intentionality, since derived intentionality has to be derived from something. And then the obvious candidates for things with original intentionality would be human minds. So not surprisingly, some very eminent philosophers who otherwise disagree sharply with Searle on many issues—for instance, Jerry Fodor and Saul Kripke—nevertheless agree with him about this. They, and the many who concur, think that human minds (or their mental states) have original intentionality and are radically unlike robot control systems in this regard.

They are all flat-out mistaken. Yes, mistaken. I mean it. Given the undeniable appeal of the distinction between original and derived intentionality, any attempt to discredit it runs the risk of being subverted by misplaced charity: "He *can't* seriously be saying that we're wrong about *that!* He must mean something else, some esoteric philosophical point he has unwisely dressed up in these preposterously provocative clothes!" Probably the best way to convince people that I really do mean it is to trot out as vivid and clear a case of *derived* intentionality as I can find, and then show that the beloved contrast between that case and human minds as cases of *original* intentionality evaporates on closer examination. It's a tall order, but here goes. I will need three linked intuition pumps to accomplish the feat.

1. The Wandering Two-Bitser. Consider a standard soft-drink vending machine, designed and built in the United States, and equipped with a transducer device for accepting and rejecting U.S. quarters. Let's call such a device a two-bitser.* Normally, when a quarter is inserted into a two-bitser, the two-bitser goes into a state, call it Q, which "means" (note the scare quotes; it sorta means) "I perceive/ accept a genuine U.S. quarter now." Such two-bitsers are quite clever and sophisticated, but hardly foolproof. They do "make mistakes." That is, unmetaphorically, sometimes they go into state Q when a slug or other foreign object is inserted into them, and sometimes they reject perfectly legal quarters—they fail to go into state Q when they are *supposed to* go into state Q. No doubt there are detectable patterns in these cases of "misperception." And no doubt at least some of the cases of "misidentification" could be predicted by someone with enough knowledge of the relevant laws of physics and the design parameters of the two-bitser's transducing machinery. It could follow quite directly from various applications of physical laws that not only legal U.S. quarters but also objects of some kind K trigger state Q, but objects of kind J (too heavy) or kind L (magnetic, unlike quarters) do not. Objects of kind K, then, would be good *slugs*—reliably "fooling" the transducer. (Look how many times I've used the **sorta** operator in this paragraph, so that I can use the **intentional stance** when giving you the specs of the two-bitser. Try to rewrite the paragraph without using the intentional stance and you will appreciate

---

* I probably shouldn't have used this obsolete slang term for a quarter-detector when I first created this intuition pump, but I did, and the term has had a fair amount of, well, currency, so let's stay with it. The obscure origin of the term "two bits" for a U.S. quarter takes us back to "pieces of eight" and doubloons and other such relics of pirate days.

how efficient it is, and how well-nigh indispensable the **sorta** operator can be for such purposes.)

If objects of kind K became more common in the two-bitser's normal environment, we would expect the owners and designers of two-bitsers to develop more advanced and sensitive transducers that would reliably discriminate between genuine U.S. quarters and slugs of kind K. Of course, trickier counterfeits might then make their appearance, requiring further advances in the detecting transducers, and at some point such escalation of engineering would reach diminishing returns, for there is no such thing as a *foolproof* mechanism. In the meantime, the engineers and users are wise to make do with standard, rudimentary two-bitsers, since it is not cost-effective to protect oneself against negligible abuses.

The only thing that makes the device a quarter-detector rather than a slug-detector, or a quarter-*or*-slug-detector, is the shared intention of the device's designers, builders, owners, and users. Only in the environment or context of those users and their intentions can we single out some of the occasions of state Q as "veridical" and others as "mistaken." It is only relative to that context of intentions that we could justify calling the device a two-bitser in the first place.

I take it that so far I have Searle, Fodor, Kripke, and others nodding their heads in agreement: that's just how it is with such artifacts; this is *a textbook case of derived intentionality*, laid bare. And so it embarrasses no one to admit that a particular two-bitser, straight from the American factory and with "Model A Two-Bitser" stamped right on it, might be installed on a Panamanian soft-drink machine, where it proceeded to earn its keep as an accepter and rejecter of quarter-balboas, legal tender in Panama and easily distinguished (by human beings) from U.S. quarters by the design and writing stamped on them, but not by their weight, thickness, diameter, or material composition.

I'm not making this up. I have it on excellent authority—Albert Erler of the Flying Eagle Shoppe, Rare Coins—that standard vending machines cannot distinguish between U.S. quarters and

Panamanian quarter-balboas minted between 1966 and 1984. Small wonder, since they were struck from U.S. quarter stock in American mints. And—to satisfy the curious, although it is strictly irrelevant to the example—the current (2011) exchange rate is one balboa equals $.98, so a quarter-balboa is, today, ever so slightly less valuable than a U.S. quarter.

Such a two-bitser, whisked off to Panama, would still normally go into a certain physical state—the state with the physical features by which we used to identify state Q—whenever a U.S. quarter or an object of kind K or a Panamanian quarter-balboa is inserted into it, but now a different set of such occasions count as the mistakes. In the new environment, U.S. quarters count as slugs, like objects of kind K, as inducers of error, misperception, misrepresentation. After all, back in the United States a Panamanian quarter-balboa is a kind of slug.

Once our two-bitser is resident in Panama, should we say that the state we used to call Q still occurs? The physical state in which the device "accepts" coins still occurs, but should we now say that we identify that physical state as "realizing" a new state, QB, instead? Well, there is considerable freedom about what we should say, since after all a two-bitser is just an artifact, and talking about its perceptions and misperceptions, its veridical and non-veridical states—its intentionality, in short—is "just metaphor." The two-bitser's internal state, call it what you like, doesn't *really* (originally) mean either "U.S. quarter here now" or "Panamanian quarter-balboa here now." It doesn't *really* mean anything—so Searle, Fodor, and Kripke (*inter alia*) would insist. Its internal state only *sorta* means something, but that will be enough to raise some problems that can also arise for us enjoyers of original intentionality. Let's look at the details.

The two-bitser was originally designed to be a detector of U.S. quarters. That was its "proper function" (Millikan, 1984), and, quite literally, its *raison d'être*, its reason for existing. No one would have bothered bringing it into existence had not this purpose occurred to them. And given that this historical fact about its origin licenses a certain way of speaking, such a device may be primarily or properly characterized as a two-bitser, a thing whose function is to detect quarters, so that *relative to that function* we can identify both its veridical states (when it gets things right) and its errors.

This would not prevent a two-bitser from being wrested from its home niche and pressed into service with a new purpose—whatever new purpose the laws of physics certify it would reliably serve—as a K-detector, a quarter-balboa-detector, a doorstop, a deadly weapon. In its new role there might be a brief period of confusion or indeterminacy. How long a track record must something accumulate before it is no longer a two-bitser, but rather a quarter-balboa-detector (a q-balber)—or a doorstop or a deadly weapon?* On its very debut as a q-balber, after ten years of faithful service as a two-bitser, is its state Q already a *veridical* detection of a quarter-balboa, or might there be a sort of force-of-habit error of nostalgia, a mistaken identification of a quarter-balboa *as* a U.S. quarter?

As described, the two-bitser differs strikingly from us in that it has no provision for memory of its past experiences—or even sorta memory of its past sorta experiences. But this could easily be provided, if it was thought to make a difference. To start with the simplest inroad into this topic, suppose the two-bitser (to refer to it by the name of its original baptism) is equipped with a counter, which after ten years of service stands at 1,435,792. Suppose it is not reset to zero during its flight to Panama, so that on its debut there the counter turns over to 1,435,793. Does this tip the support in favor of the claim that it has not yet switched to the task of correctly identifying quarter-balboas? (After all, it **sorta** misclassifies the event as yet another one of those q events—detections of U.S. quarters—it was designed to detect.) Would variations and complications on this

---

* A sad iron—like the one your great grandmother used to press the family clothes—makes a fine doorstop. If you hunt for one in antique shops and "collectibles" websites, make sure you get an authentic one, not a replica; some for sale are just iron doorstops, cast in the shape of antique sad irons. A hundred years from now somebody may manufacture quaint doorstops that look just like two-bitsers—you know, the devices your great grandparents used back when coins were used for money.

theme drive your intuitions in different directions? (Turn all the knobs on the intuition pump to see what happens to your intuitions.)

We can assure ourselves that nothing *intrinsic* about the two-bitser considered narrowly all by itself and independently of its prior history would distinguish it from a genuine q-balber, made to order on commission from the Panamanian government. Still, given its ancestry, is there not a problem about its function, its purpose, its meaning, on this first occasion when it goes into the state we are tempted to call Q? Is this a case of going into state Q (meaning "U.S. quarter here now") or state QB (meaning "Panamanian quarter-balboa here now")? I would say (along with Millikan, 1984) that whether its Panamanian debut counts as going into state Q or state QB depends entirely on whether, in its new niche, it was *selected for* its capacity to detect quarter-balboas—literally selected, for example, by the holder of the Panamanian Pepsi-Cola franchise. If it was so selected, then even though its new proprietors might have forgotten to reset its counter, its first "perceptual" act would count as a correct identification by a q-balber, for that is what it would *now* be *for*. It would have acquired quarter-balboa-detection as its proper function. If, on the other hand, the two-bitser was sent to Panama by mistake, or if it arrived by sheer coincidence, its debut would mean nothing, though its utility might soon—even immediately—be recognized and esteemed by the relevant authorities (those who could press it into service in a new role), and thereupon its subsequent states would count as tokens of QB. But until it was selected for the job, no matter how good it was at detecting quarter-balboas, its acceptance state wouldn't *mean* (in its artifactual, derived, *sorta* sort of way) "Panamanian quarter-balboa here now." Presumably Searle and colleagues would be content to let me say this, since, after all, the two-bitser is just an artifact. It has no original intentionality, so there is no "deeper" fact of the matter we might try to uncover. They would say that this is just a pragmatic question of how best to talk, when talking metaphorically and anthropomorphically about the states of the device.

Now that we have a good firm grip on *derived* intentionality, let's see what is supposed to be different about underived, *original* intentionality, *our* intentionality. Here is where Searle, Fodor, Kripke, and many others disagree with not just me, but also philosophers Ruth Millikan, Paul and Patricia Churchland, cognitive scientists Douglas Hofstadter, Marvin Minsky, and just about everybody else in the field of artificial intelligence (AI). After more than thirty years of wrangling, feelings still run high. What, then, is at issue?

2. *Twin Earth.* Suppose some human being, Jones, looks out a window and thereupon thinks he sees a horse. There may or may not be a horse out there for him to see, but the fact that he is in the mental state of thinking he sees a horse is *not at all* a matter of interpretation (Searle and company say); it is a brute fact, an instance of *original intentionality.* Let's see what happens, then, when we construct a thought experiment exactly parallel to the Panama caper. (Hint: this will be a **reductio ad absurdum** argument.) Suppose then that the planet Twin Earth was just like Earth, save for having schmorses where we have horses.* Schmorses look like horses, and are well-nigh indistinguishable from horses by all but trained biologists equipped with DNA test kits, but schmorses aren't horses any more than dolphins are fish. Twin Earthians call a schmorse a "horse," or "cheval," or "Pferd," or some other name—remember, Twin Earth is exactly like Earth except for having schmorses.

Suppose we whisk Jones off to Twin Earth, land of the schmorses, without his realizing it. (We drug him for the trip and arrange for him to wake up in his counterpart bed on Twin Earth.) When we then confront him with a schmorse, he'll naturally say, and think, "Look! A horse." When he does this, either he really is, still, provoked

---

* Philosopher Hilary Putnam (1975) invented Twin Earth many years ago, and my intuition pump is carefully modeled to reproduce the relevant details of his. My two-bitser tale is really just an elaborate resetting of the knobs of his intuition pump. There have been dozens or maybe even hundreds of other variations discussed by philosophers in the last thirty-five years. In its original telling, Putnam chose water on Earth and ersatz water (composed of XYZ, not H2O) on Twin Earth, but this raises complications not relevant to our use of the intuition pump, so let schmorses be the quarter-balboa analogues in this telling.

into the state of believing he sees a horse (a mistaken, non-veridical belief) or he is provoked by that schmorse into believing, for the first time in his life (and veridically), that he is seeing a schmorse. Which is it, and how could we tell? Is his schmorse-provoked belief true or false? If his first thought was a mistaken belief that he'd just seen a horse, how long would it take him, living among schmorses and talking with Twin Earthians about schmorses, to adjust the *meaning* of the sound "horse" in his language (without realizing it!)? If he raised some children on Twin Earth, would *their* word "horse," learned at their father's knee, mean horse or schmorse? They've never seen a horse, remember. Only schmorses.

This is obviously a bizarre, extreme example, but it does raise a good issue: What determines what our terms mean, and how? Does history count for everything, and always, or can current use overcome or overrule history? In this case, Jones has no privileged insight to offer us; he has no idea he's no longer on Earth, so he would presumably insist that his word "horse" meant *horse*. His word, the word on his lips, derives its meaning from his perceptual belief, and he knows what he believes: he's looking at a horse. That's why he said, "Look! A horse." ("What could be more obvious?" he might add.) But then suppose we told him about his journey, and the subtle but important difference between horses and schmorses. What would he say then, or what should he say then, and, more fundamentally, is there a good reason to think that whatever he says is decisive? Isn't he just doing what the rest of us would be doing, theorizing about a case in which neither he nor we have privileged information? Suppose he says his word "horse" *now* means schmorse—when he sees a schmorse and calls it a horse, he's not making a mistake. When in Rome, and all that.

Can he just declare what his words mean, and have that settle the issue? What if he later forgot what he had declared? We sometimes do things like this: "Henceforth, by 'jubjub' I will mean table salt! Please pass the jubjub!" In the context of scientific theorizing, such stipulative definition is an important and well-established practice, but it relies on a cooperative community of communicators. If Jones has original intentionality, presumably, then there should be a fact of the matter about the meaning of his terms under any circumstances, but it appears that Jones himself isn't able to consult his own original intentionality any better than we outsiders can. Suppose, for instance, we lie to Jones about our having taken him to Twin Earth, and he believes our lies (people in philosophers' intuition pumps can be mighty gullible). If he then tells us his word "horse" now means schmorse, will he be right? Perhaps what he ought to say is that he has no idea what his word "horse" means now. But then, since for all we know we too may have been whisked off to Twin Earth, shouldn't we all admit that we have no idea what we mean by "horse" either?

Those of us who are dubious about the whole idea of *original intentionality* have ready answers to all these questions, but it takes a third thought experiment to make it clear enough to have a fighting chance against traditional intuition. (So *caveat lector*! I'm going to try to cajole you into abandoning a precious hunch.)

3. The Giant Robot. Suppose you decided that you wanted to experience life in the twenty-fifth century, and suppose that the only known way of keeping your body alive that long required it to be placed in a hibernation device of sorts, where it would rest, slowed down and comatose, for as long as you liked. You could arrange to climb into the support capsule, be put to sleep, and then be automatically awakened and released in 2401.

Designing the capsule itself is not your only engineering problem, for the capsule must be protected and supplied with the requisite energy (for refrigeration or whatever) for almost four hundred years. You will not be able to count on your children and grandchildren for this stewardship, for they will be long dead before the year 2401, and you cannot presume that your more distant descendants, if any, will take a lively interest in your well-being. So you must design a supersystem to protect your capsule and to provide the energy it needs for four hundred years.

There are two basic strategies to consider. On one, you should find the ideal location, as best you can foresee, for a fixed installation that will be well supplied with water, sunlight, and whatever else your capsule (and the supersystem itself) will need for the duration. The main drawback to such an installation, or "plant," is that it cannot be moved if harm comes its way—if, say, someone decides to build a freeway right where it is located. The second alternative is much more sophisticated, but it avoids this drawback: design a mobile facility for your capsule along with the requisite sensors and early-warning devices so that it can move out of harm's way and seek out new energy sources as it needs them. In short, build a giant robot and install the capsule (with you inside) in it.

These two basic strategies are obviously copied from nature: they correspond roughly to the division between plants and animals. A third option from nature, a hardened spore or seed that can survive indefinitely inside its armor, is not available to you, since your life-support system has high energy demands, and spores are as inert and low energy as nature can make them. Since the animal strategy fits our purposes, we shall suppose that you decide to build a robot to house your capsule. You should try to design it so that above all else it "chooses" actions that will further your best interests. Bad moves and wrong turns would tend to incapacitate it for the role of protecting you until 2401—which is its sole *raison d'être*. This is clearly a profoundly difficult engineering problem, calling for the highest level of expertise in designing a "vision" system to guide its locomotion, and other "sensory" systems. And since you will be comatose throughout and thus cannot guide and plan its strategies, you will have to design it to generate its own plans in response to changing circumstances. It must "know" how to "seek out" and "recognize" and then exploit energy sources, how to move to safer territory, how to "anticipate" and then "avoid" dangers. With so much to be done, and done fast, you had best rely on economies whenever you can: give your robot no more discriminatory prowess than it will probably need to distinguish what needs distinguishing in the world.

Note once again that I've put all the intentional or "mentalistic" terms, such as "sensory" and "seek out" and "anticipate" in scare quotes, to indicate that this is a specific kind of **sorta** intentionality, *derived* intentionality, intentionality that is entirely dependent on your human purposes. This is *your* artifact, and whatever intentionality it has, it owes to you, its author. If I had left off the scare quotes, I could be accused of sneaking in some ideology, relying on the fact that engineers and others routinely use such language—without scare quotes—to talk about the specs of an information-handling device (like the **elevator**-controller). I am deliberately *not* making that move; I am granting, for the sake of argument, that *any* use of intentional language to describe or prescribe artifact talents is merely metaphorical. Note as well that, like the two-bitser, the robot's machinery is subject to economic considerations: it needs to "detect" or "discriminate" many things, but its "discriminators" will not be foolproof. It can make mistakes, but *what counts as a mistake depends ultimately on its author's needs and desires.* If the author wanted to make a droll robotic clown that apparently blundered about the world "misidentifying" things, then some of these "mistakes" would be cases of getting it right, triumphs of clown-control.

Back to the intuition pump: Your task will be made more difficult by the fact that you cannot count on your robot being the only such robot around with such a mission. If your whim catches on, your robot may find itself competing with others (and with your human descendants) for limited supplies of energy, fresh water, lubricants, and the like. (See chapter 67 for a brief discussion of the importance of the presence of other agents.) It would no doubt be wise to design your robot with enough sophistication in its control system to permit it to calculate the benefits and risks of cooperating with other robots, or of forming alliances for mutual benefit, but again, any such calculation must be a "quick and dirty" approximation, arbitrarily truncated by time pressure.

The result of this design project would be a robot capable of exhibiting a kind of self-control, since you must cede fine-grained, real-time control to your artifact once you put yourself to sleep. As such, it will be capable of deriving its own subsidiary goals from its assessment of its current state and the import of that state for its ultimate goal (which is, still, to preserve you). These secondary goals may take it far afield on century-long projects, some of which may be ill-advised, in spite of your best efforts during the design phase. Your robot may embark on actions antithetical to your purposes, even suicidal, having been "convinced" by another robot, perhaps, to subordinate its own life mission to some other.

Note too that at this point, even though all the robot's intentional states and acts are derived from your purposes, they are beginning to become detached somewhat from your purposes. Since you designed the robot to "think for itself" to some degree, its "thinking" may escape your anticipated boundaries. For a real-world, nonfictional example of such an artifact, consider a chess-playing computer that can beat its creator at chess. It is true that the only reason we can say that the computer is currently "investigating" queen-side rook options and "deciding" not to castle is that it is an artifact designed by a human artificer to do just that sort of thing. But it is also true that given the artificer's goal of making a *good* chess-playing computer, many of the artificer's decisions concerning what the computer's states are (derivedly) *about* are forced on the artificer: given the fact that a chess player needs accurate information about the rules and the state of the game, there *must* be states that concern each bishop and each pawn, and states that involve an evaluation of the game if the computer's queen captured the opponent's knight on the current move, and so forth. And no amount of authorial fiat could make a state of the computer be (derivedly) about the number of pawns remaining on the board if that state wasn't appropriately linked to locating each and every pawn on the board. Once a designer's largest goal is fixed (make a chess player, make a giant robot, make a hurricane simulator), cruel nature takes over and dictates what will work and what won't, and hence which states of which system count as mistaken or inaccurate. Poets may be able to get away with a declaration that a poem that seems to be about horses is actually about professors—William Blake tells us that the "tygers of wrath are wiser than the horses of instruction"—but computer engineers cannot similarly impose their intentions on their creations.

Let's take stock. The giant robot's simulacrum of mental states would be just that—not *real* deciding and seeing and wondering and planning, but only *as if* deciding and wondering and planning. We should pause to make sure we understand what this claim encompasses. The imagined robot is certainly much more sophisticated than the humble two-bitser; we have granted it the power to "plan" new courses of action, to "learn" from past errors, to "form allegiances," and to "communicate" with its competitors. Moreover, to do all this "planning" and "learning" and "communicating," it will have to be provided with control structures that are rich in self-reflective, or self-monitoring, power. In other words, it will have a human-like access to its own internal states and be capable of "reporting," "avowing," and "commenting upon" what it "takes" to be the import of its own internal states (when it "decides" it doesn't "want" to "lie" to us). It will have "opinions" about what these states mean, and we should no doubt take those "opinions" seriously as very good evidence— probably the best evidence we can easily get—on what those states "mean" *metaphorically speaking* (remember: it is only an artifact and has no original intentionality; we're considering its *derived* intentionality, which will be no more obvious to observers than the intentionality of us "real" agents). The two-bitser was given no such capacity to sway our interpretive judgments by issuing apparently confident "avowals" to the effect that it had no idea it was now in Panama or that it was surprised to learn about quarter-balboas.

There are several ways one might respond to this intuition pump, and we will examine them shortly, but first I want to draw out the most striking implication of standing firm on our initial presumption: no artifact, no matter how much AI wizardry is designed into it, has anything but derived intentionality. If we cling to this view, the conclusion forced on us is that our own intentionality is exactly like that of the robot, for the science-fiction tale I have told is not new; it is a variation on Richard Dawkins's (1976) vision of us and all other biological species as "survival machines" designed to prolong the futures of our selfish genes. We are artifacts, designed over the eons as survival machines for genes that cannot act swiftly and informedly in their own interests. Our interests as we conceive of them and the "interests" of our genes may well diverge—even though were it not for our genes' "interests," we would not exist. Their preservation is our original *raison d'être*, even if we can learn to ignore that goal and devise our own *summum bonum*, thanks to the intelligence, the capacity to learn, that our genes have installed in us. So our intentionality is derived from the intentionality of our "selfish" genes. They are the Unmeant Meaners, not us!

Of course our genes' intentionality is not *intrinsic* in any sense; the "meaning" of any gene is dependent on the whole evolved "alphabet" system of ACGT codons, protein synthesis, and development, for a start. But it is *original* in the sense that it is the *first* of many *representational* systems that have evolved. All the later systems have agents—intentional systems—whose representations get their intentionality from the goals they further (just like the intentionality of the giant robot).*

This vision of things, while it provides a satisfying answer to the question of whence came our own intentionality, does seem to leave us with an embarrassment, for it derives our own intentionality from entities—genes—whose intentionality is a paradigm case of mere *as if* intentionality. How could the literal depend on the metaphorical? Moreover, there is surely this much disanalogy between my science-

---

* Tecumseh Fitch's important paper "Nano-Intentionality: A Defense of Intrinsic Intentionality" (2008) proposes that eukaryotic cells—but not their ancestors, prokaryotic cells—were the first evolved entities with "intrinsic" intentionality, because their self-protective talents were, he claims, strikingly more advanced than their ancestors'. His emphasis on the autonomy, the agency, of individual cells strongly influenced the revisions to my homuncular functionalism (see chapter 20), but I disagree with his attempt to stop the finite regress at eukaryotes. Prokaryotes can no more be "replaced by a machine" than eukaryotes; the agency goes all the way down to the proteins, bottoming out at the selfish genes.

fiction tale and Dawkins's story: in my tale I supposed that there was conscious, deliberate, foresighted engineering involved in the creation of the robot, whereas even if we are, as Dawkins says, the product of a design process in which our genes are the primary beneficiaries, that is a design process that utterly lacks a conscious, deliberate, fore-sighted engineer. But this is not a good objection, as we shall see.

The chief beauty of the theory of natural selection is that it shows us how to eliminate the intelligent artificer from our account of origins. And yet the process of natural selection is responsible for designs of great cunning. It is not the genes that are the designers; genes themselves could not be more stupid; they cannot reason or represent or figure out anything. They do not do the designing them-selves; they are merely the *beneficiaries* of the design process—the clients, you might say. (In our story, they could be put in parallel with a very stupid, very rich client who hires the best engineers to build him a survival machine. If it weren't for him, the engineers would not have a well-funded assignment, and it is *his* survival that pays for the artifact they create.) Who or what does the designing? Mother Nature, of course, or more literally, the long, slow process of evolution by natural selection.

To me, the most fascinating property of the process of evolution is its uncanny capacity to mirror *some* properties of the human mind (the Intelligent Designer) while being bereft of others. There will be much more on this topic in part VI, on thinking about evolution, but in the meantime, I want to make clear the very strong link I am pro-posing between any acceptable theory of meaning and the theory of evolution. While it can never be stressed enough that natural selec-tion operates with no foresight and no purpose, we should also not lose sight of the fact that the process of natural selection has proved itself to be exquisitely sensitive to rationales, making myriads of discriminating "choices" and "recognizing" and "appreciating" many subtle relationships. To put it even more provocatively, when natu-ral selection selects, it can "choose" a particular design *for one reason rather than another*, without ever consciously—or unconsciously!—

"representing" either the choice or the reasons. Hearts were "chosen" for their excellence as blood-circulating pumps, not for the captivating rhythm of their beating, though that *might* have been the *reason* some other thing was "chosen" by natural selection.

Just as the Panamanian Pepsi-Cola franchise-holder can select the two-bitser *for* its talent at recognizing quarter-balboas, can adopt it *as* a quarter-balboa-detector, so evolution can select an organ *for* its capacity to oxygenate blood, can establish it *as* a lung. And it is only relative to just such design "choices" or evolution-"endorsed" purposes—*raisons d'être*—that we can identify behaviors, actions, perceptions, beliefs, or any of the other categories of **folk psychology**.*

The idea that we are artifacts designed by natural selection is both compelling and familiar; some would go so far as to say that it is quite beyond serious controversy.† Why, then, is it resisted not just by creationists and "Intelligent Design" ideologues, but also (somewhat subliminally) by the likes of Searle, Fodor, and company? My hunch is that it has two rather unobvious implications that some find terribly unpalatable. First, if we are "just" artifacts, then what our innermost thoughts mean—and whether they mean anything at all—is something about which we, the very thinkers of those thoughts, have no special authority. The two-bitser turns into a q-balber without ever changing its inner nature; the state that used to mean one thing now means another. The same thing could *in principle* happen to us, if we are just artifacts, if our own intentionality is thus not original but derived. (Jones, for instance, is not authoritative about whether he is thinking about horses or schmorses.) Second, if we are such artifacts, not only have we no guaranteed privileged access to deeper facts that fix the meanings of our thoughts, but *there are*

---

* For an adamant and passionate denial of everything in this paragraph, see Fodor and Piatelli-Palmarini, *What Darwin Got Wrong* (2010). Either the book you are reading is dead wrong, or that one is. For a more detailed defense of the view in this book, see part VI, and my "Evolution of Reasons" (forthcoming).

† Ruth Millikan has developed this claim in greater detail than I, in a series of brilliant books beginning in 1984. See the new volume *Millikan and Her Critics* (Ryder et al., 2013) for the current state of play.

no such deeper facts. Sometimes functional interpretation is obvious (the heart is obviously a pump; the eye is obviously for seeing), but when it is not, when we go to read Mother Nature's mind, there is no text to be interpreted. When "the fact of the matter" about proper function is controversial—when more than one interpretation is well supported—there simply is no fact of the matter.

30. RADICAL TRANSLATION AND A QUINIAN CROSSWORD PUZZLE

The claim that when two equally good functional interpretations clash there are no deeper facts that could settle the matter has been most memorably and ably defended by philosopher W. V. O. Quine (1960), in his principle of the *indeterminacy of radical translation*, which he defended with the help of a famous intuition pump. Imagine discovering an isolated island in the middle of the Pacific Ocean, let's say, inhabited by people from who knows where, speaking a language that nobody else speaks. With no bilingual interpreters available to help, the anthropologists or linguists must figure out this language from observation and trial-and-error interaction with the natives, a task Quine called "radical translation." *In principle*, Quine argued, two such investigators, given the task of deriving a translation manual for this exotic tongue, could arrive at substantially different but equally good translation manuals, which assigned different meanings to utterances made by the natives, and where there could be no fact of the matter about which translation was correct! To many philosophers, this idea has seemed too radical to take seriously—and so they simply ignore it and persist in their traditional ways. Here is a thinking tool designed to make the idea seem at least plausible, if not downright obvious. Two things need to be explained: (1) how Quine's claim could be true ("in principle"), and (2) how it could nevertheless be all but impossible to give an actual instance of it.

I regularly give this crossword puzzle to my students and ask them to solve it. In a few minutes, most of them announce success. Try it for yourself before reading on.

1.	**2.**	**3.**	**4.**
5.			
6.			
7.			

Across

1. Dirty stuff
5. A great human need
6. To make smooth
7. Movie actor

Down

1. Vehicle dependent on H_2O
2 We usually want this
3. Just above
4. U.S. state (abbrev.)

Did you solve it? If so, which solution did you discover? The puzzle has two solutions, about equally good (they are hidden later in the book, to give you a chance to find both before they are revealed). It took me hours to devise it, small as it is, because the multiple constraints that must be satisfied interact to limit the possibilities drastically. If you are skeptical, try to compose a larger, better one! (And please, send it to me if you succeed. I will use it in place of my own.)

Anybody who asks, "What word is 1 Down *really*?" stands convicted of a certain sort of misplaced realism. *There is no fact of the matter.* I deliberately set it up so there wouldn't be a fact of the matter. For instance, I didn't compose the puzzle with one set of answers (the historically first or original answers and "hence" the *real* answers) and then cast about for another set. I worked out the two solutions together, drawing from a list of pairs of four-letter words with similar meanings that I had collected.

It is possible to construct such a puzzle because there are norms for definitions that admit some flexibility. Both solutions include words that just barely fit their definitions, but the conspiracy of the surrounding fit (the holism, in the jargon of philosophers) pulls the words into two quite stable configurations. What odds would you take that there isn't going to be a third solution that competes evenly with either of these two? In general, the *cryptographer's maxim* holds: if you can find *one* solution to a puzzle, you've found *the only* solution to the puzzle. Only special circumstances permit as many as two solutions, but such cases show us that the existence of only one single solution to a question like this is not a metaphysical necessity, but just the immensely probable result of very powerful constraints.

People are much more complicated than either crossword puzzles or computers. They have convoluted brains full of neuromodulators, and these brains are attached to bodies that are deeply entwined with the world, and they have both an evolutionary and a personal history that has embedded them in the world with much more inter-penetration than the embedding of a crossword puzzle in a linguistic community. So Ruth Millikan (for instance) is right that given the nature of design constraints, it is unlikely in the extreme that there could be different ways of skinning the cat that left two radically different, globally indeterminate, tied-for-first-place interpretations. Indeterminacy of radical translation is truly negligible in practice. Still, the principle survives. The reason we don't have indeterminacy of radical translation is *not* because, as a matter of metaphysical fact, there are "real meanings" in there, in the head (what Quine called the "museum myth" of meaning, his chief target). The reason we don't have indeterminacy in the actual world is that with so many independent constraints to satisfy, the cryptographer's maxim assures us that it is a vanishingly small worry. When indeterminacy threatens in the real world, it is always just more "behavioral" or "dispositional" facts—more of the same—that save the day for a determinate reading, not some mysterious "causal power" or "intrin-sic semanticity." Intentional interpretation almost always arrives in the limit at a *single* interpretation, but in the imaginable catastrophic case in which dual interpretations survived all tests, there would be no *deeper* facts to settle which was "right." Facts do settle interpreta-tions, but it is always "shallow" facts that do the job.

31. SEMANTIC ENGINES AND SYNTACTIC ENGINES

How can meaning make a difference? It doesn't seem to be the kind of physical property, like temperature or mass or chemical composition, that could cause anything to happen. What brains are *for* is extracting *meaning* from the flux of energy impinging on their sense organs, in order to improve the prospects of the bodies that house them and provide their energy. The job of a brain is to "produce future" in the form of anticipations *about the things in the world that matter* to guide the body in appropriate ways. Brains are energetically very expensive organs, and if they can't do this important job well, they aren't earning their keep. Brains, in other words, are supposed to be *semantic engines*. What brains are *made of* is kazillions of molecular pieces that interact according to the strict laws of chemistry and physics, responding to shapes and forces; brains, in other words, are in fact only *syntactic engines*.

Imagine going to the engineers and asking them to build you a genuine-dollar-bill-discriminator, or, what amounts to the same thing, a counterfeit-detector: its specs are that it should put all the genuine dollars in one pile and all the counterfeits in another. Not possible, say the engineers; whatever we build can respond only to "syntactic" properties: physical details—the thickness and chemical composition of the paper, the shapes and colors of the ink patterns, the presence or absence to other hard-to-fake physical properties. What they *can* build, they say, is a pretty good but not foolproof counterfeit-detector based on such "syntactic" properties. It will be expensive, but indirectly and imperfectly it will test for counterfeit-hood well enough to earn its keep.

Any configuration of brain parts is subject to the same limitations. It will be caused by physicochemical forces to do whatever it does regardless of what the input means (or only **sorta** means). Don't make the mistake of imagining that brains, being alive, or made of proteins instead of silicon and metal, can detect meanings directly, thanks to the **wonder tissue** in them. Physics will always trump meaning. A genuine semantic engine, responding *directly* to meanings, is like a perpetual motion machine—physically impossible. So how can brains accomplish their appointed task? By being syntactic engines that *track* or *mimic* the competence of the impossible semantic engine.* But is this even possible? Some philosophers have argued that if the micro-causal story of how a brain works is complete (without any mysterious gaps), there is simply no room for meaning to make a difference. In chapter 33, we will encounter an intuition pump that demonstrates that this is false, by showing how semantic properties—such as truth and meaning and reference—play an *ineliminable* role in some straightforward causal processes. But before turning to that somewhat complex intuition pump, I want to examine a simpler model, which will allow us to air some suspicions about philosophers' intuition pumps in general, and, if all goes well, allay some misgivings that may be interfering with comprehension.

---

* As philosopher John Haugeland (1981, p. 23) put it, the first principle of AI is "if you take care of the syntax, *the semantics will take care of itself.*" There are different ways of thinking of this slogan; in its first, overly hopeful version, it motivated the search for an enormous database, an axiomatized formalization of world knowledge that could be maintained and exploited by a (purely syntactical) inference engine. (CYC is the best example.) This has proved (in the eyes of most experts) to be unfeasible, but the slogan survives as a good expression of the idea that the brain is a kind of computer (and hence a syntactic engine) that, thanks to its design, approximately does the work of a semantic engine.

32. SWAMPMAN MEETS A COW-SHARK

Intuition pumps are supposed to work cleanly and efficiently, pumping the sought-for intuition and then going back into storage. But a common fate of intuition pumps is to inspire a frenzy of rebuttal, counter-rebuttal, adjustment, and extension. Donald Davidson, one of America's best twentieth-century philosophers, once told me that he regretted inventing this intuition pump, since it instigated such an excessive and only intermittently illuminating wrangle. Here is Swampman, one of philosophy's favorites—if not Davidson's (1987):

> Suppose lightning strikes a dead tree in a swamp; I am standing nearby. My body is reduced to its elements, while entirely by coincidence (and out of different molecules) the tree is turned into my physical replica. My replica, The Swampman, moves exactly as I did; according to its nature it departs the swamp, encounters and seems to recognize my friends, and appears to return their greetings in English. It moves into my house and seems to write articles on radical interpretation. No one can tell the difference.
>   But there *is* a difference. My replica can't recognize my friends; it can't recognize anything, since it never cognized anything in the first place. It can't know my friends' names (though of course it seems to); it can't remember my house. It can't mean what I do by the word "house," for example, since the sound "house" it makes was not learned in a context that would give it the right meaning—or any meaning at all. Indeed, I don't see how my replica can be said to mean anything by the sounds it makes, nor to have any thoughts. [pp. 443–444]

It cannot have escaped philosophers' attention that our fellow academics in other fields—especially in the sciences—often have difficulty suppressing their incredulous amusement when such topics as Twin Earth and Swampman are posed for apparently serious consideration. Are the scientists just being philistines, betraying their tin ears for the subtleties of philosophical investigation, or have the philosophers lost their grip on reality? I'd **rather** (hint) not say.

These bizarre examples attempt to prove one conceptual point or another by deliberately reducing all but one underappreciated feature of some phenomenon to zero, so that what really counts can shine through. The Twin Earth example sets internal similarity to a maximum (you are whisked off to Twin Earth without being given a chance to register this huge shift) so that external context can be demonstrated to be responsible for whatever our intuitions tell us. The Swampman intuition pump keeps both future dispositions and internal states constant and reduces "history" to zero. Thus these thought experiments mimic scientific experiments in their design, attempting to isolate a crucial interaction between variables by holding other variables constant. A problem with such experiments is that the dependent variable is intuition—they are intuition pumps—and the contribution of imagination in the generation of intuitions is harder to control than philosophers have acknowledged. (Several of the **boom crutches** we will dismantle actually suppress the imagination of readers, distorting their intuitions and thus invalidating the "results" of the thought experiment.)

But there is also a deeper problem with such experiments. It is child's play to dream up examples to "prove" further conceptual points. Suppose a cow gave birth to something that was atom-for-atom indiscernible from a shark. Would it be a shark? If you posed that question to a biologist, the charitable reaction would be that you were making a labored attempt at a joke. Or suppose an evil demon could make water turn solid at room temperature by smiling at it; would the demon-water be ice? This is too silly a hypothesis to deserve a response. Smiling demons, cow-sharks, zombies, and

Swampmen are all, some philosophers think, logically possible, even if they are not nomologically (causally) possible, and these philosophers think this is important. I do not. Presumably the motivation for casting the net of counterfactuality so wide is so that the answer we retrieve will tell us about the *essence* of the topic in question. But who believes in real essences of this sort nowadays? Not I.

Consider a parallel question we might ask about magnets, after we noticed that there were competing candidates for the "truth-maker"—the defining property or essence—for magnets: (a) all magnets are things that attract iron, and (b) all magnets are things that have a certain internal structure (call it M-alignment). Was the old, behavioral criterion (a) eventually superseded by the new, internal structure criterion (b), or did the latter merely reductively explain the former? To find out, we must imagine posing scientists the following Swampman-style questions. Suppose you discovered a thing that attracted iron but was not M-aligned (like standard magnets). Would you call it a magnet? Or: Suppose you discovered a thing that was M-aligned but did not attract iron. Would you call it a magnet? The physicists would reply that if they were confronted with either of these imaginary objects, they would have much more important things to worry about than what to call them. Their whole scientific picture depends on there being a deep regularity between the alignment of atomic dipoles in magnetic domains and iron attraction, and the "fact" that it is *logically* possible to break this regularity is of vanishing interest to them. What is of interest, however, is the real covariance of "structural" and "behavioral" factors. If they find violations of the regularities, they adjust their science accordingly, letting the terms fall where they may.

Does Swampman have thoughts and speak English, or not? Is a cow-shark a shark? It swims like a shark, and mates successfully with other sharks. Oh, but didn't I tell you? It is atom-for-atom indiscernible from a shark, *except* that it has cow DNA in all its cells. Impossible? Not *logically* impossible (say the philosophers). Just so obviously impossible as to render further discussion unenlightening. It is just as clearly physically impossible for the "traces" of, say, Davidson's memories to appear in the structure of Swampman's brain as it is for a shark to form itself of cells containing cow DNA. Swampman may not be logically impossible, if only because cosmic coincidences of the sort imagined to produce things like Swampman are *by definition* not logically impossible, but they never happen, so who cares *what we would say* if they did?

"I do," says the philosopher who is on the lookout for **rhetorical questions**. "I think it is important always to define your terms with utmost rigor, covering all logically possible eventualities. That's the way to get to the truth." But is it? In the real world, past history and future function are bound together by multi-stranded cables of evolution, development, and learning. It is *because* Davidson's body had taken the particular trajectory that it did for years on end that Davidson had all those memories and beliefs and projects, and there is no *real* substitute for these natural accumulation processes. Settling the verdict on imaginary cases that violate these conditions serves no purpose that I can see. In fact, such labored examples strike me as manufactured opportunities to impose an imaginary dichotomy so that you can **rather** with impunity. "No," says the philosopher. "It's *not* a false dichotomy! *For the sake of argument* we're suspending the laws of physics. Didn't Galileo do the same when he banished friction from his thought experiment?" Yes, but a general rule of thumb emerges from the comparison: the utility of a thought experiment is inversely proportional to the size of its departures from reality.

Twin Earth is physically impossible, but not as impossible as Swampman! (Don't think that the many-worlds interpretation of quantum mechanics, which is gaining favor in some quarters, shows that Twin Earth is physically possible after all; even if there are an infinity of universes "out there" including (infinitely?) many that have planets that are almost like Earth, we can't send an earthling to any of them for a visit.) The two-bitser's trip to Panama, in contrast, is not just possible; instances of it may well have happened. We don't have to suspend any laws of nature to imagine it in whatever detail we like.

33. TWO BLACK BOXES

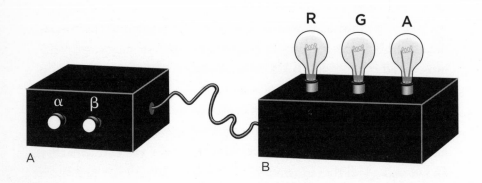

Once upon a time, there were two large black boxes, A and B, connected by a long insulated copper wire. On box A there were two buttons, marked α and β, and on box B there were three lights, red, green, and amber. Scientists studying the behavior of the boxes observed that whenever they pushed the α button on box A, the red light flashed briefly on box B, and whenever they pushed the β button on box A, the green light flashed briefly. The amber light never seemed to flash. They performed a few billion trials, under a very wide variety of conditions, and found no exceptions. They concluded that there was a causal regularity, which they conveniently summarized thus:

all α's cause reds
all β's cause greens

The causation passed through the copper wire somehow, they determined, since severing it turned off all effects in box B, and shielding the two boxes from each other without severing the wire never disrupted the regularity. So naturally they were curious to know just how the causal regularity they had discovered was passed through the wire. Perhaps, they thought, pressing button α caused a low-voltage pulse to be emitted down the wire, triggering the red light, and pressing button β caused a high-voltage pulse, which triggered the green. Or perhaps pressing α caused a single pulse, which triggered the red light, and pressing β caused a double pulse. Clearly, there had to be something that always happened in the wire when the scientists pressed button α, and something different that always happened in the wire when they pressed β. Discovering just what this was would explain the causal regularity they had discovered.

A wiretap of sorts on the wire soon revealed that things were more complicated. Whenever *either* button was pushed on box A, a long stream of pulses and gaps—ons and offs, or bits (10,000 bits, to be exact)—was sent swiftly down the wire to box B. But the pattern of bits was different each time!

Clearly there had to be a feature or property of the strings of bits that triggered the red light in one case and the green light in the other. What could it be? The scientists decided to open up box B and see what happened to the strings of bits when they arrived. Inside B the scientists found an ordinary digital, serial supercomputer, with a large memory, containing a huge program and a huge database, written, of course, in more bit strings. And when they traced the effects of the incoming bit strings on this computer program, they found nothing out of the ordinary: the input string would always make its way into the CPU (central processing unit) in normal fashion, where it would provoke a few billion operations to be performed in a few seconds, ending, always, with either of two output signals, a 1 (which turned on the red light) or a 0 (which turned on the green light). In every case, they found, they could explain each step of the causation at the microscopic level without any difficulty or controversy. They didn't suspect any occult causes to be operating, and, for instance, when they arranged to input the same sequence of 10,000 bits again and again, the program in box B always yielded the same output, red or green.

But this was mildly puzzling, because although box B always gave the same output, it didn't do so by going through the same intermediate steps. In fact, it almost always passed through different physical states before yielding the same output. This in itself was no mystery, because the program kept a copy of each input it received, and so, when the same input arrived a second or third or thousandth time, the state of the memory of the computer was slightly different each time. But the output was always the same; if the light turned red the first time a particular string was input, it always turned red for the same string thereafter, and the same regularity held for green strings (as the scientists began to call them). All strings, they were tempted to hypothesize, are either red strings (cause the red light to flash) or green strings (cause the green light to flash). But of course they didn't test all possible strings—only strings that had been emitted by box A.

The scientists decided to test their hypothesis by disconnecting A from B temporarily and inserting variations on A's output strings to B. To their puzzlement and dismay, they discovered that almost always, when they tampered with a string from A, the *amber* light flashed! It was almost as if box B had detected their intervention. There was no doubt, however, that box B would readily accept man-made versions of red strings by flashing red, and man-made versions of green strings by flashing green. It was only when a bit—or more than one bit—was changed in a red or a green string that the amber light usually—almost always—came on. "You've killed it!" somebody once blurted out, after watching a "tampered" red string turn into an amber string, and this led to a flurry of speculation that red and green strings were in some sense *alive*—perhaps male and female—while amber strings were *dead* strings. As appealing as this hypothesis was, it did not turn out to lead anywhere, although a flurry of experimentation with a few billion random variations on strings 10,000 bits long did strongly suggest to the scientists that there were really three varieties of strings—red strings, green strings, and amber strings—and amber strings outnumbered the red and green strings by many, many orders of magnitude (see chapter 35 for more on this). Almost all strings were amber strings. That made the red/green regularity they had discovered all the more exciting and puzzling.

What was it about the red strings that turned on the red light and the green strings that turned on the green light? *Of course in each particular case, there was no mystery at all.* The scientists could trace the causation of each particular string through the supercomputer in B and see that, with gratifying determinism, it produced its red or green or amber light, as the case might be. What they couldn't find, however, was a way of predicting which of the three effects a new string would have, just by examining it (without "hand-simulating" its effect on box B). They knew from their empirical data that the odds were very high that any new string considered would be amber unless it was a string known to have been emitted by box A, in which case the odds were better than a billion to one that it would be *either* red or green, but no one could tell which, without running it through box B to see how the program settled out.

Perhaps the solution to the mystery lay in box A. They opened it up and found another supercomputer, of a different make and model and running a different gigantic program, but also just a garden-variety digital computer. They soon determined that there was an internal "clock" ticking away millions of times a second, and whenever they pushed either button, the first thing the computer did was take the "time" from the clock (e.g., 10110101010101010111) and break it up into strings, which it then used to determine which subroutines to call in which order, and which part of its memory to access first in the course of its preparation of a bit string to send down the wire.

The scientists were able to figure out that it was this clock-consulting (which was as good as random) that virtually guaranteed that the same bit string was never sent out twice. But in spite of this random-ness, or pseudo-randomness, it remained true that whenever they pushed button α, the bit string the computer concocted turned out to be red, and whenever they pushed button β, the bit string eventually sent turned out to be green. Actually, the scientists did find a few anomalous cases: in roughly one in a billion trials, pushing the α

button caused a green string to be emitted, or pushing the β button caused a red string to be emitted. This tiny blemish in perfection only whetted the scientists' appetite for an explanation of the regularity.

And then one day, along came the two AI hackers who had built the boxes, and they explained it all. (Do not read on if you want to figure out the mystery for yourself.) Al, who had built box A, had been working for years on an "expert system"—a database containing "true propositions" about everything under the sun, and an inference engine to deduce further implications from the axioms that composed the database. There were Major League Baseball statistics, meteorological records, biological taxonomies, histories of the world's nations, and hosts of trivia in the database. Bo, the Swede who had built box B, had been working during the same time on a rival "world knowledge" database for his own expert system. They had each stuffed their respective databases with as many "truths" as years of work had permitted.*

But as the years progressed, they had grown bored with expert systems, and both had decided that the practical promise of this technology was vastly overrated. The systems weren't actually very good at solving interesting problems, or "thinking," or "finding creative solutions to problems." All they were good at, thanks to their inference engines, was generating lots and lots of true sentences (in their respective languages), and testing input sentences (in their respective languages) for truth and falsity, relative to their sorta knowledge. So

---

* IBM's Watson came along just in time to turn my science fiction into science fact, close enough. You could consider Watson to be in box A if you like, and box B to contain a Swedish alternative to Watson, independently developed by Bo. When I first published this thought experiment (Dennett, 1995a), the best I could say was this: "For a real-world example of such a project, see Douglas Lenat's enormous CYC (short for 'encyclopedia') project at MCC (Lenat and Guha, 1990)." See also the footnote on CYC in chapter 28. The approach to AI that Watson exemplifies was largely unimagined back in 1995, but it has been making great strides. Unlike CYC, which is largely hand-coded, Watson can graze unattended on the Internet for its own supply of truths, and make powerful use of statistical properties of the data available there. Both Watson and CYC in their different ways **sorta** understand the data in their data banks—much, much more than other computers with large databases.

Al and Bo had gotten together and figured out how the fruits of their wasted effort could be put to use. They decided to make a philosophical toy. They chose a lingua franca for translating between their two representational systems (it was English, actually, sent in standard ASCII code),* and hooked the machines together with a wire. Whenever you pushed A's α button, this instructed A to choose at random (or pseudo-random) one if its "beliefs" (either a stored axiom or a generated implication of its axioms), translate it into English (in a computer, English characters would already be in ASCII), add enough random bits after the period to bring the total up to 10,000, and send the resulting string to B, which translated this input into its own language (which was Swedish Lisp), and tested it against its own "beliefs"—its database. Since both databases were composed of truths, and roughly the same truths, thanks to their inference engines, whenever A sent B something A "believed," B "believed" it too, and signaled this by flashing a red light. Whenever A sent B what A took to be a falsehood, B announced that it judged that this was indeed a falsehood by flashing a green light.

And whenever anyone tampered with the transmission, this almost always resulted in a string that was not a well-formed sentence of English, unless all the tampering occurred only in the random junk at the end. Since B had absolutely zero tolerance for typographical errors, B responded to these by flashing the amber light. Whenever anyone chose a bit string at random, the odds were **Vast** that it would not be a well-formed truth or falsehood in English ASCII, hence the preponderance of amber strings.

So, said Al and Bo, the mysterious causal property *red* was actually the property of being a true sentence in English, and *green* was the property of being a falsehood in English. Suddenly, the search

---

* When I first wrote this intuition pump, ASCII (American Standard Code for Information Interchange) code was the standard format for almost all word-processing, e-mail, and Internet language. It has since been supplanted by an extended, backward-compatible format, UTF-8, which stands for Universal [Character-set] Transformation Format—8-bit. That is, ASCII is still a part of UTF-8.

that had eluded the scientists for years became child's play. Anyone could compose red strings *ad nauseam*. Just write down the ASCII code for "Houses are bigger than peanuts" or "Whales don't fly" or "Three times four is two less than two times seven," for instance. If you wanted a green string, try "Nine is less than eight" or "New York is the capital of Spain." Philosophers soon hit on some cute tricks, such as finding strings that were red the first hundred times they were given to B but green thereafter (e.g., the ASCII for "This sentence has been sent to you for evaluation less than a hundred and one times").

But, said some philosophers, the string properties *red* and *green* are not really *truth in English* and *falsity in English*. After all, there are English truths whose ASCII expression takes millions of bits, and besides, in spite of their best efforts, Al and Bo didn't always insert *facts* in their programs. For example, some of what had passed for common knowledge when they were working on their databases had since been disproved. There were lots of reasons why the string property—the causal property—of *redness* was not quite exactly the property of *truth in English*. So, perhaps *red* could be better defined as a *relatively short expression in English ASCII of something **sorta** believed true by box B (whose sorta beliefs are almost all true)*. This satisfied some, but others picked nits, insisting, for various reasons, that this definition was inexact, or had counterexamples that could not be ruled out in any non–*ad hoc* way, and so forth. But as Al and Bo pointed out, there were no better candidate descriptions of the property to be found, and hadn't the scientists been yearning for just such an explanation? Hadn't the mystery of red and green strings now been entirely dissolved? Moreover, now that it was dissolved, couldn't one see that there wasn't any hope at all of explaining the *causal* regularity with which we began our tale—all α's cause reds, and all β's cause greens—without using *some semantical* (or *mentalistic*) terms?

Some philosophers argued that while the newfound description of the regularity in the activity in the wire could be used to predict box B's behavior, it was not a *causal* regularity after all. Truth and falsehood (and any of the adjusted stand-ins just considered) are semantic properties, and as such are entirely abstract, and hence could not *cause* anything. Nonsense, others retorted. Pushing button α causes the red light to go on just as certainly as turning the ignition key causes your car to start. If it had turned out that what was being sent down the wire was simply high versus low voltage, or one pulse versus two, everybody would agree that this was an exemplary causal system. The fact that this system turned out to be a Rube Goldberg machine didn't show that the reliability of the link between α and red flashes was any less causal. In fact in every single case the scientists could trace out the exact micro-causal path that explained the result.[*]

Convinced by this line of reasoning, other philosophers began to argue that this showed that the properties red, green, and amber weren't *really* semantical or mentalistic properties after all, but only imitation semantical properties, mere "as if" semantical properties. What red and green were, really, were very, very complicated *syntactical* properties. These philosophers declined, however, to say anything further about just what syntactical properties these were, or to explain how even young children could swiftly and reliably produce instances of them, or recognize them. These philosophers were nevertheless convinced that there *had* to be a purely syntactic description of the regularity, since, after all, the causal systems in question were "just" computers, and computers are "just" syntactic engines, not capable of any real "semanticity."

"We suppose," retorted Al and Bo, "that if you had found *us* inside our black boxes, playing a trick on you by following the same scheme, you would then relent and agree that the operative causal property was genuine truth (or believed-truth, in any event). Can you propose any good reason for drawing such a distinction?" This led some to declare that in a certain important sense Al and Bo *had* been in the boxes, since they were responsible for creating the respective data-

---

[*] For philosophers only: Some have argued that my account of patterns in "Real Patterns" (1991b) is *epiphenomenalism* about content. This is my reply.

bases as models of their own beliefs. It led others to denying that there really were any semantical or mentalistic properties anywhere in the world. Content, they said, had been *eliminated*. The debate went on for years, but the mystery with which we began was solved.

Blocking the Exits

The tale of the two black boxes ends there. Experience teaches, however, that there is no such thing as a thought experiment so clearly presented that no philosopher can misinterpret it, so in order to forestall some of the most attractive misinterpretations, I will inelegantly draw attention to a few of the critical details and explain their roles in this intuition pump.

(1) The devices in boxes A and B are nothing but automated encyclopedias, not even "walking encyclopedias" but just "boxes of truths." Nothing in the story presupposes or implies that these devices are conscious, or *thinking things*, or even *agents*, except in the same minimal sense that a thermostat is an agent. They are utterly boring intentional systems, rigidly fixed to fulfilling a single, simple goal. (The same is true of IBM'S Watson, of course.) They contain large numbers of true propositions and the inferential machinery necessary to generate more truths, and to test for "truth" by testing a candidate proposition against their existing databases.

(2) Since the two systems were created independently, they cannot plausibly be supposed to contain (actually or even virtually) *exactly* the same truths, but for the prank to work as well as I claim it did in the story, we must suppose a very large overlap, so that it was highly unlikely that a truth generated by A would not be recognized as such by B. Two considerations, I claim, make this plausible: (i) Al and Bo may live in different countries and have different native languages, but they *inhabit the same world*, and (ii) although

there are kazillions of true propositions about that world (our world), the fact that both Al and Bo set out to create *useful* databases would guarantee a high degree of overlap between the two independently created systems. Although Al might know that on his twentieth birthday his left foot was closer to the North Pole than the South Pole, and Bo had not forgotten that his first French teacher was named Dupont, these would not be truths that either one would likely put in their respective databases. If you doubt that the mere fact that they were each intent on creating an internationally useful encyclopedia would ensure such a close correspondence between their respective databases, just add, as an inelegant detail, the convenient fact that during their years of hacking they compared notes as to topics to be covered.

(3) Why not have Al and Bob (a fellow American), or for that matter, why not simply have a duplicate of Al's system in box B? Because it is critical to my story that no simple, feasibly discoverable *syntactic* matching-up could explain the regularity. That is why Bo's system is in Swedish Lisp—to conceal from prying eyes the underlying *semantic* commonalities between the data structures consulted during A's sentence-generation task and B's sentence-translation-and-truth-testing task. Computers, as physical systems, must be, at best, syntactic engines, responding directly to physically transducible differences, not meanings. But both A and B have been designed to mirror as closely as possible the imaginary know-it-all, a *semantic* engine full of *understood* truths. When two *different* syntactic systems, A and B, have been designed to mirror the *same* semantic engine, the only way of accounting for the remarkable regularity they reveal is to ascend to the semantic-engine level, where truths are believed and assertions are intended. The idea, then, was to create two systems that exhibited the fascinating regularity of external behavior

described but that were internally as different as possible, so that *only* the fact that their respective innards were systematic *representations of a common world* could explain the regularity. (Recall that this was the theme in chapter 13.)

We might pause to ask whether or not two such systems could ever be so inscrutable as to be invulnerable to reverse engineering. Or in other words, could the scientists have remained baffled for so long? Cryptography has moved into such rarefied and arcane regions that one should think thrice at least before declaring either way. I have no idea whether anybody can make a sound argument that there are unbreakable encryption schemes or that there aren't. But encryption aside, hackers will appreciate that all the convenient **comments** and other signposts one places in the **source code** when composing a program vanish when the source code is compiled, leaving behind an *almost* impossible-to-decipher tangle of machine instructions. "Decompiling"—reverse engineering the object code and recovering the source code—is sometimes possible in practice (is it always possible in principle?), though it won't restore the comments but just render salient the structures in the higher-level language. My assumption that the scientists' efforts at decompiling the program and deciphering the databases came to naught could be strengthened by postulating encryption, if need be.

In the story as told, we can agree that it is bizarre that the scientists never thought of checking to see if there was an ASCII translation of the bit streams running through the wire. How could they be so dense? Fair enough: you can fix this flaw in the thought experiment by sending the whole gadget (boxes A and B, and the connecting wire) to "Mars," and let the alien scientists there try to figure out the regularity. The fact that all α's cause red lights, all β's cause green lights, and random-bit strings cause amber lights will be just as visible to them as to us, but they will be clueless about ASCII. To them, this gift from outer space will exhibit an utterly mysterious regularity, totally beyond all analytic probes *unless* they hit on the idea that each box contains a

description of a world, and that the descriptions are *of the same world*.*
It is the fact that each box bears multifarious semantic relationships
to the same things, though expressed in different "terminology" and
differently axiomatized, that grounds the regularity.

When I tried this thought experiment out on Danny Hillis, the
creator of the Connection Machine, a pioneering massively parallel computer built by his company, Thinking Machines, in the early
1980s, he thought immediately of a cryptographic "solution" to the
puzzle, and then granted that my solution could be profitably viewed
as a special case of his solution: "Al and Bo were using *the world* as a
'one-time pad!'"—an apt allusion to a standard technique of encryption. You can see the point by imagining a variation. You and your
best friend are about to be captured by hostile forces (space pirates,
let's say) who may know English but not much about your world. You
both know Morse code, and hit on the following impromptu encryption scheme: for a dash, speak a true sentence; for a dot, speak a false
sentence. Your captors are permitted to listen to you two speak: "Birds
lay eggs, and toads fly. Chicago is a city, and my feet are not made of
tin, and baseball is played in August," you say, answering "no" (dash-
dot; dash-dash-dash) to whatever your friend has just asked. The next
time you need to say no, you use different sentences. Even if your
captors know Morse code, unless they also can determine the truth
and falsity of these sentences, they cannot detect the properties that
stand for dot and dash. This variation could be added to our fable,
for spice, as follows: Instead of shipping the computer systems in the
boxes to Mars, we put Al and Bo in the boxes and ship them to Mars.
The Martians will be as puzzled by Al and Bo, if they play the Morse
code prank, as by the computers, unless they draw the conclusion
(obvious to us, but we're not Martians) that these things in the boxes
are to be semantically interpreted.

---

* Once the hypothesis occurs to them, the Martians can engage in a version of Quine's **radical translation**, but their task will be made doubly difficult by not being able to query their
"informants," A and B, by holding up objects and asking "ball?" "pencil?" and the like.

The point of the fable is simple. There is no substitute for the **intentional stance**; either you adopt it, and explain the pattern by finding the semantic-level facts, or you will forever be baffled by the regularity—the *causal* regularity—that is manifestly there.*

At this juncture, if you are like many philosophers, you may once again be attracted by the claim that this intuition pump "works" only because boxes A and B are artifacts whose intentionality, such as it is, is entirely derived and artifactual. The data structures in their memories get their reference (if they get any at all) by indirect reliance on the sense organs, life histories, and purposes of their creators, Al and Bo. The real source of the meaning or truth or semanticity in the artifacts lies in these human artificers. Al and Bo have original intentionality, and A and B have only derived intentionality. (That was, of course, the point of the suggestion that in a certain sense Al and Bo *were* in their respective boxes.) I *might* have told the story differently: inside the boxes were two *robots*, Al and Bo, each of which had spent a longish "lifetime" scurrying around the world gathering facts before getting in their respective boxes. I chose a simpler route, to forestall all the questions about whether box A or box B was "really thinking," but if you want to reconsider the thought experiment with this complication, note that the intuition pump about the **giant robot** survival machine has already cast doubt on the otherwise compelling idea that genuine intentionality could not arise in any artifact.

---

* The same moral can be drawn about interpreting the historical facts of evolutionary history. Even if you can describe, in matchless micro-detail, every causal fact in the history of every giraffe who has ever lived, unless you go up a level or two, and ask, "Why?"—hunting for the *reasons* endorsed by Mother Nature—you will never be able to explain the manifest regularities—the fact that giraffes have come to have long necks, for instance. (More on this in part VI.)

SUMMARY

Twenty-one thinking tools—a dozen intuition pumps and some useful concepts—lined up and put to work on the foundational concept of meaning. What have we made with their help? Do they all work well? Notice that there are two ways an intuition pump may prove valuable. If it's well made, then either the intuitions it pumps are reliable and convincing, in which case it nicely blocks some otherwise tempting path of error, or the intuitions *still* seem dubious, in which case the intuition pump may help focus attention on what is wrong with its own presuppositions. In either case, the tool is a sort of lever, like a seesaw—if one side goes up, the other side must go down—but only if the tool can't bend or break in the middle. Intuition pumps are more complicated than seesaws, so we need to turn the knobs. That's what I just did with the **two black boxes**, but there are no doubt other knobs to check before settling for its verdict.

And what are the verdicts of this long section on meaning? A mixture of pessimism and optimism. Meaning isn't going to turn out to be a simple property that maps easily onto brains, and we're not going to find "deeper" facts anywhere that just *settle* the question of what a sentence, or a thought, or a belief *really means*. The best we can do—and it is quite good enough—is to find and anchor (apparently) *best interpretations* of all the physical-stance (and design-stance) data we have. If we can find *one* solution to a Quinian quandary about meaning, we have almost certainly found *the* solution—in the sense that we may be confident that no better solution lies undiscovered. As the **two-bitser's** move to Panama showed, meaning is always relative to a context of function, and there need be no *original* intentionality beyond the intentionality of our (**sorta**) selfish genes, which derive their sorta intentionality from the functional context of evolution by natural selection, instead of from an Intelligent Designer playing the role of our rich client ordering a giant robot. And the intuition pump about the **two black boxes** shows that the **intentional stance**, with all its tolerance of **sorta** beliefs and their ilk, is *not optional* if you want to understand and explain many of the causal regularities in the world.

Our investigations into these issues are greatly enhanced, here in the twenty-first century, by the fact that, for the first time, we have ways of thinking rigorously and vigorously about mechanisms with *trillions* of moving parts—parts that work in unmysterious ways. Thanks to Turing, we can at least dimly see a path now, from brute uncomprehending matter (the physical stance) via a cascade of rearrangements (the design stance, and sorta meanings) to an appreciation of ourselves as paradigmatic believers, knowers, understanders (simplified by the intentional stance as intentional systems).

Every one of these propositions is, or has been, controversial, and there are still plenty of experts who haven't signed on to all of them. Perhaps lining up all these propositions will increase their persuasive power, and we'll get a "critical mass" phenomenon that attracts those who haven't seen the way the parts mesh so nicely. On the other hand, lining them up like this may make it easier for critics to find a common thread of mistake running through them. Either way we make progress. Or maybe we'll discover sleight of hand in many of them, obscuring the truth instead of illuminating it. To find flaws, go back and turn the knobs some more, and see what happens. At the very least, discovering such flaws amounts to a sour kind of progress: the progress of exposing tempting bad ideas, something philosophers have been doing for millennia.

I don't claim that this section gives us a *theory of meaning*. It gives us only a rather commodious logical space into which a proper, scientific theory of meaning must fit—if I am right.* Now that we have the *content* side of the mind roughly pinned in place, can we turn to

---

* I have my own hunches about what a proper scientific theory of meaning will turn out to be, replacing the rigid, Boolean (logical) constructions of GOFAI (good old-fashioned artificial intelligence) with more flexible, Bayesian (statistical, probabilistic) networks of pattern-finders, but developing those ideas is a task for another time and place.

that grand mystery of mysteries, consciousness? Not yet. We need to build some more foundations. Too many issues that arise in the quest to understand consciousness have implications about, or presuppositions about, evolution, as we have already seen in this section. Many of the themes we've begun developing have appealed to evolutionary considerations, so let's get them exposed and clarified before we go on. Besides, it's an endlessly fascinating topic.

VI.
TOOLS FOR THINKING ABOUT EVOLUTION

Darwin's idea of evolution by natural selection is, in my opinion, the single best idea that anybody has ever had, because in a single bold stroke it unites meaning with matter, two aspects of reality that appear to be worlds apart. On one side, we have the world of our minds and their meanings, our goals, our hopes, and our yearnings, and that most honored—and hackneyed—of all philosophical topics, the Meaning of Life. On the other side, we have galaxies ceaselessly wheeling, planets falling pointlessly into their orbits, lifeless chemical mechanisms doing what physics ordains, all without purpose or reason. Then Darwin comes along and shows us how the former arises from the latter, creating meaning as it goes, a bubble-up vision of the birth of importance to overthrow the trickle-down vision of tradition. The idea of natural selection is not very complex, but it is so powerful that some people cannot bear to contemplate it, and they desperately avert their attention as if it were a horrible dose of foul-tasting medicine. Here are some thinking tools to help us see how this idea illuminates the dark corners of existence, turning mysteries into puzzles that we can solve and uncovering the glories of nature as never before.

34. UNIVERSAL ACID

Did you ever hear of universal acid? This fantasy used to amuse me and some of my schoolboy friends. I have no idea whether we invented or inherited it, along with Spanish fly and saltpeter, as a part of an underground youth culture. Universal acid is a liquid so corrosive that it will eat through anything! But what do you keep it in? It dissolves glass bottles and stainless-steel canisters as readily as paper bags. What would happen if you somehow came upon or created a dollop of universal acid? Would the whole planet eventually be destroyed? What would it leave in its wake? After everything had been transformed by its encounter with universal acid, what would the world look like? Little did I realize that in a few years I would encounter an idea—Darwin's idea—bearing an unmistakable likeness to universal acid: it eats through just about every traditional concept, and leaves in its wake a revolutionized worldview, with most of the old landmarks still recognizable, but transformed in fundamental ways.*

Many Darwin-dreaders missed the point (deliberately?) when I introduced this image of Darwin's dangerous idea in 1995. I went to some lengths to reassure my readers that after the universal acid swept through their favorite topics—ethics, art, culture, religion, humor, and yes, even consciousness—what would be left behind would be just as wonderful, even more wonderful in many regards, but subtly transformed. Darwin's idea is a revolutionary idea, no doubt about it, but it does not destroy what we value in all these things; it puts them on better foundations, and unites them gracefully with the rest of knowledge. For centuries "the arts and humanities" have been

---

* Some commentators have thought that my comparison of Darwin's idea to universal acid was inspired by DNA, which is, after all, *d*eoxyribo*n*ucleic *a*cid, but I mean something more universal: DNA is not the only medium of evolution on our planet, and who knows what other instances of evolution there are throughout the universe?

considered not just separate from the sciences but somehow *protected from* the invasive examinations science engages in, but this traditional isolation is not the best way to preserve what we love. Trying to hide our treasures behind a veil of mystery prevents us from finding a proper anchoring for them in the physical world. It is a common-enough mistake, especially in philosophy.

When people sense that something they love is under threat, their first reaction is to build an "impenetrable" wall, a Maginot Line— and just to be extra safe they decide to enclose a bit more territory, a buffer zone, inside its fortifications. It seems like a good, prudent idea. It seems to protect us from the awful *slippery slope*, the insidious *thin edge of the wedge*, and as everyone knows, if you give them an inch, they'll take a mile. Dig the moat! Build the wall! And as far out as you can afford. But this policy typically burdens the defenders with a brittle, extravagant (implausible, indefensible) set of dogmas that cannot be defended rationally—and hence must be defended, in the end, with desperate clawing and shouting. In philosophy, this strategic choice often shows up as *absolutism* of one kind or another: the sanctity of (human) life is *infinite*; at the core of great art lies divine and inexplicable *genius*; consciousness is a problem too hard for us mere mortals to understand; and—one of my favorite targets—what I call *hysterical realism*: there are always deeper facts that *settle* the puzzle cases of meaning. These facts are real, *really* real, even if we are systematically unable to discover them. This is a tempting idea, in part because it appeals to our sense of proper human modesty. Who are *we* to say that there just aren't any facts to settle these issues? Einstein's notorious resistance to the indeterminacy of quantum physics is an august example of the appeal of this idea. "God does not play dice!" was his heartfelt but ultimately unreasonable ground for resistance. And, when you get right down to it, who are we—or who is Einstein—to say that God doesn't play dice? This is probably not the way to deal with such issues, and we'll see some opportunities for hysterical realism—and see how to resist it—below. Evolutionary thinking is a fine antidote.

35. THE LIBRARY OF MENDEL: *VAST* AND *VANISHING*

The *human genome* has now been sequenced by Craig Venter and others, but what does this mean? Isn't everybody's DNA different? Yes, so different, in fact, that even a rather small fragment of DNA found at a crime scene is enough to identify its owner with over 99 percent certainty. And yet human DNA is also so similar that scientists can distinguish it from the DNA of other species given only fragments of a complete genome. How is this possible? How can our personal DNA be so different and yet so similar? A good way to understand this surprising fact is by comparing DNA with the texts of books, and the Argentine writer Jorge Luis Borges (1962) has given us a little fable, "The Library of Babel," that vividly illustrates the way this difference and similarity can coexist. Borges tells of the forlorn explorations and speculations of people who find themselves living in a vast storehouse of books, structured like a honeycomb, composed of thousands (or millions or billions) of hexagonal air shafts surrounded by balconies lined with shelves. Standing at a railing and looking up or down, no one can see a top or bottom to these shafts. And nobody has ever found a shaft that isn't surrounded by six neighboring shafts. The people wonder, Is the warehouse infinite? Eventually they decide that it is not, but it might as well be, for it seems that on its shelves—in no order, alas—lie *all the possible books.*

Suppose that each book is five hundred pages long, and each page consists of forty lines, with fifty spaces for each line, so there are two thousand character-spaces per page. Each space either is blank or has a character printed on it, chosen from a set of one hundred characters (the uppercase and lowercase letters of English and other European languages, plus the blank and punctuation marks).* Somewhere in the Library of Babel is a volume consisting entirely of blank pages, and another volume is all question marks, but the vast majority consist of typographical gibberish; no rules of spelling or grammar, to say nothing of sense, prohibit the inclusion of a volume. Five hundred pages multiplied by two thousand characters per page gives a million character-spaces per book, so if we were to fill the books with every permutation of the characters, there would be $100^{1,000,000}$ different books in the Library of Babel. Since it is estimated† that there are only 100^{40} (give or take a few) *particles* (protons, neutrons, and electrons) in the region of the universe we can observe, the Library of Babel is not remotely a physically possible object, but thanks to the strict rules with which Borges constructed it in his imagination, we can think about it clearly.

Is this truly the set of *all* possible books? Obviously not, since they are restricted to being printed from "only" one hundred different characters, excluding, we may suppose, the characters of Greek, Russian, Arabic, and Chinese, thereby overlooking many of the most important *actual* books. Of course the Library does contain superb translations of these actual books, into English, French, German, Italian, and so on, as well as uncountable trillions of shoddy translations of each book. Books of more than five hundred pages are there, beginning in one volume and continuing without a break into other volumes.

It is amusing to think about some of the volumes that must be somewhere in the Library of Babel. One of them is the best, most accurate five-hundred-page biography of you, from the moment of

---

* Borges chose slightly different figures: books were 410 pages long, with 40 lines of 80 characters. The total number of characters per book is close enough to mine (1,312,000 versus 1,000,000) to make no difference. I chose my rounder numbers for ease of handling. Borges chose a character set with only 25 members, which is enough for uppercase Spanish (with a blank, a comma, and a period as the only punctuation), but not for English. I chose the more commodious 100 to make room without any doubt for the uppercase and lowercase letters and punctuation of all the Roman alphabet languages.
† Stephen Hawking (1988, p. 129) insists on putting it this way: "There are something like ten million million million million million million million million million million million million million (1 with eighty zeroes after it) particles in the region of the universe that we can observe." Michael Denton (1985) provides the estimate of 10^{70} atoms in the observable universe. Manfred Eigen (1992, p. 10) calculates the volume of the universe as 10^{84} cubic centimeters.

your birth until the moment of your death. Locating it, however, would be all but impossible, since the Library also contains kazillions of volumes that are magnificently accurate biographies of you up until your tenth, twentieth, thirtieth, fortieth birthday, and so on, and completely false about subsequent events of your life—in a kazillion different and diverting ways. But even finding one readable volume in this huge storehouse is unlikely in the extreme.

We need some terms for the quantities involved. The Library of Babel is not infinite, so the chance of finding anything interesting in it is not literally infinitesimal.* These words exaggerate in a familiar way, but we should avoid them. Unfortunately, all the standard metaphors—astronomically large, a needle in a haystack, a drop in the ocean—fall comically short. No *actual* astronomical quantity (such as the number of elementary particles in the universe, or the amount of time since the Big Bang, measured in nanoseconds) is even visible against the backdrop of these huge-but-finite numbers. If a readable volume in the Library were as easy to find as a particular drop in the ocean, we'd be in business! Dropped at random into the Library, our chance of ever encountering a volume with so much as a grammatical sentence in it is so vanishingly small that we might do well to capitalize the term, Vanishingly small, and give it a mate, Vastly, short for Very-much-more-than-astronomically.†

Here is another way of getting some sense about just how ridicu-

---

* The Library of Babel is finite, but curiously enough, it contains all the grammatical sentences of English within its walls. But that's an infinite set, and the Library is finite! Still, any sentence of English, of whatever length, can be broken down into five-hundred-page chunks, each of which is somewhere in the Library! How is this possible? Some books may get used more than once. The most profligate case is the easiest to understand: since there are volumes that contain a single character and are otherwise blank, repeated use of these one hundred volumes will create any text of any length. As Quine (1987) pointed out in his informative and amusing essay "Universal Library," if you avail yourself of this strategy of reusing volumes, and translate everything into the ASCII code your word-processor uses, you can store the whole Library of Babel in two extremely slender volumes, in one of which is printed a 0 and in the other of which appears a 1! (Quine also points out that Theodor Fechner, the psychologist, propounded the fantasy of the universal library long before Borges.)

† Quine (1987) coins the term "hyperastronomic" for the same purpose.

lously large the Library of Babel is. As just noted, only a Vanishingly small subset of the books is composed of English words. That subset is itself Vast, and a Vanishing subset within it consists of books in which the words are arranged in grammatical sentences (the Vast majority consist of volumes filled with words strings like this: "good since Paris helping easy from of which nevertheless democracy striptease tigers"). A Vast but Vanishing subset of the grammatical books is composed of sentences that make sense in sequence (the rest are composed of sentences that might be chosen at random from books in grammatical English). A Vast but Vanishing subset of those sense-making books are about somebody named John, and a Vast but Vanishing subset of *those* are about the assassination of John F. Kennedy, and a still Vast (but Vanishing) subset of *those* are true—and a Vast but Vanishing subset of those true books about the assassination of Kennedy are composed entirely of limericks! Yes, there are more *possible* true books in limericks about the death of JFK than there are volumes in the Library of Congress! Not a single one has been published, in all likelihood, which is just as well.

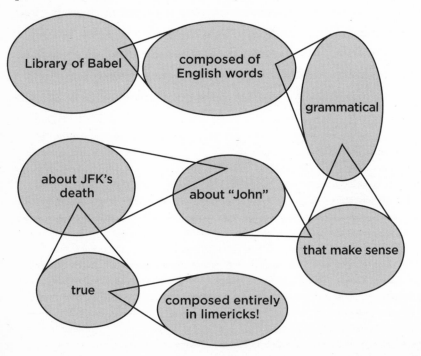

Moby-Dick is in the Library of Babel, but so are 100,000,000 mutant impostors that differ from the canonical *Moby-Dick* by a *single* typographical error. That's not yet a Vast number, but the total rises swiftly when we add the variants that differ by two or ten or a thousand typos. Even a volume with a thousand typos—two per page on average—would be unmistakably recognizable as *Moby-Dick*, and there are Vastly many of those volumes. It wouldn't matter which of these volumes you found, if only you could find one of them! Almost all of them would be equally wonderful reading, and all tell the same story, except for truly negligible—almost indiscriminable—differences. Not quite all of them, however. Sometimes a single typo, in a crucial position, can be fatal. Peter De Vries, another philosophically delicious writer of fiction, once published a novel* that began,

"Call me, Ishmael."

Oh, what a single comma can do! Or consider the many mutants that begin with "Ball me Ishmael."

In Borges's story, the books are not shelved in any order, but even if we found them scrupulously alphabetized, we would have insoluble problems finding *the* book we were looking for (for instance, the "essential" version of *Moby-Dick*). Imagine traveling by spaceship through the Moby-Dick galaxy of the Library of Babel. This galaxy is in itself Vastly larger than the whole physical universe, so no matter what direction you go in, for centuries on end, even if you travel at the speed of light, all you see are virtually indistinguishable copies of *Moby-Dick*. You will never ever reach anything that looks like anything else. *David Copperfield* is unimaginably distant in this space, even though we know that there is a path—the shortest path,

---

* *The Vale of Laughter* (De Vries, 1953). The text goes on: "Feel absolutely free to. Call me any hour of the day or night. . . ." De Vries also may have invented the game of seeing how large an effect (deleterious or not) you can achieve with a single typographical change. Some of the best: "Whose woods are these, I think I know; his house is in the *V*illage though." Others have taken up the game: in the state of nature, mutant-Hobbes tells us, one finds "the *w*ife of man, solitary, poore, nasty, brutish, and short." Or consider the question, "Am I my brothe*l*'s keeper?"

ignoring the kazillions of others—leading from one great book to the other by single typographical changes. (If you found yourself on this path, you would find it almost impossible to tell, by local inspection, which direction to go to move toward *David Copperfield*, even if you had texts of both target books in hand.)

In other words, this *logical* space is so Vast that many of our usual ideas about location, about searching and finding and other such mundane and practical activities, have no straightforward application. Borges put the books on the shelves in random order, a nice touch from which he drew several delectable reflections, but look at the problems he would have created for himself if he'd tried to arrange them in alphabetical order. Since there are only a hundred different alphabetic characters (in our version), we can treat some specific sequence of them as alphabetical order, for example, a, A, b, B, c, C, . . . z, Z, ?, ;, „ ., !,), (, %, . . . à, â, è, ê, é, . . . Then we can put all the books beginning with the same character on the same *floor*. Now our library is only a hundred stories high, shorter than the Sears (or Willis) Tower in Chicago. We can divide each floor into a hundred corridors, each of which we line with the books whose second character is the next character in alphabetical order. On each corridor, we can place a hundred shelves, one for each third-character slot. Thus all the books that begin with "aardvarks love Mozart"—and how many there are!—are shelved on the same shelf (the "r" shelf) in the first corridor on the first floor. But that's a mighty long shelf, so perhaps we had better stack the books in file drawers at right angles to the shelf, one drawer for each fourth-letter position. That way, each shelf can be only, say, a hundred feet long. But now the file drawers are awfully deep, and will run into the backs of the file drawers in the neighboring corridor, so . . . but we've run out of dimensions in which to line up the books. We need a million-dimensional space to store all the books neatly, and all we have is three dimensions: up-down, left-right, and front-back. So we will just have to pretend we can imagine a multidimensional space, each dimension running "at right angles" to all the others. We can conceive of such hyperspaces, as they are called, even if we can't visualize them. Scientists use them all the time to organize the expression of their theories. The geometry of such spaces (whether or not they count as only imaginary) is well behaved, and well explored by mathematicians. We can confidently speak about locations, paths, trajectories, volumes (hypervolumes), distances, and directions in these logical spaces.

We are now prepared to consider a variation on Borges's theme, which I will call the *Library of Mendel*. This Library contains "all possible genomes"—DNA sequences. Richard Dawkins (1986) describes a similar space, which he calls Biomorph Land, in *The Blind Watchmaker*. His discussion is the inspiration for mine, and our two accounts are entirely compatible, but I want to stress some points he chose to pass over lightly.

If we consider the Library of Mendel to be composed of *descriptions* of genomes, then it is already a proper part of the Library of Babel. The standard code for describing DNA consists of only four characters, A, C, G, and T (standing for adenine, cytosine, guanine, and thymine, the four kinds of nucleotides). All the five-hundred-page permutations of these four letters, therefore, are already in the Library of Babel. Typical genomes are much longer than ordinary books, however. The human genome has approximately three billion nucleotides, so the exhaustive description of a single human genome—such as your own—would take approximately three thousand of the five-hundred-page volumes in the Library of Babel.·

This comparison of a human genome with the volumes in the galaxy of *Moby-Dick* now gives us the explanation we need of the difference and similarity between human genomes. How can we speak of sequencing (copying down) *the* human genome if every human genome is different from every other in not just one, but hundreds or thousands of places (*loci*, in the language of genetics)? Like the proverbial snowflakes, or fingerprints, no two actual human genomes are exactly alike, including those of identical twins (the chance of typos creeping in is always present, even in the cells of a single individual). Human DNA is readily distinguishable from the DNA of any other species, even that of the chimpanzee, which is the same at over 90 percent of the loci. Every actual human genome that has ever existed is contained within a galaxy of possible human genomes that is Vastly distant from the galaxies of other species' genomes, yet within the galaxy there is plenty of room for no two human genomes to be alike. You have two versions of each of your genes, one from your mother and one from your father. They passed on to you exactly half of their own genes, randomly selected from those they received from their parents, your grandparents, but since your grandparents were also members of *Homo sapiens*, their genomes agree at almost all loci, so it makes no difference most of the time which grandparent provides either of your genes. But their genomes nevertheless differ at many thousands of loci, and in those slots, which genes you get is a matter of chance—a coin toss built into the machinery for forming your parents' contributions to your DNA. Moreover, mutations accumulate at the rate of about a hundred per genome per generation in mammals. "That is, your children will have one hundred differences from you and your spouse in their genes as a result of random copying errors by your enzymes or as a result of mutations in your ovaries or testicles caused by cosmic rays" (Ridley, 1993, p. 45).

The description of the genome for a horse or a cabbage or an octopus would be composed of the same letters, A, C, G, and T. Most animal genomes measured are smaller than the human genome, but some plants have genomes more than ten times larger than ours, and some single-celled amoebas have genomes even larger! *Amoeba dubia* is the current world record-holder, with an estimated 670 billion base-pairs, more than two hundred times larger than ours. But let us suppose, arbitrarily, that the Library of Mendel consists of all of the DNA strings described in all of the three-thousand-volume boxed sets consisting entirely of those four characters. This will capture enough of the "possible" genomes to serve any serious theoretical purpose.

I have overstated the case in describing the Library of Mendel as containing "all possible genomes." Just as the Library of Babel ignored the Russian and Chinese languages, so the Library of Mendel ignores the (apparent) possibility of alternative genetic alphabets, based on different chemical constituents, for instance. So any conclusions we come to regarding what is possible relative to *this* Library of Mendel may have to be reconsidered when we try to apply them to some broader notion of possibility. This is actually a strength rather than a weakness of our tactic, since we can keep close tabs on exactly what sort of modest, circumscribed possibility we are talking about.

One of the important features of DNA is that all the permutations of sequences of adenine, cytosine, guanine, and thymine are about equally stable, chemically. All could be constructed, in principle, in the gene-splicing laboratory, and once constructed they would have an indefinite shelf life, like a book in a library. But not every such sequence in the Library of Mendel corresponds to a viable organism. Most DNA sequences—the Vast majority—are gibberish, recipes for nothing living at all. All the genomes that we see, that actually exist today, are the products of billions of years of adjustment and revision, a mindless editorial process that is effective because most of the gibberish (all but a Vanishingly thin thread of meaningful, useful "text") is automatically discarded, while the rest is relentlessly reused, copied kazillions of times. You have more than a trillion copies of your genome in your own body right now, one copy in each human cell, and every day, as new skin cells and bone cells and blood cells are made, new copies of your genomes are installed in them. The text that *can* be copied—because it resides in a going concern, a living cell—is copied. The rest dissolves. Publish or perish.

36. GENES AS WORDS OR AS SUBROUTINES

The analogy between genes and words is useful, as we have just seen, but there is a better one that we are now equipped to understand, thanks to the interlude about computers. In his masterpiece, *The Ancestor's Tale*, Richard Dawkins (2004) gives credit to another brilliant writer on evolution, Matt Ridley, for pointing out the deep similarities between genes and software subroutines in his book *Nature via Nurture*. I would not ordinarily insert such a long quotation of somebody else's work in a book of mine, but I found that my attempts at paraphrasing this passage invariably sacrificed clarity and vividness for a smidgen of originality, so, with his permission, I am passing along the unmutated version as it appears in Dawkins's book.

> Most of the genome that we sequence is not the book of
> instructions, or master computer program, for building a
> human or a mouse, although parts of it are. If it were, we
> might indeed expect our program to be larger than the
> mouse's. But most of the genome is more like the dictionary
> of words available for writing the book of instructions—or,
> we shall soon see, the set of subroutines that are called by
> the master program. As Ridley says, the list of words in
> *David Copperfield* is almost the same as the list of words in
> *The Catcher in the Rye*. Both draw upon the vocabulary of an
> educated native speaker of English. The difference between
> the two books is the order in which those words are strung
> together.
>
> When a person is made, or when a mouse is made, both
> embryologies draw upon the same dictionary of genes: the
> normal vocabulary of mammalian embryologies. The differ-
> ence between a person and a mouse comes out of the different

orders with which the genes, drawn from that shared mammalian vocabulary, are deployed, the different places in the body where this happens and its timing. All this is under the control of particular genes whose business it is to turn other genes on, in complicated and exquisitely timed cascades. But such controlling genes constitute only a minority of the genes in the genome.

Don't misunderstand "order" as meaning the order in which the genes are strung out along the chromosomes. With notable exceptions, . . . the order of genes along a chromosome is as arbitrary as the order in which words are listed in a vocabulary—usually alphabetical, but, especially in phrase books for foreign travel, sometimes an order of convenience: words useful in airports; words useful when visiting the doctor; words useful for shopping, and so on. The order in which genes are stored on chromosomes is unimportant. What matters is that the cellular machinery finds the right gene when it needs it, and it does this using methods that are becoming increasingly well understood. . . .

In one respect the analogy with words is misleading. Words are shorter than genes, and some writers have likened each gene to a sentence. But sentences aren't a good analogy, for a different reason. Different books are not put together by permuting a fixed repertoire of sentences. Most sentences are unique. Genes, like words but unlike sentences, are used over and over again in different contexts. A better analogy for a gene than either a word or a sentence is a toolbox subroutine in a computer. . . .

The Mac has a toolbox of routines stored in ROM (Read Only Memory) or in System files permanently loaded at start-up time. There are thousands of these toolbox routines, each one doing a particular operation, which is likely to be needed, over and over again, in slightly different ways, in different programs. For example, the toolbox routine called Obscure-

Cursor hides the cursor from the screen until the next time the mouse is moved. Unseen by you, the ObscureCursor "gene" is called every time you start typing and the mouse cursor vanishes. Toolbox routines lie behind the familiar features shared by all programs on the Mac (and their imitated equivalents on Windows machines): pulldown menus, scrollbars, shrinkable windows that you can drag around the screen with the mouse, and many others. [Dawkins, 2004, pp. 155–156]

All this helps us understand why it is so easy for an expert to recognize the genome of a mammal. It has the mammal toolbox, which in addition to its specialized mammal-making tools also includes tools from the reptile toolbox, and the fish toolbox, and even the worm toolbox. The oldest tools in the kit are shared by all living things, including bacteria.

37. THE TREE OF LIFE

The genomes that exist today are connected by threads of descent to the genomes of their parents and grandparents and so on, back to the beginning of life on Earth. The image facing page 241, the Tree of Life, shows how *every* person is relatively closely related to every other person—sharing common human ancestors within the last hundred thousand years, and sharing ancestors with every dog and whale within the last two hundred million years, and every daisy and redwood tree within the last two billion years.

There are many ways of drawing the Tree of Life. In this one, the present is represented along the outer tips of the branches. Only the lineages still alive reach this outer rim. Dinosaurs (except for the birds that descended from them) are shown to have gone extinct over 60 million years ago. All the threads are connected eventually, back at the origin of life—about which more later. If we enlarged the diagram a trillionfold, we could see the family trees of every fly, fish, and frog that ever lived, seeing which died childless (most of them, of course) and which had progeny.

38. CRANES AND SKYHOOKS, LIFTING IN DESIGN SPACE

Life is amazing. When you think of the billions of solar systems that are almost certainly entirely lifeless, it is amazing that there is any way of being alive at all. And it is amazing to reflect on the variety of different ways of being alive, from bacteria to fish, birds, daisies, whales, snakes, maples, and people. Perhaps most amazing of all is the tenacity of living things, the thousands of ways they have of clinging to life and reproducing, eking out a living against formidable obstacles, thanks to millions of ingenious devices and arrangements, from the convoluted cascades of protein machinery within every cell, to echolocation in bats, to the elephant's trunk, to the capacity of our brains to reflect on every topic "under the sun" and many others as well. All that magnificent adjustment of means to ends requires an explanation, since it cannot be pure chance or happenstance. There are only two known possibilities: Intelligent Design or evolution by natural selection. In either case there is a tremendous amount of design work to be done, either miraculously by an Intelligent Designer or ploddingly, unforesightedly, stupidly—but non-miraculously—by natural selection. Call the design work *R & D* (the standard abbreviation in industry for research and development), and recognize that R & D is always costly. It takes time and energy. The beauty of Darwin's great idea is that he saw how, given billions of years in which to work, and a prodigious amount of "waste" motion (zillions of trials ending in errors), design improvements could non-miraculously accumulate, automatically, without intention or foresight or understanding. Robert Beverley MacKenzie, one of Darwin's most ardent critics, put it eloquently:

> In the theory with which we have to deal, Absolute Ignorance
> is the artificer; so that we may enunciate as the fundamental

principle of the whole system, that, IN ORDER TO MAKE A PERFECT AND BEAUTIFUL MACHINE, IT IS NOT REQUISITE TO KNOW HOW TO MAKE IT. This proposition will be found, on careful examination, to express, in condensed form, the essential purport of the Theory, and to express in a few words all Mr. Darwin's meaning; who, by a strange inversion of reasoning, seems to think Absolute Ignorance fully qualified to take the place of Absolute Wisdom in all the achievements of creative skill. [1868]

Exactly. And ever since Darwin proposed this amazing idea, skeptics have wondered whether there was enough time to do all that creative work the plodding way. A convenient way to imagine the design work that needs to have been done is to think of it as *lifting* in Design Space. What is Design Space? Like the Library of Babel and the Library of Mendel, it can best be conceived as a multidimensional space. In fact Design Space contains both of those libraries and more, because it includes not only all the (designed, authored) books and the (designed, evolved) organisms, but all other things that are well described by the design stance (see chapter 18), such as houses, mousetraps, battleaxes, computers, and spaceships. And just as most of the Library of Babel is gibberish, most of the places in Design Space are filled with junk, things that can't do anything well at all. If you are like me, you can imagine just three dimensions at a time, but the more you play around with the idea in your imagination, the easier it gets to think of the familiar three dimensions as standing in for many. (This is a thinking tool that improves with practice.)

When we imagine placing the Tree of Life in the Library of Mendel, we can see how all the living things that have ever actually existed on this planet are connected to each other by lines of descent. Those lineages transmit the basic design improvements "discovered" by natural selection, preserving the earliest R & D for use in all subsequent living things. (The "machinery" inside every cell, from bacteria to brain cells, includes thousands of brilliantly designed nano-devices that have been cranking away for over three billion years, the basic engine room of life that we share with trees and birds and yeast cells.) At the multi-cell level we find hearts, lungs, eyes, arms, legs, and wings, reusing and improving on designs that were first developed "only" two billion years ago. But in addition to the parts of organisms, there are the artifacts of organisms: spider webs and bird nests and beaver dams, for example. These also show unmistakable evidence of R & D, and the fruits of that R & D have to have been transmitted somehow along the same lineage lines—either in the genes or by offspring copying their parents. Every now and then a novelty arises—by mutation or experimentation or accident—that is an improvement, and it gets copied and copied and copied. Failed experiments go extinct. Again, publish or perish.

Then there are the human artifacts, the plows and bridges and cathedrals, the paintings, plays, poems, and printing presses, the airplanes and computers and lawnmowers, and . . . the thinking tools. What about them? Do they not hang off the branches of one part of the Tree of Life—the human lineage? Each of them depends on at least one author or inventor, and most depend on uncounted thousands or millions of contributors to the R & D that lies behind them. Beethoven didn't have to invent the symphony, which was already there for him to adapt, and Shakespeare didn't have to invent the sonnet. A chainsaw is composed of dozens or hundreds of "off the shelf" elements, already invented, already optimized. Some of our human artifacts are probably copied from the artifacts of other animals. Did the weaverbird's nest inspire the invention of weaving cloth? Was the raised snow shelf on the floor of an Inuit igloo, which permits the cold air to drain out the lower entryway, copied from the similar raised floor in polar bear dens, or are these independent inventions (or did polar bears copy from the Inuit)?

The deep similarities of function between hearts and pumps, bat echolocation and sonar and radar, beaver dams and irrigation dams, eyes and cameras are no accident; similar processes of exploration—of R & D—have shaped and honed and improved them over the centuries. Put them all in a common space: Design Space, the space of *all possible* designs.

This move is contentious among biologists, for reasons I think I understand, and deplore. Many biologists are extremely reluctant to talk about "design" in living things, because they think it gives aid and comfort to the Intelligent Design movement, that disingenuous, pseudo-scientific, crypto-religious campaign to undermine the richly deserved authority of evolutionary biology. (Among these resisters are two of my most esteemed colleagues and friends, evolutionary biologists Richard Dawkins and Jerry Coyne.) By speaking of purpose and design in nature, we (apparently) give the Intelligent Design gang half their case; it is better, some think, to maintain a stern embargo on such themes and insist that *strictly speaking* nothing in the biosphere is designed unless it is designed by human artificers. Nature's way of generating complex systems (organs, behaviors) is so unlike an artificer's way, they think, that we should not use the same language to describe them. Thus Richard Dawkins speaks (on occasion—e.g., 1996, p. 4) of *designoid* features of organisms, and in *The Ancestor's Tale* (2004, p. 457), he says, "The illusion of design conjured by Darwinian natural selection is so breathtakingly powerful." I disagree with this policy of austerity, which can backfire badly. I recently overheard a conversation among some young people in a bar about the marvels of the nano-machinery discovered inside all cells. "When you see all those fantastic little robots working away, how can you possibly believe in evolution!" one exclaimed, and another nodded wisely. Somehow these folks had gotten the impression that evolutionary biologists thought that life wasn't all that complex, wasn't made of components that were all that wonderful. These evolution-doubters were not rednecks; they were Harvard Medical students! They hugely underestimated the power of natural selection because evolutionary biologists had told them, again and again, that there is no *actual* design in nature, only the *appearance* of design. This episode strongly suggested to me that "common knowledge" is beginning to incorporate the mistaken idea that evolutionary biologists are reluctant to "admit" or "acknowledge" all the obvious design in nature.

Consider in this regard Christoph Schönborn, Catholic archbishop of Vienna, the chap duped by the Intelligent Design folks. He wrote, notoriously, in a *New York Times* op-ed piece entitled "Finding Design in Nature,"

> The Catholic Church, while leaving to science many details about the history of life on earth, proclaims that by the light of reason the human intellect can readily and clearly discern purpose and design in the natural world, including the world of living things. Evolution in the sense of common ancestry might be true, but evolution in the neo-Darwinian sense—an unguided, unplanned process of random variation and natural selection—is not. Any system of thought that denies or seeks to explain away the overwhelming evidence for design in biology is ideology, not science.

Which campaign do we evolutionists want to lead? Do we want to try to convince laypeople that they don't really see the design that is stunningly obvious at every scale in biology, or would we rather try to show that, wonderful to say, what Darwin has shown is that there can be design—real design, as real as it gets—without an Intelligent Designer? We have persuaded the world that the earth goes around the sun and that time is relative, not absolute. Why shrink from the pedagogical task of showing that there can be design without a designer? So I am defending here (once again, with new emphasis) the following claim:

The biosphere is utterly saturated with design, with purpose, with reasons. What I call the design stance predicts and explains features throughout the living world using the same assumptions that work so well when we are reverse engineering artifacts made by (somewhat) intelligent human designers. Evolution by natural selection is a set of processes that "find" and "track" reasons for things to be arranged one way rather than another. The chief difference between the reasons found by evolution and the reasons found by human designers is that the latter are typically (but not always) represented in the minds of the designers, whereas the reasons uncovered by natural selection are typically represented for the first time by the human investigators who succeed in reverse engineering nature's productions. That is to say, human designers *think about* the reasons for the features of their artifacts, and hence *have ideas* that represent the reasons. They typically notice, appreciate, formulate, refine, and then convey, discuss, criticize the reasons for their designs. Evolution doesn't do any of this; it just sifts mindlessly through the variation it generates, and the good stuff (which is good for reasons, reasons undreamed of or unrepresented by the process of natural selection) gets copied.

There could be a good use for the term *designoid* to mark merely apparent design, but it is not in biology. When I think of the mere appearance of design, I think of how cartoonists set the stage for cartoons about scientists by showing some bearded eggheads standing in front of a blackboard covered with (actually nonsensical) symbols, or in a chemistry lab stocked with an impressive-looking forest of tubes and beakers, or by showing us the mad inventor working on his time machine, bristling with dials and antennas and hi-tech gizmos. These things couldn't actually do any work; they only appear to be functional. But the designs of nature are truly effective. In fact, they are often demonstrably much more efficient and powerful than any human-designed counterpart yet invented.

An example of a designoid inscription:

"WHAT EVER HAPPENED TO ELEGANT SOLUTIONS?"

A healthy young man can walk, carrying all the food and water he needs to survive, for about a week, stopping and resting whenever he chooses, traveling perhaps 150 miles. (Water is the key burden: carrying fifty pounds of water and sixteen pounds of food and ten pounds of gear makes a very heavy pack; if he could find water on the way, he could go for months.) For comparison, consider the brainchild of Cornell University roboticist Andy Ruina and his colleagues, who have built by far the longest walking robot, Ranger, which traveled nonstop 65.2 kilometers (40.5 miles) in a robot ultra-marathon in Japan on May 1–2, 2011. Ranger's designers take advantage of the dynamical properties of limbs to create a superbly energy-efficient walker (around and around on a flat track for hours on end, guided by a human being with a joystick). Another magnificent four-legged walker robot, Big Dog, is about fifteen times less energy-efficient, but has much more impressive capacities to accommodate difficult terrain. Humans are still considerably more efficient transport devices than Ranger by a factor of four or five, and unlike Ranger, they can respond autonomously to all manner of features in the world. (See Ruina, 2011.)

Something has to give. Either we *define* "design" as the product of an intelligent designer, such as a designer of poems or cars, for instance, or we acknowledge that there can be design—genuine design—without an intelligent designer. Tradition and etymology might seem to favor the former course, but consider this: *atom*—from the Greek *a* [without] + *tomos*, from *temnein*, to cut or slice. *Atom* originally meant "unsplittable thing," but science discovered that splitting the atom, after all, was not a contradiction in terms. Science has also discovered, I submit, that design without a designer (lacking a designer with a mind, with foresight and intention) is not only possible but all around us. Design-by-evolution is a real, well-understood process. It differs in interesting ways from design-by-engineer, but it is also deeply similar, capable of humbling "ingenuity." Time and again, biologists baffled by some apparently futile or maladroit bit of bad design in nature have eventually come to see that they have underestimated the sheer brilliance in one of Mother Nature's creations. Francis Crick mischievously baptized this trend in the name of a colleague, Leslie Orgel, speaking of what he called Orgel's Second Law: "evolution is cleverer than you are." (This apparently reckless tactic of personifying the process of natural selection as Mother Nature, this in-your-face anthropomorphizing, will be defended in due course. It is not just an entertaining metaphor; it is a thinking tool in its own right.)

Back to Design Space, the multidimensional space of all *possible* designs, including not just the actual organisms and automobiles and poems, but—like the books in the Library of Babel—all the never-evolved, never-constructed designs: the talking kangaroos and flying snakes, nuclear-powered popcorn poppers and underwater roller-skates. What should our *alphabet* of basic design elements be? Since we aren't going to try to *make* Design Space, but just think about it, we might as well be profligate: let's say, all possible configurations of atoms, drawn from the periodic table of elements. (This Vast space will include atom-for-atom duplicates of all the *undesigned* things as well, such as every pebble on every beach, and Mt. Everest, but that is as it should be since there is nothing to prevent somebody from deciding to design and build replicas of these entities.) Where will Brahms's Third Symphony be in Design Space? Well, the *score* (in spots of ink on paper, etc.) will be in kazillions of places, and tape recordings and vinyl stereo records will be in others, so it will be in Design Space for sure. A song that was never written down or recorded but rather preserved and transmitted in an oral tradition will be harder to tie down to families of atoms, but a suitably convoluted subsection of Design Space over time will house it well enough. Just as the Library of Babel is filled mainly with junk, unreadable books of nonsense, Design Space is filled mainly with nonsensical stuff of no interest or function or competence at all, but here and there, Vanishingly thin threads of actual and possible design shine through; things that can *do things* aside from just waiting around to crumble under the inexorable edict of the second law of thermodynamics.

With just this roughed-out idea of Design Space in our heads, we can now see "at a glance" how to frame a series of questions that have haunted debate about evolution ever since Darwin's time: Are there *any* actual designs, natural or artificial, that are not ultimately derived from that single Tree of Life, either directly or indirectly?

Here are some answers to consider:

1. No.
2. Yes, some marvels of nature are just too wonderful, too "irreducibly complex," to have been arrived at by the plodding uphill process of design-by-evolution. They must have been independently created by an Intelligent Designer.
3. Yes, some human artifacts, such as the plays of Shakespeare and Gödel's theorem, are too wonderful to be "mere" products of evolved human brains; they are works of miraculous *genius* and are inexplicable by—unreachable by—the plodding uphill process of design-by-evolution.

We can characterize answers (2) and (3) as relying heavily on the contrast between the utterly inefficient, plodding process of natural selection ("Absolute Ignorance," as MacKenzie called it), and the swift, apparently effortless brilliance of Mozart (or any other "God-like" genius you choose). (Chapter 49 explores this.) Using our analogy between *lifting* and R & D, we can say that they each proclaim the need for a *skyhook*.

> *skyhook*, orig. Aeronaut. An imaginary contrivance for attachment to the sky; an imaginary means of suspension in the sky. [*Oxford English Dictionary*]

The first use noted by the *Oxford English Dictionary* is dated 1915: "an aeroplane pilot commanded to remain in place (aloft) for another hour, replies 'the machine is not fitted with skyhooks'." The skyhook concept is perhaps a descendant of the *deus ex machina* of ancient Greek dramaturgy: when second-rate playwrights found their plots leading their heroes into inescapable difficulties, they were often tempted to crank down a god onto the scene, like Superman, to save the situation supernaturally. Or skyhooks may be an entirely independent creation of convergent folkloric evolution. Skyhooks would be wonderful things to have, great for lifting unwieldy objects out of difficult circumstances, and speeding up all sorts of construction projects. Sad to say, they are impossible.*

There are *cranes*, however. Cranes can do the lifting work our imaginary skyhooks might do, and they do it in an honest, non-question-begging fashion. They are expensive though. They have to be designed and built, from everyday parts already on hand, and they have to be located on a firm base of existing ground. Skyhooks are miraculous lifters, unsupported and insupportable. Cranes are no less excellent as lifters, and they have the advantage of being real. Anyone who, like me, is a lifelong onlooker at construction sites will have noticed with some satisfaction that it sometimes takes a small crane to set up a big crane. And it must have occurred to many other onlookers that in principle this big crane could be used to enable or speed up the building of a still more spectacular crane. Cascading cranes is a tactic that seldom if ever gets used more than once in real-world construction projects, but in principle there is no limit to the number of cranes that could be organized in series to accomplish some mighty end.†

---

* Well, not quite impossible. Geostationary satellites, orbiting in unison with the earth's rotation, are a kind of real, non-miraculous skyhook. What makes them so valuable—what makes them financially sound investments—is that we often do want very much to attach something (such as an antenna or camera or telescope) to a place high in the sky. Satellites are impractical for *lifting*, alas, because they have to be placed so high in the sky. The idea has been carefully explored. It turns out that a rope of the strongest artificial fiber yet made would have to be over a hundred meters in diameter at the top—it could taper to a nearly invisible fishing line on its way down—just to suspend its own weight, let alone any payload. Even if you could spin such a cable, you wouldn't want it falling out of orbit onto the city below!

†I was pleased to see the *sky crane* invented to help lower *Curiosity*, the robotic rover, to the surface of Mars on August 6, 2012, and especially pleased that it is called a sky *crane* not a sky*hook*, since it is the product of stunning engineering but no miracle.

Now imagine all the "lifting" that has to get done in Design Space to create the magnificent organisms and other artifacts we encounter in our world. Huge distances must have been traversed since the dawn of Life with the earliest, simplest, self-replicating entities, spreading outward (diversity) and upward (excellence). Darwin has offered us an account of the crudest, most rudimentary, stupidest imaginable lifting process—the wedge or inclined plane of natural selection. By taking tiny—the tiniest possible—steps, this process can gradually, over eons, traverse these huge distances. Or so Darwin claims. At no point would anything miraculous—from on high—be needed. Each step has been accomplished by brute, mechanical, **algorithmic** climbing, from the base already built by the efforts of earlier climbing.

It does seem incredible. Could it really have happened? Or did the process need a "leg up" now and then (perhaps only at the very beginning) from one sort of skyhook or another? For over a century, skeptics have been trying to find proof that Darwin's idea just can't work, at least not *all the way*. They have been hoping and hunting for skyhooks, as exceptions to what they see as the bleak vision of Darwin's algorithm churning away. And time and again, they have come up with truly interesting challenges—leaps and gaps and other marvels that do seem, at first, to need skyhooks. But then along have come the cranes, discovered in many cases by the very skeptics who were hoping to find a skyhook.

It is time for some more careful definitions. Let us understand that a *skyhook* is a "mind-first" force or power or process, an exception to the principle that all design, and apparent design, is ultimately the result of mindless, motiveless mechanicity. A *crane*, in contrast, is a subprocess, or a special feature of a design process that can be demonstrated to permit the local speeding up of the basic, slow process of natural selection, *and* that can be demonstrated to be itself the predictable (or retrospectively explicable) product of the basic process. Some cranes are obvious and uncontroversial; others are still being argued about, very fruitfully. Just to give a general sense of the breadth and application of the concept, let me point to three very different examples.

Symbiosis is a crane. One of my favorite examples is the symbiotic origin of the eukaryotic cell. If you look at the Tree of Life (facing p. 241), you will notice that the glorious fan-out of multicellular life, including all plants and animals, occurs after the evolution of eukaryotes. For about a billion years on this planet, the only living things were single-celled organisms, bacteria and archaea, together known as prokaryotes. Then one lucky day, one prokaryote happened to bump into another (it no doubt happened very often then, as it still does today), and instead of one of them engulfing and dismantling the other (eating it), or repelling it, the two joined forces, forming a brand new kind of living thing, with (roughly) twice as many working parts and a greater variety of working parts. Two R & D lineages that had been chugging along separately for millions of years, each honing its own peculiar talents, came together and the result was— happened to be—an overnight success. ("Technology transfer" does not always or even often yield good results, but when it does, it can be spectacular.) Neither lineage had to go to the plodding trouble of reinventing all the tricks and systems of the other, and since the combination of their talents happened to be a net gain (*synergy* is the buzzword for this), this *eu-karyote* ("good" + "cell") was fitter than either by itself, so the lineage of eukaryotes prospered. The claim that the origin of eukaryotes was such an event of symbiosis used to be controversial, but so many lines of evidence support it that it is now solidly in the textbooks. (It would be gratifying to report that the origin of the bacterial flagellum, long the flagship example of "irreducible complexity" among the Intelligent Design crowd, has also proved to be due to the helping crane of symbiosis, and although Lynn Margulis, the late biologist and champion of the symbiotic origin of the eukaryotes, vigorously defended this claim, the evidence currently favors alternative evolutionary accounts of the source of the flagellum. Given this embarrassment of riches, the claim that flagella need a skyhook is looking particularly forlorn now.)

As we can see at a glance in the Tree of Life, eukaryotes set the stage for all of multicellular life. All the multicolored lineages to the right of the bacteria and archaea are eukaryotes. To a first approximation, every living thing that can be seen by the naked eye is a eukaryote. The eukaryotic revolution opened up huge regions of Design Space, but it did not happen *in order to* make all these designs accessible. Cranes must be "paid for" locally, in terms of the immediate benefits they convey to those that have the design innovations. But once established they can have profound further effects. (Similarly, computers were not invented *in order to* make word-processing and the Internet possible, but once the space of possible computer applications was rendered accessible, design processes went into overdrive creating all the "species" we now rely on every day.)

Evolutionary theorists now generally agree that *sex* is a crane. Species that reproduce sexually can move through Design Space at a greater speed than species that reproduce asexually. Moreover, they can "discern" design improvements along the way that are all but "invisible" to asexually reproducing species (Holland, 1975). This cannot be the *raison d'être* of sex, however. Evolution cannot see way down the road, so anything it builds must have an immediate payoff to counterbalance the cost. As recent theorists have insisted, the "choice" of reproducing sexually carries a huge *immediate* cost: organisms send along only 50 percent of their genes in any one transaction (to say nothing of the effort and risk involved in securing a transaction in the first place). So the *long-term* payoff of heightened efficiency, acuity, and speed of the redesign process—the features that make sex a magnificent crane—is as nothing to the myopic, local competitions that must determine which organisms get favored in the very next generation. Some other, short-term benefit must have maintained the positive selection pressure required to make sexual reproduction an offer few species could refuse. There are a variety of compelling—and competing—hypotheses that might solve this puzzle, which was first forcefully posed for biologists by John Maynard Smith (1978). For a lucid introduction to this important topic in evolutionary biology, see

Matt Ridley's book *The Red Queen: Sex and the Education of Human Nature* (1993).

Sex reveals that a crane of great power may exist that was not created *in order to exploit* that power; it was created for other reasons, although its power as a crane may help explain why it has been maintained ever since. A crane that was obviously created to be a crane is *genetic engineering*. Genetic engineers can now unquestionably take huge leaps through Design Space, creating organisms that would never have evolved by "ordinary" means. This is no miracle *provided that genetic engineers (and the artifacts they use in their trade) are themselves wholly the products of earlier, slower evolutionary processes*. If the creationists were right that mankind is a species unto itself, divine and inaccessible via brute Darwinian paths, then genetic engineering would not be a crane after all, having been created with the help of a major skyhook. I don't imagine that any genetic engineers think of themselves this way, but it is a logically available perch, however precarious. Less obviously silly is this idea: if the bodies of genetic engineers are products of evolution, but their *minds* can do creative things that are irreducibly non-algorithmic or inaccessible by all algorithmic paths, then the leaps of genetic engineering might involve a skyhook. We will briefly explore this prospect later.

39. COMPETENCE WITHOUT COMPREHENSION

MacKenzie described Darwin's idea of Absolute Ignorance being the source of "all the achievements of creative skill" as a "strange inversion of reasoning," since it turns upside down one of the most "obvious" ideas we have: comprehension is the *source* of competence. Why do we send our children to school, and why do we emphasize "concepts" over "rote learning"? Because we think that the best route to competence, in any sphere of activity, is comprehension. Don't settle for being a mindless drudge! *Understand* the principles of whatever we're doing so we can do it better! This is surely excellent advice in most arenas of human activity. We recognize extreme exceptions, such as gifted musicians who "play by ear" and can't read a note of music, or natural athletes who always seem to do the best thing but can't explain how or why they do it, and hence can't coach others. Then there are "idiot savants" with bizarre combinations of incompetence in most regards and superhuman prowess in some limited domain. But in general, the rule of thumb is hard to deny: comprehension is usually the key to (human) competence.

And Darwin really does invert that reasoning, showing, as MacKenzie so vividly put it, that Absolute Ignorance is the artificer. The process of natural selection is breathtakingly competent—think of Orgel's Second Law—but utterly mindless. Moreover, the organisms it designs get the benefits of all their exquisite equipment without needing to understand why or how they are so gifted. My favorite example is the cuckoo. Cuckoos are *brood parasites* that don't make their own nests. Instead, the female cuckoo surreptitiously lays her egg in the nest of a host pair of some other species of birds, where it awaits the attentions of its unwittingly adoptive parents. Often, the female cuckoo will roll one of the host eggs out of the nest—just in case the host parents can count! And as soon as the cuckoo chick is hatched (and it tends to incubate more quickly than the host eggs), the fledgling cuckoo goes to great efforts to roll any remaining eggs out of the nest! Why? To maximize the attention it will get from its adoptive parents.

40. FREE-FLOATING RATIONALES

Natural selection is an automatic reason-finder; it "discovers" and "endorses" and "focuses" reasons over many generations. The scare quotes are to remind us that natural selection doesn't have a mind, doesn't itself have reasons, but it is nevertheless competent to perform this "task" of design refinement. This is itself an instance of competence without comprehension. Let's just be sure we know how to cash out the scare quotes. Consider a population with lots of variation in it. Some members of the population do well (at multiplying); most do not. In each case we can ask *why*. Why did this one have surviving offspring while these others did not? In many cases, most cases, there is *no reason at all*; it's just dumb luck, good or bad. But if there is a subset, perhaps a very small one, of cases in which there is an answer, a difference that happens to make a difference, then what those cases have in common provides the germ of a reason. This permits functionality to accumulate by a process that blindly tracks reasons, creating things that have purposes but don't need to know them. The Need to Know principle reigns in the biosphere, and natural selection itself doesn't need to know what it's doing.

So there were reasons before there were reason-representers. The reasons tracked by evolution I have called "free-floating rationales," a term that has apparently jangled the nerves of more than a few thinkers, who suspect I am conjuring up ghosts of some sort, strange immaterial ideas that have no business appearing in a sober materialist's account of reality. Not at all. Free-floating rationales are no more ghostly or problematic than numbers or centers of gravity. There were nine planets before people invented ways of articulating arithmetic, and asteroids had centers of gravity before there were physicists to dream up the idea and calculate with it. It is a mistake to confuse *numbers* with the *numerals* (Arabic or Roman or whatever) that we use as their names. Numerals are human inventions; numbers are not. Reasons, in the sense I am using the term, are like numbers, not numerals. We should all be happy to speak of the reasons uncovered by evolution before they were ever expressed or represented by human investigators or any other minds. Consider the strikingly similar constructions in the figures facing page 240.

The termite castle and Antoni Gaudí's La Sagrada Familia are very similar in shape but utterly different in genesis and construction. *There are reasons* for the structures and shapes of the termite castle, but they are not represented by any of the termites. There is no Architect Termite who planned the structure, nor do any individual termites have the slightest clue about why they build the way they do. Competence without comprehension. There are also reasons for the structures and shapes of Gaudí's masterpiece, but they are (in the main) Gaudí's reasons. Gaudí *had* reasons for the shapes he ordered created; *there are* reasons for the shapes created by the termites, but the termites don't *have* those reasons. There are reasons why trees spread their branches, but they are not in any strong sense the trees' reasons. Sponges do things for reasons; bacteria do things for reasons; even viruses do things for reasons. But they don't *have* the reasons; they don't need to have the reasons.

There are reasons aplenty for these behaviors, but in general, organisms need not understand them. They are endowed with behaviors that are well designed by evolution, and they are the beneficiaries of these designs without needing to know about it. This feature is everywhere to be seen in nature, but it tends to be masked by our tendency, adopting the **intentional stance,** to interpret behavior as more mindful and rational than it really is. How clever the termites are to air-condition their castles with well-placed ventilation shafts! How sagacious the squirrel is to store away food for the winter! How wily the pickerel is to hover motionless as its prey approaches! These are indeed excellent strategies for success in the unrelentingly competitive world of nature, but their beneficiaries need not appreciate what we do when we figure them out. We are the first minds to represent the reasons that account for the success of these arrangements.

41. DO LOCUSTS UNDERSTAND PRIME NUMBERS?

Just to drive home the point about the independence of numbers and numerals, free-floating rationales and represented reasoning, consider the case of the seventeen-year locusts. In 1977, Stephen Jay Gould wrote an insightful and admiring chapter about the curious fact that cicadas (such as the "seventeen-year locust") have reproductive cycles with lengths, in years, equal to prime numbers—thirteen years, or seventeen, but never fifteen or sixteen, for instance. "As evolutionists," Gould (p. 99) says, "we seek answers to the question, why. Why, in particular, should such striking synchronicity evolve, and why should the period between episodes of sexual reproduction be so long?" The answer—which makes beautiful sense, in retrospect—is that by having a large prime number of years between appearances, the cicadas minimize the likelihood of being discovered and later tracked as a predictable feast by predators who themselves show up every two years, or three years, or five years. If the cicadas had a periodicity of, say, sixteen years, then they would be a rare treat for predators who showed up every year, but a more reliable source of food for predators who showed up every two or four years, and an even-money gamble for predators who got in phase with them on an eight-year schedule. If the length of their reproductive period is not a multiple of any lower number, however, they are not worth "trying" to track for any species that isn't lucky enough to have exactly the same periodicity (or some multiple of it—the mythical Thirty-Four-Year Locust-Muncher would be in fat city).

It should be clear that the soundness of this explanation (which may not yet be established) does not depend on any hypothesis suggesting that locusts understand arithmetic, let alone prime numbers. Nor does it depend on the process of natural selection *understanding* prime numbers. The mindless, uncomprehending process of natural selection can *exploit* this important property of some numbers without having to understand it at all. For another example: neither bees nor Mother Nature need to *understand* the geometry that declares the hexagon the ideal shape for cells in a honeycomb. Many more examples of evolution's mathematical competence-without-comprehension could be cited.

42. HOW TO EXPLAIN STOTTING

Remember the baffling regularity revealed in the intuition pump about the **two black boxes**? You didn't have to have a semantic or intentional interpretation of the boxes to see it: α caused red, and β caused green—an obvious pattern in need of explanation. In each instance of button-pressing, the scientists understood exactly how each step in the computing and transmitting process worked, but they couldn't explain the generalization. You do need a semantic interpretation to explain why the regularity exists. In other words, the "macro-causal" level at which the explanation is expressed does not "reduce" to the "micro-causal" level.

Here is another instance of this very general phenomenon. You have probably seen video of gazelles being chased across the plain by a predator, and noticed that some of the gazelles are leaping high into the air during their attempts to escape their pursuer. This is called stotting. Why do gazelles stot? It is clearly beneficial, because gazelles that stot seldom get caught and eaten. This is a causal regularity that has been carefully observed, just like the regularity between buttons and lights. And it too can baffle. No account of the actions of all the proteins in all the cells of all the gazelles and the predators chasing them could reveal why this regularity exists. For that we need the branch of evolutionary theory known as costly signaling theory (Zahavi, 1987; FitzGibbon and Fanshawe, 1988). The strongest and fastest of the gazelles stot to advertise their fitness to the pursuer, signaling in effect, "Don't bother chasing me; I'm too hard to catch; concentrate on one of my cousins who isn't able to stot—a much easier meal!" and the pursuer takes this to be an honest, hard-to-fake signal and ignores the stotter. This is the free-floating rationale, and it need not be appreciated by either gazelle or predator. That is, the gazelle may be entirely oblivious to why it is a good idea to stot if it can,

and the predator, say, a lion, may not understand why it finds stotting gazelles relatively unattractive prey, but if the signaling wasn't
honest, costly signaling, it couldn't persist in the evolutionary arms
race between predator and prey. (If evolution tried using a "cheap"
signal, like tail-flicking, which every gazelle, no matter how strong
or weak, could send, it wouldn't be worth it for lions to pay attention
to it, so they wouldn't.) These explanations in terms of free-floating
rationales are not reducible to explanations at lower levels, such as the
molecular level, but it is important to recognize that even though the
explanation of why and how stotting works is from the **intentional
stance** (in terms of what it would be rational for a lion to conclude
from the stotting of the gazelle), the individual lion or gazelle need
not understand the meaning of stotting for it to work; they need only
sorta understand it.

43. BEWARE OF THE PRIME MAMMAL

You may think you're a mammal, and that dogs and cows and whales are mammals, but really there aren't any mammals at all. There couldn't be! Here's a philosophical argument to prove it (drawn with alterations from Sanford, 1975):

1. Every mammal has a mammal for a mother.
2. If there have been any mammals at all, there have been only a finite number of mammals.
3. But if there has been even one mammal, then by (1), there have been an infinity of mammals, which contradicts (2), so there can't have been any mammals. It's a contradiction in terms.

Since we know perfectly well that there are mammals, we take this argument seriously only as a challenge to discover what fallacy is lurking within it. It's a straightforward *reductio ad absurdum*, so something has to give. And we know, in a general way, what has to give: if you go back far enough in the family tree of any mammal, you will eventually get to the *therapsids*, strange, extinct bridge species between the reptiles and the mammals. A gradual transition occurred from clear reptiles to clear mammals, with a lot of hard-to-classify intermediaries filling in the gaps. What should we do about drawing the lines across this spectrum of gradual change? Can we identify a mammal, the Prime Mammal, that didn't have a mammal for a mother, thus negating premise (1)? On what grounds? Whatever the grounds are, they will compete with the grounds we could use to support the verdict that that animal was *not* a mammal—after all, its mother was a therapsid. What could be a better test of therapsid-hood than that? Suppose we list ten major differences used to distinguish therapsids from mammals, and declare that having five or more of the mammal marks makes an animal a mammal. Aside from being arbitrary—why ten differences instead of six or twenty, and shouldn't they be ordered in importance?—any such dividing line will generate lots of unwanted verdicts, since during the long, long period of transition between obvious therapsids and obvious mammals there will be plenty of instances in which mammals (by our five-plus rule) mated with therapsids (less than five mammal marks) and had offspring that were therapsids born of mammals, mammals born of therapsids born of mammals, and so forth! Of course we would need a time machine to see all these anomalies, since the details are undetectable after all those millions of years. It's just as well, since the details don't really matter in the long run. What should we do? *We should quell our desire to draw lines.* We don't need to draw lines. We can live with the quite unshocking and unmysterious fact that all these gradual changes accumulated over many millions of years and eventually produced undeniable mammals. Similarly the differences between lakes, ponds, and wetlands or marshes do not need to be calibrated, even by limnologists (those who study inland waters).

Philosophers, however, tend to be tidy, fussy users of words. Ever since Socrates persisted in demanding to be told precisely what marked the defining features of virtue, knowledge, courage, and the like, philosophers have been tempted by the idea of stopping a threatened infinite regress like this one by identifying something that is—must be—*the* regress-stopper: the Prime Mammal, in this case. It often lands them in doctrines that wallow in mystery, or at least puzzlement, and it commits them to *essentialism*. The Prime Mammal must be whichever mammal in the set of mammals was the first to have all the *essential* mammalian features. If there is no definable essence of *mammal*—and evolutionary biology shows us that there are no such essences—these philosophers are in trouble. So, as a general rule, consider ignoring the philosophers' demand for an essence, a defining feature, a "truth-maker." It typically—not always—starts a wild goose chase that may be diverting but is only moderately illuminating at best.

242 INTUITION PUMPS AND OTHER TOOLS FOR THINKING

Abandoning this demand is a really bitter pill for many philosophers to swallow. The rational methods for doing philosophy that have been handed down since Socrates almost always call for "defining your terms" in such a way as to commit everybody in the discussion to a doctrine of essentialism, even if only *for the sake of argument*, as we say. If we have to abandon essentialism, some of our favorite argument forms are rendered almost useless. Consider, for instance, the structure of arguments that start with an apparently trivially true *disjunction*:

> Either A or not-A (how can you argue with *that?*)
> If you choose path A, then blahblahblah, so you arrive at conclusion C;
> and if you start with not-A, then blahblahblah, you *also* arrive at C!
> Therefore C is established.

But what if there are apparently lots of intermediate cases about which it isn't clear whether they are A or not-A (mammals or not mammals, alive or not alive, conscious or not conscious, a belief or not a belief, moral or not moral, etc.)? In order to brush aside this worry, you must "draw a line" distinguishing the A from the not-A and banishing all **sorta** talk. Without that sharp boundary, marking the essence of whatever is at stake, the argument simply can't be constructed. Such arguments work brilliantly in mathematics, where you really *can* draw the lines. Every integer really is odd or even, and every number really is rational or not rational, and every polygon really is a (three-sided) triangle or not. Outside of such abstract domains, these arguments fare less well.

The insistence that there must be a Prime Mammal, even if we can never know when and where it existed, is an example of *hysterical realism*. It invites us to reflect that if we just knew enough, we'd see— we'd *have* to see—that there is a special property of mammal-hood that defines mammals once and for all. To deny this, philosophers

Termite Castle and La Sagrada Famiglia (See p. 235 for discussion.)

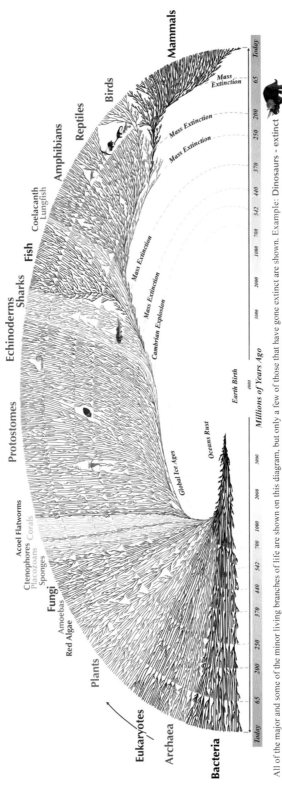

All of the major and some of the minor living branches of life are shown on this diagram, but only a few of those that have gone extinct are shown. Example: Dinosaurs - extinct

Mammals

Birds

Reptiles

Amphibians

Coelacanth
Lungfish

Fish

Sharks

Echinoderms

Protostomes

Acoel Flatworms
Ctenophores   Corals
Placozoans
Sponges

Fungi

Amoebas
Red Algae

Plants

Eukaryotes

Archaea

Bacteria

Mass Extinction
Mass Extinction
Mass Extinction
Mass Extinction
Mass Extinction
Cambrian Explosion

Earth Birth

Global Ice Ages

Oceans Rust

Millions of Years Ago

Today   65   200   250   370   440   542   700   1000   2000   3000   4000   3000   2000   1000   700   542   440   370   250   200   65   Today sometimes say, is to confuse metaphysics with epistemology: the study of what there (really) *is* with the study of what we can *know* about what there is. I reply that there may be occasions when thinkers do go off the rails by confusing a metaphysical question with a (merely) epistemological question, but this must be shown, not just asserted.

44. WHEN DOES SPECIATION OCCUR?

A curious feature of evolution by natural selection is that it depends crucially on events that "almost never" happen. For instance, speciation, the process in which a new species is generated by wandering away from its parent species, is an exceedingly rare event, but each of the millions of species that have existed on this planet got its start with an event of speciation. Every birth in every lineage is a potential speciation event, but speciation almost never happens, not once in a million births. Mutation in DNA almost never happens—not once in a trillion copyings—but evolution depends on it. Moreover, the vast majority of mutations are either deleterious or neutral; a fortuitously "good" mutation almost never happens. But evolution depends on those almost rarest of rare events.

Consider an intuition pump about a remarkable possibility: At this time, so far as we know, there is just one species of hominid on the planet, *Homo sapiens*. But suppose that fifty years from now, all but a lucky handful of our descendants are wiped out by a virus that leaves only two groups of survivors: a thousand Inuit living on remote Cornwallis Island off Greenland, and a thousand Andamanese living in splendid isolation on islands in the middle of the Indian Ocean. These two populations have been isolated from each other for thousands of years and have developed distinct physiological differences in response to their very different environments, but we have no good reason to question the standard assumption that they are members of our species. Suppose these populations remain both geographically and reproductively isolated for another ten thousand years, eventually repopulating the globe with two species—as they learn when they finally encounter each other and discover they have no interest in mating with each other, and besides, their few inadvertent attempts at mating are fruitless, a standard mark of *allopatric speciation*, reproductive isolation produced over time by geographical isolation. They might wonder, When precisely did the speciation occur? It is probably the case that their last common ancestor lived more than thirty thousand years ago, but speciation didn't occur then and there (and so far as we know, it hasn't occurred yet), but it still might emerge in a few thousand years that speciation had occurred at some time before the two populations were reunited. Did speciation occur before the dawn of agriculture or after the creation of the Internet? There is no nonarbitrary answer we could comfortably defend. There must have been a last common ancestor, or *concestor* to use Dawkins's (2004) term, living maybe thirty thousand years ago, and the offspring of this individual could eventually turn out in the fullness of time *to have been* the founders of two different species, but it still isn't settled today, one way or the other, whether a speciation event started then.

Here we would have an event, a birth that could turn out to have played a pivotal role in human (and post-human) history, one that occurred in a precise time and place but didn't acquire its special status until millennia of *sequelae* had fixed that role, which was never a foregone conclusion. All it would take to prevent that birth from ever having been a speciation event would be a single boatload (or planeload) of islanders making a journey that led to the "premature" reuniting of the branches. One can *imagine* that speciation actually occurred at some precise but unknowable moment in the interval between initial isolation of the lineages and the eventual demonstration of their status as two species, but how could such a tipping point be defined? Presumably as the earliest time at which, thanks to the accumulation of chromosomal divergence between the two lineages, *if* any cross-lineage matings had been attempted, they *would have* proved infertile. But surmises about such counterfactuals are of scant significance.

The building of the transcontinental railroad split the herds of American bison into reproductively isolated populations, but Buffalo Bill Cody and his colleagues nipped that potential speciation event in the bud in no time by pretty much wiping out all but one

246 INTUITION PUMPS AND OTHER TOOLS FOR THINKING

of the populations. Populations of conspecifics often get divided by environmental events into two (or more) isolated groups, which stay reproductively isolated from each other for a few generations, and almost always either these groups reunite again or one group goes extinct. So although such first steps to speciation must happen fairly often, they almost never lead to speciation, and when they do, it is an outcome that takes many hundreds of generations to establish. Absolutely nothing about the circumstances of the initial separation could tell you whether they were the beginnings of a speciation event, even if you had perfect physical knowledge of every molecule in the world at the time. The very concept of a species is a **sorta** concept. Domestic dogs, coyotes, and wolves are named as species, and yet coydogs and dog-wolf offspring are quite common, so "officially" maybe we should consider these as three mere varieties, not even subspecies, of Canidae. Generalizations about the possibility of hybridizing—creating offspring from parents of different species—are hard to establish, which is not surprising when you reflect that every individual of every species exhibits subtle differences from every other individual of that species. This does not particularly worry biologists; they have learned not to fret over definitions or essences, since the processes that create all the intermediate cases are well understood.

45. WIDOWMAKERS, MITOCHONDRIAL EVE, AND RETROSPECTIVE CORONATIONS

A woman in New York City may suddenly acquire the property of being a widow by virtue of the effects that a bullet has just had on some man's brain in Dodge City, over a thousand miles away. (In the days of the Wild West, there was a revolver nicknamed the Widowmaker. Whether a particular revolver lived up to its nickname on a particular occasion might not be settled by even the most exhaustive examination of the scene of the crime.) The example gets its curious capacity to leap through space and time from the conventional nature of the relationship of marriage, in which a past historical event, a wedding, is deemed to create a permanent relation—a formal relation, not a causal relation—of interest in spite of subsequent wanderings and concrete misfortunes (the accidental loss of a ring, or the destruction of the marriage certificate, for instance).

The system of genetic reproduction is natural, not conventional, but it works like clockwork, and that very systematicity permits us to think *formally* about causal chains extending over millions of years, causal chains that would otherwise be virtually impossible to designate or refer to or track. This permits us to become interested in, and reason rigorously about, even more distant and locally invisible relationships than the formal relationship of marriage. Speciation, like marriage, is a concept anchored within a tight, formally definable system of thought, but unlike marriage it has no conventional saliencies—weddings, rings, certificates—by which it can be observed. As we just saw, speciation is also a curiously "long-distance" phenomenon, in both space and time. Species are fuzzy-edged collections over time, and we could only retrospectively (and arbitrarily) identify some individual organism in such a crowd as the Prime Mammal (so don't bother). We can see this feature of speciation in a better light by looking first at another instance of retrospective crowning, the conferring of the title of Mitochondrial Eve, which is not arbitrary.

Individual organisms have rather crisper bounders and hence clearer identities than species, but even with them there are plenty of fence-sitters. Let's take the most striking instance: of the ten trillion or so cells that are crowded together inside your clothes, nine out of ten are not human! Yes, symbiont visitors in thousands of species outnumber your host cells—the cells that descended from the zygote formed by your parents' union. There are not only bacteria but also eukaryotes, both single-celled microbes and multicellular organisms: fungi, mites in your eyelashes and elsewhere, worms microscopic and bigger, and who knows what else. You are a walking ecosystem, and while some of the visitors are unwanted (the fungi that cause athlete's foot, or the bacteria that lead to bad breath or crowd around any infection), others are so essential that if you succeeded in evicting all the trespassers, you would die. Since these symbiont cells are generally much smaller than your human cells, by *weight* you are mostly human, but their combined weight is not negligible either—probably several pounds, and maybe as much as ten. Then there are the viruses, in even greater numbers.

Still, in spite of your porous boundaries, you—like other individual organisms—are readily distinguished from the others, and sometimes we can single out a specific individual organism for a specific role in evolutionary history. Mitochondrial Eve is one of the most famous. Mitochondrial Eve is the woman who is the *most recent* direct ancestor, in the female line, of every human being *alive today*. We all have mitochondria in our cells, and they are passed to us through the maternal line alone, so all the mitochondria in all the cells in all the people alive today are direct descendants of the mitochondria in the cells of a particular woman, named Mitochondrial Eve by Rebecca Cann, Mark Stoneking, and Allan Wilson (1987).

Mitochondria are tiny organelles in our cells that play a central role in metabolism, capturing energy from food to use in all the body's projects, and mitochondria have their own DNA, a telling trace of their symbiotic origin several billion years ago. By analyzing the patterns in the mitochondrial DNA of the different people alive today, scientists have been able to deduce roughly how recently Mitochondrial Eve lived, and even where she lived. Early calculations suggested that Mitochondrial Eve lived in Africa about three hundred thousand years ago, but that number has been refined more recently: she lived (in Africa, almost certainly) only two hundred thousand years ago. Deducing *where* and *when* is a far trickier task than deducing *that* there was a Mitochondrial Eve, something no biologist doubts. Consider a few of the things we already know about Mitochondrial Eve, setting aside the controversies. We know that she had at least two daughters who had surviving daughters. (If she had just one daughter, her daughter would wear the crown of Mitochondrial Eve.) To distinguish her title from her proper name, let's call her Amy. Amy bears the title of Mitochondrial Eve; that is, she just happens to have been the maternal founder of today's line of people. It is important to remind ourselves that *in all other regards*, there was probably nothing remarkable or special about Mitochondrial Eve; she was certainly not the First Woman, nor the founder of the species *Homo sapiens*. Many earlier women were unquestionably of our species, but none of them, as it happens, was the most recent source of all the mitochondria in all the people living today. It is also true that although Mitochondrial Eve had daughters and granddaughters, she was probably not noticeably stronger, faster, more beautiful, or more fecund than the other women of her day.

To bring out just how un-special Mitochondrial Eve—that is, Amy—probably was, suppose that tomorrow, thousands of generations later, a virulent new disease were to spread around the earth, wiping out 99 percent of the human race in a few years. The survivors, fortunate to have some innate resistance to the disease virus, would probably be quite closely related. *Their* closest common direct female ancestor—call her Betty—would be some woman who lived hundreds or thousands of generations later than Amy, and the crown of Mitochondrial Eve would pass to her, retroactively. She may have been the source of the mutation that centuries later became a species-saver, but it probably didn't do *her* any good, since the virus against which it triumphs probably didn't exist in its virulent form then. The point is that Mitochondrial Eve can only be *retrospectively* crowned. This historically pivotal role is determined not just by the accidents of Amy's own time, but by the accidents of later times as well. Talk about massive contingency! If Amy's uncle hadn't saved her from drowning when she was three, none of *us* (with our particular mitochondrial DNA, thanks ultimately to Amy) would ever have existed! If all of Amy's granddaughters had starved to death in infancy—as so many infants did in those days—the same oblivion would be ours.

The same logical argument establishes that there is—must be—an Adam as well: the closest direct male ancestor of every man and boy alive today. We can call him Y-chromosome Adam, since all our Y-chromosomes pass down through the paternal line just the way our mitochondria pass through the maternal line.* Was Y-chromosome Adam the husband or lover of Mitochondrial Eve? Not a chance. Paternity being a much less time- and energy-consuming business than maternity, what is *logically* possible is that Y-chromosome Adam lived *very* recently, and was very, very busy in the bedroom—leaving Errol Flynn in his, um, dust. If the oldest living man today is, say, 110 years old, it is *logically* possible that Y-chromosome Adam was his father, an early-twentieth-century Don Juan who is also the father or grandfather or great-grandfather, and so on, of all the younger living males. We males make billions of sperm, after all, hundreds of millions in each ejaculation, so it wouldn't take Y-chromosome Adam more than a week to make enough sperm to father the whole human race (in principle)! But by counting all the genetic differences in men's Y-chromosomes around the world, and calculating how long it would take for that much mutation to accumulate, we can

---

* Note one important difference between the legacies of Mitochondrial Eve and Y-chromosome Adam: we all, male and female, have mitochondria in our cells, and they all come from our mothers; if you are male, you have a Y-chromosome and got it from your father, whereas virtually all—but not quite all—females have no Y-chromosome at all.

estimate the actual date for Y-chromosome Adam as somewhat less than one hundred thousand years ago. And again, if a plague struck down half, say, the male population, in all likelihood the crown of Y-chromosome Adam would pass to a much more recent progenitor.*

A curious fact about every individual organism—you, or me, or your dog, or your geranium, for instance—is that it is a *potential* founder of a new species, the first of a long line of whatchamacallits, but it will be hundreds or thousands of generations before whatchamacallits stand out from the crowd enough to be recognized as a species, so the coronation would have to occur long after you, or I, or your dog, or your geranium had returned to dust. Your parents could thus turn out to be the most recent common ancestors of all the members of two humanoid species, but don't hold your breath. Chihuahuas and Great Danes are members of the same species, *Canis familiaris*, but if civilization collapses and their respective offspring go feral, they could more readily achieve the breakaway of speciation than, say, beagles and Basset Hounds, since without human help, fertilization of Chihuahuas by Great Danes, or vice versa, is unlikely. In all likelihood, however, both lineages would go extinct, as have most lineages over the eons, before that happened.

It is estimated that well over 99 percent of all the organisms that have ever lived have died without having had offspring. And yet here you are: of all your billions of ancestors over the years, from single cells to worms to fish to reptiles to mammals to primates, not a single one of them died childless. How lucky you are! Of course every blade of grass has an equally long and proud heritage, and every mosquito, and every elephant and every daisy.

---

* Setting logical possibility aside and looking at actual history, we see that there have been men who tried to monopolize the siring in their populations, and apparently sometimes succeeded to an astonishing degree: powerful kings and warriors who took and impregnated hundreds of women. They probably have made a disproportionate contribution to our human gene pool, for better or worse.

46. CYCLES

Everybody knows about the familiar large-scale cycles of nature: day follows night follows day; summer-fall-winter-spring-summer-fall-winter-spring; the water cycle of evaporation and precipitation that refills our lakes, scours our rivers, and restores the water supply of every living thing on the planet. But not everybody appreciates how cycles—at every spatial and temporal scale from the atomic to the astronomic—are quite literally the hidden spinning motors that power all the wonderful phenomena of nature. Nikolaus Otto built and sold the first internal-combustion gasoline engine in 1861, and Rudolf Diesel built his engine in 1897, two brilliant inventions that changed the world. Each exploits a cycle, the four-stroke Otto cycle and the two-stroke Diesel cycle, that accomplishes some work and then restores the system to the original position so that it is ready to accomplish more work. The details of these cycles are ingenious, and they have been discovered and optimized by an R & D cycle of invention that is several centuries old. An even more elegant, micro-miniaturized engine is the Krebs cycle, which was discovered in 1937 by Hans Krebs, but invented over millions of years of evolution at the dawn of life. It is the eight-stroke chemical reaction that turns fuel—food—into energy in the process of metabolism that is essential to all life, from bacteria to redwood trees.

Biochemical cycles like the Krebs cycle are responsible for all the motion, growth, self-repair, and reproduction in the living world, wheels within wheels within wheels, a clockwork with trillions of moving parts, and each clock needing to be rewound, restored to step one so that it can do its duty again. All of these cycles have been optimized by the grand Darwinian cycle of reproduction, generation after generation, picking up fortuitous improvements over the eons.

At a completely different scale, our ancestors discovered the efficacy of cycles in one of the great advances of human prehistory: the role of repetition in manufacture. Take a stick and rub it with a stone and almost nothing happens—a few scratches are the only visible sign of change. Bring the stick back to the starting point and do it again. Still you have almost nothing to show for your efforts. Rub it a hundred times and there is still hardly anything to see. But rub it just so, for a few thousand times, and you can turn it into an uncannily straight arrow shaft. By the accumulation of imperceptible increments, the cyclical process creates something altogether new. The combination of foresight and self-control required for such projects was itself a novelty, a vast improvement over the repetitive but largely instinctual and mindless building and shaping processes of other animals. And that novelty was itself a product of the Darwinian cycle, enhanced eventually by the swifter cycle of cultural evolution, in which the reproduction of the technique wasn't passed on to offspring through the genes but transmitted among non-kin who picked up the trick of imitation.

The first ancestor who polished a stone into a handsomely symmetrical hand axe must have looked pretty stupid in the process. There he sat, rubbing away for hours on end, to no apparent effect. But hidden in the interstices of all the mindless repetition was a process of gradual refinement that was well-nigh invisible to a naked eye designed by evolution to detect changes occurring at a much faster tempo.* The same appearance of futility has occasionally misled sophisticated biologists. In his elegant book *Wetware*, the molecular and cell biologist Dennis Bray (2009) describes cycles in the nervous system:

---

* Dale Peterson has drawn my attention to the fact that chimpanzee hammer stones get gradually polished by continual use over long periods of time, and this provides a good "missing link" in a series that begins with more or less randomly picking up a stone and smashing a nut with it, then choosing the best-shaped stone you can see in the vicinity for that job, then looking far and wide for a better-shaped stone, then noticing (with your naked eye and visual memory) that your favorite stone is getting better from use, until finally you reach the sophistication of setting out to shape a stone for an anticipated task.

In a typical signaling pathway, proteins are continually being modified and demodified. Kinases and phosphates work ceaselessly like ants in a nest, adding phosphate groups to proteins and removing them again. It seems a pointless exercise, especially when you consider that each cycle of addition and removal costs the cell one molecule of ATP—one unit of precious energy. Indeed, cyclic reactions of this kind were initially labeled "futile." But the adjective is misleading. The addition of phosphate groups to proteins is the single most common reaction in cells and underpins a large proportion of the computations they perform. Far from being futile, this cyclic reaction provides the cell with an essential resource: a flexible and rapidly tunable device. [p. 75]

The word "computations" is aptly chosen. Computer programmers have been exploring the space of possible computations for less than a century, but their harvest of invention and discovery so far includes millions of loops within loops within loops. It turns out that all the "magic" of cognition depends, just as life itself does, on cycles within cycles of recurrent, "re-entrant," reflexive information-transformation processes ranging from the nano-scale biochemical cycles within each neuron, through the generate-and-test cycles of predictive coding in the perceptual systems (see Clark, 2013, for a brilliant survey), to the whole brain sleep cycle, large-scale waves of cerebral activity and recovery that are revealed by EEG recordings. The secret ingredient of improvement everywhere in life is always the same: practice, practice, practice.

It is useful to remember that Darwinian evolution is just one kind of accumulative, refining cycle. There are plenty of others. The problem of the origin of life can be made to look insoluble ("irreducibly complex"—Behe, 1996) if one argues, as Intelligent Design advocates have done, that since evolution by natural selection depends on reproduction, there cannot be a *Darwinian* solution to the problem of how the first living, reproducing thing came to exist. It was surely breathtakingly complicated, beautifully designed—it must have been a miracle. If we lapse into thinking of the pre-biotic, pre-reproductive world as a sort of featureless chaos of chemicals (like the scattered parts of the notorious jetliner assembled by a windstorm that creationists invite us to imagine), the problem does look daunting and worse, but if we remind ourselves that the key process in evolution is cyclical repetition (of which genetic replication is just one highly refined and optimized instance), we can begin to see our way to turning the mystery into a puzzle: How did all those seasonal cycles, water cycles, geological cycles, and chemical cycles, spinning for millions of years, gradually accumulate the preconditions for inaugurating the biological cycles? Probably the first thousand "tries" were futile, near misses. But as the wonderfully sensual song by George Gershwin and Buddy DeSylva reminds us, see what happens if you "do it again" (and again, and again).*

A good rule of thumb, then, when confronting the apparent magic of the world of life and mind is to look for the cycles that are doing all the hard work.

---

* The role of abiotic cycles in changing the probability of the emergence of reproducing cells is discussed in more detail in my "Evolution of Reasons" (forthcoming).

47. WHAT *DOES* THE FROG'S EYE TELL THE FROG'S BRAIN?

One of the early classics of cognitive science is the famous paper "What the Frog's Eye Tells the Frog's Brain," by J. Y. Lettvin and colleagues (1959). It showed that the frog's visual system is sensitive to small moving dark spots on the retina, tiny shadows cast in almost all natural circumstances by flies flying in the vicinity. This "fly-detector" mechanism is appropriately wired to the hair trigger in the frog's tongue, which handily explains how frogs feed themselves in a cruel world and thereby help propagate their kind. Now what *does* the frog's eye tell the frog's brain? That there is a fly out there, or that there is a fly-or-a-"slug" (a fake fly of one sort or another), or a thing of kind *K* (whatever kind of thing reliably triggers this visual gadget—recall the **two-bitser**)? Darwinian meaning theorists (such as Ruth Millikan, David Israel, and I) have discussed this very case, and the arch-critic of evolutionary theory, Jerry Fodor, has pounced on it to show what is wrong, by his lights, with any evolutionary account of such meanings: They are too indeterminate. They fail to distinguish, as they ought, between such frog-eye reports as "fly here now" and "fly or small dark projectile here now" and so forth. But this is false. We can use the frog's environment of selection (to the extent that we can determine what it has been) to distinguish between the various candidates. To do this, we use exactly the same considerations we used to settle the questions about the meaning of the state in the two-bitser. And to the extent that there is nothing in the selective environment that uniquely singles out a particular class of occasions, there is also no fact of the matter about what the frog's-eye-report *really* means. This can be brought home vividly by sending the frog to Panama—or more precisely, sending the frog to a novel selective environment.

Suppose scientists gather up a small population of frogs from some fly-grabbing species on the brink of extinction, and put them under protective custody in a new environment—a special frog zoo in which there are no flies, but rather zookeepers who periodically arrange to launch little food pellets past the frogs in their care. To the keepers' delight, the system works; the frogs thrive by zapping their tongues for these pellets, and after a while there is a crowd of descendant frogs who have never seen a fly, only pellets. What do *their* eyes tell *their* brains? If you insist on saying the meaning hasn't changed, you are in a bind. The case of the frogs is simply an artificially clear instance of what happens in natural selection all the time: *exaptation*—the reuse of an existing structure for a new function. As Darwin was careful to remind us, the reuse of machinery for new purposes is one of the secrets of Mother Nature's success. We can drive home the point, to anyone who wishes some further persuasion, by supposing that not all the captive frogs do equally well. Variation in pellet-detecting prowess in their visual systems causes some to eat less heartily than others, and then to leave less progeny as a result. In short order there will have been undeniable selection for pellet detection—though it would be a mistake to ask e*xactly when* enough of this has occurred for it to "count." Don't listen for a bell to ring indicating that what the frog's eye is saying has *just now* been revised. There was no Prime Mammal and there is no Prime Pellet Detection.

Unless there were "meaningless" or "indeterminate" variation in the triggering conditions of the various frogs' eyes, there could be no raw material (blind variation) for selection for a *new* purpose to act upon. The indeterminacy that Fodor (and others) see as a flaw in Darwinian accounts of the evolution of meaning is actually a precondition for any such evolution. The idea that there must be *something determinate* that the frog's eye *really* means—some possibly unknowable proposition in froggish that expresses *exactly* what the frog's eye is telling the frog's brain—is just essentialism applied to meaning (or function). Meaning, like function, on which it so directly depends, is not something determinate at its birth. It arises not by saltation— huge leaps in Design Space—or special creation, but by a (typically gradual) shift of circumstances.

48. LEAPING THROUGH SPACE IN THE LIBRARY OF BABEL

In 1988, Otto Neugebauer, the great historian of astronomy, was sent a photograph of a fragment of Greek papyrus that had a few numbers written in a column on it. The sender, a classicist, had no clue about the meaning of this bit of papyrus and wondered if Neugebauer had any ideas. The eighty-nine-year-old scholar recomputed the line-to-line differences of the numbers, found their maximum and minimum limits, and determined that this papyrus had to be a translation of part of "Column G" of a Babylonian cuneiform tablet on which was written a Babylonian "System B" lunar ephemeris! (An ephemeris is a tabular system for computing the location of a heavenly body for every time in a particular period.) How *could* Neugebauer make this Sherlock Holmesian deduction? Elementary: he recognized that what was written in Greek (a sequence of sexagesimal—not decimal—numbers) was part—column G!—of a highly accurate calculation of the moon's location that had been worked out by the Babylonians. There are lots of different ways of calculating an ephemeris, and Neugebauer knew that anyone working out their own ephemeris independently, using their own system, would not have come up with exactly the same numbers, though they might have been close. The Babylonian system B was excellent, so the design had been gratefully conserved, in translation, with all its fine-grained particularities (Neugebauer, 1989).

Neugebauer was a great scholar, but you can probably execute a parallel feat of deduction, following in his footsteps. Suppose you were sent a photocopy of the text below, and asked the same question: What does it mean? Where might this be from?

> Freunde, Römer, Mitbürger, gebt mir Gehör!
> Ich komme, Cäsars Leiche zu bestatten, nicht, ihn zu loben.

Before reading on, try it. You can probably figure it out even if you don't know how to read the old German *fraktur* typeface—and even if you don't know German! Look again, closely. Try to pronounce the words with great emphasis and sonority and don't worry about mispronunciation. Did you get it? Impressive stunt! Neugebauer may have his Babylonian column G, but you quickly determined, didn't you, that this fragment *must be* part of a German translation of lines from an Elizabethan tragedy (act III, scene 2, lines 79–80 to be exact). Once you think about it, you realize that it could hardly be anything else! The odds against *this* particular sequence of German letters getting strung together under any other circumstances are **Vast**.*

The R & D that went into creating that sequence is too specific to be duplicated by chance. Why? What is the particularity that marks such a string of symbols? Nicholas Humphrey (1987) makes the question vivid by posing a more drastic version: if you were forced to "consign to oblivion" one of the following masterpieces, which would you choose: Newton's *Principia*, Chaucer's *Canterbury Tales*, Mozart's *Don Giovanni*, or Eiffel's tower? "If the choice were forced," Humphrey *answers*,

I have little doubt which it should be: the *Principia*
would have to go. How so? Because, of all those works,
Newton's was the only one that was not *irreplaceable*.
Quite simply: if Newton had not written it, then someone
else would—probably within the space of a few years. . . .
The *Principia* was a glorious monument to human intellect,
the Eiffel Tower was a relatively minor feat of romantic
engineering; yet the fact is that while Eiffel did it *his* way,
Newton merely did it God's way.

---

* Here is the fragment of German in an easier-to-read modern font: *Freunde, Römer, Mitbürger, gebt mir Gehör! Ich komme, Cäsars Leiche zu bestatten, nicht, ihn zu loben.*

49. WHO IS THE AUTHOR OF *SPAMLET*?

Suppose Dr. Frankenstein designs and constructs a monster, Spake-sheare, which thereupon sits up and writes out a play, *Spamlet*.

Who is the author of *Spamlet*?

First, let's take note of what I claim to be irrelevant in this intuition pump. I haven't said whether Spakesheare is a robot, constructed out of metal and silicon chips, or, like the original Frankenstein's monster, constructed out of human tissues—or nano-engineered out of cells, or proteins, or amino acids, or carbon atoms. As long as Dr. Frankenstein carried out the design work and the construction, it makes no difference to the example what the materials are. It might well turn out that the only way to build a robot small enough and fast enough and energy-efficient enough to sit on a stool and type out a play is to construct it from artificial cells filled with beautifully crafted motor proteins and other carbon-based nano-robots. That is an interesting technical and scientific issue, but not of concern here. For exactly the same reason, if Spakesheare is a metal-and-silicon robot, it may be larger than a galaxy if that's what it takes to get the requisite complication into its program—and we may have to repeal the speed limit for light so that we can imagine it taking place in a human length of time. These technical constraints are commonly declared to be off-limits in such intuition pumps, and this time we may go along with the gag, since nothing will hinge on it. (Turn the knobs and see if this is so.) If Dr. Frankenstein chooses to make his artificial intelligence (AI) robot out of proteins and the like, that's his business. If his robot is cross-fertile with normal human beings and hence capable of creating what is arguably a new species by giving birth to a child, that is fascinating, but what we will be concerned with is Spakesheare's purported brainchild, *Spamlet*. Back to our question: Who is the author of *Spamlet*?

In order to get a grip on this question, we have to look inside and see what happens in Spakesheare. At one extreme, we find inside a file (if Spakesheare is a robot with a computer memory) or a basically *memorized* version of *Spamlet*, all loaded and ready to run. In such an extreme case, Dr. Frankenstein is surely the author of *Spamlet*, using his intermediate creation, Spakesheare, as a mere storage-and-delivery device, a particularly fancy word processor. *All* the R & D work was done earlier and copied to Spakesheare by one means or another.

We can visualize this more clearly by imagining *Spamlet* and its galaxy of near neighbors in the **Library of Babel**. How did *Spamlet* get there? What was the trajectory of R & D that created it? If we find that the whole journey was already completed by the time Spakesheare's memory was constructed and filled with information, we know that Spakesheare played no role at all in the search. Working backward, if we find that Spakesheare's only role was running the stored text through a spell-checker before using it to guide its typing motions, we will be unimpressed by claims of Spakeshearian authorship. This is a measurable, but **Vanishing**, part of the total R & D. There is a sizable galaxy of near-twin texts of *Spamlet*—roughly a hundred million different minor mutants but a single uncorrected typo in them, and if we expand our horizon to include one typo per page, we have begun to enter the land of Vast numbers of variations on the theme. Working back a little further, once we graduate from typos to *thinkos*,* those arguably mistaken, or suboptimally chosen, words, we have begun to enter the land of serious authorship, as contrasted with mere copy-editing. The relative triviality of copy-editing, and yet its unignorable importance in shaping the final product, get well represented in Design Space, where every little bit of lifting counts

---

* This excellent coinage is a computer hacker's way of referring to a coding error at the semantic level, not the syntactic level. Leaving out a parenthesis is a typo; forgetting to declare a local variable is a thinko. In any human activity with a semantic or intentional interpretation, and clear canons of correctness or elegance, there is room for *thinkos*. Describing a lady as meretricious instead of meritorious is a thinko, not a typo. See Dennett, 2006b.

for something, and sometimes a little bit of lifting moves you onto a whole new trajectory. As usual, we may quote Ludwig Mies van der Rohe at this juncture: "God is in the details."

Now let's turn the knobs on our intuition pump and look at the other extreme, in which Dr. Frankenstein leaves most of the work to Spakesheare. The most realistic scenario would surely be that Dr. Frankenstein equipped Spakesheare with a virtual past, a lifetime stock of pseudo-memories of experiences on which to draw while responding to its Frankenstein-installed obsessive desire to write a play. Among those pseudo-memories, we may suppose, are many evenings at the theater, or reading books, but also some unrequited loves, some shockingly close calls, some shameful betrayals, and the like. Now what happens? Perhaps some scrap of a "human interest" story on the network news will be the catalyst that spurs Spakesheare into a frenzy of generate-and-test, ransacking its memory for useful tidbits and themes, transforming what it finds, jiggling the pieces into temporary, hopeful structures that compete for completion, most of them dismantled by the corrosive processes of criticism that nevertheless expose useful bits now and then, and so forth. All of this multileveled search would be somewhat guided by multilevel, internally generated evaluations, including evaluation of the evaluation of the evaluation functions as a response to evaluation of (evaluation of) the products of the ongoing searches (**cycles** within cycles within cycles).

Now if the amazing Dr. Frankenstein had actually anticipated all this activity down to its finest grain at the most turbulent and chaotic level, and had hand-designed Spakesheare's virtual past, and all its search machinery, to yield just this product, *Spamlet*, then Dr. Frankenstein would be, once again, the author of *Spamlet*, but also, in a word, God. Such Vast foreknowledge would be simply miraculous. Restoring a smidgen of realism to our fantasy, we can set the knobs at a less extreme position and assume that Dr. Frankenstein was unable to foresee all this in detail, but rather delegated to Spakesheare most of the hard work of completing the trajectory in **Design Space** to *one literary work or another*, something to be determined by later R & D occurring within Spakesheare itself. We have now arrived, by this simple turn of the knob, in the neighborhood of reality itself, for we already have actual examples of impressive artificial authors that Vastly outstrip the foresight of their own creators. Nobody has yet created an artificial playwright worth serious attention, but both an artificial chess player—IBM's Deep Blue—and an artificial composer—David Cope's EMI—have achieved results that are, *in some respects*, equal to the best that human creative genius can produce.

Who beat Garry Kasparov, the reigning World Chess Champion? Not Murray Campbell or any members of his IBM team. Deep Blue beat Kasparov. Deep Blue designs better chess games than any of them can design. None of them can author a winning game against Kasparov. Deep Blue can. Yes, but. Yes, but. You may be tempted to insist at this point that when Deep Blue beats Kasparov at chess, its brute-force search methods are *entirely* unlike the exploratory processes that Kasparov uses when he conjures up his chess moves. But that is simply not so—or at least it is not so in the only way that could make a difference to the context of this discussion of the Darwinian perspective on creativity. Kasparov's brain is made of organic materials and has an architecture importantly unlike that of Deep Blue, but it is still, so far as we know, a massively parallel search engine that has built up, over time, an outstanding array of heuristic pruning techniques that keep it from wasting time on unlikely branches. There is no doubt that the investment in R & D has a different profile in the two cases; Kasparov has methods of extracting good design principles from past games, so that he can recognize, and know enough to ignore, huge portions of the game space that Deep Blue must still patiently canvass *seriatim*. Kasparov's "insight" dramatically changes the shape of the search he engages in, but it does not constitute "an *entirely* different" means of creation. Whenever Deep Blue's exhaustive searches close off a *type* of avenue that it has some algorithmic way of identifying as probably negligible (a difficult, but not impossible task), it can reuse that R & D whenever it is appropriate, just as Kasparov does. Deep Blue's designers have done much of this analytical work and given it as an innate endowment to Deep Blue, but Kasparov has likewise benefitted from the fruits of hundreds of thousands of person-years of chess exploration transmitted to him by players, coaches, and books and subsequently installed in the habits of his brain.

It is interesting in this regard to contemplate a suggestion Bobby Fischer once made. He proposed to restore the game of chess to its intended rational purity by requiring that the major white pieces be *randomly* placed in the back row and the major black pieces be arranged in the same random order (mirror image) in the opposite back row at the start of each game (but always ensuring that each side has a white-square and black-square bishop, and the king was between the rooks). This would instantly render the mountain of memorized openings almost entirely obsolete, for humans and machines alike, since only rarely would any of this lore come into play. One would be thrown back onto a reliance on fundamental principles; one would have to do more of the hard design work in real time, with the clock running. It is far from clear whether this change in rules would benefit human beings more than computers. It all depends on which type of chess player is relying most heavily on what is, in effect, rote memory—reliance *with minimal comprehension* on the R & D of earlier explorers.

The fact is that the search space for chess is too big for even Deep Blue to explore exhaustively in real time, so like Kasparov, it prunes its search trees by taking calculated risks, and like Kasparov, it often gets these risks precalculated. Both presumably do massive amounts of "brute-force" computation on their very different architectures. After all, what do neurons know about chess? Any work *they* do must be brute-force work of one sort or another.

It may seem that I am begging the question in favor of a computational, AI approach by describing the work done by Kasparov's brain in this way, but the work has to be done somehow, and no *other* way of getting the work done has ever been articulated. It won't do to say that Kasparov uses "insight" or "intuition," since that just means that Kasparov himself has no privileged access, no insight, into how the good results come to him. So, since nobody—least of all Kasparov—knows how Kasparov's brain does it, there is not yet any evidence to support the claim that Kasparov's means are "entirely unlike" the means exploited by Deep Blue. One should remember this when tempted to insist that "of course" Kasparov's methods are hugely different. What on earth could provoke one to go out on a limb like that? Wishful thinking? Fear?

But that's just chess, you say, not art. Chess is *trivial* compared to art (now that the World Chess Champion is a computer). This is where composer and computer hacker David Cope's Experiments in Musical Intelligence, or EMI for short (2000, 2001), come into play. Cope set out to create a mere efficiency-enhancer, a composer's aid to help him over the blockades of composition any creator confronts, a high-tech extension of the traditional search vehicles (the piano, staff paper, the tape recorder, etc.). As EMI grew in competence, it promoted itself into a whole composer, incorporating more and more of the generate-and-test process. When EMI is fed music by Bach, it responds by generating musical compositions in the style of Bach. When given Mozart, or Schubert, or Puccini, or Scott Joplin, it readily analyzes their styles and then composes new music in those styles, better pastiches than Cope himself—or almost any human composer—can write. When fed music by two composers, EMI can promptly compose pieces that eerily unite their styles, and when fed, all at once (with no clearing of the palate, you might say) all these styles, it proceeds to write music based on the totality of its musical "experience." The compositions that result can then also be fed back into it, over and over, along with whatever other music comes along in MIDI format,* and the result is EMI's own "personal" musical style, a style that candidly reveals its debts to the masters while being an unquestionably idiosyncratic integration of all this "experience."

---

* Roughly, MIDI is to music what ASCII code is to writing: the *lingua franca* between computer programs and the outside world.

EMI can now compose not just two-part inventions and art songs but whole symphonies—and has composed over a thousand, when last I heard. They are good enough to fool experts (composers and professors of music), and I can personally attest to the fact that an EMI-Puccini aria brought a lump to my throat. David Cope can no more claim to be the composer of EMI's symphonies and motets and art songs than Murray Campbell can claim to have beaten Kasparov in chess.

To a Darwinian, this new element in the cascade of **cranes** is simply the latest in a long history, and we should recognize that the boundary between authors and their artifacts should be just as penetrable as all the other boundaries in the cascade. When Richard Dawkins (1982) notes that the beaver's dam is as much a part of the beaver phenotype—its *extended phenotype*—as its teeth and its fur, he sets the stage for the further observation that the boundaries of a human author are exactly as amenable to extension. In fact, we have known this for centuries and have carpentered various semi-stable conventions for dealing with the products of Rubens, of Rubens's *studio*, of Rubens's various students. Wherever there can be a helping hand, we can raise the question of just who is helping whom, what is creator and what is creation.

50. NOISE IN THE VIRTUAL HOTEL

Consider the difference between virtual worlds and real worlds. If you want to make a real hotel, you have to put a lot of time, energy, and materials into arranging matters so that the people in adjacent rooms can't overhear each other. When you go to make a virtual hotel, you get that insulation for free. In a virtual hotel, if you want the people in adjacent rooms to be able to overhear each other, you have to add that capacity. You have to add *non*-insulation. You also have to add shadows, aromas, vibration, dirt, footprints, and wear-and-tear. All these nonfunctional features come for free in the real, concrete world. The generic term for what must be added to virtual worlds to make them more realistic is *collision detection*. If you have ever tried to make a computer video game, you probably soon realized that putting shapes in motion on the screen is not enough. The shapes pass right through each other without any effect unless you build collision detection into the update loop (a cycle in your program that incessantly intervenes in whatever the program object is doing and asks, *Am I colliding with anything?*).

In his book *Le Ton Beau de Marot*, Doug Hofstadter (1997) draws attention to the role of what he calls *spontaneous intrusions* into a creative process. In the real world, almost everything that happens leaves a wake, makes shadows, has an aroma, makes noise, and this provides a bounty of opportunities for spontaneous intrusions. It is also precisely what is in short supply in a virtual world. Indeed one of the chief beauties of virtual worlds, from the point of view of computer modelers, is that quietness: nothing happens except what you provide for, one way or another. This permits you to start with a clean slate and add features to your model one at a time, seeing what the minimal model is that will produce the sought-for effects.

This absence of noise makes computer simulations of evolution extremely limited, since evolution by natural selection feeds on noise, turning fortuitously encountered noise into signal, junk into tools, bugs into features. An early computer simulation of evolution that is still one of the most impressive is Karl Sims's *Evolved Virtual Creatures* (1994), which can be seen at http://www.karlsims.com/evolved-virtual-creatures.html.

Sims started with *random assemblies* of virtual jointed blocks with virtual muscles to move the joints, and then let them evolve in their virtual world with its virtual physics. The program automatically selected the assemblages that moved the farthest on their trials for virtual mating, and then repeated the cycle with the resulting off-spring. Better and better swimmers, walkers, and jumpers evolved, untouched by any intelligent designer's hand. The far-from-random designs that resulted demonstrated how efficiently (virtual) evolution could **sorta** discover good design principles and **sorta** reinvent a striking variety of features found in nature.

It is a spectacular example of getting a lot from a *relatively* simple model, but it also shows the narrow limits of virtual world evolution. Sims designed the simple "developmental" system that takes whole genomes as inputs and yields novel organisms as outputs, but that process is all backstage, not part of the virtual world being simulated. As a result an accidental bump or shock or collision with a bit of (virtual) debris cannot shorten or lengthen a genome, or change the rules of gene expression. All of that machinery is simply not in the virtual world with its virtual stuff, and hence is immutable. There is no way, for instance, for a Sims creature to evolve a new chromosome. Its whole genetic system is outside the model, not facing natural selection itself but merely conveying genetic information by fiat between generations. (For another example of this phenomenon, see chapter 51.)

In a computer model of creativity there should be junk lying around that your creative processes can bump into, noises that your creative processes can't help overhearing. The spontaneous intrusion of that little noise from the next room may tweak what those processes are doing in a way that is serendipitous, or in a way that is destructive, but either way this opens up new possibilities. The exploitation of accidents is the key to creativity, whether what is being made is a new genome, a new behavior, or a new melody.

Let me clarify what I'm *not* saying. The problem with Sims's evolved creatures is not that they are not made of carbon, or that they contain no protein or hemoglobin. The problem is that they are virtual. And by being virtual, they live in a world many orders of magnitude simpler than the world of biological evolution. The same thing is true of Cope's EMI. Wonderful as it is, EMI is orders of magnitude simpler than the world of human musical composition. What's delightful about both cases is the discovery of just how much you can get from something so clean, so noise-free, so abstract.

We can imagine improving Cope's EMI, or Sims's work, or any other such project in artificial life or artificial creativity, by adding more and more and more junk, more and more opportunities for collisions, into the world. This would provide more virtual stuff for their sims to cope with, and you never can tell when serendipity will strike, if given an opportunity. But consider how counterintuitive such advice would appear:

> No matter what you're modeling, make sure that every phe-
> nomenon, every subroutine, everything that happens in that
> world broadcasts a variety of nonfunctional effects through
> the world: makes extraneous noises, leaves a wake, sheds
> dust, causes vibrations, and so forth.

Why? What is all this noise for? It's not for anything; it's just there so that every other process has that noise as a potential source of signal, as something that it *might* turn, by the alchemy of the creative algorithm, into function, into art, into meaning. Every increment of design in the universe begins with a moment of serendipity, the undesigned intersection of two trajectories yielding something that turns out, retrospectively, to be more than a mere collision. But to the extent that computer modelers follow this advice, they squander the efficiency that makes computers such great tools. So there is a sort of homeostasis here. We can see that, not for any mysterious reason, computer modeling of creativity confronts diminishing returns. In order to get closer and closer to the creativity of a human composer, the model has to become ever-more concrete; it has to model more and more of the incidental collisions that impinge on an embodied composer.

51. HERB, ALICE, AND HAL, THE BABY

The late great evolutionary theorist George Williams insisted that it was a mistake to identify genes with DNA molecules. That would be approximately the same mistake as thinking that *Hamlet* is made out of ink. Of course any actual copy of Shakespeare's play has to be made out of something (if not ink, then maybe letter-shaped patterns on a computer screen, or even strings of binary code burned into a CD), but the play is an abstract, informational thing that can hop from medium to medium. Genes, as recipes for making proteins, are also abstract, informational things, according to this way of thinking—which has always struck me as the right way. But there have been those who disagree, who doubt the value of conceiving of genes in this way. For them, and in particular for philosopher of biology Peter Godfrey-Smith, I constructed a little intuition pump:

Herb and Alice want to have a baby, but here's how they do it:

1. They both have their genomes sequenced. They receive in the mail a data file consisting of their genomes, spelled out in two sequences of approximately three billion letters, A, C, G, T, ...
2. Then they write a little computer program that does the meiosis algorithm on both their genomes, (randomly) creating virtual sperm and eggs, which are then (randomly) united *in silico*, to create a new genome specification (which passes all the forensic tests for being the specification of the DNA of an offspring of Herb and Alice). (So far this is all done literally in terms of the symbols A, C, G, T, a purely computational process of string-rewriting.)

3. This specification is then used to construct, codon by codon, an actual DNA implementation of the entire genome, A = adenine, C = cytosine, G = guanine, and T = thymine. (Craig Venter's lab can now do this.)

4. This genome is then implanted in the nucleus of a human egg (does it matter whose egg this is, since its own DNA will be removed before nucleus implantation?), and becomes a "test tube baby" in one of the usual ways.

Is the resulting infant, Hal, the child of Herb and Alice? It seems to me to be quite obvious that Hal is indeed their biological offspring, since it avails itself of all the genetic information they would contribute if Hal were conceived in the normal way. This intuition pump highlights the importance of what matters in reproduction: information, and the causal transmission of information (in this case, in the form of ASCII code for "A," "C," "G," and "T," not in the form of molecules). The causal link might, for instance, pass through telecommunication satellites, instead of taking the more direct, biochemical routes. [Drawn with revisions from personal correspondence, April 26, 2010]

Godfrey-Smith agreed with me that Hal is the offspring of Herb and Alice, but he had some reservations about my way of putting it (which can be read, unabridged, in Dennett, 2010; Godfrey-Smith, 2011). In the same spirit of constructive criticism, I acknowledged that there *is* a biologically important difference between the process Herb and Alice used to procreate and the way we normally do. What if everybody did it Herb and Alice's way? Since the genetic information from Herb does not ride in its usual vehicle—a sperm cell—on its route to the egg, *sperm motility* would no longer be under selection pressure, and would, other things being equal, decline over the generations. Use it or lose it. Still, I maintain—and think this intuition pump illustrates clearly—that the molecular structure that stays roughly constant over the generations is preserved *because* it embodies the information that it does.

If there were alternate structures that preserved the information, evolution would continue unimpeded. This claim can be further examined in yet another intuition pump. Imagine that on another planet, "odd-numbered" generations used the DNA rungs A, C, G, and T, and "even-numbered" generations used a different double helix, call it XNA, with rungs made of P, Q, R, and S (some other molecules). We can suppose that the offspring's XNA molecules were made from DNA templates from their parents by a mechanism rather like messenger RNA, but "translating" between the two different biochemical languages. These messages would be translated back by another messenger mechanism in the next generation, and so forth. You'd have to find a mate whose genes were written in the same language if you wanted offspring, but those offspring would have genomes written in the other language. Oedipal unions would be infertile—which is probably just as well—but there might be many Romeo-and-Juliet–style tragedies in which lovers could not procreate since they came from opposite communities. (They could always settle for a barren sex life and adopt babies of either type, or even play egg donor and sperm donor and raise half-siblings galore.) In such a world, aside from these complications, evolution would continue as always, transmitting genetic information about valuable adaptations (and heritable diseases, etc.) through the generations in alternative coding systems that could be as structurally different as you please. Same genes, different molecules. Each gene would have two forms, as different as "cat" and "*chat*," "house" and "*maison*." (Note the parallel with the case of the **two black boxes**: what the two syntactically, structurally different vehicles in both cases have in common is the *same information*, the same semantics.)

52. MEMES

I haven't mentioned memes yet, which may make some readers wonder if I have abandoned them. Not at all. The concept of memes is one of my favorite thinking tools, and I have a lot to say about it—too much to put in this book! I have already said a great deal about memes elsewhere (Dennett, 1990, 1991a, 1995a, to cite a few examples). For various reasons many people have a visceral dislike of the concept, so they tend to fall for the many criticisms that have been raised. I have decided that I should try one more time to make the case for memes and deal with all the critics, both the serious critics and the white-knuckled meme-haters, but that will take a small book of its own. In the meantime, those who want to know more about memes should take a look at my essay on them, "The New Replicators" (2002; also in Dennett, 2006a).

But here, as a preview, is a brief introduction to the *serious* concept of memes (in contrast to its over-popular loose usage by Internet denizens). As Dawkins (1976) pointed out, when he introduced the concept of the meme as a cultural item that gets itself copied, the fundamental principle of biology is

> that all life evolves by the differential survival of replicating entities. . . .

> The gene, the DNA molecule, happens to be the replicating entity which prevails on our own planet. There may be others. If there are, provided certain other conditions are met, they will almost inevitably tend to become the basis for an evolutionary process.
>
> But do we have to go to distant worlds to find other kinds of replication and other, consequent, kinds of evolution? I

think that a new kind of replicator has recently emerged on this very planet. It is staring us in the face. It is still in its infancy, still drifting clumsily about in its primeval soup, but already it is achieving evolutionary change at a rate which leaves the old gene panting far behind. [p. 206]

Two main insights that flow from this thinking tool dramatically alter the landscape of our imaginations when we think about human culture and creativity. First, memes shatter the otherwise seductive idea that there are only two routes to good Design: it's either *genes* or *genius*. For most thinkers, until memes open their eyes, if something in human life exhibits the telltale signs of adaptation of means to ends or functional efficiency, it must be either a product of *genetic* natural selection or a product of deliberate, comprehending, intending human thinking—*intelligent* design. Orgel's Second Law—evolution is cleverer than you are—might seem to enshrine the two options, but in fact there is a third possibility, and it is everywhere instanced: nongenetic, cultural selection, accomplished by the same process of mindless natural selection that gives us the genes. A vivid example is provided by an observation about Polynesian canoes more than a century old: "every boat is copied from another boat. . . . it is the sea herself who fashions the boats, choosing those which function and destroying the others" (Alain, 1908). This is natural selection, plain as day: the islanders have a simple rule: if it returns from the sea intact, copy it! They may have considerable comprehension of the principles of naval architecture that retrospectively endorse their favorite designs, but it is strictly unnecessary. Evolution takes care of the quality control. The same is true of grammatical rules, words, religious practices, and many other bedrock features of human culture: *nobody* designed them, and they're not "in our genes," but they are nevertheless quite excellently designed.

The second insight is that the price we pay for having this extra information highway, this bounteous medium of design and transmission that no other species enjoys, is that memes *have their own fitness*, just like all the other symbionts that thrive in our company, and their fitness is to some degree independent of our own fitness. Blindness to this idea is endemic, and is particularly evident when people discuss evolutionary accounts of religion. "Oh, so you're working on an evolutionary theory of religion. What good do *you* think religions provide? They *must* be good for something, since apparently every human culture has religion in some form or other." Well, every human culture has the common cold too. What is it good for? It's good for itself. We should be prepared to find cultural replicators that are not beneficial but that manage to thrive nevertheless. This evens the playing field of theories of cultural evolution, replacing the blinkered idea that cultural innovations—just like genetic innovations—always enhance the fitness of those who transmit them. Memes are informational symbionts, and like the mutualist symbionts by the trillions that also inhabit us, we couldn't live without them, but that doesn't mean they are all our friends. Some are harmful plagues we could well do without.

SUMMARY

In this section I have tried to demonstrate that Darwinian thinking does live up to its billing as universal acid: it turns the whole
traditional world upside down, challenging the top-down image of
designs flowing from that genius of geniuses, the Intelligent Designer,
and replacing it with the bubble-up image of mindless, motiveless
cyclical processes churning out ever-more robust combinations until
they start replicating on their own, speeding up the design process
by reusing all the best bits over and over. Some of these earliest
offspring eventually join forces (one major crane, symbiosis), which
leads to multicellularity (another major crane), which leads to the
more effective exploration vehicles made possible by sexual reproduction (another major crane), which eventually leads in one species to
language and cultural evolution (cranes again), which provide the
medium for literature and science and engineering, the latest cranes
to emerge, which in turn permits us to "go meta" in a way no other
life form can do, reflecting in many ways on who and what we are
and how we got here, modeling these processes in plays and novels,
theories and computer simulations, and ever-more thinking tools to
add to our impressive toolbox.

This perspective is so widely unifying and at the same time so
generous with detailed insights that one might say it's a power tool,
all on its own. Those who are still strangely repelled by Darwinian
thinking must consider the likelihood that if they try to go it alone
with only the hand tools of tradition, they will find themselves labor-
ing far from the cutting edge of research on important phenomena as
diverse as epidemics and epistemology, biofuels and brain architecture, molecular genetics, music, and morality.

VII

TOOLS FOR THINKING
ABOUT CONSCIOUSNESS

Well armed with dozens of thinking tools, we finally arrive at the topic that many regard as the most puzzling phenomenon in the whole universe. Indeed not a few folks have claimed that it is terminally mysterious. We will never *ever* understand consciousness, they declare; it will systematically defy the best efforts of our science and philosophy until the end of time. Since there are no *good* reasons to believe in this intellectual roadblock, I have to conclude that it is wishful thinking. Some folks hate the idea of our uncovering the secrets of how the conscious mind works, and just to make sure we don't impose our understanding on them, they counsel that we give it up as a lost cause. If we take their advice, they will be right, so let's ignore them and get on with this difficult, but not impossible, quest.

53. TWO COUNTER-IMAGES

Many of the tools I have introduced earlier deal in one way or another with the mind—believing, thinking, and so forth—but I postponed the knotty problems of consciousness until now. There is a reason: when people start musing about consciousness, they have a way of inflating their notions of what consciousness must be, of bamboozling themselves. They tackle the hardest issues before they have had a chance to see how much of the work (and play) of the mind can be accounted for without first settling the perennial questions about conscious experience. Now that we have built a base camp, are we ready to tackle the summit? Yes, but if we think of it that way, we are already making a mistake of imagination! Our minds don't have a single magnificent summit, consciousness. Contrary to a tradition going back at least to Descartes in the seventeenth century, conscious phenomena are neither the most "central" nor the "highest" phenomena in our minds (Jackendoff, 1987; Dennett, 1991a). A seductive bad image needs a counter-image to neutralize it, so here is a simple imagination-adjuster to start us off: recall Cole Porter's wonderful song "You're the Top" and reflect that maybe you're *not* the top—not the summit of the mountain, but the whole mountain, and what you know and can tell about the mountain that is you is not the view from the summit, but various views from halfway up. You might like to think of the phenomena of consciousness as rather like the fringe of hair around a bald man's pate. Bear that in mind.

And here is another: consciousness is *not* a medium, like television, into which information can get transduced or recorded, and there is no place in the brain where "it all comes together" for the appreciation of some Central Witness—I call this imaginary place the Cartesian Theater (Dennett, 1991a). Consciousness is *more like fame than television*: fame in the brain, cerebral celebrity, a way in which some contents come to be more influential and memorable than the competition. Instead of arguing for this (for the arguments, see Dennett, 1991a, 2005b), I am simply offering you this thinking tool, take it or leave it, with some friendly advice: whenever you find yourself thinking of entry into consciousness as Arrival at Head-quarters or as Translation from unconscious neural spike-signals into Something Else, remind yourself of these counter-images and ask yourself if you might be mis-imagining the phenomena.

54. THE ZOMBIC HUNCH

Most people have a hunch—it's no better than that, really—that no robot (made of silicon and metal and plastic, etc.) could ever be conscious the way we humans are. There is something about our living, breathing, organic bodies and brains that is necessary for consciousness. This is an intuition that hardly needs pumping, so ubiquitous is it, and maybe these people are right. But now that we have some insight into the way our bodies and brains can themselves be seen as made of robots made of robots made of robots, and so on, all the way down to below the neuron level where the motor proteins and other nanobots trudge along making the whole system work, we can see that *maybe* that hunch is just an artifact of impoverished imagination: folks have been thinking about robots that are too simple, by many orders of magnitude. A friend once responded to this opening gambit of mine by trying to nip it in the bud: "I just can't conceive of a conscious robot!" Nonsense, I replied. What you mean is that you *won't* conceive of a conscious robot. You think it is silly and preposterous to try to take the idea seriously. But it's actually child's play to conceive of a conscious robot, or, for that matter, a conscious choo-choo train (The Little Engine That Could) or a conscious Christmas tree (all those sappy children's stories about lonely little fir trees that pine for a home). Anybody who has seen *Star Wars* has spent an hour or so conceiving of R2D2 and C3PO as conscious. We have done this since we were children, "without a second thought" for the most part. It's not just easy, it's almost irresistible when we are confronted with something that acts—and especially, talks—like a human being.

Here's an interesting fact: since the pioneering work of neuroscientist Wilder Penfield in Montreal back in the 1950s, there have been many operations that exposed the brains of wide-awake patients who were able to say what it was like when their brains were stimulated *there* or *just there*. I don't think any participant or observer of one of these operations has ever thought, "Oh my gosh! This isn't a person. This is a zombie. It has to be, because when we look inside, all we find is gray matter." No, it is just too obvious—look! listen!—that the patient is conscious. And it would be just as obvious, really, if we were to open up somebody's skull while he or she is conversing with us and find the cranial cavity packed with microchips. We'd learn, perhaps to our surprise, that a conscious robot was not just easy to conceive of or imagine, but actual.

Some philosophers think that your imagination would be playing a trick on you if you *fell for* this "merely behavioral" evidence of consciousness and *jumped* to that conclusion. "Don't fall, don't jump!" might be their motto. *Proving* that another person is conscious is much harder than that, since that person might—it's at least a logical possibility—be a "zombie." Not a voodoo-style zombie of the sort that one sees in movies or dresses up as at Halloween. The walking dead are readily distinguishable from normal people by their behavior (and their horrible appearance). Philosophers' zombies, in contrast, can be delightful company, the life of the party, as loving and joyous and spontaneous as anybody you know. Some of your best friends might be zombies. Philosophers' zombies are (by definition) behaviorally indistinguishable from normal conscious human beings, but "there's nobody home"—they entirely lack any inner life, any conscious experience. They just appear from the outside to be conscious. If you agree with these philosophers that this is a serious issue, if you wonder—given the logical possibility of philosophers' zombies—how there could ever be a scientific, materialistic theory of consciousness, then you are gripped by the *Zombic Hunch*.*

Let me acknowledge right away that I can feel the Zombic Hunch

---

* One reader of an early draft of this book thought I was making all of this up. If you share that suspicion, check out the long, deadly serious article on philosophical zombies in the august *Stanford Encyclopedia of Philosophy*, online at http://plato.stanford.edu/entries/zombies/.

as vividly as anyone. When I squint just right, it *does* sort of seem that consciousness must be something in addition to all the things it does for us and to us, some kind of special private glow or *here-I-am-ness* that would be absent in any robot, and that is all but unimaginable as a "mere" physical activity of the brain. But I've learned not to credit the hunch. I think it is a flat-out mistake, a failure of imagination, not an insight into necessity. Convincing others of this, however, proves to be no easy task, and we will need several different intuition pumps to loosen the grip of the Zombic Hunch.

To start, we may get our bearings on this logical possibility by comparing it with a few others. It is *logically* possible that you are living in the Matrix, and all of the life you see around you and apparently participate in is a virtual reality show designed to keep you calm as your actual body lies motionless in a high-tech pod of some kind. It is *logically* possible that there aren't really any carbon atoms; what appear to scientists to be carbon atoms are actually kazillions of tiny spaceships piloted by aliens whose life work is to pretend that they are carbon atoms. It is *logically* possible that the entire universe was created about six thousand years ago, with all the so-called fossils in place and photons streaming in as if from galaxies light-years away. (It's *logically* possible that the world was created ten minutes ago, complete with all the purported memories of your past installed in your brain.) We may find such logical possibilities amusing premises for fiction, but we don't take them seriously as signs that our physics and chemistry and biology need to be overhauled or abandoned. Is there anything that makes the Zombic Hunch more substantial, more worthy of consideration? Many serious thinkers have thought so.

Perhaps the grandfather of all intuition pumps designed to yield something like the Zombic Hunch was invented hundreds of years ago by Gottfried Wilhelm Leibniz, the philosopher/mathematician who shares credit with Isaac Newton for inventing calculus. He was as smart and ingenious as any thinker in his age, and yet he fell for this intuition pump of his own devising.

And supposing there were a machine, so constructed as to think, feel, and have perception, it might be conceived as increased in size, while keeping the same proportions, so that one might go into it as into a mill. That being so, we should, on examining its interior, find only parts which work one upon another, and never anything by which to explain a perception. *Thus* [my italics] it is in a simple substance, and not in a compound or in a machine, that perception must be sought for. [Leibniz, 1714, para. 17]

This "Thus" is one of the most glaring *non sequiturs* in all of philosophy. Leibniz doesn't give us any intervening argument for the conclusion; he thinks it is too obvious to need any. Recall William Bateson, the early-twentieth-century geneticist who couldn't imagine that genes could be material entities (see p. 100). Just as Bateson had no way of taking seriously the extravagant idea of three-billion base-pairs in a double helix inside every cell (preposterous!), Leibniz had no way of taking seriously the idea of a "mill" with *trillions* of moving parts. He would insist, no doubt, that "just adding more parts" couldn't take you from machinery to mind, but that would be only his hunch, not anything he could claim to demonstrate. But if Darwin, Crick, and Watson have exposed Bateson's failure of imagination, Turing has rendered Leibniz's intuition pump obsolete. Except that he hasn't. Not yet. In due course, I think, the Zombic Hunch will fade into history, a curious relic of our spirit-haunted past, but I doubt that it will ever go extinct. It will not survive in its current, mind-besotting form, but it will survive as a less virulent mutation, still psychologically powerful but stripped of authority. We've seen this happen before. It still *seems* as if the earth stands still and the sun and moon go around it, but we have learned that it is wise to disregard this as mere appearance. It still *seems* as if there's a difference between a thing at absolute rest and a thing that is merely not accelerating within an inertial frame, but we have learned not to trust this feeling. I anticipate a day when philosophers and scientists and laypeople will chuckle over the fossil traces of our earlier bafflement about consciousness: "It still *seems* as if these mechanistic theories of consciousness leave something out, but of course we now understand that that's an illusion. They do, in fact, explain everything about consciousness that needs explanation."

Continuing allegiance to the Zombic Hunch is actually fostered by many philosophers' thought experiments, such as John Searle's famous **Chinese Room,** the inspiration for my coinage, "intuition pump." It will soon get dismantled in front of your eyes. But first I want to explore the concept of philosophical zombies a bit more carefully.

55. ZOMBIES AND ZIMBOES

When people say they can conceive of (philosophical) zombies, we are entitled to ask them how they know. Conceiving is not easy! Can you conceive of more than three dimensions? The curvature of space? Quantum entanglement? Just imagining something is not enough—and in fact, Descartes tells us, it is not conceiving at all. According to Descartes, imagining uses your (ultimately mechanistic) body, with all its limitations (nearsightedness, limited resolution, angle, and depth); conceiving uses just your mind, which is a much more powerful organ of discernment, unfettered by the requirements of mechanism. He offers a compelling example of the difference: the chiliagon, a regular thousand-sided polygon. Can you conceive of one? Can you imagine one? What is the difference? Let's try imagining one first. Start with a pentagon, say, then imagine a decagon. It's hard, but you know what to do: bend each side of the pentagon in the middle and push out a little bit, turning five equal sides into ten. How far should you push out? Just inscribe the pentagon inside a circle and push the new sides out till they intersect the circle. Now do it again, making an icosagon, with twenty sides.

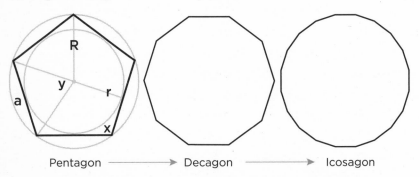

Pentagon ⟶ Decagon ⟶ Icosagon

Do it again, and again seven more times, and you'll have a regular 1,280-sided polygon, which is well-nigh indistinguishable from a circle *in imagination*, but is as distinct *in conception* from a circle—and from a chiliagon—as a square is distinct from a circle. If I ask you to imagine a circle inside a chiliagon inside a circle inside a chiliagon inside a circle, making a sort of bull's-eye target, can you tell *in your mental image* which are the circles and which are the chiliagons? No, they all look just like circles, but you have no difficulty *conceiving* of the circumstance you've been asked to think about.

Descartes doesn't tell you to perform such constructions; to him conception, like imagination, is a kind of direct and episodic mental act, *glomming without bothering to picture*, or something like that. You somehow just grasp (mentally) the relevant concepts (SIDE, THOUSAND, REGULAR, POLYGON), and *shazam*! You've got it. I have always been suspicious of this Cartesian basic act of *conceiving*. If you can do it, good for you, but I find that I can't (any more than I can conceive a baby, in another sense of the term). I am not confident that I have *succeeded* in conceiving of something until I have manipulated the relevant ideas for some time, testing out implications in my mind, doing exercises, in effect, until I get fluent in handling the tools involved. (And when I do these mental gymnastics, I make heavy use of my imagination, exploring various diagrams and pictures in my head, for instance. In short, I exploit what Descartes would disparage as merely my imagination to accomplish what he would celebrate as my conception.) Can you conceive of string theory? Do you find all that talk about umpteen dimensions filled with superstrings and "branes" and the like easy to make sense of, easy to test for logical consistency? It is *unintelligible* to me, but for that very reason I wouldn't be willing to declare it inconceivable or impossible (Ross, 2013). I am unconvinced, but I am also not so confident in my own conceptual abilities as to dismiss it as nonsense. I haven't been able to conceive of the truth of string theory *yet*. We should not put much weight on blithe verdicts of conceivability or inconceivability in the absence of careful demonstrations. Bateson said that a material gene was "inconceivable," but if he were alive today, he could readily learn to conceive of one. After all, children in grade school learn about the double helix with all its rungs, a phenomenon that proves readily conceivable to them once they get the hang of it. But no amount of new information and techniques of imagination will help us conceive of a round square (a regular four-sided polygon whose boundaries are everywhere equidistant from its center), or a largest prime number.

I am pretty sure that a philosophers' zombie is conceptually incoherent, impossible, a bankrupt idea. But don't take my word for it. What could you do to convince yourself that you *can* conceive of a philosophers' zombie? Suppose you try to imagine that your friend Zeke "turns out to be" a zombie. What would convince you or even tempt you to conclude that this is so?* What difference would make all the difference? Remember, nothing Zeke could *do* should convince you that Zeke is, or isn't, a zombie. I find that many people don't do this exercise correctly; that is, they inconveniently forget or set aside part of the definition of a philosophers' zombie when they attempt their feat of conception. It may help you see if you are making this mistake if we distinguish a special subspecies of zombies that I call zimboes (Dennett, 1991a). All zombies have nonconscious (of course) control systems that extract information from the world (via their zombie eyeballs and ears) and exploit that information to avoid walking into walls and to turn when you call, and so on. They are all intentional systems, in other words. But a zimbo is special, a zombie that is also blessed with equipment that permits it to monitor its own activities, both internal and external, so it has internal (nonconscious) higher-order informational states that are *about* its other internal states. Further self-monitoring allows a zimbo to have and use information about those very self-monitoring states, and so on, indefinitely. A zimbo, in other words, is equipped with *recursive self-representation*—*unconscious* recursive self-representation, if that

---

* This is another one of those places where some philosophers would like to accuse me of confusing a metaphysical question with an epistemological question: "Don't ask *how we would know* someone is a zombie! Ask *what it is* to be a zombie!" Metaphysics so isolated from epistemology is, at best, an exercise in fantasy.

makes any sense. It is only in virtue of this special talent that a zimbo can participate in the following sort of conversation:

You: Zeke, do you like me?

Zeke: Of course I do. You're my best friend!

You: Did you mind my asking?

Zeke: Well, yes, it was almost insulting. It bothered me that you asked.

You: How do you know?

Zeke: Hmm. I just recall feeling a bit annoyed or threatened or maybe just surprised to hear such a question from you. Why did you ask?

You: Let me ask the questions, please.

Zeke: If you insist. This whole conversation is actually not sitting well with me.

Remember: since a philosophical zombie is declared to be behaviorally indistinguishable from a conscious person, behaviors like carrying out this conversation are within its repertoire, and in order to control such behaviors the zombie is going to need recursive self-representation. It can "think" (in its unconscious zombie way) about how it feels about how it felt about what it was thinking of when it wondered whether . . . , and so forth. It is easy enough to imagine your dreadful suspicions being aroused if Zeke just draws a blank, becoming weirdly unresponsive when you query him this way, but that would be discovering that if Zeke is a zombie, he isn't a zimbo. You should always make sure you're thinking of a zimbo when you ask if a philosophers' zombie is a real possibility, for only a being with recursive self-representation would be able to hold its own in everyday interactions like this conversation, to say nothing of writing poetry, framing novel scientific hypotheses, and acting in dramas, all of which are within the competences of zimboes—by definition.

Unless you go to the trouble of imagining, in detail, how indistinguishable "normal" Zeke would be from zimbo Zeke, you haven't really tried to conceive of a philosophers' zombie. You're like Leibniz, giving up without half trying. Now ask yourself a few more questions. Why would you *care* whether Zeke is a zimbo? Or more personally, why would you care whether you are, or became, a zimbo? In fact, you'd never know.

Really? Does Zeke have beliefs? Or does he just have *sorta* beliefs, "you know, the sort of informational states-minus-consciousness that guide zimboes through their lives the way beliefs guide the rest of us"? Only here, the *sorta* beliefs are exactly as potent, as competent, as "the real thing," so this is an improper use of the sorta operator. We can bring this out by imagining that left-handers (like me, DCD) are zimboes; only right-handers are conscious!

DCD: You say you've proved that we lefties are zombies? I never would have guessed! Poor us? In what regard?

RIGHTIE: Well, by definition you're not conscious—what could be worse than that?

DCD: Worse for whom? If there's nobody home, then there's nobody in the dark, missing out on everything. But what are you doing, trying to have a conversation with me, a zimbo?

RIGHTIE: Well, there *seems to me* to be somebody there.

DCD: To me too! After all, as a zimbo, I have all manner of higher-order self-monitoring competences. I know when I'm frustrated, when I'm in pain, when I'm bored, when I'm amused, and so forth.

RIGHTIE: No. You function *as if* you knew these things, but you don't really *know* anything. You only *sorta* know these things.

DCD: I think that's a misuse of the *sorta* operator. What you're calling my *sorta* knowledge is indistinguishable from your so-called *real* knowledge—except for your "definitional" point: zimbo knowledge isn't real.

RIGHTIE: But there *is* a difference, there *must be* a difference!

DCD: That sounds like bare prejudice to me.

If this isn't enough rehearsal of what it would be like to befriend a zimbo, try some more. Seriously, consider writing a novel about a zimbo stuck in a world of conscious people, or a conscious person marooned on the Island of the Zimboes. What details could you dream up that would make this a credible tale? Or you could take an easier path: read a good novel while holding onto the background hypothesis that it is a novel about zimboes. What gives it away or disconfirms your hypothesis? Novelists have a choice of standpoints or *narrative modes*, including the *first-person narrative* used by Herman Melville in *Moby-Dick* and by J. D. Salinger in *The Catcher in the Rye*:

> "Call me Ishmael."

> "When I really worry about something, I don't just fool around. I even have to go to the bathroom when I worry about something. Only, I don't go. I'm too worried to go. I don't want to interrupt my worrying to go."

Other novelists opt for the *third-person omniscient narrative*. Curiously, the first-person narrative mode might seem to lend itself more to sustaining the zombie hypothesis. After all, the entire story merely depicts that narrative *behavior* of Zimbo Ishmael or Zimbo Holden Caulfield. We see only their outsides, and *what they purport to be* accounts drawing on their inner lives! Compare those first-person narratives to these third-person narratives in Jane Austen's *Persuasion* and Fyodor Dostoevsky's *Crime and Punishment*, for example:

> She [Elizabeth] felt that Mrs Musgrove and all her party ought to be asked to dine with them, but she could not bear to have the difference of style, the reduction of servants, which a dinner must betray, witnessed by those who had been always so inferior to the Elliots of Kellynch. It was a struggle between propriety and vanity; but vanity got the better, and then Elizabeth was happy again.

He [Raskolnikov] looked at Sonia and felt how great her love
for him was, and, strange to say, he felt distressed and pained
that he should be loved so much. Yes, it was a queer and
dreadful sensation.

Here, it seems, the authors let us "look right into the minds"
of Elizabeth and Raskolnikov, so how could they be zimboes? But
remember: where conscious people have a stream of consciousness,
zimboes have a stream of *unconsciousness*. After all, zimboes are not
supposed to be miraculous; their behaviors are controlled by a host
of internal goings-on of tremendous informational complexity, and
modulated by functional emotion-analogues that amount to happi-
ness, distress, and pain. So both Elizabeth and Raskolnikov could
be zimboes, with Austen and Dostoevsky using the terms we all
know and love from **folk psychology** to render descriptions of their
inner goings-on, just as chess programmers talk about the iterated
"searches" and risky "judgments" of their computer programs. A
zimbo can be embarrassed by a loss of social status, or smothered
by love.

Never forget William Bateson's failure of imagination. When I
try my hardest to avoid that trap, hunting for loopholes in my background assumptions, keeping my eye peeled for ways in which I could
be proved wrong about zombies, I always come up with imagined
discoveries that show, at most, that the whole concept of consciousness is seriously confused. For instance, I can imagine that there
might be two (or seven, or ninety-nine) different sorts of so-called
consciousness, and lefties have one, and righties have another, and
lobsters have yet another. But the only way I can imagine this (so far)
is by imagining that *they are distinguishable by the following functional
differences*: lefties can't do X, and righties can't do Y, and so on. But
those distinguishable differences just go to show that we're not talking about philosophical zombies after all, for (by definition) there
are no distinguishable-from-the-outside differences between philosophical zombies and "genuinely conscious" people. And nobody has

yet been able to articulate a distinguishable-from-the-inside mark of genuine consciousness that doesn't somehow involve the putatively conscious person being *able to do* something "mental" that convinces us (and her) that she is conscious. But whatever this mental difference is would presumably have its counterpart sham version in the zombie's "stream of unconsciousness." If not, why not? So I am quite confident that the whole idea of a philosophical zombie is a sort of intellectual hallucination, an affliction one can outgrow. Try it. I'll provide some further assistance for this task of self-persuasion later in this section.

56. THE CURSE OF THE CAULIFLOWER

I see you tucking eagerly into a helping of steaming cauliflower, the merest whiff of which makes me faintly nauseated, and I find myself wondering how you could possibly relish *that taste*, and then it occurs to me that to you, cauliflower probably tastes (must taste?) different. A plausible hypothesis, it seems, especially since I know that the very same food often tastes different to me at different times. For instance, my first sip of breakfast orange juice tastes much sweeter than my second sip if I interpose a bit of pancakes and maple syrup, but after a swallow or two of coffee, the orange juice goes back to tasting (roughly? exactly?) the way it did during the first sip. **Surely** (ding!) we want to say (or think about) such things, and surely (ding!) we are not wildly wrong when we do, so . . . surely (ding!) it is quite okay to talk of *the way the juice tastes to Dennett at time t*, and ask whether it is just the same as or different from *the way the juice tastes to Dennett at time t'*, or *the way the juice tastes to Jones at time t*. Call these ways things can seem to us *qualia*.

This "conclusion" seems innocent, but right here we have already made the big mistake. The final step presumes that we can isolate the "qualia" from everything else that is going on—at least in principle or for the sake of argument. What counts as *the way the juice tastes to x* can be distinguished, one supposes, from what is a mere accompaniment, contributory cause, or by-product of this "central" way. One dimly imagines taking such cases and stripping them down gradually to the essentials, leaving their common residuum, the way things look, sound, feel, taste, smell to various individuals at various times, independently of how those individuals are stimulated or non-perceptually affected, and independently of how they are subsequently disposed to behave or believe. The mistake is not in supposing that we can in practice ever or always perform this act of purification with certainty, but the more fundamental mistake of supposing that there is such a residual property to take seriously, however uncertain our actual attempts at isolation of instances might be.

The examples that seduce us are abundant in every modality. I cannot imagine, will never know, could never know, it seems, how Bach sounded to Glenn Gould. (I can barely recover in my memory the way Bach sounded to me when I was a child.) And I cannot know, it seems, what it is like to be a bat (Nagel, 1974), or whether you see what I see, color-wise, when we look up at a clear "blue" sky. These everyday cases convince us of the reality of these special properties—those subjective tastes, looks, aromas, sounds—that we then apparently isolate for definition by this act of philosophical distillation. Thus are qualia born.

"Qualia" is a "technical" term for something that could not be more familiar to each of us: the *ways things seem to us*. Nothing, it seems, could you know more intimately than your own qualia; let the entire universe be some vast illusion, some mere figment of Descartes's evil demon, and yet what the figment is *made of* (for you) will be the *qualia* of your hallucinatory experiences. Descartes claimed to doubt everything that could be doubted, but he never doubted that his conscious experiences had qualia, the properties by which he knew or apprehended them.

This definition of qualia may seem clear enough—*the ways things seem to* us—but although qualia thus introduced have been the subject of much analysis and discussion by philosophers, there is still no consensus about just what the term means or implies, technically speaking. Many cognitive scientists have made the charitable assumption that philosophers must know what they are talking about when they use this special term, and have added the term to their working vocabulary, but this is a tactical mistake. Controversy still rages on what qualia are and aren't, quite independently from any empirical issues. Some years ago, in an essay, I (1988a) proposed that the root concept of qualia has four conditions. Qualia are

1. ineffable,
2. intrinsic,
3. private, and
4. directly apprehensible ways things seem to one.

That is to say, they are (1) somehow atomic to introspection, and hence indescribable ("you had to be there"); (2) not relational or dispositional or functional (the color red may be anxiety-provoking to some people, but that subjective disposition is not a quale of red); (3) "You had to be there, but you can't be; they're mine and mine alone!"; and (4) your qualia are known to you more intimately than anything else.

This is still regarded as a good starting place in most circles, but since the point of that essay was to show that nothing could meet these four conditions, there has been ample discussion of revised or improved versions of the concept, with no emerging consensus. It is not unusual for a much-used and generally highly regarded technical term to have multiple incompatible definitions—think of "gene" or "species" in biology and "cause" almost everywhere in science—but the disarray surrounding "qualia" strikes me as worse, a Trojan horse to anyone in other disciplines who thinks of the concept as a gift from philosophy that might come in handy in their own research.

I trotted out thirteen other intuition pumps (in addition to the cauliflower) in that essay, and I will not repeat any of them here, since over the years I have devised other, probably more powerful tools to wield in my continuing battle against the complacency expressed in a famous response to the challenge to say what, exactly, qualia are. Ned Block (1978, p. 281) dismissed this obstreperous query "only half in jest" by invoking Louis Armstrong's legendary reply when he was asked what jazz was: "If you got to ask, you ain't never gonna get to know." This amusing tactic perfectly expresses the presumption that is my target. If I succeed in my task, this response of Block's, which still passes muster in most circles today, will look as quaint and insupportable as a jocular expression of disbelief by a vitalist who, when confronted with a person—"a living thing, mind you!"—claimed to doubt the very existence of *élan vital*.

57. VIM: HOW MUCH IS THAT IN "REAL MONEY"?

It is a common opinion that although you could construct a robotic model of color vision, say, that exhibited all the familiar phenomena we humans experience, such as complementary afterimages and color contrast illusions, and although the robot would have similar internal processes that accounted for its afterimages and so forth, since "it's just a robot" it couldn't have red and blue *qualia*. The functional states that signaled or represented colored things in front of the robot's television camera eyes would not have that extra something that we have. Thomas Nagel's famous essay "What Is It Like to Be a Bat?" (1974) provides us with a standard way of alluding to the conscious states, if any, of an entity. It wouldn't *be like* anything to be a robot having an afterimage. Why do so many people think this is obvious? It might be because they are imagining a relatively simple robot and failing to note that you can't draw conclusions about *all* robots from facts about all *simple* robots. Of course if you *define* qualia as *intrinsic properties* of experiences considered in isolation from all their causes and effects, and logically independent of all dispositional properties, then qualia are logically guaranteed to elude all functional analysis. No amount of clever engineering could endow a robot with qualia—but this is an empty victory, since there is no reason to believe such intrinsic properties exist.

To see this, compare the *qualia* of experience to the *value* of money. Some naïve Americans seem to think that dollars, unlike euros and yen, have *intrinsic value*. The tourist in the cartoon asks, "How much is that in *real money*?" meaning how much is that in dollars. Let's push this idea a little farther: These naïve Americans are willing to exchange dollars for euros; they are happy to "reduce" the value of other currencies to their exchange rate with dollars (or goods and services), but when they do this, they have a sense that

dollars are different. Every dollar, they declare, has something logically independent of the functional exchange powers it shares with
all other currencies in circulation. A dollar has a certain *je ne sais
quoi*. When you contemplate it, you can detect that it has an aura
of value—less than in the olden days, perhaps, but still discernible:
let's call it the dollar's *vim* (from the Latin, *vis*, meaning power).
Officially, then, vim is the non-relational, non-dispositional, *intrinsic*
economic value of a dollar. Pounds sterling and euros and the like
have no intrinsic value—they are just symbolic stand-ins; they are
redeemable for dollars, and hence have *derived* economic value, but
they don't have vim! How sad for those Europeans! Their currencies
lack intrinsic economic value! How do they bear it? How do they
motivate themselves to earn their pay, these poor *vimbies!* Those of
us fortunate enough to get paid in dollars acquire items with a good
helping of vim attached. No wonder the U.S. dollar has been adopted
as the currency of choice in so many nations! Even foreigners can
sense the vim of a dollar.

So say our imaginary American tourists. So defined, the vim of
each dollar is guaranteed to elude the theories of economists forever,
since no economic theory could ever account for *intrinsic economic
value*. So much the worse for economics? The existence of vim would
render economics a seriously incomplete science, but fortunately, we
have no good reason to believe that there is such a thing as intrinsic
economic value. Vim is quite obviously a figment of the imagination,
an artifact of the heartfelt hunches of those naïve Americans, and we
can explain the artifact without honoring it.

Some participants in the consciousness debates are rather like the
imaginary tourists. They simply insist, flat out, that their intuitions
about *intrinsic phenomenal properties* are a nonnegotiable starting
point for any science of consciousness. Such a conviction should be
considered an interesting *symptom* deserving a diagnosis, a datum
that any science of consciousness must account for, in the same spirit
that economists and psychologists might set out to explain why so
many people succumb to the potent illusion that money has intrinsic

value. (When Europe switched to the euro, people who were used to conceiving of prices in terms of francs and marks and lire and the like went through an awkward period when they could no longer rely on "translations" into *their* home-grown versions of "real money." See Dehaene and Marques, 2002, for a pioneering exploration of this phenomenon.)

There are many properties of conscious states that can and should be subjected to further scientific investigation right now, and once we get accounts of them in place, we may well find that they satisfy us as an explanation of what consciousness is. After all, this is what happened in the case of the erstwhile "mystery" of what *life* is. Vitalism—the insistence that there is some big, mysterious extra ingredient in all living things, dubbed *élan vital* —turns out to have been a failure of imagination. Vitalism today is all but extinct, though there are still a few cranks around who haven't given up. Inspired by that happy success story, we can proceed with our scientific exploration of consciousness. If the day arrives when all the demonstrable features of consciousness are explained, all the acknowledged intellectual debts are paid, and we plainly see that something big *is* missing (it should stick out like a sore thumb at some point, if it is really important), those with the unshakable hunch will get to say they told us so. In the meantime, they can worry about how to fend off the diagnosis that they, like the vitalists before them, have been misled by an illusion. Here is the challenge, then, to those who believe in qualia as intrinsic properties of experiences: How do they distinguish their conviction from the mistake of the naïve Americans? (Or are the Americans right? Dollars *do* have vim, as anybody can just intuit!)

58. THE SAD CASE OF MR. CLAPGRAS

So what are qualia, then, if not *intrinsic* properties of conscious experiences? One evening, over a fine bottle of Chambertin, the philosopher Wilfrid Sellars said to me, "Dan, qualia are what make life worth living!" That's an attractive idea. Let's consider what it would imply about qualia. To see what is at issue, I will present an intuition pump against a background of recent work in cognitive neuroscience on several bizarre and counterintuitive pathologies: *prosopagnosia* and *Capgras delusion*.

Prosopagnosics have normal vision in most regards, but they cannot recognize faces. They can tell a male from a female, old from young, African from Asian, but faced with several close friends of the same gender and age, they are unable to tell which is which until they hear a voice or detect some other identifying peculiarity. Given a row of photographs of people, including famous politicians and movie stars, family members, and anonymous strangers, a prosopagnosic asked to identify any who are known to him will generally perform at chance. Those of us who are not prosopagnosics may find it difficult to imagine what it's like to look right at one's mother, say, and be unable to recognize her. Some may find it hard to believe that prosopagnosia exists. When I tell people about these phenomena, I often discover skeptics who are quite confident that I am making these facts up. But we must learn to treat such difficulties as measures of our frail powers of imagination, not insights into impossibility. Prosopagnosia (from the Greek *prosopon*, which means "face," and *agnosia*, "not knowing") is a well-studied, uncontroversial pathology afflicting thousands of people.

One of the most interesting facts about (many) prosopagnosics is that in spite of their inability to identify or recognize faces as a conscious task, they can respond differently to familiar and unfamiliar faces, and even respond in ways indicating that *unbeknownst to themselves*, or *covertly*, they were able to identify the faces they were unable to identify when asked. For instance, such covert recognition is demonstrated when prosopagnosics are shown pictures and given five candidate names from which to choose. They choose at chance, but their galvanic skin response—a measure of emotional arousal— shows a distinct rise when they hear the correct name associated with the picture. Or consider this simple test: Which of the following are *names* of politicians: Marilyn Monroe, Al Gore, Margaret Thatcher, Mike Tyson? You should be able to execute this task swiftly, but if each name were shown with the wrong picture of the person, your response would be markedly delayed. This could be explained only if *at some level*, you were actually identifying the faces, even though it was strictly irrelevant to the task. It seems, then, that there are (at least) two largely independent visual face-recognition systems in the brain: the impaired *conscious* system, which cannot help the subjects in the task presented by the experiment, and the unimpaired *unconscious* system, which responds with agitation to the mismatched names and faces. Further tests show that the impaired system is "higher," in the visual cortex, while the unimpaired system has connections to the "lower," limbic system. This oversimplifies a richer story about the varieties of prosopagnosia and what is now known about the brain areas involved, but it will do for our purposes, when we turn to the even stranger pathology known as Capgras delusion (first described by the French psychiatrist Jean Marie Joseph Capgras in 1923).

People who suffer from Capgras delusion suddenly come to believe that a loved one—a spouse or lover or parent, in most cases—has been covertly replaced with a replica impostor. Capgras sufferers are not insane; they are otherwise quite normal people who, as a result of brain injury, suddenly acquire this particular belief, which they maintain with such confidence, in spite of its extravagance or its utter unlikeliness, that in some cases they kill or seriously harm the "impostor"—actually their loved one. At first glance it must seem simply impossible for any brain damage to have precisely *this* weird effect. (Should we also expect there to be people who get hit on the head and thereafter believe that the moon is made of green cheese?) But cognitive neuroscientist Andrew Young saw a pattern, and proposed that the Capgras delusion was simply the "opposite" of the pathology that produces prosopagnosia. In Capgras, the conscious, cortical face-recognition system is spared—that's how the deluded sufferer recognizes the person standing in front of him as the spitting image of his loved one—but the unconscious, limbic system is disabled, draining the recognition of all the emotional resonance it ought to have. The *absence* of that subtle contribution to identification is so upsetting ("Something's missing!") that it amounts to a pocket veto on the positive vote of the surviving system's identification of the familiar person: the emergent result is the sufferer's heartfelt conviction that he or she is looking at an impostor. Instead of blaming the mismatch on their own faulty perceptual system, Capgras sufferers blame the world, in a way that is so metaphysically extravagant, so improbable, that there can be little doubt of the power (the political power, in effect) that the impaired unconscious face-recognition system normally has in us all. When this particular system's epistemic hunger goes unsatisfied, it throws such a fit that it overthrows the contributions of the other systems.

Haydn Ellis and Young first proposed this hypothesis in 1990, and since then Young and neuroscientist Chris Frith and others have confirmed and elaborated it. There are, of course, complications that I will not dwell on, since I want to use this particular bit of imagination-stretching cognitive neuroscience to open our minds to yet another possibility, not yet found but imaginable. This is the *imaginary* case of poor Mr. *Clapgras*, a name I have made up to remind us of its inspiration: the real syndrome of Capgras delusion. (This scenario joins a large throng of philosophers' intuition pumps exploring imaginable disruptions in a person's consciousness that might bear on the nature of qualia.)

Mr. Clapgras earns a modest living as an experimental subject in

Norfolk Library and Information Service

Please keep your receipt

Title	Due Date
ntuition pumps and her tools for thinking / ardback]	06/09/2019

psychological and psychophysical experiments, so he is far from naïve about his own subjective states. One day he wakes up and cries out in despair as soon as he opens his eyes: "Aargh! There's something wrong! The whole world is just . . . *weird*, just . . . *awful*, somehow *wrong!* I don't know if I want to go on living in *this* world!" Clapgras closes his eyes and rubs them; he cautiously opens them again, only to be confronted yet again by a strangely disgusting world, familiar but also different in some way that defies description. That's what he says. "What do you see when you look up?" he is asked. "Blue sky, with a few fleecy white clouds, some yellowish-green buds on the springtime trees, a bright red cardinal perched on a twig," he replies. Apparently his color vision is normal, but just to check, he is given the standard Ishihara test, which shows he is not color-blind, and he correctly identifies a few-dozen Munsell color chips. Almost everybody is satisfied that whatever poor Mr. Clapgras's ailment is, it doesn't involve his color vision, but one researcher, Dr. Chromaphil, holds out for a few more tests.

Chromaphil has been conducting research on color preferences, emotional responses to color, and the effects of different colors on attention, concentration, blood pressure, pulse rate, metabolic activity, and a host of other subtle visceral responses. Over the past six months he has accumulated a huge database of Mr. Clapgras's responses, both idiosyncratic and common, on all these tests, and he wants to see if there have been any changes. He retests Clapgras and notices a stunning pattern: all the emotional and visceral responses Clapgras used to exhibit to blue he now exhibits to yellow, and vice versa. His preference for red over green has been reversed, as have all his other color preferences. Food disgusts him—unless he eats in the dark. Color combinations he used to rate as pleasing he now rates as jarring, while finding the combinations of their "opposites" pleasing, and so forth. The shade of shocking pink that used to set his pulse racing he still identifies as shocking pink (though he marvels that anybody could call *that* shade of pink shocking), but it is now calming to him, while its complement, a shade of lime green that used to be calming, now excites him. When he looks at paintings, his trajectory of saccades—the swift jumps our eyes make as they scan anything—is now profoundly unlike his earlier trajectories, which were apparently governed by subtle attention-grabbing, gaze-deflecting effects of the colors on the canvas. His ability to concentrate on mental arithmetic problems, heretofore seriously depressed by putting him in a bright-blue room, is now depressed by putting him in a bright-yellow room.

In short, although Clapgras does not complain about any problems of color vision, and indeed passes all standard color-naming and color-discriminating tests with, well, flying colors, he has undergone a profound inversion of all his emotional and attentional reactions to colors. What has happened to Clapgras, Dr. Chromaphil tells his amazed and skeptical colleagues, is simple: he's undergone a total color *qualia* inversion, while leaving intact his merely high-level cognitive color talents—his ability to discriminate and name colors, for instance, the talents a color-sensitive robot could have.

Now what should *we* say? Have Clapgras's qualia been inverted? Since the case is imaginary, it seems that we can answer it however we like, but philosophers have been taking other imaginary cases seriously for years, thinking that profound theoretical issues hinge on how they are decided, so we mustn't just dismiss the case. First, is this a *possible* case? It may depend on what kind of possibility we are talking about. Is it logically possible? Is it physiologically possible? These are profoundly different questions. Philosophers have tended to ignore the latter as quite irrelevant to philosophical concerns, but in this case they may relent. I can see no way of arguing that the case is logically impossible. Clapgras, as described, has a strange combination of spared abilities and shocking new inabilities; dispositions that are normally tightly linked are here dissociated in unprecedented ways, but is his condition any more radical in this regard than either prosopagnosia or Capgras delusion? I am not sure Clapgras's condition is even physiologically impossible; there are well-studied cases of subjects who can discriminate colors just fine but not name them (color anomia), and of subjects who become color-blind but don't notice their new deficit, blithely confabulating and naming colors at chance without any recognition that they are guessing. Clapgras, like a Capgras sufferer, has no problems with recognition or naming; it is the subtle ineffable flavoring that has gone all askew in him—all the personal dispositions that make paintings worth looking at, rooms worth painting, color combinations worth choosing. The effects of colors that contribute to making life worth living are what changed in Clapgras—in other words (if Sellars was right), his color *qualia*.

Suppose we put the issue to Clapgras and ask him if his color qualia have been inverted. He has three possible answers: *Yes, No,* and *I don't know*. Which should he answer? If we compare my story of Clapgras with the many tales of inverted qualia that have been soberly promulgated and discussed at great length by philosophers, the most disturbing innovation is the prospect that Clapgras might have his qualia inverted and be none the wiser. Remember that Dr. Chromaphil had to propose this hypothesis to his skeptical colleagues, and Clapgras may well share their skepticism. After all, he not only hasn't complained of any problem with his color qualia (as in the standard stories), but also has satisfied himself that his color vision is just fine in the same way he satisfied the researchers: by easily passing the standard color vision tests. This feature of the story ought to cause some discomfort, for it is commonly assumed in the philosophical literature that such behavioral self-testing is irrelevant: **surely** (ding!) *those* tests have no bearing at all on qualia. Those tests are standardly characterized as having no power at all to illuminate or constrain qualia quandaries. But, as my variation shows, philosophers' imaginations have overlooked the prospect of somebody being at least tempted to *rely on* these tests to secure his own confidence that his qualia have not changed.

Can your qualia stay constant while you undergo a change in "affect"? Philosophers are divided over how to answer such definitional questions about qualia. Consider the effect of monosodium glutamate (MSG), the flavor enhancer. There is no doubt that it makes food seem tastier, more strongly flavored, but does it *change the qualia* of food, or does it merely heighten the sensitivity of people to the qualia they were already enjoying? This is an appeal for a clarification of the concept of qualia, not an empirical question about the site of action of MSG, or the variation in human responses to MSG as shown by subjects' reports, since until we settle the conceptual question one way or another, any discoveries about the underlying neural processes or **heterophenomenology** of the subject would be systematically ambiguous. What I want to know is simply how philosophers mean to use the word "qualia"—do they identify all changes in subjective response as changes in qualia, or is there some privileged subset of responses that in effect anchor the qualia? Is the idea of changing one's aesthetic opinion about—or response to—a particular quale nonsense or not? Until one makes decisions about such questions of definition, the term is not just vague or fuzzy; it is hopelessly ambiguous, equivocating between two (or more) fundamentally different ideas.

Have Clapgras's color qualia been inverted? Some philosophers say that I haven't given enough detail in describing his condition. I have described his behavioral competences—he recognizes, and discriminates, and names colors correctly, while responding "wrong" in many other regards—while avoiding describing his subjective state. I haven't said whether, when he looks at a ripe lemon, he experiences *intrinsic subjective yellow* or, say, *intrinsic subjective blue*. But that is the point: I am challenging the presumption that these terms name any real properties of his experience at all. Suppose I add that when asked, Clapgras *says*, "Since I still see ripe lemons *as* yellow, of course my experience includes the property of intrinsic subjective yellow." Does that settle anything? Do we have any confidence that he knows what he means when he says these words? Should we believe him, or might he be in the grip of a philosophical theory that does not deserve his allegiance?

Here is the main weakness in the philosophical methods standardly used in these cases: philosophers tend to assume that all the competences and dispositions that normal people exhibit regarding, say, colors, form a monolithic block, invulnerable to decomposition or dissociation into independent sub-competences and sub-dispositions. This handily excuses them from addressing the question of whether qualia are to be anchored to some subset or specific disposition. For instance, philosophers George Graham and Terry Horgan (2000, p. 73) speak of "direct acquaintance with phenomenal character itself, acquaintance that provides the experiential basis for [a person's] recognitional/discriminatory capacities." How do they know that this "direct acquaintance" is the "basis" for recognition or discrimination? Prosopagnosics presumably have direct acquaintance with the faces they see, or at least with the "visual qualia" of those familiar faces, but prosopagnosics cannot recognize them as the qualia that are experienced when they are looking at the faces of their friends and family. If, to harken back to Wilfrid Sellars once again, qualia are what make life worth living, then qualia may *not* be the "experiential basis" for our ability to recognize colors from day to day, to discriminate colors, to name them.

59. THE TUNED DECK

In a famous paper, the philosopher David Chalmers (1995) distinguishes the "easy" problems about consciousness from what he calls the (capital "H") Hard Problem of consciousness. What Chalmers would consider "easy" is still difficult enough. Consider, for example, these really challenging questions about consciousness:

1. How does consciousness enable us to talk about what we see, the sounds we hear, the aromas we smell, and so on? (Oversimplifying, how does the information from the perceiving parts of the brain get used by the language parts of the brain to form the reports and answers we can give?)

2. When we are doing a routine activity (one we can "almost do in our sleep"), why does our consciousness kick in whenever we run into a problem, and how does consciousness help us with the problem encountered?

3. How many independently moving things can we consciously track simultaneously, and how do we do it? (The answer is at least four; you can see for yourself by experiencing an amazing demonstration of this phenomenon, known as FINST indexing, at http://ruccs .rutgers.edu/finstlab/MOT-movies/MOT-Occ-baseline .mov.)

4. When you have something "on the tip of your tongue"—when you know you know it and can *almost* retrieve the answer—what is going on?

5. Why do you have to be conscious of a joke to find it funny? (See Hurley, Dennett, and Adams, 2011, for the book-length answer to this one.)

These problems are relatively easy, according to Chalmers, because they involve the cognitive *functions* of consciousness, the things we can *do*, using the information-processing and attention-directing processes in the brain, the tracking and reminding and recalling activities that we engage in during our waking lives. However hard it may be to think up promising solutions to them, the solutions will be testable and refinable by experiments, and in fact we're making great progress on these "easy" problems. We can build *relatively* simple computer models, for instance, that replicate these functions quite persuasively, so we can be quite sure the brain accomplishes them without magic or anything unparalleled in the rest of nature. A robot that exhibited all these phenomena could be constructed, if not today then in the foreseeable future.

The Hard Problem, for Chalmers, is the problem of *"experience,"* *what it is like* to be conscious, the inexpressible, unanalyzable *thusness* of being conscious. A robot could behave *just as if* it were conscious, answering all our questions, tracking all the moving spots, succumbing to and recovering from the tip-of-the-tongue phenomenon, laughing at the right times, and being (unconsciously) puzzled or dumfounded at the right times, but in fact there would be nobody home in there. The robot would be a zombie, without the faintest shadow of the inner life you and I, as normal conscious people, enjoy.

According to Chalmers, you, gentle reader, and I know we are conscious whenever we are up and about. A philosophers' zombie doesn't know any such thing—it is never awake and has no inner life—it just *seems from the outside* to be conscious. And of course it insists, convincingly, that it is just as conscious as you and I are, and if given a lie-detector test when it says this, it passes the test for sincerity—but, being a zombie, it is mistaken! (Zombies are also indistinguishable from normal conscious people when neuroscientists probe their inner brain states using fMRI machines, and the like.) This makes it clear that telling a conscious person from a zombie is certainly a hard problem—if it is any problem at all. And if *that* is a problem, explaining how this difference can exist is an even harder problem; it is *the* Hard Problem. Some of us, myself included, think the Hard Problem is a figment of Chalmers's imagination, but others—surprisingly many—have the conviction that there is or would be a real difference between a conscious person and a perfect zombie and that this is important.

Let me review this curious situation: some of us doubt the very existence of the Hard Problem, but others think we must be crazy to doubt this: nothing, they say, could be more obvious, more immediately intuited by any conscious being, than his or her own special consciousness, and it is this wonderful property we enjoy that defies scientific understanding (so far) and thus deserves to be called the Hard Problem. There is no way to nudge these two alternative positions closer to each other. One side or the other is flat wrong. I have tried for years to show that however tempting the intuition may be, it must be abandoned. I am quite sure that the tempting idea that there is a Hard Problem is simply a mistake, but I cannot prove this. Or, better, even if I could prove this, my proof would often fall on deaf ears, since I am assured by some philosophers that their intuition here is invulnerable bedrock, an insight so obvious and undeniable that no argument could make it tremble, let alone shatter it. So I won't make the tactical error of trying to dislodge with rational argument a conviction that is beyond reason.

This attitude reminds me of the heartfelt convictions often expressed by those who have just seen a spectacular display of stage magic. Every magician knows that people have a tendency to inflate their recollections of any good magic trick they have seen. The shock and bafflement of the moment amplifies their memories, and they earnestly and sincerely insist that they have just seen something that goes beyond what the magician tried to fool them into seeing. Some people want very much to believe in magic. Recall Lee Siegel's comment about "real magic," discussed in chapter 22, on **wonder tissue**: *"Real magic . . .* refers to the magic that is not real, while the magic that is real, that can actually be done, is *not real magic."* (See p. 98)

To many people consciousness is "real magic." If you're not talking about something that is supercalifragilisticexpialidocious, then you're not talking about consciousness, the Mystery Beyond All Understanding. The science journalist Robert Wright (2000) expresses the attitude succinctly:

> Of course the problem here is with the claim that consciousness is "identical" to physical brain states. The more Dennett et al. try to explain to me what they mean by this, the more convinced I become that what they really mean is that consciousness doesn't exist. [p. 398]

Any bag of tricks in the brain just *couldn't be* consciousness, not *real* consciousness. But even those who don't make this preemptive mistake often have a weakness for exaggerating the phenomena of consciousness. (That's why so much of my book *Consciousness Explained*, 1991a, had to be devoted to *deflation*, whittling consciousness—real consciousness—down to size, showing people that the phenomena were not as spectacular as most of them think. This exercise in deflation then inspired many readers to joke that my book should have been entitled *Consciousness Explained Away* or—as Wright suggests—*Consciousness Denied*.) For those who doubt that they could be flummoxed into an inflated view of consciousness, I want to strike a glancing blow, hoping to banish their complacency by drawing attention to a delicious and disturbing parallel from the world of card magic: The Tuned Deck.

> For many years, Mr. Ralph Hull, the famous card wizard from Crooksville, Ohio, has completely bewildered not only the general public, but also amateur conjurors, card connois-

seurs and professional magicians with the series of card tricks
which he is pleased to call "The Tuned Deck" . . .

—John Northern Hilliard, *Card Magic* (1938)

Ralph Hull's trick looks and sounds roughly like this:

Boys, I have a new trick to show you. It's called "The Tuned
Deck." This deck of cards is magically tuned [Hull holds
the deck to his ear and riffles the cards, listening carefully
to the buzz of the cards]. By their finely tuned vibrations, I
can *hear* and *feel* the location of any card. Pick a card, any
card. . . . [The deck is then fanned or otherwise offered
for the audience, and a card is taken by a spectator, noted,
and returned to the deck by one route or another.] Now I
listen to the Tuned Deck, and what does it tell me? I hear
the telltale vibrations, . . . [buzz, buzz, the cards are riffled
by Hull's ear and various manipulations and rituals are
enacted, after which, with a flourish, the spectator's card is
presented].

Hull would perform the trick over and over for the benefit of his
select audience of fellow magicians, challenging them to figure it out.
Nobody ever did. (Remember that a cardinal rule of card magic is
never to repeat a trick for the audience; this great trick audaciously
flouted that rule.) Magicians offered to buy the trick from him, but
he would not sell it. Late in his life he gave his account to his friend,
Hilliard, who published the account in his privately printed book.
Here is what Hull had to say about his trick:

For years I have performed this effect and have shown it to
magicians and amateurs by the hundred and, to the very
best of my knowledge, not one of them ever figured out the
secret. . . . *the boys have all looked for something too hard* [my
italics].

Like much great magic, the trick is over before you even realize it has begun. The trick, in its entirety, is in the name, "The Tuned Deck," and more specifically, in one word—"The"! As soon as Hull had announced his new trick and given its name to his eager audience, the trick was over. Having set up his audience in this simple way, and having passed the time with some obviously phony and misdirecting chatter about vibrations and buzz-buzz-buzz, Hull would do a relatively simple and familiar card presentation trick of type A (at this point I will draw the traditional curtain of secrecy; the further mechanical details of legerdemain, as you will see, do not matter). His audience, savvy magicians, would see that he might possibly be performing a type A trick, a hypothesis they could test by being stubborn and uncooperative spectators in a way that would thwart any attempt at a type A trick. When they then adopted the appropriate recalcitrance to test the hypothesis, Hull would "repeat" the trick, this time executing a type B card presentation trick. The spectators would then huddle and compare notes: Might he be doing a type B trick? They test *that* hypothesis by adopting the recalcitrance appropriate to preventing a type B trick, and still he does "the" trick—using method C. When they test the hypothesis that he's pulling a type C trick on them, he switches to method D— or perhaps he goes back to method A or B, since his audience has "refuted" the hypothesis that he's using method A or B. And so it would go, for dozens of repetitions, with Hull staying one step ahead of his hypothesis-testers, exploiting his realization that he could always do *some trick or other* from the pool of tricks they all knew, and concealing the fact that he was doing a grab bag of different tricks by the simple expedient of the definite article: *The* Tuned Deck. As Hull explained it to Hilliard,

Each time it is performed, the routine is such that one or more ideas in the back of the spectator's head is exploded, and sooner or later he will invariably give up any further attempt to solve the mystery.

Hull's trick was introducing a single common word: *"the"*—for heaven's sake! This modest monosyllable seduced his audience of experts, paralyzing their minds, preventing them from **jootsing**. They found themselves stuck in a system in which they were sure that they had to find a big, new trick, so they couldn't see that their problem(s) had not one solution but many; they failed to jump out of the system.

I am suggesting, then, that David Chalmers has—unintentionally—perpetrated the same feat of conceptual sleight of hand in declaring to the world that he has discovered "The Hard Problem." Is there *really* a Hard Problem? Or is what appears to be the Hard Problem simply the large bag of tricks that constitute what Chalmers calls the Easy Problems of Consciousness? These all have mundane explanations, requiring no revolutions in physics, no emergent novelties. They succumb, with much effort, to the standard methods of cognitive science.

I cannot prove that there is no Hard Problem, and Chalmers cannot prove that there is one. He has one potent intuition going for him, and if it generated some striking new predictions, or promised to explain something otherwise baffling, we might join him in trying to construct a new theory of consciousness around it, but it stands alone, hard to deny but otherwise theoretically inert.

The inventory of known effects of consciousness is large and growing, and they range from the mundane to the exotic. It's hard to keep track of them all, so we must be alert to the possibility that we are being victimized by an error of arithmetic, in effect, when we take ourselves to have added up all the Easy Problems and discovered a residue unaccounted for. That residue may already have been accommodated, without our realizing it, in the set of mundane phenomena for which we already have explanations—or at least un-mysterious paths of explanation still to be explored. How could we commit this "error in arithmetic" and then overlook it? By double counting the phenomena or by forgetting that we had already explained some phenomenon, and hence should have erased it from our list of "Still-to-Be-Explained Phenomena." Is it plausible that we are making such a mistake? Consider this: when we looked at poor Mr. Clapgras, we saw that *something* was seriously amiss with him, but there seemed to be two importantly different ways of putting his plight:

A. His aesthetic and emotional *reactions* to his color qualia had all been inverted (while his qualia remained constant).

B. His color qualia had been inverted, even though his competence to distinguish, identify, and name colors had been preserved.

Consider how one might argue (rather like the baffled magicians trying to figure out Hull's trick): "A cannot be right, because the only reason we have for saying his color qualia have remained constant is that his *naming and discriminating behavior* has stayed constant, but that proves nothing about his qualia; those behaviors are (merely) cognitive, functional facts, and qualia are, of course, independent of those. And B cannot be right, because it is *only* his reactions that have changed; Clapgras doesn't complain that colors *look different* to him now, but just that those very same subjective colors don't appeal to him now the way they used to. So maybe his color qualia changed and maybe they didn't, and—you'll note—there is no empirical way of telling which hypothesis is true! This is truly a Hard Problem!"

This argument overlooks the possibility that the qualia discussed in A and B aren't doing any work. In both A and B, we see that the discrimination machinery is working just as before, while Clapgras's reactions to the deliverances of that machinery are inverted. The qualia are interposed as a sort of hard-to-pin-down intermediary that is imagined to provide the basis or raw material or ground of the emotional reactions, and there seem then to be two places where the inversion could happen: before the qualia are "presented" to the appreciation machinery, or after "presentation," in the way the appreciation machinery responds to those presented qualia. This is one presentation process too many. We know, for instance, that negative (alarming, fear-inducing) reactions can be triggered quite early in the perceptual process, and they then "color" all subsequent processing of that perceptual input, in which case we could say that the emotional reactions *cause* the qualia to have the subjective character they had for Clapgras, rather than (vice versa) that the "intrinsic" nature of the qualia cause or ground the emotional reactions. But if we've already arrived at the emotional (or aesthetic or affective) reactions to the perceptual input, we have no more "work" for the qualia to do, and, of course, a zimbo would be just as bummed out by inverted reactions-to-perceptions as a conscious person is.

What does the story about the Tuned Deck add to all the other intuition pumps about qualia? Just a real-life example of how very clever, knowledgeable experts can be induced to create a phantom problem simply by the way an issue is presented to them. It has happened. It can happen again. And this yields a novel perspective on the impasse, creating a new burden of proof: How do you know that you have *not* fallen for something like the Tuned Deck? I'm not suggesting that this is conclusive, but just that it ought to give those who credit the **Zombic Hunch** some second thoughts about how "obvious" it is.

60. THE CHINESE ROOM

In the late 1970s there was a wave of ballyhoo about AI—artificial intelligence—that oversold both the existing and the prophesied progress in the field. Thinking machines were just around the corner! Berkeley philosopher John Searle was sure he could see through this, and concocted a thought experiment to prove it. In 1980, he published "Minds, Brains and Programs," his famous Chinese Room thought experiment purporting to show that "Strong AI" was impossible. He defined Strong AI as the claim that "the appropriately programmed computer literally has cognitive states and that the programs thereby explain human cognition" (Searle, 1980, p. 417), and later clarified his definition: "the appropriately programmed digital computer with the right inputs and outputs would thereby have a mind in exactly the sense that human beings have minds" (Searle, 1988, p. 136). The 1980 article appeared in *Behavioral and Brain Sciences*, the flagship journal of cognitive science, and *BBS*, as it is known, has a special format: each issue contains several long "target articles" accompanied by several-dozen commentaries by experts in the field and a response by the author(s). Since *BBS* is energetically interdisciplinary, these experts typically come from a variety of disciplines, giving the reader a useful and timely cross section of reactions. Seeing how—and whether—these other experts take the target article seriously is a great way of gauging how to use or ignore it in your own work. You also can learn a lot about the difficulties of interdisciplinary communication, with very confident people furiously talking past each other, or participating in academic tag team wrestling of the highest caliber. Searle's target article provoked a fire storm of rebuttal, including mine (Dennett, 1980), in which I coined the term "intuition pump," in the service of trying to show what was deeply misleading about his thought experiment.

It was my term, but credit should also be given to Doug Hofstadter, for my coinage grew out of discussions with him about Searle's essay, which we reprinted, with commentary, in our anthology, *The Mind's I* (Hofstadter and Dennett, 1981). We found his thought experiment fascinating because it was, on the one hand, so clearly a fallacious and misleading argument, yet, on the other hand, just as clearly a tremendous crowd-pleaser and persuader. How—and why—did it work? We looked at it from the point of view of *reverse engineering*, and Doug came up with the tactic of "turning all the knobs" to see what makes it work. Is the story robust under deformation, or does it critically depend on details that *ought* to be optional?*

That was over thirty years ago, and I must grant that Searle's Chinese Room has had tremendous appeal and staying power. It is a classic, presented in probably thousands of undergraduate courses and debated over and over to this day. I have used it for years in my own classes, and have learned a lot about how it works and how to show people what's wrong with it.†

For it is, I will now show, a defective intuition pump, a **boom crutch** that can disable your imagination unless you handle it very carefully. But before I turn to that delicate task, I want to acknowl-

---

* Doug zeroed in on the phrase "bits of paper" in Searle's essay, and showed how it encouraged people to underestimate the size and complexity of the software involved by many orders of magnitude. His commentary on Searle in our book featured this criticism, and led to a ferocious response from Searle (1982) in the pages of the *New York Review of Books*, because, although we had reprinted his article correctly, in his commentary Doug slipped and wrote "a few slips" where Searle had said "bits," and this, Searle claimed, completely misrepresented his argument! If Searle is right about this, if that small inadvertent mutation transformed the machinery, this actually proved our point, in a way: if such a tiny adjustment disables or enables a thought experiment, that is something that should be drawn to the attention of all whose intuitions are up for pumping.

† Check out Hofstadter's own virtuoso demonstration in *The Mind's I* (Hofstadter and Dennett, 1981), showing that the Chinese Room is an intuition pump with (at least) five knobs, which he proceeds to turn, one at a time, to derive a family of different thought experiments with different invited conclusions. In the closing reflections, I noted,

> Each setting of the dials on our intuition pump yields a slightly different narrative, with different problems receding into the background and different morals drawn. Which version or versions should be trusted is a matter to settle by examining them carefully, to see which features of the narrative are doing the work. If the oversimplifications are the *source* of the intuitions, rather than just devices for suppressing irrelevant complications, we should mistrust the conclusions we are invited to draw. [p. 460]

edge that many of you are probably silently rolling your eyes, or even groaning. You don't want me to disable this device; you like the conclusion so much—Strong AI is impossible, *whew!*—that your eyes glaze over at the prospect of being dragged through a meticulous critique of a vivid, entertaining argument that supports your fervent hope. I used to respond to this reaction with scorn. Those of you responding this way love the fact that an eminent Berkeley professor has a famous argument that purports to show that you are right, and you are happy to take it on his authority. The details don't really interest you, only the conclusion. What an anti-intellectual copout!

But then I caught myself doing much the same thing and reconsidered my harsh verdict. I confess that I have always found quantum mechanics somehow repellent, deeply disorienting, and even, well, something I would prefer not to be true! I know that it is stunningly successful at predicting and explaining many phenomena, including everyday phenomena such as the reflection and refraction of light, and the operation of the proteins in our retinas that permit us to see. It lies at the very heart of science, but it is famously hard to make sense of, even by the experts. My several attempts to master the mathematics of quantum mechanics have failed, so I am an interested but ultimately incompetent bystander on the scientific controversies surrounding its interpretation, but this hasn't prevented me from being deeply suspicious of much that has been said about this by supposedly knowledgeable experts. And then I read Murray Gell-Man's book *The Quark and the Jaguar: Adventures in the Simple and the Complex* (1995, a science book for nonspecialists like me. To my delight, Gell-Mann adopts a no-nonsense, demystifying tone, and just beats the daylights out of some of the more dubious pronouncements that have gained favor. (Read his chapter "Quantum Mechanics and Flapdoodle" to see what I mean.) I found myself thinking, "Hit them again, Murray! Sock it to them!" Here was a world-famous Nobel laureate physicist supporting my prejudice, using arguments that I understood. This was my kind of quantum physics! But then it hit me. Did I really understand his arguments, or just **sorta** understand them? Could I be sure that I wasn't just falling for his rhetoric? I hoped there weren't other physicists who would want to drag me back through the technicalities, showing me that I had been taken in by this authoritative dismissal. I liked his conclusion so much I didn't have any stomach for the details. Same copout.

But not quite. I have conscientiously tried to assess Gell-Mann's verdicts in the light of what others have written since (and so far, so good). And I remain open to the distinct possibility that Gell-Mann's "common sense," which I find so appealing, will turn out some day to be one more case of failure of imagination instead of deep insight. I would beg you to attempt to adopt the same open-minded attitude toward my effort to dismantle and neutralize Searle's Chinese Room. I'll make the bitter pill as palatable as I can.

Way back in 1950 Alan Turing had proposed what he claimed would be the acid test of intelligence in a machine, now known as the Turing test, in which a judge has a probing conversation with two entities, one a human being and the other a computer, both hidden from view and communicating by "teletype" (think: screen and keyboard). The human being tries to demonstrate her genuine humanity to the judge, and the computer tries to fool the judge into thinking that it is the human being. If the judge can't reliably tell the difference, the computer (program) has passed the Turing test and would be declared not just to be intelligent, but to "have a mind in exactly the sense that human beings have minds," as Searle put it in 1988. Passing the Turing test would be, in the eyes of many in the field, the vindication of Strong AI. Why? Because, they thought (along with Turing), you can't have such a conversation without understanding it, so the success of the computer conversationalist would be proof of its understanding.* Notice that the

---

* As has often been pointed out, this conviction echoes that of Descartes, who proposed in his *Discourse on Method* way back in 1637 that the best way to tell a machine from a person with an immaterial soul was to have a conversation with it.

It is indeed conceivable that a machine could be so made that it would utter words, and even words appropriate to the presence of physical acts or objects which cause some change in its organs; as, for example, if it was touched in some spot that it

Turing test doesn't—can't—distinguish between a zimbo and a "really conscious" person, since whatever a conscious person can *do*, a zimbo can do exactly as well. As many have remarked, the claim that an entity that passes the Turing test is not just intelligent but *conscious* flies in the face of the **Zombic Hunch**. This may seem all by itself to disqualify the Turing test as a good test of mind, but we should reserve judgment on that until we *look at the details*. The program that passes the Turing test may have only a zimbo's stream of *unconsciousness* where we have a stream of consciousness, but we have just seen a challenge to the Zombic Hunch that insists that this marks a real difference. Is the zimbo program only *sorta* conscious? In what dimension, exactly, does it fall short? Perhaps Searle's intuition pump will shed light on that question: it appears to be a *reductio ad absurdum* argument to discredit the idea of Strong AI.

He invites us to imagine him locked in a room, hand-simulating a giant AI program, which putatively understands Chinese. He stipulates that the program passes the Turing test, foiling all attempts by human interlocutors to distinguish it from a genuine understander of Chinese. Searle, who knows no Chinese, locked in the room and busily manipulating the symbol strings according to the program, doesn't thereby gain understanding of Chinese (obviously), and there is nothing else in the room that understands Chinese either. (It is empty, aside from Searle and the "bits of paper" on which Searle's instructions are written. By following them precisely he is "hand-simulating" the giant program.) If Searle doesn't understand Chinese, surely (ding!) Searle plus bits of paper doesn't understand Chinese. Ergo, there is no understanding of Chinese in the Chinese Room, in spite of its conversational prowess, which is good enough

would ask what you wanted to say to it; if in another, that it would cry that it was hurt, and so on for similar things. But it could never modify its phrases to reply to the sense of whatever was said in its presence, as even the most stupid men can do.

Nobody knows if Turing got the inspiration for his intuition pump from Descartes's intuition pump.

to fool native Chinese-speakers. Searle, like a computer, identifies the Chinese symbols by their shape only; they are just different meaningless "squiggles" to him and to a computer, so Searle-in-the-Chinese-Room just *is* an implementation of the computer program at issue. It does its job without any understanding of Chinese, whether it is running on silicon or on Searle.

This is so simple and convincing! Can there possibly be anything wrong with this thought experiment? Well, yes. When Searle presented it at Berkeley, the computer scientists retorted with what Searle calls the Systems Reply (Berkeley):

> While it is true that the individual person who is locked in the room does not understand the story, the fact is that he is merely part of the whole system, and the system does understand the story. The person has a large ledger in front of him in which are written the rules, he has a lot of scratch paper and pencils for doing calculations, he has "data banks" of sets of Chinese symbols. Now, understanding is not being ascribed to the mere individual; rather it is being ascribed to this whole system of which he is a part. [Searle, 1980, p. 419]

Searle says something very telling in the course of responding to this reply:

> Actually I feel somewhat embarrassed . . . because the theory seems to me so implausible to start with. The idea is that while a person doesn't understand Chinese, somehow the *conjunction* of that person and bits of paper might understand Chinese. It is not easy for me to imagine how someone who was not in the grip of an ideology would find the idea at all plausible. [Searle, 1980, p. 419]

What Searle finds so implausible is nothing other than the fundamental insight Turing had when he created the idea of a stored-program computer! The competence is all in the software. Recall that the register machine in chapter 24 doesn't understand arithmetic at all, but the register machine in conjunction with the software does perfect arithmetic. The central processing unit in your laptop doesn't know anything about chess, but when it is running a chess program, it can beat you at chess, and so forth, for all the magnificent competences of your laptop. What Searle describes as an ideology is at the very heart of computer science, and its soundness is demonstrated in every walk of life. The way to reproduce human competence and hence comprehension (eventually) is to stack virtual machines on top of virtual machines on top of virtual machines—the power is in the system, not in the underlying hardware. Darwin's "strange inversion of reasoning" is nicely echoed by Turing's strange inversion of reasoning (Dennett, forthcoming): whereas we used to think (before Turing) that human competence had to flow from comprehension (that mysterious fount of intelligence), we now appreciate that comprehension itself is an effect created (bubbling up) from a host of competences piled on competences.

Details matter. Searle never tells his reader at what level he is hand-simulating the giant AI program. This is his account of what it is like when he works through the program:

> Now suppose that after this first batch of Chinese writing [the input] I am given a second batch of Chinese script together with a set of rules for correlating the second batch with the first batch. The rules are in English, and I understand these rules as well as any other native speaker of English. They enable me to correlate one set of formal symbols with another set of formal symbols. . . . Now suppose also that I am given a third batch of Chinese symbols together with some instructions, again in English, that enable me to correlate elements of this batch with the first two batches, and these rules instruct me how to give back certain Chinese symbols with certain sorts of shapes

in response to certain sorts of shapes given me in the third batch. [Searle, 1980, p. 418]

He contrasts this "correlation" between "batches of symbols" with what happens when instead an English sentence or story is input, and he responds in his native English.

From the external point of view—from the point of view of somebody reading my "answers"—the answers to the Chinese questions and the English questions are equally good. But in the Chinese case, unlike the English case, I produce the answers by manipulating uninterpreted formal symbols. [Searle, 1980, p. 418]

What a contrast! But look what Searle has still left out. We know he gets his "set of rules" (instructions) in English, but are they along the lines of "add the contents of register 39021192 to the contents of register 215845085" (machine code), or "Define a constant: queue-size and set it at 100" (**source code**)? Is he down in the basement, doing arithmetic at a furious rate (trillions of operations per second), or is he following the source code of a program, implemented many layers higher? And if he's following the source code, does he get to read any comments? Better not, since they are not officially part of the program, and they would give him lots of hints about what was going on ("This parses the sentence, yielding nouns, pronouns, verbs, and modifiers, and identifies it as a question, declarative, imperative or interjection," and then, a few billion operations later, "pun discovered; switch to repartee mode . . . ," and then a more detailed set of billions of operations, in which references are refined, alternative answers are evaluated rather like different chess moves, and then finally an output sentence is generated). If the program Searle is hand-simulating is able to carry on an impressive conversation in Chinese, it will have to consult huge data banks not just of "sets of Chinese symbols," as he puts it, but of everyday knowledge that Chinese speakers share, and that is the least of it. When Searle hand-simulates, does he get any hints of all this layered cognitive activity, or is it just a whole lot of arithmetic to him?

Think of how Searle would handle the following question in English:

> Imagine taking a capital letter D and turning it counterclock-wise 90 degrees on its side. Now place it on top of a capital letter J. What sort of weather does that remind you of?

Now imagine that Searle is given an analogous challenge in Chinese when he is hard at work in the Chinese Room.

> On June 4, 2012, the following posting of characters was blocked on Sohu Weibo [a Chinese blogging service]. Can you figure out why?

占占占占人　占占占点　占占点占　占点占占　点占占占　灬占占占占

These are actual Chinese characters (Searle's "squiggles"), but the sequence is utter gibberish. Why would it be blocked by the authori-ties? Because June 4 is the anniversary of the Tiananmen Square massacre in which hundreds of protesters were killed by the army. ("June 4" is as evocative to the Chinese as "9/11" is to Americans.) The most famous images that emerged were of a single brave man who faced down the tanks. You can see him ("人" means person) confront-ing four tanks on the left, which then roll over him and over him and over him and then leave at the right.*

The Chinese Room ought to "get it," but unless Searle had access to the comments on the source code, he would be none the wiser, since it would never be apparent to him that his rule-following was

---

* Thanks to linguist, sinologist, and polymath David Moser for the example, which was cre-ated in China just as I was casting about for such an example.

framing a "mental image" and manipulating it and then using the result as a probe of memory. That is, the *system* would go through a set of activities before responding to the Chinese question that are strikingly parallel to the activities Searle went through knowingly to respond to the English question. You could say that the system has a mind of its own, unimagined by Searle, toiling away in the engine room.

Any program capable of passing the Turing test would *have* to go through "mental" operations that very closely mimicked the mental operations we go through in the course of a conversation. Suppose, for instance, the questioner in the Turing test began tutoring the candidate in quantum physics, using the Socratic question-and-answer method, giving the student simple problems to solve. Searle, in the engine room, would be obliged to take the system through elaborate intellectual exercises in order to hold up its end of the conversation, but Searle would emerge from the ordeal as uncomprehending of quantum physics as when he went in. The system, in contrast, would now have a much better working understanding of the field than it had before the Turing test began, because it had *done the exercises*. This particular instance of the Turing test would install a new virtual machine in the program: the simple quantum physics machine.

Such facts are completely obscured by Searle's image of "bits of paper" and "rules" that permit him to "correlate" Chinese symbols. I'm not saying that Searle deliberately concealed the complexity of the program he imagined he was hand-simulating, but just that he ignored the implications of the complexity. If you think of the program as a relatively simple bunch of rules, then, like Bateson thinking of "particles of chromatin, indistinguishable from each other and indeed almost homogeneous under any known test," you are likely to find the purported comprehension powers of programs, like the powers of DNA, "inconceivable."

Look at what we've just done. We've turned the knob on Searle's intuition pump that controls the level of description of the program being followed. There are always many levels. At the highest level, the comprehending powers of the system are not unimaginable; we even get insight into just how the system comes to understand what it does. The system's reply no longer looks embarrassing; it looks obviously correct. That doesn't mean that AI of the sort Searle was criticizing actually achieves a level of competence worth calling understanding, nor that those methods, extended in the ways then imagined by those AI researchers, would likely have led to such high competences, but just that Searle's thought experiment doesn't succeed in what it claims to accomplish: demonstrating the flat-out impossibility of Strong AI.

There are other knobs to turn, but that task has been carried out extensively in the huge literature the Chinese Room has provoked. Here I am concentrating on the thinking tool itself, not the theories and propositions it was aimed at, and showing that it is a defective tool: it persuades by clouding our imagination, not exploiting it well.

61. THE TELECLONE FALL FROM MARS TO EARTH

You see the moon rise in the east. You see the moon rise in the west. You watch two moons moving toward each other across the cold black sky, one soon to pass behind the other as they continue on their way. You are on Mars, millions of miles from home, protected from the killing, frostless cold of the red Martian desert by fragile membranes of terrestrial technology—protected but stranded, for your spaceship has broken down beyond repair. You will never ever return to Earth, to the friends and family and places you left behind.

But perhaps there is hope. In the communication compartment of the disabled craft, you find a Teleclone Mark IV teleporter and instructions for its use. If you turn the teleporter on, tune its beam to the Teleclone receiver on Earth, and then step into the sending chamber, the teleporter will swiftly and painlessly dismantle your body, producing a molecule-by-molecule blueprint to be beamed to Earth, where the receiver, its reservoirs well stocked with the requisite atoms, will almost instantaneously produce—from the beamed instructions—you! Whisked back to Earth at the speed of light, into the arms of your loved ones, who will soon be listening with rapt attention to your tales of adventures on Mars.

One last survey of the damaged spaceship convinces you that the Teleclone is your only hope. With nothing to lose, you set the transmitter up, flip the right switches, and step into the chamber. Five, four, three, two, one, FLASH! You open the door in front of you and step out of the Teleclone receiver chamber into the sunny, familiar atmosphere of Earth. You've come home, none the worse for wear after your long-distance Teleclone fall from Mars. Your narrow escape from a terrible fate on the red planet calls for a celebration, and as your family and friends gather around, you notice how everyone has changed since last you saw them. It has been almost three years, after all, and you've all grown older. Look at Sarah, your daughter, who must now be eight and a half. You find yourself thinking, "Can this be the little girl who used to sit on my lap?" Of course it is, you reflect, even though you must admit that you do not so much recognize her as extrapolate from memory and deduce her identity. She is so much taller, looks so much older, and knows so much more. In fact, most of the cells now in her body were not there when last you cast eyes on her. But in spite of growth and change, in spite of replacement of cells, she's the same little person you kissed good-bye three years ago.

Then it hits you: "Am I, really, the same person who kissed this little girl good-bye three years ago? Am I this eight-year-old child's mother or am I actually a brand new human being, only several hours old, in spite of my memories—or apparent memories—of days and years before that?" Did this child's mother recently die on Mars, dismantled and destroyed in the chamber of a Teleclone Mark IV?

Did I die on Mars? No, certainly *I* did not die on Mars, since I am alive on Earth. Perhaps, though, *someone* died on Mars—Sarah's mother. Then I am not Sarah's mother. But I must be! The whole point of getting into the Teleclone was to return home to my family. But I keep forgetting; maybe *I* never got into that Teleclone on Mars. Maybe that was someone else—if it ever happened at all.

Is that infernal machine a tele*porter*—a mode of transportation—or, as the brand name suggests, a sort of murdering twinmaker? Did Sarah's mother survive the experience with the Teleclone or not? She thought she was going to. She entered the chamber with hope and anticipation, not suicidal resignation. Her act was altruistic, to be sure—she was taking steps to provide Sarah with a loved one to protect her—but also selfish—she was getting herself out of a jam and into something pleasant. Or so it seemed. "How do *I* know that's how it seemed? Because I was *there*; I *was* Sarah's mother thinking those thoughts. I *am* Sarah's mother. Or so it seems."

A song or a poem or a movie can undoubtedly be teleported. Is a self the sort of thing—a thing "made of information"—that can be teleported without loss? Is our reluctance to admit the teleportation of people a bit like the anachronistic resistance, recently overcome in most quarters, to electronically scanned legal signatures on documents? (I learned in 2011 that Harvard University's Society of Fellows would not accept a scanned signature on my letter of recommendation; they required some dry ink that had actually been laid down by the motion of my actual hand, and it took me half a day of riding around in taxis in Beirut to get, sign, and express-mail back the relevant form—on cream-colored bond paper. It is my understanding that the Society has now changed its policy, but I hope Harvard still insists on putting wax seals on their diplomas. There is a place for tradition, in all its glorious gratuitousness.)

62. THE SELF AS THE CENTER OF NARRATIVE GRAVITY

What is a self? Philosophers have been grappling with this question for centuries. The Christian concept of an immortal soul, immaterial and inexplicable, captivated thinkers and deflected serious investigation for centuries, but it is losing adherents daily. The idea of a mind-thingy that goes to Heaven when somebody dies grows more incoherent every day. The wishful thinking that prevents us from just discarding it, along with the goblins and witches, is only too apparent. So those of us who are materialists, confident that the mind is the brain (properly understood), have to confront the question of why it *seems* that each of us has some such mind-thingy, or better: that each of us *is* some such mind-thingy inhabiting a body, and more particularly a brain. Do we simply find our selves when we look inside?

David Hume famously disparaged this idea in 1739:

> For my part, when I enter most intimately into what I call *myself*, I always stumble on some particular perception or other, of heat or cold, light or shade, love or hatred, pain or pleasure. I never can catch *myself* at any time without a perception. . . . If anyone, upon serious and unprejudiced reflection, thinks he has a different notion of *himself*, I must confess I can reason no longer with him. All I can allow him is, that he may be in the right as well as I, and that we are essentially different in this particular. He may, perhaps, perceive something simple and continued, which he calls *himself*; though I am certain there is no such principle in me. [1964, I, iv, sect. 6]

Hume's tongue-in-cheek acknowledgment that others may be different echoes to this day among those who muse about whether I, for instance, am a zombie (a zimbo, of course) innocently extrapolating from my own impoverished experience to how it is with others. An amusing conjecture, but I don't think anybody takes it seriously.

It is clear what a self isn't. It isn't a part of the brain, like the amygdala or hippocampus. The frontal lobes play a crucial role in evaluating situations, intentions, perceptions, and the like, but I don't think anybody has made the mistake of *locating the self* in the frontal lobes. (A prefrontal lobotomy is a dire surgery, leaving behind someone who really is "a shadow of his former self," but it isn't a self-ectomy. As the old joke has it, I'd rather have a free bottle in front of me than a prefrontal lobotomy, but in either case I'd be there to experience it.) Then what might the self be? I propose that it is the same *kind* of thing as a center of gravity, an abstraction that is, in spite of its abstractness, tightly coupled to the physical world. You, like every other material object, have a center of gravity (or more properly a center of mass, but we'll ignore that nicety here). If you are top-heavy, your center of gravity is higher than average for people of your height, you have to work harder to stay upright, and so forth. There are many ways of locating your center of gravity, which, depending on such factors as the shoes you have on and when you last ate a meal, moves around in a smallish area in the middle of your body. It is a mathematical point, not an atom or molecule. The center of gravity of a length of steel pipe is not made of steel and indeed is not made of anything. It is a point in space, the point on the midline running through the center of the pipe that is equidistant from the ends (roughly, depending on imperfections, etc.).

The concept of a center of gravity is a very useful thinking tool in its own right. In effect it averages over all the gravitational attractions between every particle of matter in a thing and every particle of matter on the planet, and tells us that we can boil all that down to two points—the center of the earth (its center of gravity) and the center of gravity of the thing—and calculate the behavior of the thing under varying conditions. For instance, if a thing's center of gravity at any time falls outside all the points of its supporting base, it will topple.

Of course, we had an intuitive understanding of centers of gravity long before Newton figured out gravity. ("Sit down! You're rocking the boat.") Now we can explain how and why the concept works in detail, and if we're designing vehicles or floor lamps, for example, the goal of lowering a center of gravity, or moving it to a more effective location, shows the near indispensability of the concept in many of our activities. It may be a "theorist's fiction," but it is a very valuable fiction from which a lot of true predictions can be generated. Can such an abstract entity, having no material existence, actually *cause* anything? Not directly, but explanations that cite a center of gravity compete with explanations that are clearly causal. Why didn't that coffee mug tip over when the sailboat heeled so drastically? "Because it has an unusually low center of gravity" competes with "Because it is glued to the deck."

We may call a center of gravity a theorist's *fiction* because it shares with fictional characters the curious property of indeterminacy of properties. Sherlock Holmes, as described by Arthur Conan Doyle in the Sherlock Holmes mystery stories, has many properties, but where Conan Doyle was silent, there is no fact of the matter. We can extrapolate a bit: The author never mentions Sherlock having a third nostril, so we are entitled to assume that he didn't (Lewis, 1978). We can also agree that he was not a bigamist with one wife in Paris and another in New York. But for many such questions there is no answer: Did he have a mole on his left shoulder blade? Was he a first cousin of Oscar Wilde? Did he own a cottage in Scotland? These questions and kazillions more about any *real* human being must have true answers, even if we can never discover them. Not so for Sherlock; being fictional he has only properties his author says or implies that he has. A naïve reader who thinks the Sherlock Holmes stories are true might wonder whether the conductor on the train to Aldershot was taller or shorter than Holmes, but if you understand what fiction is, you know better than to ask. The same is true of centers of gravity. If you wondered whether they might eventually "turn out to be neutrinos," you would be missing the point of them as theorist's fictions.

What then is a center of *narrative* gravity? It is also a theorist's fiction, posited in order to unify and make sense of an otherwise bafflingly complex collection of actions, utterances, fidgets, complaints, promises, and so forth, that make up a person. It is the organizer of the **personal level** of explanation. Your hand didn't sign the contract; you did. Your mouth didn't tell the lie; you did. Your brain doesn't remember Paris; you do. You are the "owner of record" of the living body we recognize as you. (As we say, it's your body to do with what you like.) In the same way that we can simplify all the gravitational attractions between all the parts of the world and an obelisk standing on the ground by boiling it down to two points, the center of the earth and the center of gravity of the obelisk, we can simplify all the interactions—the handshakes, the spoken words, the ink scrawls, and much more—between two selves, the seller and the buyer, who have just completed a transaction. Each self is a person, with a biography, a "backstory," and many ongoing projects. Unlike centers of gravity, selves don't just have trajectories through space and time; they gather as they go, accumulating memories and devising plans and expectations.

There are parts of the backstory that each person would probably wish to disavow, but what's done is done; that part of the narrative cannot be revised. It can be reinterpreted, however, in the light of later biographical elements. "I wasn't myself when I did that," is a familiar refrain, and our tolerance for this apparently self-contradictory claim is often wise. What the person means is that he was in an extreme "out of character" state when he did that, and he is imploring us not to judge him in the present or extrapolate from that behavior into the future. Sometimes this is very plausible, sometimes not. Another familiar move: "Well, if you didn't do that, who did?" "The devil made me do it." Again, we often accept this claim, not on its face value, but as a sincere disavowal of the character and motivations that guided the action. This raises issues about responsibility and free will that we will tackle in the next chapter; just note, for now, how we need the concept of the self to draw a line (however arbitrary it may often turn out to be) between what you *do* and what happens to you.

Every physical object has a center of gravity and every living human body has a self, or rather, every living human body is owned by a self, a sort of live-in manager. Only one owner? Could a body be shared by two or more selves? The condition known as dissociative identity disorder (it used to be called multiple personality disorder) is apparently an example of many selves sharing a single body, with a dominant self (the "host") and a group of "alters." I say "apparently" because controversy rages about the diagnosis, running from outright fraud through *folie à deux* (in which a naïve psychiatrist unintentionally encourages a troubled patient to develop the symptoms) to acceptance of a few rare and genuine cases surrounded by various flavors of *wannabes*. After studying the phenomenon (and the people studying and treating the phenomenon) for several years, psychologist Nicholas Humphrey and I (1989) decided that everyone is right! There are frauds, exaggerations, gullible therapists with eager patients, and yes, a few cases in which the condition seems to have existed in at least rudimentary form prior to any elaboration at the hands of a fascinated interlocutor. This is not surprising, when we recognize that it is an intensification of something quite normal that we all experience to various degrees. Most of us lead several fairly distinct lives, at work, at home, at play, and acquire habits and memories in each context that turn out not to travel well to other contexts.

As sociologist Erving Goffman (1959) recounted in his classic book on the subject, *The Presentation of Self in Everyday Life*, we all engage in presenting ourselves as characters in real-life dramas (Professor Dennett, Dan from up the road, Dad, Grandpa, etc.), and we effortlessly enlist the help of the supporting cast, who are similarly presenting themselves. We feed each other lines we can handle readily, becoming complicit in each other's campaign of self-presentation, or we can disrupt these smoothly running scenarios by playing out of character, with results that are awkward, comic, or worse. It takes nerves of steel to do this. Can you imagine asking a person newly introduced to you at a party to show you some identification, a driver's license, perhaps, or a passport—or, heading in the other direction, attempting to give her a passionate embrace? When people are put in extremely difficult positions, they sometimes adopt extreme measures, and what starts out as feigning in desperation becomes almost second nature. When the going gets tough, you simply *depart*, leaving behind a different center of narrative gravity, a different character, better equipped to deal with the problem at hand.

Humphrey and I learned that when you interview a putative sufferer of dissociative identity disorder, expect to find a naïve virtuoso in the art of deflecting obtrusive inquiry. To raise the questions that cry out for answers* or—better—to set little traps to see whether one alter really doesn't have any memories of what the other alter was doing and saying, you will have to be downright rude, and risk giving serious offense, so in all likelihood you will find yourself politely going along with the gag, an accomplice enlisted without so much as a wink. Con artists do this deliberately, with great skill, but so do innocent victims of this personality disorder, without any recognition of what they are doing. So do we all, to one degree or another. But *their* alters are just fictional characters, right? The *real* person is the host, right? Well, it isn't quite that straightforward.

That thing that is *you*, the person you play, whether you play multiple roles or really just one monolithic role, is your center of narrative gravity. It is how your friends recognize you ("You're not yourself today!"), and how you see yourself for the most part, but it is also somewhat idealized ("Oh my God! Did *I* do that? *I* would never do that!"). Professional novelists, like con artists, create narratives with cunning and deliberate attention to the details. The rest of us are talented amateurs, spinning our tales cleverly but (in the main) unwittingly, rather the way a spider spins a web. It is nature, not art.

---

* Such as: How do you folks decide who is host and who are alters? How have you explained to yourself that your memory of recent experiences consists of brief episodes of *being there* surrounded by hours or days of oblivion? Doesn't that strike you as alarming?

It is not so much that *we,* using our brains, spin our yarns, as that our brains, using yarns, spin *us.* There is a core of undeniable true biography, to be sure, but over the years large parts of it become as good as gone, inert and of no relevance to who you are now. Some of it you may actively disavow, jettison, "forget," in the process of self-maintenance and self-improvement.*

Consider how easily you can answer some questions about your past. Have you ever danced with a movie star? Have you ever been to Paris? Have you ever ridden a camel? Have you ever strangled somebody to death with your bare hands? These are easy for almost all of us, whether the answer is yes or no. (Imagine someone who was asked the last question and who paused, thoughtfully, scratching his chin, before answering. Give him a wide berth!) We know the answers to these questions because we know enough about ourselves—our *selves*—to know that had we ever danced with a movie star, been to Paris, ridden a camel, or strangled someone, we'd now be recollecting it. When "nothing comes to mind," we interpret this absence as a negative. (How else could we be so sure? Do you keep a list of all the things you've never done? All the places you've never been?) Contrast those questions with these superficially similar questions: Have you ever danced with a person named Smith? Have you ever been to a drug store that sold floor polish? Have you ever ridden in a blue Chevrolet? Have you ever broken a white coffee mug? Some may be easy to answer, and others may lead you to say you have no idea, and some may inspire you to give false answers without realizing it, just because they are so unimportant. Why would you remember it if you had done any of these things? A lot that has happened to us is just not memorable; a lot of things that we have done, good and bad, have been shed by our centers of narrative gravity; and a lot that

---

* In T. S. Eliot's verse play, *Murder in the Cathedral,* Becket is asked about an event in his past and he replies:

> *You talk of seasons that are past. I remember*
> *Not worth forgetting.*

never happened has been added, innocently enough, because for one reason or another it just fits us to a *t*. What you are is that rolling sum of experience and talent, solemn intention and daydreaming fantasy, bound together in one brain and body and called by a given name. The idea that there is, in addition, a special indissoluble nugget of *you*, or ego, or spirit, or soul, is an attractive fantasy, but nothing that we need in order to make sense of people, their dreams and hopes, their heroism and their sins.

This center of narrative gravity may not be a mysterious nugget of mind stuff, but if it is just an abstraction, can it be studied scientifically? Yes, it can.

63. HETEROPHENOMENOLOGY

Heterophenomenology is not an intuition pump, but another example of *staging* that is well worth putting in place before we tackle some difficult questions. The study of human consciousness involves phenomena that at first glance seem to occur in something rather like another dimension: the private, subjective, "first-person" dimension that each of us occupies with regard to our own consciousness, and to which nobody else can gain direct access. What, then, is the relation between the standard "third-person" objective methodologies for studying meteors or magnets (or human metabolism or bone density), and the methodologies for studying human consciousness? Do we have to create some radical or revolutionary alternative science, or can the standard methods be extended in such a way as to do justice to the phenomena of human consciousness? I defend the claim that there is a straightforward, conservative extension of objective science that handsomely covers *all* the ground of human consciousness, doing justice to all the data without ever having to abandon the rules and constraints of the experimental methods that have worked so well in the rest of science. This third-person methodology, heterophenomenology (phenomenology of an *other* not oneself), is the sound way to take the *first*-person point of view as seriously as it can legitimately be taken.

Why the multisyllabic name? "Phenomenology" originally meant a catalogue of phenomena, of one sort or another, before there is a good theory of them. In the sixteenth century, William Gilbert compiled a good phenomenology of magnetism, but it was centuries before all the magnetic phenomena he carefully described could be explained. In the early twentieth century, Edmund Husserl, and a group of psychologists and philosophers influenced by him, adopted the term, "Phenomenology" (with a capital "P"), for a presumably scientific study of the phenomena of subjective experience, to be observed using a "first-person" introspective method that attempted to be theory-neutral and without presuppositions. The school of thought continues to this day, embattled or ignored for the most part, for reasons good and bad. In spite of some very tantalizing results, well worth further exploration, as a first-person approach it has been shunned by objective, empirical science, which insists on data that can be accessible to all investigators. But we can study consciousness objectively, and the method is really just a simple twist on Phenomenology, so I call it heterophenomenology, to contrast it with Husserlian *autophenomenology*. Heterophenomenology is the study of first-person phenomena from the third-person point of view of objective science.

Obviously the key difference between experiments with rocks, roses, and rats on the one hand, and experiments with awake, cooperative human subjects on the other, is that the latter can communicate in language and hence can collaborate with experimenters, by making suggestions, interacting verbally, and telling them what it is like under various controlled conditions. That is the core of heterophenomenology: it exploits our capacity to *perform* and *interpret* speech acts, yielding a catalogue of *what the subject believes to be true about his or her conscious experience*. This catalogue of beliefs fleshes out the subject's *heterophenomenological world*, the world according to S, the subjective world of one subject. The total set of details of heterophenomenology, plus all the data we can gather about concurrent events in the brains of subjects and in the surrounding environment, comprise the total data set a theory of human consciousness must explain. It leaves out no objective phenomena and no subjective phenomena of consciousness.

The interpretation required to turn *raw* data about speech sounds and button pressings into reports and expressions of beliefs involves adopting the **intentional stance**: it requires the working hypothesis that the subject is an agent whose actions are rationally guided by beliefs and desires that are themselves rational, given the subject's perceptual history and needs. For instance, the constraints of the intentional stance can be clearly discerned in the standard precautions taken in such experiments to prevent subjects from having experiences that might give them either beliefs or desires that would tend to bias their responses in ways that would distort our interpretation of their actions: we keep them in the dark about what we hope they will say, for instance, while at the same time taking steps to assure ourselves that they understand the tasks we set them. This adoption of the intentional stance is not an irreparably subjective and relativistic affair. Rules of interpretation can be articulated; standards of intersubjective agreement on interpretation can be set and met; deviations can be identified; the unavoidable assumption of rationality can be cautiously couched and treated as an adjustable, defensible, and evolutionarily explicable assumption. (The details of these processes are articulated in Dennett, 1991a.)

This is not a proposal for a new methodology for studying consciousness. I am just being self-conscious about the standard methods already adopted by researchers in cognitive psychology, psychophysics (which studies the relationships between physical stimuli and subjective reactions), and neuroscience, and explaining and defending them. These methods, correctly understood and followed, obviate the need for any radical or revolutionary "first-person" science of consciousness, and leave no residual phenomena of consciousness inaccessible to controlled scientific study.

What kinds of things does this methodology commit us to? Beyond the unproblematic things all of science is committed to (neurons and electrons, clocks and microscopes), it commits us just to *beliefs*—the beliefs expressed by subjects and deemed constitutive of their subjectivity—and to *desires*—the desires to cooperate with the experimenters, and to tell them the truth as candidly as possible. (An important part of the method involves controlling these beliefs and desires, and any experimental result that shows evidence of failure to do this must be discarded.) What kind of things are beliefs and desires? We may stay maximally noncommittal about this—pending the confirmation of theory—by treating beliefs and their contents or objects as *theorists' fictions* or *abstractions* similar to centers of mass, the equator, and parallelograms of forces.

Mermaid-sightings are real events, however misdescribed, whereas mermaids don't exist. Similarly, a catalogue of beliefs about experience is not the same as a catalogue of experiences themselves. Philosopher Joseph Levine (1994, p. 117) has objected that "conscious experiences themselves, not merely our verbal judgments about them, are the primary data to which a theory must answer." This can't be right. How, in advance of theory, could we catalogue the experiences themselves? Consider the evidence we get from putting subjects into experimental situations and querying them (and asking them to perform whatever other actions we want them to perform). These sources are naturally nested by the cascade of interpretations we have to perform, ranked here from least raw to most raw:

(a) "conscious experiences themselves"
(b) beliefs about these conscious experiences
(c) the "verbal judgments" Levine mentions
(d) the utterances of one sort or another that (can be interpreted to) express those verbal judgments

In one sense of "primary," the utterances are primary data—recorded sounds and motions. Electroencephalographic (EEG) readings and functional magnetic resonance imaging (fMRI) readings and the like can be added to the primary data, as circumstances permit. Reliable methods of interpretation can take us to (c) and (b), so we have a catalogue of subjects' beliefs about what it is like to be them under these conditions. But should we push on to (a) in advance of theory? This is not a good idea, for two reasons.

First, if (a) outruns (b)—if you have conscious experiences you don't believe you have, then those extra conscious experiences are just as inaccessible *to you* as to the external observers.

So Levine's proposed alternative garners no more usable data than heterophenomenology does.

> Second, if (b) outruns (a)—if you believe you have conscious experiences that you don't in fact have, then it is your beliefs that we need to explain, not the nonexistent experiences.

Sticking to the heterophenomenological standard, then, and treating (b) as the maximal set of *primary* data, is the way to avoid any commitment to spurious data, while ensuring that all phenomena accessible to *anybody* get included.

What if some beliefs are inexpressible in verbal judgments? There is nothing to prevent heterophenomenologists and subjects from collaborating on devising analogue or other nonlinguistic modes of belief expression. For instance,

> Draw a vertical line across the line segment indicating how intense [in one dimension or another] the experience is:

> Barely noticeable————————————Overpowering

Or subjects can press a button with variable pressure to indicate severity of pain (or anxiety or boredom or even distrust in the experiment). Then there are a host of physiological dependent variables to measure, from galvanic skin response and heart rate to changes in facial expression and posture. And if you, the subject, believe that there are *still* ineffable residues unconveyed after exhausting such methods, you can tell this to the heterophenomenologists, who can add that belief to the list of beliefs in your primary data:

> S claims that he has ineffable beliefs about X.

If this belief is true, then science has the obligation to explain what such beliefs are and why they are ineffable. If this belief is false, science still has to explain why S believes (falsely) that there are these particular ineffable beliefs.*

---

* The defense of heterophenomenology as the methodology of choice for the scientific study of consciousness has occasioned substantial controversy. Some researchers regard it as a game-changing clarification of the conditions under which science can study consciousness, some regard it as just rehearsing the obvious, and still others continue to object. See Sources for references to some of the best work on this that has appeared to date.

64. MARY THE COLOR SCIENTIST: A BOOM CRUTCH UNVEILED

Australian philosopher Frank Jackson's thought experiment about Mary the color scientist, often called "the Knowledge Argument," has been pumping philosophers' intuitions with remarkable vigor since it first appeared in 1982. For sheer volume and reliability, this must count as one of the most successful intuition pumps ever devised by an analytical philosopher. It is a classic, perennially on the list of required reading in undergraduate courses in the philosophy of mind all over the English-speaking world, and several weighty anthologies have been devoted to essays reflecting on its implications. It is interesting to note that its author has subsequently recanted, declaring that he no longer accepts its conclusion—but that has not diminished its popularity.

Here it is in its entirety, drawn slightly out of context perhaps, but still clear as can be:

Mary is a brilliant scientist who is, for whatever reason, forced to investigate the world from a black and white room *via* a black and white television monitor. She specializes in the neurophysiology of vision and acquires, let us suppose, all the physical information there is to obtain about what goes on when we see ripe tomatoes, or the sky, and use terms like "red", "blue", and so on. She discovers, for example, just which wavelength combinations from the sky stimulate the retina, and exactly how this produces *via* the central nervous system the contraction of the vocal chords and expulsion of air from the lungs that results in the uttering of the sentence "The sky is blue". (It can hardly be denied that it is in principle possible to obtain all this physical information from black and white television, otherwise the Open University would *of necessity* need to use color television.) What will happen when Mary is released from her black and white room or is given a color television monitor? Will she *learn* anything or not? It seems just obvious that she will learn something about the world and our visual experience of it. But then it is inescapable that her previous knowledge was incomplete. But she had *all* the physical information. *Ergo* there is more to have than that, and Physicalism [i.e., materialism, the denial of dualism] is false. [Jackson, 1982, p. 130]

Is it a good intuition pump? Let's turn all the knobs and see what makes it work. Actually, that would take us too long, but the job has been done, in the sizable literature on the topic. Here I will simply illustrate a few knobs that need to be examined, and leave the result as an exercise for you. (If you want, you can check your own results against the literature; two recent anthologies are referenced in Sources. Can you come up with a new twist?) More than twenty years ago, I conducted a preliminary exploration of the knobs, and issued a killjoy verdict that has been largely dismissed or disregarded: "Like a good thought experiment, its point is immediately evident even to the uninitiated. In fact it is a bad thought experiment, an intuition pump that actually encourages us to misunderstand its premises!" (Dennett, 1991a, p. 398). Let's see if this is so. I claim that it is much more difficult to imagine the scenario correctly than people suppose, so they imagine something easier, and draw their conclusions from that mistaken base.

First knob: "a black and white room *via* a black and white television monitor."

Presumably she wears black or white gloves and is forbidden to look at herself when she bathes, but the idea of cutting off all "external sources" of color is forlorn in any case. Would we have to rig some device that prevented her from rubbing her eyes (to create "phos-phenes"—try it)? And couldn't she have colors in her dreams before actually seeing them? If not, why not? Do the colors have to "get in via the eyes" before she can "store" them in her brain? A tangle of bad folk theory of color lies behind this simple suggestion.

> Second knob: she "acquires, let us suppose, all the physical information there is to obtain about what goes on when we see ripe tomatoes, or the sky, and use terms like 'red', 'blue', and so on."

All the physical information there is to obtain? How much is that? Is that like having all the money in the world? What would that be like? It's not easy to imagine, and nothing less than all will serve to make the thought experiment's intended point. It must include all the information about all the variation in responses in all the brains, including her own, especially including all the emotional or affective reactions to all the colors under all conditions. So she will know in exquisite detail which colors calm her, annoy her, would grow on her with exposure, distract her, repel her, and so on. Is she forbidden to perform experiments on herself (without cheating, without smuggling any colored things into her cell)? If you didn't imagine all this (and more), you didn't follow directions. It's like being asked to conceive of a chiliagon and imagining a circle instead. Lots of implications follow from one of these exercises of mental representation that don't follow from the other. In this case, for instance, are we supposed to ignore the fact that if Mary acquired all this information, she would no doubt be in a state of total mental collapse, burdened with thousands of encyclopedia articles and diagrams?

If Jackson had stipulated that Mary had the God-like property of being "physically omniscient"—not just about color but about every physical fact at every level from the quark to the galaxy—many if not all readers would resist, saying that imagining such a feat is just too fantastical to take seriously. But stipulating that Mary knows *merely* all the physical facts *about color vision* is not substantially less fantastical.

"Imagine that Mary has a billion heads. . . ."
"Don't be silly!"
"Ok. Make it a million heads. . . ."
"No problem!" (Really?)

In an earlier attempt to dramatize this problem of imagination, I encouraged people to consider a variant ending:

And so, one day, Mary's captors decided it was time for her to see colors. As a trick, they prepared a bright blue banana to present as her first color experience ever. Mary took one look at it and said "Hey! You tried to trick me! Bananas are yellow, but this one is blue!" Her captors were dumfounded. How did she do it? "Simple," she replied. "You have to remember that I know *everything*—absolutely everything—that could ever be known about the physical causes and effects of color vision. So of course before you brought the banana in, I had already written down, in exquisite detail, exactly what physical impression a yellow object or a blue object (or a green object, etc.) would make on my nervous system. So I already knew exactly what *thoughts* I would have (because, after all, the 'mere disposition' to think about this or that is not one of your famous qualia, is it?). I was not in the slightest surprised by my experience of blue (what surprised me was that you would try such a second-rate trick on me). I realize it is *hard for you to imagine* that I could know so much about my reactive dispositions that the way blue affected me came as no surprise. Of course it's hard for you to imagine. It's hard for anyone to imagine the consequences of someone knowing absolutely everything physical about anything!'" [Dennett, 1991a, pp. 399–400]

It is standardly assumed that things could not proceed this way. As Jackson disarmingly put it, "It seems just obvious that she will learn something about the world and our visual experience of it." Or as George Graham and Terry Horgan (2000, p. 72) say, "**Surely**, [ding!], we submit, she should be both surprised and delighted." That is a mistake, and that is what is wrong with Mary as a thought experiment. It just feels so good to conclude that Mary has a revelation of *some* sort when she first sees color that nobody wants to bother showing that this is how the story must go. In fact, it needn't go that way at all.

Jackson's intuition pump excellently exposes to the light a lot of naïve thinking about the nature of color experience and the brain that no doubt serves people well most of the time, so we might grant that he nicely draws out some of the implications of folk theory. But his aim was to refute a hypothesis about the capacity of the physical sciences to account for all color phenomena. Of course in any real-world situation, somebody in Mary's imagined position would learn something new because however much she knew about color, there would be lots of facts about physical effects of color she didn't know. It is only the stipulated extreme case that makes Jackson's "just obvious" and Graham and Horgan's "surely" out of place. If you are still inclined to think that my suggested alternative ending of the story would have to be impossible, see if you can work out an argued reason for your belief. It would be interesting to see if you come up with a consideration that has escaped the hundreds of philosophers who have labored over this for years. (Of course, that very fact might be taken to show that this is after all a wonderful intuition pump: it has provided employment for philosophers for three decades.)

SUMMARY

A besetting problem for the scientific study of consciousness has been the fact that *everybody* is an expert! Not really, of course, but just about everybody who has reflected for more than a few minutes on the topic seems to think the deliverances of those reflections are as authoritative as the results of any high-tech experiment or any mountain of statistics. It can be downright comical to hear them during the question-and-answer sessions at scientific conferences firmly *correcting* the *mistakes* they have just detected in the presenter's work, by citing a recent experience they (think they) had. If we were, as these people typically think, infallible judges of the nature of our own personal experiences, they would be right!

But you *can* misremember, misinterpret, misdescribe your own most intimate experiences, covertly driven by some persuasive but unreliable bit of ideology. Here is a simple demonstration you can perform at home that may surprise you. Sit in front of a mirror so you can monitor your own compliance with the directions, which are to stare intently into your own eyes, fixating on them as a target instead of letting your eyes get attracted to peripheral goings-on. Now, without looking, take a card from the middle of a well-shuffled deck of cards and hold it, *face-side toward you,* at arm's length just outside the boundaries of your peripheral vision. Wiggle the card. You will know you are doing it, but you won't see it, of course. Start moving the card into your field of view, wiggling it as you do so. First you can see motion (the wiggling) *but no color!* You can't tell whether it's a red card or a black card or a face card, and you certainly can't identify its number. As you move it more and more centrally, you will be amazed at how close to straight ahead it has to be for you to identify its color, or the fact that it is a face card or not. As the card gets closer and closer to your fixation point, you must concentrate on not cheating, stealing a glance at the card as it moves in. When you are finally able to identify the card, it is almost directly in front of you. Surprising? I don't know anybody who wasn't surprised the first time they experienced this. Here you've thought all along that your vision was roughly equally detailed and colored "all the way out to the periphery," and now you learn that although that seems to "stand to reason," and seems confirmed by casual introspection, it is simply not true. This is just one dimension, one phenomenon among many, in which the apparently rich, continuous, detailed presentation of the world in our (visual) consciousness is an illusion. The moral is unmistakable: don't think you understand the phenomena of consciousness until you see what science has discovered about it in recent years. The armchair theories of philosophers who ignore this moral are negligible at best and more often deeply confused and confusing. What you "learn" about your consciousness "through introspection" is a minor but powerfully misleading portion of what *we* can learn about *your* consciousness by adopting the heterophenomenological framework and studying consciousness systematically.

There are still difficulties aplenty in need of resolution, hard problems that are not the Hard Problem. If when we have solved all these "easy" problems there is still a deeply mysterious residue, it will then be time to reconsider our starting point and cast about for some radical departure from current assumptions about biology, physics, and even logic. In the meantime, let's see how far we can get with business-as-usual science, the science that has brought us our current understanding of everything from asteroids and plate tectonics to reproduction, growth, repair, and metabolism in living things.

VIII.
TOOLS FOR THINKING ABOUT FREE WILL

The chasm between **the manifest image** and **the scientific image** is at its most treacherous when the topic is free will. Like the questions of what color is, what it *really* is, and what dollars are, *really*, when you get right down to it the question of whether free will is an illusion or something we actually have invites us to use the scientific image to investigate this issue, which is posed in the traditional terms of the manifest image. And the invitation has been enthusiastically accepted in recent years. There has been quite a chorus of eminent scientists saying, point blank, that free will is an illusion: neuroscientists Wolf Singer, Chris Frith, and Patrick Haggard; psychologists Paul Bloom and Daniel Wegner; and a few rather well-regarded physicists, Stephen Hawking and Albert Einstein. Could so many brilliant scientists be wrong? Many—not all, and maybe not most—philosophers say yes. They say this *is* a job for philosophy! Are they right? I think so.

The scientists have typically been making a rookie mistake: confusing the manifest image with what we might call the *folk ideology* of the manifest image. The folk ideology of color is, let's face it, bonkers; color just isn't what most people think it is, but that doesn't mean that the manifest world doesn't really have any colors; it means that colors—real colors—are quite different from what most folks think they are. The folk ideology of consciousness is also bonkers—

resolutely dualistic and mysterian; if *that* were what consciousness had to be, then Wright would be right (see p. 313): we'd have to say that consciousness doesn't exist. But we don't have to treat consciousness as "real magic"—the kind that doesn't exist, made of **wonder tissue**; we can recognize the reality of consciousness as a phenomenon by acknowledging that folks don't yet have a sound ideology about it. Similarly, free will isn't what some of the *folk ideology* of the manifest image proclaims it to be, a sort of magical isolation from causation. I've compared free will in this sense to levitation, and one of the philosophical defenders of this bonkers vision has frankly announced that a free choice is a "little miracle." I wholeheartedly agree with the scientific chorus that *that* sort of free will is an illusion, but that doesn't mean that free will is an illusion in any morally important sense. It is as real as colors, as real as dollars.

Unfortunately, some of the scientists who now declare that science has shown that free will is an illusion go on to say that this "discovery" matters, in a morally important sense. They think it has major implications for morality and the law: nobody is ever *really* responsible, for instance, so nobody ever *deserves* to be either punished or praised. They are making the mistake people make when they say that nothing is ever solid, not *really*. They are using an unreconstructed popular concept of free will, when they should be adjusting it first, the way they do with color and consciousness (and space and time and solidity and all the other things that the *ideology* of the manifest image gets wrong).

The intuition pumps in this part are designed to wean you from that ideology about free will and get you to see a better concept, the concept of real free will, practical free will, the phenomenon in the manifest image that matters. The controversies that have swirled around the topic of free will for several millennia are too many and too tangled to be settled in any one part or book, but we have to start somewhere, and these are thinking tools that work rather like crowbars, jimmying you out of well-worn ruts into rather new terrain with better perspectives. The first is designed to show why this is such an important task.

65. A TRULY NEFARIOUS NEUROSURGEON

We are at the dawn of neurosurgical treatment of debilitating psychological conditions. Deep brain stimulation by implanted electrodes
is showing striking effects in treating obsessive-compulsive disorder
(OCD), for instance, as reported in a pioneering study by neuropsy-
chiatrist Damiaan Denys and his colleagues (2010) in Amsterdam.
That is fact, but this is fiction: One day a brilliant neurosurgeon said
to a patient on whom she had just performed an implantation procedure in her shiny high-tech operating theater:

> The device I've implanted doesn't just control your OCD; it
> controls your every decision, thanks to our master control
> system, which maintains radio contact with your microchip
> twenty-four hours a day. In other words, I've disabled your
> conscious will; your sense of free will henceforth will be an
> illusion.

In fact she had done no such thing; this was simply a lie she decided
to tell her patient to see what would happen. It worked; the poor
fellow went out into the world convinced that he was not a responsible agent, but rather a mere puppet, and his behavior began to show
it: he became irresponsible, aggressive, and negligent, indulging his
worst whims until he got caught and put on trial. Testifying in his
own defense, he passionately protested his non-responsibility because
of the implant in his brain, and the neuroscientist, when called to
testify, admitted what she had said, and added, "But I was just mess-
ing with his head—a practical joke, that's all. I never thought he'd
believe me!"

It really doesn't matter whether the court believed his testimony
or hers, whether it sentenced him or her; either way she ruined his
life with her ill-considered assertion, robbing him of his integrity

and crippling his power to make decisions. In fact, her false "debriefing" of her patient actually accomplished nonsurgically much of what she claimed to accomplish surgically: she disabled him. But if she is responsible for this dire consequence, the neuroscientists currently filling the media with talk about how their science shows that free will is an illusion are risking mass-production of the same harm to all the people who take them at their word.* Neuroscientists, psychologists, and philosophers need to take seriously their moral obligation to think through the presuppositions and implications of their public pronouncements on these issues with the same care that is demanded of people who hold forth on global warming or impending asteroid strikes. For just one example, consider the message that wily social critic and observer Tom Wolfe (2000 p. 100) finds in the pronouncements of these neuroscientists:

> The conclusion people out beyond the laboratory walls are
> drawing is:
> *The fix is in! We're all hardwired!* That, and: *Don't blame me!*
> *I'm wired wrong!*

Wired wrong? What would it be, then, to be wired right—or have scientists "discovered" that nobody is, or could be, wired right for moral responsibility?

---

* If you doubt that instilling such a belief could have such consequences, see Vohs and Schooler (2008) and the subsequent literature for experimental evidence.

66. A DETERMINISTIC TOY: CONWAY'S GAME OF LIFE

When physicist Richard Feynman found himself listening to a scientific talk in a field he didn't know well, he had a favorite question to ask the speaker: Can you give me a really simple example of what you're talking about? If the speaker couldn't oblige, Feynman got suspicious, and rightly so. Did this person really have something to say, or was this just fancy technical talk parading as scientific wisdom? If you can't make a hard problem relatively simple, you are probably not going about it the right way. Simplification is not just for beginners.

Biology has its "model organisms"—species that have been carefully chosen to ease the path of the experimenter; they reproduce swiftly in the lab, are relatively safe and easy to handle, and—once they have been studied by many teams—are well mapped and understood: the fruit fly, the laboratory rat, the zebra fish, the squid (for its giant nerve axon), the nematode worm *Caenorhabditis elegans*, and *Arabidopsis thaliana*, a hardy, fast-growing plant related to mustard, the first plant to have its entire genome sequenced. Artificial intelligence (AI) has its own simple cases, known as "toy problems," which, as the name suggests, are deliberately oversimplified versions of "serious" real-world problems. Many of the most interesting programs devised in AI are solutions to toy problems—such as getting a computer program to build simple structures in the *blocks world*, a virtual world consisting of a tabletop with a bunch of movable children's blocks on it. Playing chess is a toy problem; it is certainly much more tractable than driving a car from Maine to California, or solving the Arab–Israeli conflict, or even making a sandwich of appropriate ingredients found in a kitchen. Ethicists have their *trolley problems*: In the simplest version, a runaway trolley is heading down a track where if it is not diverted it will hit and kill five people who cannot get off the track; there is a switch that you can throw that will divert the trolley to a side track—where it will hit and kill a single person. Do you throw the switch?

Here is a toy world for helping people think about *determinism*, the idea that the facts at one moment in time—the location, mass, direction, and velocity of every particle—determine what happens in the next moment, and so on, forever. Physicists and philosophers and others have argued for several millennia about whether our universe is deterministic, or whether there are some genuinely undetermined events: utterly unpredictable "random" events that just *happen* without anything causing them to happen. Even experienced thinkers may find new insights by playing around with Life, the breathtakingly simple model of a deterministic world created by the mathematician John Horton Conway and his graduate students in 1970.

Life is played on a two-dimensional grid, such as a checkerboard, using simple counters, such as pebbles or pennies—or one could also go high-tech and play it on a computer screen. It is not a game one plays to win; if it is a game at all, it is solitaire. The grid divides the plane into square cells, and each cell is either ON or OFF at each moment. (If it is ON, place a penny on the square; if it is OFF, leave the square empty.) Notice that each cell has eight neighbors: the four adjacent cells—north, south, east, and west—and the four diagonals—northeast, southeast, southwest, and northwest.

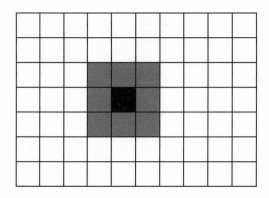

Figure 1

Time in the Life world is discrete, not continuous; it advances in ticks, and the state of the world changes between each tick according to the following rule:

> *Life Physics*: For each cell in the grid, count how many of its eight neighbors are ON at the present instant. If the answer is exactly two, the cell stays in its present state (ON or OFF) in the next instant. If the answer is exactly three, the cell is ON in the next instant whatever its current state. Under all other conditions the cell is OFF.

That's the only rule of the game. You now know all there is to know about how to play Life. *The entire physics of the Life world is captured in that single, unexceptioned law.* While this is the fundamental law of the "physics" of the Life world, it helps at first to conceive this curious physics in biological terms: think of cells going ON as births, cells going OFF as deaths, and succeeding instants as generations. Either overcrowding (more than three inhabited neighbors) or isolation (less than two inhabited neighbors) leads to death. Consider a few simple cases.

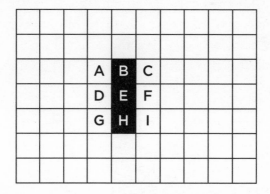

Figure 2

In the configuration in figure 2, only cells D and F have exactly three neighbors ON, so they will be the only birth cells in the next generation. Cells B and H each have only one neighbor ON, so they die in the next generation. Cell E has two neighbors ON, so it stays on. So the next "instant" will look like figure 3.

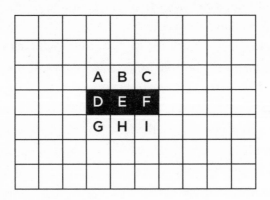

Figure 3

Obviously, the configuration will revert back in the next instant, and this little pattern will flip-flop back and forth indefinitely, unless some new ON cells are brought onto the scene somehow. It is called a *flasher* or traffic light. What will happen to the configuration in figure 4?

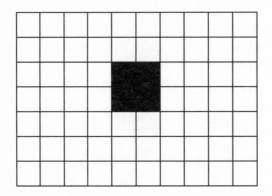

Figure 4

Nothing. Each ON cell has three neighbors ON, so it is reborn just as it is. No OFF cell has three neighbors ON, so no other births happen. This configuration is called a *still life*.

By the scrupulous application of our single law, one can predict with perfect accuracy the next instant of any configuration of ON and OFF cells, and the instant after that, and so forth. *In other words, the Life world is a toy world that perfectly instantiates the determinism made famous by the early-nineteenth-century French scientist Pierre Laplace: given the state description of this world at an instant, we observers can perfectly predict the future instants by the simple application of our one law of physics.* Or we could put it this way: when we *adopt the physical stance* toward a configuration in the Life world, our powers of prediction are perfect: there is no noise, no uncertainty, no probability less than one. Moreover, it follows from the two-dimensionality of the Life world that nothing is hidden from view. There is no backstage; there are no hidden variables; the unfolding of the physics of objects in the Life world is directly and completely visible.

If you find following the simple rule a tedious exercise, there are computer simulations of the Life world in which you can set up configurations on the screen and let the computer execute the algorithm for you, changing the configuration again and again according to the single rule. In the best simulations, the scale of both time and space can be changed, alternating between close-up and bird's-eye views.

One soon discovers that some simple configurations are more interesting than others. Consider a diagonal line segment, such as the one shown in figure 5.

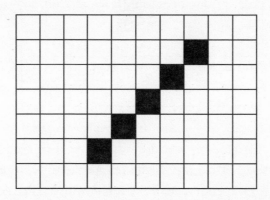

Figure 5

This pattern is *not* a flasher; each generation, the two ON cells at either end of the row die of isolation and there are no birth cells. The whole segment soon evaporates. In addition to the configurations that never change—the still lifes—and those that evaporate entirely, such as the diagonal line segment, there are configurations with all kinds of periodicity. The flasher, we saw, has a two-generation period that continues *ad infinitum*, unless some other configuration encroaches. Encroachment is what makes Life interesting: among the periodic configurations are some that swim, amoeba-like, across the plane. The simplest is the *glider*, the five-pixel configuration shown taking a single stroke to the southeast in figure 6.

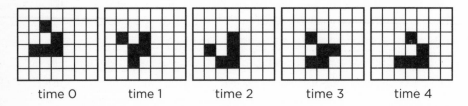

time 0   time 1   time 2   time 3   time 4

Figure 6

Then there are the eaters, the puffer trains and space rakes, and a host of other aptly named denizens of the Life world that emerge as recognizable objects at a new level (analogous to the *design level*). This level has its own language, a transparent foreshortening of the tedious descriptions one could give at the physical level. For instance:

> An eater can eat a glider in four generations. Whatever is being consumed, the basic process is the same. A bridge forms between the eater and its prey. In the next generation, the bridge region dies from overpopulation, taking a bite out of both eater and prey. The eater then repairs itself. The prey usually cannot. If the remainder of the prey dies out as with the glider, the prey is consumed. [Poundstone, 1985, p. 38]

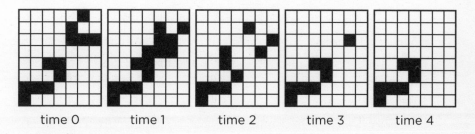

| time 0 | time 1 | time 2 | time 3 | time 4 |

Figure 7

Notice that something curious happens to our "ontology"—our catalogue of what exists—as we move between levels. At the physical level there is no motion, only ON and OFF, and the only individual things that exist, cells, are defined by their fixed spatial location. At the design level we suddenly have the motion of persisting objects; it is one and the same glider (though each generation is composed of different cells) that has moved southeast in figure 5, changing shape as it moves; and there is one less glider in the world after the eater has eaten it in figure 7.

Notice too that whereas at the physical level, there are absolutely no exceptions to the general law, at this level our generalizations have to be hedged: they require "usually" or "provided nothing encroaches" clauses. Stray bits of debris from earlier events can "break" or "kill" one of the objects in the ontology at this level. Their *salience as real things* is considerable, but not guaranteed. To say that their salience is considerable is to say that one can, with some small risk, ascend to this design level, adopt its ontology, and proceed to predict—sketchily and riskily—the behavior of larger configurations or systems of configurations, without bothering to compute the physical level. For instance, one can set oneself the task of designing some interesting super-system out of the "parts" that the design level makes available.

This is just what Conway and his students set out to do, and they succeeded majestically. They designed, and proved the viability of the design of, a self-reproducing entity composed entirely of Life cells. Grinding away deterministically on its infinite plane, it would copy itself perfectly, and then its copy would copy itself, and so forth. It was also (for good measure) a Universal Turing machine: a two-dimensional computer that in principle can compute any computable function! What on earth inspired Conway and his students to create first this world and then this amazing denizen of that world? They were trying to answer at a very abstract level one of the central questions of biology: What is the minimal complexity required for a self-reproducing thing? They were following up the brilliant early speculations of John von Neumann, who had been working on the question at the time of his death in 1957. Francis Crick and James Watson had discovered the structure of DNA in 1953, but how it worked was a mystery for many years. Von Neumann had imagined in some detail a sort of floating robot that picked up pieces of flotsam and jetsam that could be used to build a duplicate of itself, and that would then be able to repeat the process. His description (posthumously published, 1966) of how an automaton would read its own blueprint and then copy it into its new creation anticipated in impressive detail many of the later discoveries about the mechanisms of DNA expression and replication, but in order to make his proof of the possibility of a self-reproducing automaton mathematically rigorous and tractable, von Neumann had switched to simple, two-dimensional abstractions, now known as *cellular automata*. Conway's Life world cells are a particularly agreeable example of cellular automata.

Conway and his students wanted to confirm von Neumann's proof in detail by actually creating a two-dimensional world with a simple physics in which such a self-replicating construction would be a stable, *working* structure. Like von Neumann, they wanted their answer to be as general as possible, and hence as independent as possible of actual (earthly? local?) physics and chemistry. They wanted something dead simple, easy to visualize and easy to calculate, so they not only dropped from three dimensions to two but also "digitized" both space and time: all times and distances, as we saw, are in whole numbers of "instants" and "cells." It was von Neumann who had taken Alan Turing's abstract conception of a mechanical computer (now called a Turing machine) and engineered it into the specification for a general-purpose stored-program serial-processing computer (now called a von Neumann machine), and in his brilliant explorations of the spatial and structural requirements for such a computer, he had realized—and proved—that a Universal Turing machine (see part IV) could in principle be "built" in a two-dimensional world.* Conway and his students also set out to confirm this with their own exercise in two-dimensional engineering.†

It was far from easy, but they showed how they could "build" a working computer out of simpler Life forms. Glider streams can provide the input-output "tape," for instance, and the tape-reader can be some huge assembly of eaters, gliders, and other bits and pieces. What does this machine look like? Poundstone (1985) calculated that the whole construction would be on the order of 10^{13} cells or pixels.

> Displaying a 10^{13}-pixel pattern would require a video screen about 3 million pixels across at least. . . . [Imagine a screen with the high resolution of your laptop or iPad, a half a mile wide.] Perspective would shrink the pixels of a self-reproducing pattern to invisibility. If you got far enough away from the screen so that the entire pattern was comfortably in view, the pixels (and even the gliders, eaters and guns) would be too tiny to make out. A self-reproducing pattern would be a hazy glow, like a galaxy. [pp. 227–288]

In other words, by the time you have built up enough pieces into something that can reproduce itself (in a two-dimensional world), it is roughly as much larger than its smallest bits as an organism is larger than its atoms. You probably can't do it with anything much less complicated, though this has not been strictly proved.

---

* See Dennett, 1987, chapter 9, for more on the theoretical implications of this trade-off in space and time.
† For a completely different perspective on two-dimensional physics and engineering, see A. K. Dewdney's *Planiverse* (1984), a vast improvement over Edwin A. Abbott's *Flatland* (1884), and a magnificent thinking tool in its own right.

The game of Life illustrates many important principles and can be used to construct many different arguments or thought experiments, but I will use it to illustrate just three points, leaving you to discover others for yourself: First, notice how the distinction between the physical stance and the design stance gets blurred here. Do gliders, for instance, count as designed things, or as natural objects—like atoms and molecules? The tape-reader that Conway and his students cobbled out of gliders and eaters and the like must count as designed if anything does, but its ingredients are quite raw materials—the simplest "things" in the Life world. Nobody had to design or invent the glider; it was *discovered* to be implied by the physics of the Life world. But that, of course, is actually true of *everything* in the Life world. Nothing happens in the Life world that isn't strictly implied— logically deducible by straightforward theorem-proving—by the physics and the initial configuration of cells. Some of the things in the Life world are just more marvelous and unanticipated (by us, with our puny intellects) than others. There is a sense in which the Conway self-reproducing computer pixel-galaxy is "just" one more Life macromolecule with a very long and complicated periodicity in its behavior. This nicely illustrates a parallel point about biology and the origin of life: amino acids, one might say, just are; they didn't have to be designed. But proteins, composed of nothing but amino acids, are too fancy; they are at least **sorta** designed. Darwin's gradualism makes yet another appearance.

Second, the Life world, being deterministic, has a perfectly predictable future for every possible configuration, but, somewhat surprisingly, its past is often perfectly inscrutable! Consider the still life consisting of four ON pixels in a square. You can't tell from looking at it, or even looking at it and its neighborhood, what its past was. To see this, note that any three of the four pixels ON would lead, in the next generation, to this still life of four pixels ON. Whether any of those cells were OFF in the past is an **inert historical fact**.

Third, recall how important "noise" and collisions were in creating the mutations that evolution—like other creative processes—feeds on.

Conway's huge construction reproduced itself, but it couldn't mutate. It would always make a *perfect* copy of itself, and in order to introduce mutations into the picture, the whole construction would have to be enlarged many fold. Why? Because the Life world is deterministic, so the only way a "random" mutation can occur is if some stray bit of stuff wanders (pseudo-randomly) onto the scene and breaks something. But the smallest moving thing is a glider, so think of it as like a single photon, or cosmic ray, moving at the speed of (Life physics) light. A single glider can do a lot of damage; if it must barely "tweak" something in the genome of the self-reproducing thing without destroying the genome, that genome is going to have to be very large, relative to the glider, and quite robust. It might well be provable that evolution could not occur in the Life world, no matter how large we made the entities, if it turned out that these galaxy-sized assemblages were just too fragile to survive an occasional rain of gliders.

67. ROCK, PAPER, AND SCISSORS

Probably every one of you knows the game of rock, paper, and scissors. Two people face each other, and count, "One, two, three, shoot!" and each, simultaneously, extends a hand either clenched in a fist (rock), with a pair of fingers extended (scissors), or with the palm flat open facing down (paper). Rock breaks (beats) scissors, scissors cut (beat) paper, and paper covers (beats) rock. Unless both players display the same hand symbol—a tie—one player wins and the other loses. It's a tantalizing game because if you can outguess your opponent, you can seem to read her mind and come up with the right hand shape to win consistently. It's unnerving when that happens. Can some people play the game better than others? Apparently, since there have been tournaments with large cash prizes in which national and international winners have emerged, and—this is important since every tournament has to be won by somebody even if there is no skill involved—the better players have a history of winning.

How do they do it? Perhaps by picking up subtle hints from the faces and postures of their opponents. Poker players speak of reading the "tell" of another player, sensing when they are bluffing and when they aren't, while maintaining a "poker face" of their own. Perhaps most people who play rock, paper, and scissors have a tell that they can't control and that the best players pick up at the last instant. So what is the best strategy to use to prevent your opponent from picking up a pattern from your outer demeanor? Playing absolutely randomly is the best, since if you play a random sequence of moves, there is simply no pattern for your opponent to detect. (While you are playing randomly, and breaking even, you can try to find a pattern in your opponent's moves, and use that pattern to craft a nonrandom strategy, and then strike.)

People are notoriously bad at creating actually random series. They tend to switch too often, avoiding choosing the same move two or three times in a row, for instance (which ought to occur fairly often in a genuinely random series). Knowing that your casual effort to create a genuinely patternless series is apt to fail, you should consider a better strategy: get a table of random numbers from the library (or online). Put your finger "at random" somewhere on the table, and copy down the next hundred digits. Throw out all the 0s (say), and then replace each 1, 2, or 3 with "R" (for rock), each 4, 5, and 6, with "P" (for paper), and each 7, 8, and 9 with "S" (for scissors). This will give you a sequence of approximately ninety moves (since you threw out approximately ten 0s), which should be enough for a match.

Now you're ready to play, and the cardinal rule is: *keep your list secret.* If your opponent gets to peek at it, you will be completely at her mercy. As the saying goes, she will turn you into a money pump. If she has no way of getting at your list, on the other hand, she will have to start trying to second-guess you, anticipating your line of thinking as best she can. (In short, she will have to treat you from the **intentional stance** and reason about your reasoning, instead of treating you as a simple mechanism whose behavior she can reliably read off your list.)

This simple principle of keeping your intended choices secret from your opponent turns out to be one of the central pivots in the long-standing controversies over free will. In fact, the invention of *game theory* by von Neumann and Morgenstern (1944) began with the recognition that while a solitary agent (or intentional system) trying to predict the future from the information it gathers can get by with a calculation of *expected utility* using probability theory (of one sort or another), as soon as there are two agents, two intentional systems in the environment, the circumstance is changed radically. Now each agent has to take into account the attempts at prediction by the other agent, and include the other agent's observation of, and attempts to anticipate and exploit, its own behavior, creating feedback loops of indefinite complexity.*

---

* A delicious example of runaway higher-order second-guessing appears in the film *The Princess Bride*, in the scene in which Wallace Shawn as Vizzini tries to outwit Cary Elwes as Westley in the "Which cup has the poison?" encounter, and ends up outwitting himself. See http://www .dailymotion.com/video/xhr71a_never-go-in-against-a-sicilian-when-death-is-on-the-line_shortfilms.

This fundamental fog of inscrutability or unpredictability of agents by each other creates the conditions in which game theory flourishes. Evolution has discovered this, and many species can be seen to apply the principles of game theory (**competence without comprehension!**) in their interactions. Gazelle **stotting** is just one simple example. Another is the erratic flight of butterflies, whose trajectories are hard for insectivorous birds to predict, though evolution has helped the birds by giving them a faster "flicker fusion rate" than we have, for instance (they see more "frames per second" than we do—a movie would look like a slide show to them).

Be unpredictable, and look out for others following this advice! "Appreciation" of this principle can be seen in the widespread instinct found in animals who, when confronted with any complicated moving entity, try to treat it as an agent—"*Who* goes there, and what do you want?" not just "What's that?"—in order to be safe, because maybe it *is* an agent and it wants to eat the animal, or to mate with it, or to fight over some prize. This instinctual response is the source in evolution of the invention of all the invisible elves, goblins, leprechauns, fairies, ogres, and gods that eventually evolve into God, the ultimate invisible intentional system (Dennett, 2006a).

Like animals who adopt this strategy without having to know why, we human beings appreciate the tactic of preserving our unpredictability without having to understand why this is such a good idea. But it's pretty obvious, most of the time. When you are shopping and spot an antique that you have to have, you know better than to gush over it before you've learned the selling price. You'll get scalped by the seller if you don't. When you advertise something for sale, you put a reasonable asking price on it—one you would be content to receive—because you can't tell when a buyer would actually pay more, and you hope that the buyer can't tell how much less you would accept than your asking price. (You can refuse to bargain, of course.) Auctions are ways of exploring this terra incognita, and if you trust the auctioneer with an advance bid, you are counting on his integrity not to reveal your maximum to the other bidders.

Similarly, when you fall head over heels in love at first sight of somebody, you do your best not to swoon and pant, keeping as reserved and casual as possible; you don't want to scare this paragon off or, alternatively, let this delight have too much of the upper hand, wrapping you around her little finger. A poker face is not just for poker. In general, you improve your chances of getting what you want by keeping the competition—the other agents in the neighborhood—off balance, so they don't have good enough hunches about which way you're going to leap to prepare for your landing. (It's costly to prepare another agent's environment, so your opponents won't try to anticipate you unless they have very good evidence of what you will do.)

Magicians know how to do a "psychological force" to get you to pick from the deck ("of your own free will") the card they want you to take. There are many methods, all subtle and hard to detect, and a really good magician can do it most of the time. This is a genuine abridgement of your agency, a manipulation that turns you into a tool, a pawn, an extension of the magician's will, not a free agent.

Contrary to ancient ideology, we don't want our free choices to be utterly uncaused. What we all want, and should want, is that when we act, we act based on good information about the best options available to us. If only the environment will *cause* us to have lots of relevant true beliefs about what's out there, and also *cause* us to act on the most judicious assessment of that evidence we could achieve! That would give us *almost* everything we want as agents—except this: we wouldn't want the environment to include a manipulative agent that usurps control from us, so we wouldn't want the environment to make our best moves too obvious to all the other agents out there, for then they can exploit us, knowing too much about what we want and how much we want it. So add to our wish list the capacity to keep our thought processes and our decisions to ourselves, even if it means on occasion choosing our second-best option, just to keep the others off balance. (Clegg, 2012, provides a pioneering formal analysis of this.)

Some people, dimly appreciating the importance of this unpredictability, think that "just to be safe" they should hold out for *absolute* unpredictability, which can be achieved only if, down in the basement of our brains, matters are physically indeterministic. Here is how the philosopher Jerry Fodor (2003) once put it with characteristic vividness:

> One wants to be what tradition has it that Eve was when she bit the apple. Perfectly free to do otherwise. So perfectly free, in fact, that even God couldn't tell which way she'd jump. [p. 18]

But why does "one want" this? Is this absolute unpredictability any better, really, than practical unpredictability? Many philosophers, over several thousand years, have insisted on absolute unpredictability as a condition of genuine free will. Do they know something that we don't know? If so, they are keeping it secret. To almost all of them, the idea that free will is incompatible with determinism has seemed too obvious to need an argument. I say that the burden of proof is on them. Show us why we ought to despair if we can't have *absolute* unpredictability. I've shown why we—like evolution itself—are wise to arrange for as much *practical* unpredictability as we can. Tell us, please, why that is not enough.

I will give you one good reason: if you plan to play rock, paper, and scissors with God, for high stakes (salvation, maybe), then you have reason, just as Fodor says, to want "perfect" freedom. I, for one, don't anticipate that contest, so I am content with the practical freedom I have by just keeping my counsel and staying away from sleight-of-hand artists and other manipulators when the stakes are high.

68. TWO LOTTERIES

Compare the following two lotteries for fairness. In Lottery A—for "After"—all the tickets are sold, their stubs are placed in a suitable mixer and mixed, as randomly as you like, and *then* the winning ticket is blindly drawn. (Most lotteries we encounter are like this.) In Lottery B—for "Before"—the mixing of stubs and the blind drawing of the winner take place *before* the tickets are sold (and the winning stub is put in a safe), but otherwise the lotteries are conducted the same way. Someone might think the second lottery is unfair because the winning ticket is determined before people even buy their tickets. One of those tickets is *already* the winner (even if nobody knows which one); the other tickets are worthless paper, and selling them to unsuspecting people is some sort of fraud. But in fact both lotteries are equally fair. Everyone who buys a ticket has an equal chance of winning; the timing of the selection of the winner is an utterly inessential feature.

The drawing in most lotteries is postponed until after the sale of the tickets in order to provide the public with firsthand eyewitness evidence that there have been no shenanigans. No sneaky person with inside knowledge has manipulated the distribution of tickets, because the knowledge of the winning ticket did not (and could not) exist in any agent until after the tickets were sold. It is interesting that not all lotteries follow this practice. Publisher's Clearing House used to mail out millions of envelopes each year that had written on them in bold letters "YOU MAY ALREADY HAVE WON"—a million dollars, or some other prize. (The organization now runs its lottery largely online.) These expensive campaigns are based on market research showing that in general people do think lotteries with preselected winners are fair so long as they are honestly conducted. But perhaps people go along with these lotteries uncomplainingly because they get their tickets for free. Would many people *buy* a ticket in a lottery in which the winning stub, sealed in a special envelope, was known to have been deposited in a bank vault from the outset? People buy scratch tickets by the millions, and whether or not any ticket is a winner is already determined when it is bought. Apparently these people consider themselves to have a real opportunity to win. I think they are right, but whether they are right or wrong, their calm conviction that such lotteries are fair, and that they have a real opportunity to win, should undo the confidence of the philosophers (going back two millennia to Democritus and Lucretius) who have somehow convinced themselves that no opportunity is a *real* opportunity unless the outcome is undetermined up to the last instant. These philosophers have maintained that without a continuing supply of truly random, undetermined *branch points* to break up the fabric of causation, there is no possibility of free choices, no *real* chances to do the right thing.

The two lotteries give us a new perspective on the problem of determinism. If the world is determined, then we have pseudo-random number generators in us, not truly (quantum-mechanical) random randomizers. If our world is determined, all our lottery tickets were drawn at once, in effect, about fourteen billion years ago at the moment of the Big Bang, put in an envelope for us, and doled out as we needed them through life. Whenever you need to "flip a coin" or in some less ostentatious way make a chancy decision, your brain opens the envelope and takes out the next "random" number, letting its value *determine* what you do, just like the list of moves in "rock, paper, and scissors." "But that is unfair," someone may say, "for some people will have been dealt more winners than others." Indeed, on any particular deal, some people have more high cards than others, but one should remember that in the long run the luck averages out. "But if all the drawings take place before we are born, some people are *determined* to get more luck than others!" That will be true, however, even if the drawings are not held before we are born, but periodically, on demand, throughout our lives. Even in a perfectly random and unbiased drawing, a genuinely undetermined drawing, it is still *determined* that some people will get more winners than others. Even in a perfectly fair, perfectly random, coin-tossing tournament, it is determined that someone—or other—will win, and everybody else in the tournament will lose. The winner cannot properly claim it was his "destiny" to win, but whatever advantages accrue to winning are his, destiny or not, and what could be fairer than that? Fairness does not consist in everybody winning.

Probably the most frequently cited reason for hoping for indeterminism is that without it, when we choose an act, "we could not have done otherwise," and **surely** (ding!) that is something that should be important to us. This, too, is not as obvious as it has often seemed, and in order to get a glimpse at how this familiar idea might be misleading us, consider the curious category of inert historical facts.

69. INERT HISTORICAL FACTS

An inert historical fact is any fact about a perfectly ordinary arrangement of matter in the world at some point in the past that is no longer discernible, a fact that has left no footprints *at all* in the world today. My favorite example of an inert historical fact is this:

> A. Some of the gold in my teeth once belonged to Julius Caesar.

Or maybe this:

> B. It is false that some of the gold in my teeth once belonged to Julius Caesar.

Now (logic tells us) one of these two must be a fact. (Hang on: Wasn't the moral of the **sorta** operator chapter that we should distrust these "obvious" disjunctions? Let's check this one out. How could it be the case that neither A nor B had a clear claim on truth? Well, what if *ownership* in Caesar's day was either vague or ill defined so that Caesar only **sorta** owned some of his gold—perhaps the way the Queen of England to this day is the owner of all the swans in the land?*) Assuming that the relevant concept of ownership is nicely demarcated, the way the concept of gold is, one of the two sentences must express a fact, but which of the two is true is

---

* According to the official royal website, "Today, the Crown retains the right to ownership of all unmarked mute swans in open water, but The Queen only exercises her ownership on certain stretches of the Thames and its surrounding tributaries. This ownership is shared with the Worshipful Company of Vintners and the Worshipful Company of Dyers, who were granted rights of ownership by the Crown in the fifteenth century. Nowadays, of course, the swans are no longer eaten."

almost certainly not discoverable by any physical investigation, no matter how sophisticated it is and no matter how long it takes to conduct it.

Really? We can imagine cases where we could be almost certain that either A or B is the true alternative. If it turned out that, because of various well-recorded historical processes, the "provenance" of some of the gold in my teeth was scrupulously controlled and recorded through the millennia (like the "chain of custody" for exhibits of evidence in murder trials), we could be quite sure that A is true. Let's say that my dentist purchased an ancient gold ring from a museum, the famous "Caesar's pinky ring," which a host of documents attest had been handed down over the centuries from monarch to monarch until it arrived in the museum, and there is a videotape showing the dentist melting the ring and pouring the molten gold into the plaster cast for my filling. Outlandish, sure, but clearly within the bounds of physical possibility. Or alternatively, suppose that I am a gold-panning hobbyist and made a trip to the base of a receding glacier in Alaska that had covered the land for ten thousand years, where I carefully collected all the gold that subsequently went into my teeth. Then B would be even more certainly the truth. But if nothing like these extreme tales is well evidenced, then it is as good as certain that we could never know which of A or B is true. The true one, whichever it is, is an inert historical fact.

Quantum physics raises an interesting difficulty: even if the trajectory of each atom of gold in my teeth could be traced back through the centuries, if there were occasions when two or more gold atoms—one from the Caesar legacy and one from outside sources—collided (or just got *very* close to each other), it would be impossible in principle to tell which atom was which after the "collision." Atoms and smaller particles don't have anything like fingerprints or other distinguishing characteristics, and cannot be *continuously* tracked, so the continuing identity of particles does not always make sense, adding another barrier to knowing the facts about the gold.

Now whether or not the whole universe is deterministic, computers are designed to be deterministic in the face of submicroscopic noise and even quantum randomness, absorbing these fluctuations by being digital, not analog. (We saw a vivid example of that with **Conway's game of Life** in chapter 66, but digital determinism is everywhere.) The fundamental idea behind digitizing in order to produce determinism is that we can *create* inert historical facts by design. Forcibly sorting all the pivotal events into two categories—high *vs.* low; ON *vs.* OFF; o *vs.* 1—guarantees that the micro-differences (between different high voltages, different flavors of being ON, different shades of o) are ruthlessly discarded. Nothing is allowed to hinge on them, and they vanish without a trace, facts about actual historical variations that make *no difference at all* to the subsequent series of states through which the computer passes. For instance, your friend downloads a song from a website and burns it onto two CDs. These two unlabeled CDs—we'll call them A and B, but we won't write their names on them—will be digital duplicates, of course. Ask him to "copy" one of them onto your laptop in a pitch-black room. Don't tell him which CD to use, and have him handle both CDs after completing the action (wiping out the possibility of using fingerprint evidence, or DNA traces) before depositing them in a bag full of other CDs and shaking it vigorously. Now we have two candidate inert historical facts:

(a) Your laptop has a copy made from the A disc.
(b) Your laptop has a copy made from the B disc.

Any actual physical encoding of the bit stream of the song will have a microscopically fine structure that differs from the fine structure of any other encoding. And when you "copy" one of the CDs to RAM (random-access memory), the voltage patterns in RAM will also have a unique fine structure, and if we then "copy" the file from RAM to a hard disk or a flash drive, these too will contain microscopic differences that distinguish them. What is conveniently called copying is always the creation of yet another continuous or analog physical signal that has its own unique fine structure because that's the way the world is way down among the electrons and protons. But the genius of digitization is that all this fine structure is "ignored," wiped out in the "correction to the norm." When you have norms, like an alphabet, it doesn't make any difference wH*at f*LAv*O*r the individual symbols have; they all read the same. In a computer it's all os and is.

So unless one of the CDs happens to have an "error" discernible at the level of the digital idealization (has a *flipped bit*, that is—a o instead of a i, or vice versa), there will be no way of telling. The digitization prevents the *propagation* of the individuality of the two CDs to later versions, and ultimately to the digital-to-analog conversion that drives the speakers or ear buds. Some music lovers are reputed to be "golden eared," able to tell vinyl records from the best digital CDs, and compressed (e.g., MPEG) from uncompressed digital files, but no music lover could do better than chance if asked whether two successive playings of some music were from the same, or different, CDs. That is an inert historical fact, undetectable not just by human ears but by electron microscopy of the fine structure of their "copies" in RAM. Any human being who could do this would be a strong candidate for having supernatural ESP, since digitization creates a physical barrier to the information transmission that would enable a guesser to do better than chance.

Because a computer is a digital device, it is trivial to get it to execute a few trillion steps, and then place it back in *exactly* the same (digital) state it was in before, and watch it execute *exactly* the same few trillion (digital) steps again, and again, and again.

Wait a minute, comes an objection: You say computers are deterministic? You can get them to replay exactly the same trillion steps over and over? Gimme a break! Then why does my laptop crash every so often? Why does my word processor freeze on Tuesday when I was doing the very same thing that worked just fine on Monday?

You weren't doing the *very* same thing. It froze not because it is indeterministic, but because it was not in *exactly* the same state on Tuesday that it was in on Monday. Your laptop must have done something in the interval that raised a hidden "flag" or called up some part of the word processor that had never before been activated by you, which flipped a bit somewhere that got saved in its new position when you shut down, and now the word processor has stubbed its toe on that tiny change and crashed. And if you somehow manage to put it back in *exactly* the same Tuesday-morning state a second time, it will crash again.

> What about the "random-number generator"? I thought my computer had a built-in device for creating randomness on demand.

Every computer these days comes equipped with a built-in "random number" generator that can be consulted whenever needed by any program running on it. (Before there were computers you could buy a book that was nothing but a table of random numbers to use in your research, page after page of digits that had been scrupulously generated in such a way as to pass all the tests of randomness that mathematicians had devised. Of course each copy of a particular edition of such a book had exactly the same sequence of random numbers in it. RAND Corporation published one of the best books in 1955; it consisted of a million random digits.) The sequence of numbers generated by a so-called random-number generator isn't really random, but just pseudo-random: it is "mathematically compressible" in the sense that this infinitely long sequence can be captured in a finitely specified mechanism that will crank it out. Suppose, for instance, your random-number generator is a program that can be specified in, say, a megabyte—eight million bits—but it generates a sequence (the same sequence every time) that is actually infinite. If you wanted to send somebody this infinite series, you wouldn't have to do so in an infinitely long e-mail message recording the series *verbatim*. You could just send them your megabyte-long algorithm and they'd have access to the entire infinite series. That is the fundamental idea of a pseudo-random-number generator. Whenever you start the random-number generator from a cold start—whenever you reboot your computer, for instance—it will always yield *exactly* the same sequence of digits, but a sequence that is as *apparently* patternless as if it were generated by genuinely random quantum fluctuations. It is a built-in "table of random numbers," you might say, rather like what you would get on a very long loop of videotape, recording the history of a fair roulette wheel over millions of spins. The loop always returns to "the beginning" when you start up your computer. Sometimes this matters. Computer programs that avail themselves of randomness at various "choice" points will nevertheless spin out exactly the same sequence of states if run over and over again from a cold start, and sometimes, if you want to test a program for bugs, you will always test the same "random sample" of states, unless you take steps (easy enough) to jog the program to dip elsewhere, now and then, into the stream of digits for its next "random" number.

70. A COMPUTER CHESS MARATHON

It is fiendishly difficult to think clearly about determinism and choice. If determinism is true, are there ever any *real* choices? If an agent that apparently has free will is actually deterministic, living in a deterministic world, does this remove all choice, all *opportunity*? Here is an intuition pump that explores the question by looking at a simplified world—chess playing—in an artificially constructed deterministic world: the world of activity performed by a computer.

Suppose you install two different chess-playing programs on your computer and yoke them together with a little supervisory program that pits them against each other, game after game, in a potentially endless series. Will they play the same game, over and over, until you turn off the computer? You *could* set it up like that, but then you wouldn't learn anything interesting about the two programs, A and B. Suppose A beats B in this oft-repeated game. You couldn't infer from this that A is a better program in general than B, or that A would beat B in a different game, and you wouldn't be able to learn anything from the exact repetition about the strengths and weaknesses of the two different programs. Much more informative would be to set up the tournament so that A and B play a succession of different games. This can be readily arranged. If either chess program consults the random-number generator during its calculations (if, for instance, it periodically "flips a coin" to escape from situations where it has no handy reason for doing one thing versus another in the course of its searching for a good move), then in the following game the state of the random-number generator will have changed (unless you arrange to have it re-initialized), and hence different alternatives will be explored, in a different order, leading on occasion to different moves being "chosen." A variant game will blossom, and the third game will be different in different ways, resulting in a series in which no two games, like no two snowflakes, are alike. Nevertheless, if you turned off the computer and then restarted it running the same program, exactly the same variegated series of games would spin out, because the same pseudo-random series of numbers would determine all the "coin flips" used by both programs.

Suppose, then, we set up such a chess universe involving two programs, A and B, and study the results of a run of, say, a thousand games. We will find lots of highly reliable patterns. Suppose we find that A always beats B, in a thousand *different* games. That is a pattern that we will want to explain, and saying, "Since the program is deterministic, A was *caused* always to beat B," would utterly fail to address our very reasonable curiosity. We will want to know what it is about the structure, the methods, the dispositions, of A that accounts for its superiority at chess. A has a competence or power that B lacks, and we need to isolate this interesting factor. It might be that the explanation lies at a low level; it might turn out, for instance, that program A and program B are actually the same program, *identical* chess-move evaluators at the **source code** level, but program A is more efficiently compiled than B so that it can explore the game further than program B can in the same number of machine cycles. In effect A "thinks exactly the same thoughts" about chess as B, and B "knows" everything about chess that A does, but A just thinks faster. (Serious chess, tournament chess, is always played with a time clock; if you run out of time before you've made all your moves, you lose.) More likely the superiority of A to B would require explanation at a higher-level perspective at which the everyday topics of chess decision-making appear: *representations* of board positions, *evaluations* of possible continuations, *decisions* about which continuations to pursue further, and so forth. Thus program A may adjust the relative value of its pieces as the game progresses, or have better evaluation functions of board positions, or decide to terminate certain sorts of explorations earlier or later. It doesn't "think the same thoughts" as B; it "thinks better, more sophisticated thoughts." (It **sorta** thinks these thoughts, of course. It isn't a conscious person.)

It might actually be more telling if one program didn't always win. Suppose A *almost* always beats B, and suppose A evaluates moves using a different set of principles. Then we would have something even more interesting to explain. To investigate *this* causal question, we would need to study the history of the thousand different games, looking for further patterns. We would be sure to find plenty of them. Some of them would be endemic to chess wherever it is played (e.g., the near certainty of B's loss in any game where B falls a rook behind), and some of them would be peculiar to A and B as particular chess players (e.g., B's penchant for getting its queen out too early). We would find the standard patterns of chess strategy, such as the fact that when B's time is running out, B searches less deeply in the remaining nodes of the game tree than it does when it has more time remaining and is in the same local position. In short, we would find a cornucopia of *explanatory* regularities, some exceptionless (in our run of a thousand games) and others statistical.

These recognizable chess-move patterns are salient moments in the unfolding of a deterministic pageant that, observed from the perspective of micro-causation, is pretty much all the same. What from one vantage point appear to us to be two chess programs in suspenseful combat can be seen through the "microscope" (as we watch instructions and data streaming through the computer's CPU) to be a single deterministic automaton unfolding in the only way it can, its jumps already predictable by examining the precise state of the pseudo-random-number generator and the rest of the program and data. There are no "real" forks or branches in its future; all the "choices" made by A and B are already determined by the total state of the computer and its memory. Nothing, it seems, is really *possible* in this world other than what actually happens. Suppose, for instance, that an ominous *mating net* (a guaranteed win that might be hard to discern) looms over A at time *t*, but it collapses when B runs out of time and terminates its search for the key move one pulse too soon. That mating net *was never going to happen*. (This is something we could prove, if we doubted it, by running exactly the same tournament another day. At the same moment in the series, B would run out of time again and terminate its search at exactly the same point.)

So what are we to say? Is this toy world really a world without prevention or avoidance, without offense and defense, without lost opportunities, without the thrust and parry of genuine agency, without genuine possibilities? Admittedly, our chess programs, like insects and fish, are much too simple agents to be plausible candidates for morally significant free will, but the determinism of their world does not rob them of their different powers, their different *abilities* to avail themselves of the *opportunities* presented. If we want to understand what is happening in that world, we may, indeed must, talk about how their informed *choices* cause their circumstances to change, and about what they *can* and *cannot* do. If we want to uncover the *causal regularities* that account for the patterns we discover in those thousand games, we have to take seriously the perspective that describes the world as containing two agents, A and B, trying to beat each other in chess.

Suppose we rig the tournament program so that whenever A wins, a bell rings, and whenever B wins, a buzzer sounds. We start the marathon and an observer who knows nothing about the program notes that the bell rings quite frequently, the buzzer hardly ever. What explains this regularity, she wants to know. The regularity with which A beats B can be discerned and *described* independently of adopting the **intentional stance**, but it stands in need of *explanation*. The only explanation—the right explanation—may be that A generates better "beliefs" about what B will do if . . . than B generates about what A will do if . . . In such a case, adopting the intentional stance is *required* for finding the explanation (see chapters 33 and 42 for other examples of causal links that are utterly inexplicable until you adopt the intentional stance).

So far so good, but these "decisions" and "choices" seem to be only **sorta** decisions and choices. They lack something, it seems, that genuine choices have: "could have done otherwise." But let's look more closely at a specific example, since appearances can be deceiving. It will help to add a third chess-playing program, C, to our tournament program, and let's suppose that C is better than A and B, beating them both almost all the time, and let's suppose that the first twelve moves in a pair of these games are exactly the same, and that C wins both games, beating both A and B, though by somewhat different routes after those first twelve moves. The experts huddle in retrospect and figure out that at move 12, the last common move, if either A or B had castled, C would likely have lost. Castling at move 12 was the key to victory, missed by both A and B.

The designer of program A shrugs and says, "Well, A could have castled," and the designer of B adds, "My program too; B could have castled." *But the designer of A was right and the designer of B was wrong!* How could this be? The tournament program T is deterministic, and if we run through the games again, in *exactly* the same state, neither A nor B castles. Isn't the designer of A kidding herself? Not necessarily. What are we trying to find out when we ask if A could have done otherwise? Looking at *precisely* the same case, again and again, is utterly uninformative, but looking at *similar* cases is in fact diagnostic. If we find that in many similar circumstances in other games, A *does* pursue the evaluation slightly farther, discovering the virtues of such moves and making them, then we support the designer's conviction that A could have castled then.

We might find, in the minimal case, that flipping a single bit in the (pseudo-)random-number generator would have resulted in A's castling. Suppose A's designer digs deep down into the actual execution of the program and shows that on this occasion A stopped "thinking" one pulse too early. (Every chess program, no matter how brilliant, has to truncate its searches arbitrarily at some point.) A considered castling, and had begun its analysis of that outcome, but since time was running out, it consulted its random-number generator, flipping a coin, in effect, and settled on the move it had so far identified as the best—and it wasn't castling. But if the pseudo-random number had been a 1 instead of a 0, A would have gone on considering for a little while longer, and castled instead. "Just flip one bit in the random number and A wins!" says the designer. We would say that in this case A's failure to castle was a fluke, bad luck with the random-number generator.

When we turn to the designer of B, no such story in support of the claim that B could have castled under the circumstances is forthcoming. It is true that B "knows" that castling is legal under these conditions, and perhaps actually briefly "considered" castling, but B was nowhere near choosing castling on this occasion. Castling was a *deep* move, the sort of move that is followed by "(!)" in the newspaper chess columns, and far beyond program B's limited analytical powers. So here we have an entirely deterministic world—program T—in which A could have castled but B could not have castled. The difference between A and B is real and explanatory, a difference in competence or ability. One way we could put it is apparently paradoxical:

A could have castled at time *t* but the universe couldn't have had a castling event at time *t*.

What could possibly license this way of describing the situation? Simply this: if we consider A *divorced from its immediate environment—which includes the random-number generator*—then whether A castles or not is undetermined. It depends on something that is strictly speaking outside A. Given the way the rest of the universe was arranged at *t*, castling was not possible for A, but that is "not A's fault." B, in contrast, could not have castled; it was not in B's nature to castle. To imagine B castling would require too many alterations of reality.

This is a useful discovery: a distinction between what A and B "could do" that does *not* depend on indeterminism. Even in a deterministic world we can see that A *can do* kinds of things that B *cannot do*, and this difference is part of the *explanation* of why A beats B. The fact that, because determinism is true in this world, A and B can only do what they actually do on the specific occasion (and would do it again and again if *exactly* the same circumstances were repeated) is simply not interesting, not relevant to the explanation we get of the perfectly objective and visible regularity: A beats B.

A chess-playing program is not a moral agent, and it is not morally responsible for the choices it makes—its world is entirely amoral, and violating one of the rules of chess is simply unthinkable for a chess program, and hence requires no penalties for violations. But as we have just seen, even in the simple deterministic world of computer chess we can make a real and important distinction between A and B. Sometimes when A does something stupid or clever we can say, "A could have done otherwise, but B could not have done otherwise." If you think that this must be a mistake "because neither A nor B could *ever* have done otherwise since the world is deterministic," it is you making the mistake.

A and B differ in chess competence, and "could have done otherwise" nicely captures an aspect of that difference, as we have just seen. What about *moral* competence? When people say of some human beings who act badly that "they could have done otherwise," and use this as their justification for not excusing them, while agreeing that other human beings in similar circumstances could *not* have done otherwise, they are not making a mistake either—and this is independent of whether or not determinism is true. They are pointing to a *real difference in moral competence* that does not depend on either indeterminism or determinism, and that can ground a difference in our response.

To see this more clearly, take the perspective of the programmer who designed program B. She wants to know if she has uncovered a weakness in B. Here is a game in which not castling cost B the victory; could B have castled then? If all it would take for that to happen was the flip of a single bit in the random-number generator, then perhaps no design improvements are called for. As often as not, in similar circumstances, B will castle, and perhaps that's as good as anyone could hope for. A program must always use random numbers now and then (as coin flips) to terminate search and get on with the game, and hence there will always be cases where thanks to the flip, the search stops just this side of discovery. And notice that the situation is not improved if we give program B (or program A) a quantum random-number generator, say, a Geiger counter that spews out bits based on the undetermined trajectories of subatomic particles. Then consider what we would say about B in the case where B doesn't castle because of a single o where a 1 might have been. If the quantum number generator yields a o, B castles; if it yields a 1, B doesn't castle. "B could have castled," says an observer when the 1 comes up. Yes, but B is no freer for all that. In a series of games in which this sort of opportunity comes up, half the time B will castle and half the time B won't, whether B's random-number generator is "genuine" or "pseudo." The philosopher David Wiggins (1973, p. 54) once wrote of the "cosmic unfairness" of determinism, but what our intuition pump about the computer chess tournament shows is the equal "cosmic unfairness" of indeterminism. B is "at the mercy of" its random-number generator *or* its pseudo-random-number generator. (So, of course, is A; so are we all.) There is no reason to prefer the genuinely random-number generator—unless of course you plan to play chess against an omniscient God who can see into your pseudo-random-number generator and plan accordingly!

So we're still looking for a reason to want indeterminism to be true. Perhaps we can have all the free will worth wanting without indeterminism playing any role. Here's another candidate reason:

I can't change the past, but if indeterminism is true, I can change the future!

Nope. Change the future from what to what? From what it *was* going to be to what it *is* going to be? You can no more *change the future* than you can *change the past*. The concept is incoherent. So:

If determinism is true, I can't change the future, and if determinism is false, I can't change the future. So it follows that I can't change the future.

Why does it seem that we want to change the future? Because we want to be able to foresee disasters and do something so those disasters don't happen. And we *can* do this, independently of indeterminism. If somebody throws a brick at you, and you see it and duck, you can avoid being hit by the brick. Good for you. Was the collision going to happen? In one sense yes, since the brick was clearly on a trajectory right for your head, but since you saw it (since you were caused to see it by the light bouncing off of it into your eyes, where your brain calculated the risk and was caused to take action), you avoided it. Of course, if you had wanted to *avoid avoiding* it (if some reason had occurred to you for why you might actually do better by letting it hit you), you could do just that. Some observer might not be able to tell, right up to the last moment, whether you were going to take the hit or not. And if he was betting on you to duck, he'd lose. We're back at our reason for wanting to be unpredictable, which does not require indeterminism.

What does this intuition pump accomplish? It takes the familiar phrase "could have done otherwise" and shows that contrary to widespread but ill-examined opinion, a valuable version of it does *not* depend on indeterminism. If there is a sense of "could have done otherwise" that is both incompatible with determinism and morally important—not merely a metaphysical curiosity, you might say—this has yet to be established, and the burden of proof lies with those who think so. One more "obvious" point exposed as not so obvious after all.

71. ULTIMATE RESPONSIBILITY

So far, we've been looking at trivial choices, not involving moral responsibility at all: rock, paper, scissors; chess moves; and brick-ducking. Perhaps it is when we are specifically looking at our attempts to be *moral* agents, not just intentional systems like chess-playing computers and stotting gazelles, that indeterminism is truly desirable. Many thinkers have thought so. For them, these exercises are just so much distraction. Here is a nice clear version of what some thinkers take to be the decisive argument. It is due in this form to the philosopher Galen Strawson (2010):

1. You do what you do, in any given situation, because of the way you are.
2. So in order to be ultimately responsible for what you do, you have to be ultimately responsible for the way you are—at least in certain crucial mental respects.
3. But you cannot be ultimately responsible for the way you are in any respect at all.
4. So you cannot be ultimately responsible for what you do.

The first premise is undeniable: "the way you are" is meant to include your total state at the time, however you got into it. Whatever state it is, your action flows from it non-miraculously. The second premise observes that you couldn't be "ultimately" responsible for what you do unless you were "ultimately" responsible for getting yourself into that state—at least in some regards. But according to step (3) this is impossible.

So step (4), the conclusion, does seem to follow logically. Several thinkers have found this argument decisive and important. But is it really? Let's look more closely at step (3). Why can't you be ultimately responsible for *some* respects, at least, of the way you are? In everyday life we make exactly this distinction, and it matters morally. Suppose you design and build a robot and send it out into the world unattended and unsupervised and knowing full well the sorts of activities it might engage in, and suppose it seriously injures somebody. Aren't you responsible for this, at least in some respects? Most people would say so. You made it; you should have foreseen the dangers—indeed you *did* foresee some of the dangers—and now you are to blame, at least in part, for the damage done. Few would have any sympathy for you if you insisted that you weren't responsible *at all* for the harm done by your robot.

Now consider a slightly different case: you design and build a person (yourself at a later time) and send yourself out into the risky world knowing full well the possible dangers you would encounter. You get yourself drunk in a bar and then get in your car and drive off. Aren't you responsible, at least in part, for the "way you were" when you crashed into a school bus? Common sense says of course. (The bartender, or your compliant host, may share the responsibility.) But how could this be, in the face of Strawson's knockdown argument? Well, remember that Strawson says you can't be *absolutely* responsible for the way you are. Okay, but so what? Who would think it was important to be *absolutely* responsible? That is indeed a state that is utterly impossible, *even if indeterminism is true!* (So much for the idea that this argument gives us a reason for hoping for indeterminism.) Here is what Strawson (2010) says:

> To be absolutely responsible for what one does, one would have to be *causa sui*, the cause of oneself, and this is impossible (it certainly wouldn't be more possible if we had immaterial souls rather than being wholly material).

Absolute responsibility is a red herring, a blessing nobody should hanker for. Strawson (2003) thinks otherwise, and criticizes me for neglecting it:

He doesn't establish the kind of absolute free will and moral responsibility that most people want to believe in and do believe in. That can't be done, and he knows it.

He's exactly right: I don't establish the kind of free will most people want to believe in, and I know it. But I think they are *wrong* to want to believe in it, and wrong to believe in it if they do. The burden falls on Strawson and others to show *why* we ought to care about ultimate responsibility—or the determinism/indeterminism issue—in our lives. They can define a variety of free will that is incompatible with determinism, and show that lots of folks think that's important, but they also need to show that those folks aren't deceiving themselves. Why should anybody care? (Note my rhetorical question. I'm leading with my chin. I would be happy for Strawson or somebody else to step up to the plate and try to answer it, but so far there are no volunteers.)

Before leaving Strawson's argument, let me ask if you have noticed its uncanny resemblance to an earlier argument. I will revise the earlier argument into a form a little closer to Strawson's to bring out the similarities.

1. A mammal is a mammal, in any given context, because of the way it is.
2. In order to be a mammal, you have to become the way you are by having a mammal for a mother.
3. But this must be true of your mother, and her mother, and so forth *ad infinitum*, which is impossible.
4. So you cannot be a mammal because mammals are utterly impossible.

You should always be leery of any such "ancestral" argument. It is almost certain to be a disguised instance of the ancient fallacy known as the *sorites* (or "heap") argument:

1. A single grain of wheat is not a heap.

2. Adding a grain to a single grain does not make a heap.
3. You can't make a non-heap into a heap by adding a single grain.
4. Therefore there are no such things as heaps!

Philosophers have written about the sorites paradox and the problems of the vague boundaries of terms (which is what the paradox obviously depends on) for thousands of years, and there is still no resolution of just how to diagnose and avoid the fallacy. (See the *Stanford Encyclopedia of Philosophy* online for an excellent and up-to-the-minute survey.) There are even a few brave philosophers who declare the sorites to be valid, and they try to live with the "fact" that there are no bald men and no non-bald men either. Tough position to defend! But as chapter 43 showed, Darwin taught us how to turn our backs on the sorites; we don't need to find "principled" dividing lines between categories ranked in ancestral order.

To my knowledge I am the first to point out the resemblance of Strawson's argument—and the other arguments of this ilk in the free-will literature—to a sorites paradox, but there it is. I think it is just as obvious that people can gradually become morally responsible during their passage from infancy to adulthood as it is that lineages of reptiles and then therapsids can gradually become a lineage of mammals over the eons. You don't have to be an *absolute mammal* to be a mammal, and you don't have to be *absolutely responsible* to be responsible, or have *absolute* free will to have a kind of free will worth wanting. In fact, since absolute free will would be miraculous, there really needs to be a powerful argument to show why anybody would covet such a thing. Do they want to be God? Too bad, they're out of luck, but the next best thing is quite a good thing to be.

72. SPHEXISHNESS

Doug Hofstadter (1982) coined the term "sphexishness" for a familiar sort of rigid, robotic mindlessness that is often mistaken for great cleverness. The defining example of sphexishness, and the source of the term, is a wasp with a curious behavior. Doug and I had independently been struck by a passage in a popular science book, *The Machinery of the Brain*, written by Dean Wooldridge (1963), who described the *Sphex* wasp thus:

> When the time comes for egg-laying, the wasp *Sphex* builds a burrow for the purpose and seeks out a cricket which she stings in such a way as to paralyze but not kill it. She drags the cricket into the burrow, lays her eggs alongside, closes the burrow, then flies away, never to return. In due course, the eggs hatch and the wasp grubs feed off the paralyzed cricket, which has not decayed, having been kept in the wasp equivalent of deep freeze. To the human mind, such an elaborately organized and seemingly purposeful routine conveys a convincing flavor of logic and thoughtfulness—until more details are examined. For example, the wasp's routine is to bring the paralyzed cricket to the burrow, leave it on the threshold, go inside to see that all is well, emerge, and then drag the cricket in. If the cricket is moved a few inches away while the wasp is inside making her preliminary inspection, the wasp, on emerging from the burrow, will bring the cricket back to the threshold, but not inside, and will then repeat the preparatory procedure of entering the burrow to see that everything is all right. If again the cricket is removed a few inches while the wasp is inside, once again she will move the cricket up to the threshold and re-enter the burrow for a final check. The wasp

never thinks of pulling the cricket straight in. On one occasion this procedure was repeated forty times, always with the
same result. [p. 82]

A perfect example, it seems, of the imperfect, uncomprehending
competence that we unmask when we expose the superficial, pseudo-
understanding of a second-rate computer program. We have recently
learned, however, that Wooldridge gave us—as popular science writers so often do—an oversimplified sketch of the phenomenon. The
psychologist Lars Chittka, in a note to me, quoted from the work of
Jean-Henri Fabre (in 1879), which had apparently been the source for
Wooldridge, who, if he had read on in Fabre, would have found that
in fact only some *Sphex* wasps are sphexish. In fact, Fabre was eager
to make the point. If at first blush you thought *Sphex* was clever, and
at second blush you thought *Sphex* was stupid, try third blush, and
find that some *Sphex* wasps are not so sphexish after all. Chittka
sent me the German translation of Fabre (I still haven't located the
French), which includes the following sentence: "*Nach zwei oder drei
Malen, . . . packt ihre Fuehler mit den Kieferzangen und schleift sie in die
Hoehle. Wer war nun der Dummkopf?*" (After two or three times, . . .
she grabbed her [the prey's] antennae with her pincers and slid it into
the hole. Now who's the dummy?)

So the adjective *sphexish* is a bit of a misnomer, but since it has
caught on, the *Sphex* wasps will just have to endure the insult. They
are lucky, in a way, to be in the limelight of nonspecialist attention,
which probably has a nonnegligible fitness enhancement. (Which
habitat would you vote to protect, *Sphex* habitat or *Humdrumbeetle*
habitat?) *Sphex* wasps may not be "charismatic" like elephants and
tigers and wolves, but they are rather well known—for their problematic sphexishness.

Sphexishness is an important property not so much because
so many whole, simple animals—insects, worms, fish—exhibit it
(though they do, in varying degrees), but because it gives us a term
for the limited, robotic, myopic, competences out of which we can
build fancier, more versatile, comprehending minds. The building

blocks in any mind model had better be sphexish! Or, as I noted earlier, the building blocks should be **sorta** minds, pale shadows of our minds. Sphexishness is also useful to distinguish morally competent minds from morally incompetent minds. To the extent that a human being is sphexish, because of a brain tumor or brain injury or serious imbalance of neuromodulators or mental illness or sheer ignorance or immaturity, that human being could not have done otherwise in the relevant sense.

The persistent biologist interfering with the *Sphex* wasp in order to expose its sphexishness is the very model of the manipulative agent we rightly dread. Many philosophers' thought experiments about free will depend on invoking just such a puppeteer, or a nefarious neurosurgeon who has secretly wired someone up to do his bidding. Presumably the moral of these scary tales is that even if there is no actual puppeteer, the fact that our behavior is caused by various features of our environments, as processed through our perceptual systems and brains, shows that there might as well be a puppeteer. (The cover illustration of Sam Harris's little book *Free Will* (2012) is a set of puppeteer control strings.) But this invited conclusion is a clear *non sequitur*. When the "control" by the environment runs through our well-working perceptual systems and our undeluded brains, it is nothing to dread; in fact, nothing is more desirable than our being caused by the things and events around us to generate true beliefs about them that we can then use in modulating our behavior to our advantage. Photons bouncing off air holes in the tidal flats into my eyes are apt to cause me to grab my clam rake and basket and start digging. If this is a case of being controlled by my environment, I'm all for it. And, like most people, I do not feel threatened or manipulated when my friends offer me sumptuous meals, knowing full well that I will be unable to resist the temptation to eat them.

Another thing you will notice about the puppeteer and neurosurgeon examples in the literature on free will is that the intervention is always—always—secret. Why should this be? Because it is only when we are *unwittingly* being caused to act or choose by some other, secret agent that the intuitions flood in to the effect that our will is not free. The reason for this is not far to seek, and harks back to the insight that inaugurated game theory: when an agent knows about the attempt at manipulation by another agent, it thereupon seeks countermeasures, and at the very least adjusts its behavior to better cope with this discovery. The competitive interactions between the two agents involve multiple levels of feedback, and hence diminishing "control" by the would-be manipulator. And if the intervention is not only not secret, but requested by the "puppet," the tables are turned completely.

This we can demonstrate by simply altering the standard cases slightly, turning the knobs on the intuition pumps. The philosopher Harry Frankfurt (1969) invented an intuition pump in which a person is being monitored by secretly implanted neurostimulation gadgetry that is controlled by a neurosurgeon who makes sure that that person decides the way he wants that person to decide. If you, as that person, are faced with a dilemma and choose option A rather than B, then if this is what the neurosurgeon wanted you to choose, he does nothing; if instead his gauges show that you are about to choose option B, he hits the button and prevents you from choosing option B, and you choose A after all. You don't feel a thing. Did you choose freely in either case? Over the years philosophers have written hundreds of pages about "Frankfurt cases" with many variations, but one turning of the knobs that makes a huge difference has never to my knowledge been explored. Here it is:

Wanting to tame your profligate love of rich desserts, you have contracted with the good doctor to implant this device, and you are paying him a handsome fee to monitor your every meal, providing a safety net that keeps you from ordering the hot fudge sundaes and slices of cheese cake. Both of you hope he never has to deploy his button, and soon you almost forget that he or his assistant is electronically at your elbow; you are cured and the gadget has recorded an unbroken string of hundreds of A choices ("No thanks, just a cup of black coffee"). If those aren't examples of *you* choosing responsibly and freely, why not? Wasn't it wise of you to get help with your somewhat fragile willpower?

73. THE BOYS FROM BRAZIL: ANOTHER BOOM CRUTCH

In 2004, the psychologists Joshua Greene and Jonathan Cohen co-authored "For the Law, Neuroscience Changes Everything and Nothing," which was published in the prestigious journal *Philosophical Transactions of the Royal Society*. This influential article conjures up a revolution in the law, triggered by scientific discoveries.

> [T]he law *says* that it presupposes nothing more than a metaphysically modest notion of free will that is perfectly compatible with determinism. However, we argue that the law's intuitive support is ultimately grounded in a metaphysically overambitious, libertarian [indeterministic] notion of free will that is threatened by determinism and, more pointedly, by forthcoming cognitive neuroscience. [p. 1776]

The case they make is subtle; it has to be, because they grant that there are a wealth of arguments in support of compatibilism (the view defended by me here), but they want to show that actually "we are all of two minds" about free will. They offer a thought experiment designed to reveal the dependence of *everyday* commonsense thinking on indeterminism. Note that this is pretty much what I've just been calling for: show us, please, both *that* and *why* we should care about indeterminism. Their thought experiment was inspired by the film *The Boys from Brazil*, about Nazi scientists who raise Hitler clones (thanks to some salvaged DNA). Here it is:

> Let us suppose, then, that a group of scientists has managed to create an individual—call him Mr Puppet—who, by design, engages in some criminal behavior: say, a murder done during a drug deal gone bad. [p. 1780]

Here is what they say about their thought experiment:

> Yes, he is as rational as other criminals, and, yes, it was
> his desires and beliefs that produced his actions. But those
> beliefs and desires were rigged by external forces, and that
> is why, intuitively, he deserves our pity more than our moral
> condemnation. . . . what is the real difference between us
> and Mr Puppet? One obvious difference is that Mr Puppet
> is the victim of a diabolical plot whereas most people, we
> presume, are not. But does this matter? The thought that
> Mr Puppet is not fully responsible depends on the idea that
> his actions were externally determined. . . . But the fact that
> these forces are connected to the desires and intentions of
> evil scientists is irrelevant, is it not? What matters is only
> that these forces are beyond Mr Puppet's control, that they're
> not really his. [p. 1780]

What do you think? Is this a good intuition pump for its purpose, or not? Amusingly, the authors note that this is a question worth considering: "Daniel Dennett might object that the story of Mr Puppet is just a misleading 'intuition pump.'" Indeed I do. I say it's a **boom crutch**. But they shrug off this hunch and carry on: "It seems to us that the more one knows about Mr Puppet and his life the less inclined one is to see him as truly responsible for his actions and consider our punishing him as a worthy end in itself."

So let's take a closer look, turning the knobs on this intuition pump to see what is actually doing the work. I propose to adjust four knobs. First, let's get rid of the diabolical plot—which the authors themselves insist does not matter. I am surprised that they are so blithe about introducing a "nefarious neurosurgeon" and supposing that this is obviously innocent, since doubts have been expressed for years about such a move, but we can test their conviction by replacing "a group of scientists" with "an indifferent environment":

BEFORE: Let us suppose, then, that *a group of scientists* has managed to create an individual—call him Mr Puppet—who, by design, engages in some criminal behavior: say, a murder done during a drug deal gone bad.

AFTER: Let us suppose, then, that *an indifferent environment* has managed to create an individual—call him Mr Puppet—who, by design, engages in some criminal behavior: say, a murder done during a drug deal gone bad.

Second knob: With the plotters gone, we have to replace "by design" with "with high probability":

BEFORE: Let us suppose, then, that an indifferent environment has managed to create an individual—call him Mr Puppet—who, *by design*, engages in some criminal behavior: say, a murder done during a drug deal gone bad.

AFTER: Let us suppose, then, that an indifferent environment has managed to create an individual—call him Mr Puppet—who, *with high probability*, engages in some criminal behavior: say, a murder done during a drug deal gone bad.

Third knob: I want to change the motivation of the crime—still a murder, but in a rather different setting. (That shouldn't matter, should it?)

BEFORE: Let us suppose, then, that an indifferent environment has managed to create an individual—call him Mr Puppet—who, with high probability, engages in some criminal behavior: say, a murder done *during a drug deal gone bad*.

AFTER: Let us suppose, then, that an indifferent environment has managed to create an individual—call him Mr Puppet—who, with high probability, engages in some criminal behavior: say, a murder done *to cover up an embezzlement*.

Fourth knob: Let's change the culprit's name. After all, it's just a name.

> BEFORE: Let us suppose, then, that an indifferent environment has managed to create an individual—call him *Mr Puppet*—who, with high probability, engages in some criminal behavior: say, a murder done to cover up an embezzlement.
>
> AFTER: Let us suppose, then, that an indifferent environment has managed to create an individual—call him *Captain Autonomy*—who, with high probability, engages in some criminal behavior: say, a murder done to cover up an embezzlement.

What intuitions does this pump for you now? The same intuitions? Are you more inclined to pity than condemnation? Maybe it would help if we fleshed out the details a little further. Here is my friendly amendment to Greene and Cohen's intuition pump:

> Captain Autonomy majored in economics at Harvard, and after graduation he went to work at Lehman Brothers, where all around him people were cheating and making fortunes in the process. He fell in love with a gold-digging heartbreaker, who threatened to leave him if he didn't get rich quick. He saw his chance, a virtually undetectable embezzlement, almost surely an invisible crime, and he knowingly took the risk, but, alas, against all the odds a witness arose, who made the mistake of standing too close to the railing on the penthouse garden, . . . a quick "stumble"—Oops!—and the witness was sent to his death on the avenue below. Suspicions were aroused, and soon enough Captain Autonomy was under arrest.

Are you still inclined to think that *because his actions were externally determined* he is "not truly responsible"? Even if you are still tempted to see Captain Autonomy as a *victim* of his (posh) environment, I think you have to agree that the temptation is much diminished, and might even be a hangover of sorts from the earlier telling. (Or maybe I've just exploited your emotions in the opposite direction, counting on your bloodthirsty desire to punish the greedy Wall Street types for their role in our economic malaise.) I'm not claiming that my variations prove that people are or can be responsible in spite of being determined; I am just claiming that this particular intuition pump is not at all to be trusted, since the (available, permissible) knob settings are interfering so much with our judgments. It may not have been designed to blow smoke, but it certainly manages to hinder clear thinking.

SUMMARY

People care deeply about having free will, but they also seem to have misguided ideas about what free will is or could be (like their misguided ideas about color and consciousness). Our decisions are not little miracles in the brain that violate the physics and chemistry that account for the rest of our bodies' processes, even if many folk think this must be what happens if our decisions are to be truly free. We can't conclude from this, however, that then we *don't* have free will, because free will in this bonkers sense is not the only concept of free will. The law, according with common sense, contrasts signing a contract "of your own free will" with signing a contract under duress or under the influence of hallucination or other mental derangement. Here is a perfectly familiar sense of free will, a distinction presupposed by many of the practices and attitudes that comprise our manifest image, that has no demonstrated dependence on the bonkers sense.

For hundreds of years there have been philosophers who have insisted that this sense of free will is the important sense, the one we should care about, and it is compatible with determinism, with materialism, with physics and chemistry reigning unchallenged. The intuition pumps and other thinking tools in this part are designed to support and advance the understanding of this prospect, *compatibilism*. It has had many versions over the years, and is probably the consensus not only among philosophers but also among judges, lawyers, and others who have to make distinctions about who is responsible for what and who is excused because they didn't have free will when they acted. Some scientists are now challenging this consensus, and they may of course be right to do so. Let's take a hard look at the arguments.

Maybe science is teaching us something radical, even revolutionary: that nobody is ever responsible for anything they do, and there is no sound basis for distinguishing some acts as praiseworthy and others as blameworthy. But such a revolutionary conclusion needs a lot more conscientious attention to detail than it has so far received from the scientists declaring it. The nefarious neurosurgeon disabled her patient with nothing but a false idea; a mistaken view promulgated by influential scientists could rob people of a legitimate and life-enhancing variety of free will. Caution is called for, on all sides.

Compatibilism, for all its popularity among philosophers, has always provoked suspicion. Immanuel Kant famously called it a "wretched subterfuge," and writers today often express doubts about the sincerity of those of us who maintain it. This is as it should be, actually. Science teaches us to be especially on guard against wishful thinking, and many of the rules of scientific investigation are specifically designed to prevent us from being taken in by our hopes when we think we are being convinced by the evidence. Imagine that some astronomers announce that a giant asteroid is going to strike our planet in ten years, obliterating all life, and then another group of astronomers claim that their reanalysis of the data shows that we can all breathe easily; the asteroid will miss Earth by a narrow margin. Good news, but how do we know the second group of astronomers aren't deceiving themselves—or just deceiving us with a benign lie? Check and recheck their calculations; mount an independent attempt at replication; don't just gratefully accept their conclusion because it doesn't contain any obvious errors and it appeals to you. But also never forget that it is possible that they are right. Don't make the opposite mistake of discrediting—on "general principles"—something that seems "too good to be true."

Is compatibilism too good to be true? I think not; I think it *is* true, and we can soundly and roundly dismiss the alarmists, at the same time reforming and revising our understanding of what underwrites our concept of moral responsibility. But that is a task for the future, and it should be the work of many hands. So far as I can see, it is both the most difficult and the most important philosophical problem confronting us today. The stakes are high, the issues thorny, and emotions tend to cloud our judgment. We will need all our thinking tools and more, which we will have to make as we go along.

IX

WHAT IS IT LIKE TO BE A PHILOSOPHER?

When we are too close to something, it is hard to see what it is. In recent years I have spent less time interacting with other philosophers than I used to, and more time interacting with scientists and other kinds of thinkers. I am still a philosopher (no matter what some philosophers say!), and I relish the task of explaining to non-philosophers why philosophy is worth doing. To those utterly outside philosophy, it often looks preposterous, the very paradigm of use-less cleverness. They are missing something (recall **Sturgeon's Law**: 90 percent of everything is crap; they are missing the 10 percent). Having spent fifty years inside philosophy, I am familiar with it; now that I spend so much time far away from philosophy, I can also see its strange side vividly. Some of my scientific friends and colleagues con-fess that they cannot for the life of them see why I don't abandon ship and join them. The short answer is that I have managed, by strad-dling the boundaries, to have the best of both worlds. By working with scientists I get a rich diet of fascinating and problematic *facts* to think about, but by staying a philosopher without a lab or a research grant, I get to think about all the theories and experiments and never have to do the dishes. To quote one of my favorite Gershwin songs, it's "nice work if you can get it."

It seems to me that these days, happily, scientists are paying more respectful attention to philosophers than they used to, especially in my main area, the mind, where the phenomena that cognitive scientists study are almost exactly the phenomena that philosophers have been thinking about for centuries: perception, memory, meaning, volition, and consciousness. And philosophers—some of them—have earned the attention by informing themselves of the relevant science and coming up with useful proposals for clarifying and advancing the scientific research and composing better ways of explaining the results to the nonscientific world. There are still large failures of communication when the tribes try to interact, however, and I am going to address a few of the differences with the goal of achieving more mutual understanding in the future.

74. A FAUSTIAN BARGAIN

For several years, I have been posing the following choice for my fellow philosophers: If Mephistopheles offered you the following two options, which would you choose?

(A) You *solve* the major philosophical problem of your choice so conclusively that there is nothing left to say (thanks to you, part of the field closes down forever, and you get a footnote in history).

(B) You write a book of such tantalizing perplexity and controversy that it stays on the required reading list for centuries to come.

Some philosophers reluctantly admit that they would have to go for option (B). If they had to choose, they would rather be read than right. Like composers, poets, novelists, and other creators in the arts, they tend to want their work to be experienced, over and over, by millions (billions, if possible!). But they are also tugged in the direction of the scientists' quest. After all, philosophers are *supposed* to be trying to get at the truth.

When I present the same Faustian bargain to scientists, they tend to opt for (A) without any hesitation—it's a no-brainer for them. And then they shake their heads in wonder (or disgust?) when they learn that this is a hard choice for many philosophers, some of whom opt, somewhat sheepishly, for (B). But this reaction by scientists misses the important point made by Nicholas Humphrey (1987) (see chapter 48):

In *Two Cultures*, C. P. Snow extolled the great discoveries of science as "scientific Shakespeare," but in one way he was

fundamentally mistaken. Shakespeare's plays were Shakespeare's plays and no one else's; scientific discoveries, by
contrast, belong—ultimately—to no one in particular.

If Shakespeare hadn't existed, nobody else would have written *Hamlet*
or *Romeo and Juliet* or *King Lear*. If Van Gogh hadn't existed, nobody
else would have painted *Starry Night*. This may be a slight exaggeration, but there's something to it. On the one hand, there is an individuality to the contributions of great artists that seems to be not just
rare in science, but positively beside the point. The famous priority
disputes in science, and the races for one Nobel Prize clincher or
another, are ferocious precisely because somebody else *could* make
exactly the contribution you were striving to make—and you won't
get points for style if you come in second. These contests have no
parallel in the arts, where a different set of goals reigns.

Some scientists aspire to reach large readerships, and to delight
the readers they catch, and the best write works of surpassing literary
value. Darwin's books come to mind. But the goal of getting it right,
of persuading the readers of a discovered truth, still comes first, as we
can tell at a glance by comparing Darwin's *Voyage of the Beagle* with
Melville's *Moby-Dick*. One can learn a great deal about whales and
whaling from *Moby-Dick*, but Melville didn't write it to be an artful
and persuasive compendium of whaling facts.

Bearing in mind the difference between the goals of science and
the goals of art, then, here is a question for scientists that appropriately
parallels the teaser I ask my philosophical colleagues: If Mephistopheles offered you the following two options, which would you choose?

1. You win the race (and the accompanying Nobel Prize)
   for pinning down a discovery that becomes the basis for
   a huge expansion of scientific knowledge but that, in
   retrospect, epitomized Humphrey's epithet, belonging to
   no one in particular. (Crick and Watson come to mind;
   there is scant doubt that if they hadn't won the race when

they did, Linus Pauling or somebody else would have
done so soon.)

2. You propose a theory so original, so utterly unimagined
   before your work, that your surname enters the language,
   but your theory turns out to be mostly wrong, though it
   continues to generate years—even centuries—of valuable
   controversy. (I think of Cartesian dualism about the mind,
   Lamarckian theories of evolution, Skinnerian behaviorism, and Freudian views of everything from infant sexual-
   ity and neurosis to art, music, and literature.)

A better, though less well-known example of option (2) might be
Descartes's ambitious work on physics, which was so influential and
so brilliantly wrong that it was a major provocation for Isaac Newton,
whose world-changing *Philosophiae Naturalis Principia Mathematica*
(written in 1687) deliberately echoed the title of Descartes's *Principia
Philosophiae* (of 1644) to make it clear what worldview he intended
to replace. And then there is Chomskian linguistics. It certainly
passes the originality test. Like the victory of the *America* in the race
that gave the America's Cup its name, there was no second place
anywhere in sight when Chomsky burst on the scene. In subsequent
years the original theoretical seed—the "transformational" theory of
Chomsky's *Syntactic Structures* (published in 1957)—has been largely
abandoned, superseded by descendant theories in several species as
different from their common ancestor as ostriches, hummingbirds,
and albatrosses are from the dinosaurs from whom they evolved. Was
Chomsky fruitfully wrong in 1957, or did he **rather** (ding!) discover a
great truth? "Yes" answers the question pretty well.

We honor scientists who are wrong in useful ways—recall Wolfgang Pauli's insult about the theorist who "isn't even wrong." But
forced to choose, would you trade being first and right for being
original and provocative? Not quite so easy to decide, is it?

75. PHILOSOPHY AS NAÏVE AUTO-ANTHROPOLOGY

Patrick Hayes, the artificial intelligence researcher, once set out on a project to axiomatize the naïve (or folk) physics of liquids. The idea was to provide a robot with the propositions it would need to use as its core beliefs if it was going to interact with people (who rely on folk physics every day). It proved to be more challenging than he had anticipated, and he wrote an interesting paper about the project, "The Naïve Physics Manifesto" (Hayes, 1978). In the naïve physics of liquids, everything that strikes naïve folks as counterintuitive is, of course, ruled out: siphons are "impossible" and so are pipettes, but you can mop up liquid with a fluffy towel, and pull water out of a well with a suction pump. A robot equipped with such a store of "knowledge" would be as surprised by a siphon as most of us were when first we saw one in action. Hayes's project was what I would call *sophisticated* naïve physics, because he was under no illusions; he knew the theory he was trying to axiomatize was false, however useful in daily life. This was an exercise in what might be called axiomatic anthropology: you treat what the folks say—and agree about—as your axioms or theorems, and try to render the data set consistent, resolving any contradictions encountered. And, of course, he didn't bother rounding up any actual informants; he figured that he knew the naïve physics of liquids as well as any normal person did, so he used himself as his sole informant: axiomatic *auto*-anthropology.*

Now compare Hayes's project with the philosophical projects

---

* Hayes's work inspired others. See the anthology edited by Bobrow (1985). Authors of one of the essays therein remark, "Naïve physics is in itself an ambiguous term. Is it just bad physics? Is it psychology? Artificial intelligence? Physics?" (Bobrow, 1985, p. 13). The answer, I submit, is that naïve physics is the attempt to make the physics part of our manifest image rigorous enough to support automated deductive reasoning.

in *analytic metaphysics*, which often strike me as *naïve* naïve auto-anthropology since the participants in this research seem to be convinced that their program actually gets at something true, not just something believed true by a particular subclass of human beings (Anglophone philosophers of the analytic metaphysics persuasion). Otherwise, the programs seem identical: you gather your shared intuitions, test and provoke them by engaging in mutual intuition-pumping, and then try to massage the resulting data set into a consistent "theory," based on "received" principles that count, ideally, as axioms. I've asked a number of analytic metaphysicians whether they can distinguish their enterprise from naïve naïve auto-anthropology of their clan, and have not yet received any compelling answers.

The alternative is *sophisticated* naïve anthropology (both auto- and hetero-)—the anthropology that reserves judgment about whether any of the theorems adduced by the exercise deserve to be trusted—and this is a feasible and frequently valuable project. I propose that this is the enterprise to which analytic metaphysicians should turn, since it requires rather minimal adjustments to their methods and only one major revision of their *raison d'être*: they must roll back their pretensions and acknowledge that their research is best seen as a preparatory reconnaissance of the terrain of the manifest image, suspending both belief and disbelief the way anthropologists do when studying an exotic culture: let's pretend for the nonce that the natives are right, and see what falls out. Since at least a large part of philosophy's task, in my vision of the discipline, consists in negotiating the traffic back and forth between the **manifest and scientific images**, it is a good idea for philosophers to analyze what they are up against in the way of folk assumptions before launching into their theory-building and theory-criticizing.

One of the hallmarks of sophisticated naïve anthropology is its openness to counterintuitive discoveries. As long as you're doing naïve anthropology, counterintuitiveness (to the natives) counts against your reconstruction; when you shift gears and begin asking which aspects of the naïve "theory" are true, counterintuitiveness loses its force as an objection and even becomes, on occasion, a sign of significant progress. In science in general, counterintuitive results are prized, after all.

One of the weaknesses of auto-anthropology is that one's own intuitions are apt to be distorted by one's theoretical predilections. Linguists have known for a long time that they get so wrapped up in their theories they are no longer reliable sources of linguistic intuition. Can you really say in English, "The boy the man the woman kissed punched ran away," or is my theory of clause embedding tricking my "ear"? Their raw, untutored intuitions have been sullied by too much theory, so they recognize that they must go out and ask nonlinguists for their linguistic intuitions. Philosophers have recently begun to appreciate this point, in the new enthusiasm for so-called experimental philosophy (see Knobe and Nichols, 2008). It is early days still, and some of the pioneer efforts are unimpressive, but at least philosophers are getting used to the idea that they can no longer declare various propositions to be obviously true on the sole grounds that they seem smashingly obvious *to them*. (In a similar vein, Hayes *might* have surprised himself about the chief tenets of folk physics if he had gone to the trouble of interviewing a random sample of folk instead of just treating himself as exemplary.)

So here is a project, a particular sort of sophisticated naïve anthropology, that philosophers should seriously consider undertaking as a survey of the terrain of the commonsense or manifest image of the world before launching into their theories of knowledge, justice, beauty, truth, goodness, time, causation, and so on, to make sure they actually aim their analyses and arguments at targets that are relevant to the rest of the world, both lay concerns and scientific concerns. Such a systematic inquiry would yield something like a catalogue of the unreformed conceptual terrain that sets the problems for the theorist, the metaphysics of the manifest image, if you like. This is where we philosophers have to start in our attempts to negotiate back and forth between the latest innovations in the scientific image, and it wouldn't hurt to have a careful map of this folk terrain instead of just eyeballing it. This is the other half, one might say, of the reform that turned philosophy of science from an armchair fantasy field into a serious partnership with actual science, when philosophers of science decided that they really had to know a lot of current science from the inside. Once we think about our philosophical tasks with this image in mind, we can see that a great deal of the informal trudging around, backing and filling, counterexample-mongering and intuition-busting that fills the pages of philosophy journals is—at best—an attempt to organize a mutually acceptable consensus about this territory.

76. HIGHER-ORDER TRUTHS
OF CHMESS

Consider this chess puzzle.* White to checkmate in two.

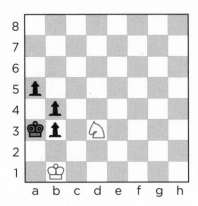

WHITE TO PLAY
Hint: Checkmate
in 2 moves.

Solution: 1. Nb2 a4
(the only legal move)
2. Nc4 mate (from
a study by Gurevich).

It appeared recently in the *Boston Globe,* and what startled me was
that I had thought it had been proved that you can't checkmate
with a lone knight (and a king, of course). I was wrong; as David
Misialowski pointed out to me in a recent e-mail, it has been proved
that you cannot checkmate your opponent's king when only his king
and your king and knight are on the board. The fact that the proposition *you can never checkmate with a lone knight and king* is *not* a truth of
chess is a *higher-order* truth of chess.

Philosophy is traditionally an *a priori* discipline, like mathematics, or at least it has an *a priori* methodology at its core, and this fact
cuts two ways. On the one hand, it excuses philosophers from spend-
ing tedious hours in the lab or out in the field, and from learning

---

* With regard to another puzzle in this book, for one thing, the *slop* I *love* is *even* followed by
Laura *Dern,* and for another, in spite of the *smut,* I *hope* to *iron* Sean *Penn's* shirt.

data-gathering techniques, statistical methods, geography, history, foreign languages, empirical science, and so on, so they have plenty of time for honing their philosophical skills. On the other hand, as is often noted, philosophy can be created out of just about anything, and this is not always a blessing. For those of you younger readers who are thinking of undertaking a career in the field, and I hope some of you are, this chapter is a warning that the very freedom and abstractness of philosophy can be weaknesses. This chapter is also a travel guide for outsiders about some of the folkways and pitfalls of philosophy.

Consider, as a paradigm of *a priori* truths, the truths of chess. It is an empirical fact that people play chess, and there are mountains of other empirical facts about chess, about how people have been playing it for centuries, how they often use handsomely carved pieces on inlaid boards, and so forth. No knowledge of these empirical facts plays an indispensable role in the activity of working out the *a priori* truths of chess, which also exist in abundance. All you need to know are the rules of the game. There are exactly twenty legal opening moves (sixteen pawn moves and four knight moves); a king and a lone bishop cannot achieve checkmate against a lone king, and neither can a king and a lone knight, and so forth. Working out these *a priori* truths about chess is not always easy. Proving just what is and is not possible within the rules of chess is an intricate task, and mistakes can be made. For instance, a few years ago, a computer chess program discovered a mating net—a guaranteed or forced win—consisting of more than two hundred moves without a capture. This disproved a long-standing "theorem" of chess and has forced a change in the rules of the game. It used to be that fifty moves without a capture by either side constituted a draw (stalemate), but since this lengthy mating net is unbreakable, and leads to a win, it is unreasonable to maintain the fifty-move stalemate. (Before computers began playing chess, nobody imagined that there *could* be a guaranteed win anywhere near this length.) All this can be pretty interesting, and many highly intelligent people have devoted their minds to investigating this system of *a priori* truths of chess.*

Some philosophical research projects—or problematics, to speak with the more literary types—are rather like working out the truths of chess. A set of mutually agreed-upon rules are presupposed—and seldom discussed—and the implications of those rules are worked out, articulated, debated, refined. So far, so good. Chess is a deep and important human artifact, about which much of value has been written. But some philosophical research projects are more like working out the truths of *chmess*. Chmess is just like chess except that the king can move two squares in any direction, not one. I just invented it—though no doubt others have explored it in depth to see if it is worth playing. Probably it isn't. It probably has other names. I didn't bother investigating these questions because although they have true answers, they just aren't worth my time and energy to discover. Or so I think. There are just as many *a priori* truths of chmess as there are of chess (an infinity), and they are just as hard to discover. And that means that if people actually did get involved in investigating the truths of chmess, they would make mistakes, which would need to be corrected, and this opens up a whole new field of *a priori* investigation, the *higher-order* truths of chmess, such as the following:

1. Jones's (1989) proof that *p* is a truth of chmess is flawed: he overlooks the following possibility. . . .
2. Smith's (2002) claim that Jones's (1989) proof is flawed

---

* A delicious chess hoax appeared on the Internet on April Fools' Day, 2012 ("Rajlich: Busting the King's Gambit," *ChessBase News*, April 2, 2012, http://chessbase.com/newsdetail. asp?newsid=8047). It claimed that a gigantic consortium of computers working around the clock for over four months had proved that the King's Gambit (an opening long discredited but never "disproved") had now been shown definitively to be defeatable in all but one unlikely condition. The hoax fooled me—which was particularly embarrassing since I had written about an earlier hoax by Martin Gardner (in the introduction to Hurley, Dennett, and Adams, 2011). For the explanation of how the hoax was created, see "The ChessBase April Fools Prank," *ChessBase News*, April 4, 2012, http://chessbase.com/newsdetail.asp?newsid=8051.

presupposes the truth of Brown's lemma (1975), which has
recently been challenged by Garfinkle (2002). . . .

Now none of this is child's play. In fact, one might be able to demonstrate considerable brilliance in the group activity of working out the
higher-order truths of chmess. Here is where psychologist Donald
Hebb's dictum comes in handy:

> If it isn't worth doing, it isn't worth doing well.

Probably every philosopher can readily think of an ongoing controversy in philosophy whose participants would be out of work if
Hebb's dictum were ruthlessly applied, but we no doubt disagree on
just which cottage industries should be shut down. Probably there is
no investigation in our capacious discipline that is not believed by
some school of thought to be a wasted effort, brilliance squandered on
taking in each other's laundry. Voting would not yield results worth
heeding, and dictatorship would be even worse, so let a thousand
flowers bloom, I say. But just remember: if you let a thousand flowers
bloom, count on 995 of them to wilt. The alert I want to offer you is
just this: try to avoid committing your precious formative years to a
research agenda with a short shelf life. Philosophical fads quickly go
extinct, and there may be some truth to the rule of thumb: the hotter
the topic, the sooner it will burn out.

One good test to make sure a philosophical project is not just
exploring the higher-order truths of chmess is to see if people aside
from philosophers actually play the game. Can anybody outside of
academic philosophy be made to *care* about whether Jones's counter-
example works against Smith's principle? Another such test is to try
to teach the stuff to uninitiated undergraduates. If they don't "get it,"
you really should consider the hypothesis that you're following a self-
supporting community of experts into an artifactual trap.

Here is one way the trap works. Philosophy is to some extent an
unnatural act, and the more intelligent you are, the more qualms and

reservations you are likely to have about whether you get it, whether you're "doing it right," whether you have any talent for this discipline, and even whether the discipline is worth entering in the first place. So bright student Jones is *appropriately* insecure about going into philosophy. Intrigued by Professor Brown's discussion, Jones takes a stab at it, writing a paper on hot topic *H* that is given an "A" by Professor Brown. "You've got real talent, Jones," says Brown, and Jones has just discovered something that might be suitable lifework. Jones begins to invest in learning the rules of this particular game and in playing it ferociously with the other young aspirants. "Hey, we're good at this!" they say, egging each other on. Doubts about the enabling assumptions of the enterprise tend to be muffled or squelched "for the sake of argument." Publications follow.

So don't count on the validation of your fellow graduate students *or* your favorite professors to settle the issue. They all have a vested interest in keeping the enterprise going. It's what they know how to do; it's what they are good at. This is a problem in other fields too, and it can be even harder to break out of. Experimentalists who master a technique and equip an expensive lab for pursuing it sometimes get stuck filling in the blanks of data matrices that nobody cares about any longer. What are they supposed to do? Throw away all that expensive apparatus? It can be a nasty problem. It is actually easier and cheaper for philosophers to retool. After all, our "training" is not, in general, high-tech. It's mainly a matter of learning our way around in various literatures, learning the moves that have been tried and tested. And here the trap to avoid is simply this: You see that somebody eminent has asserted something untenable or dubious in print; Professor Goofmaker's clever but flawed piece is a sitting duck, just the right target for an eye-catching debut publication. Go for it. You weigh in, along with a dozen others, and now you must watch your step, because by the time you've all cited each other and responded to the responses, you're a budding expert on how to deal with how to deal with responses to Goofmaker's minor overstatement. (And remember, too, that if Goofmaker hadn't made his thesis a little too bold, he never would have attracted all the attention in the first place; the temptation to be provocative is not restricted to graduate students on the lookout for a splashy entrance into the field.)

Some people are quite content to find a congenial group of smart people with whom to share "the fun of discovery, the pleasures of cooperation, and the satisfaction of reaching agreement," as the philosopher John Austin (1961, p. 123) once put it in a published lecture, without worrying about whether the joint task is worth doing. And if enough people take up the task, it eventually becomes a phenomenon in its own right, worth studying. As philosopher Burton Dreben used to say to the graduate students at Harvard, "Philosophy is garbage, but the history of garbage is scholarship." Some garbage is more important than other garbage, however, and it's hard to decide which of it is worthy of scholarship. In another lecture published in the same book, Austin (1961) gave us the following snide masterpiece:

> It is not unusual for an audience at a lecture to include some
> who prefer things to be important, and to them now, in case
> there are any such present, there is owed a peroration. [p. 179]

Austin was a brilliant philosopher, but most of the very promising philosophers who orbited around him, no doubt chuckling at this remark, have vanished without a trace, their oh-so-clever work in *ordinary language philosophy* (a school Austin more or less invented) duly published and then utterly and deservedly ignored within a few years after publication. It has happened many times.

So what should you do? The tests I have mentioned—seeing if folks outside philosophy, or bright undergraduates, can be made to care—provide only warning signs; they are not definitive. Certainly there have been, and will be, forbiddingly abstruse and difficult topics of philosophical investigation well worth pursuing, in spite of the fact that the uninitiated remain unimpressed. I certainly don't want to discourage explorations that defy the ambient presumptions about what is interesting and important. On the contrary, the best bold strokes in the field will almost always be met by stony incredulity or ridicule at first, and these should not deter you. My point is that you should not settle complacently into a seat on the bandwagon just because you have found some brilliant fellow travelers who find your work on the issue as unignorable as you find theirs. You may all be taking each other for a ride.

77. THE 10 PERCENT THAT'S GOOD

So if **Sturgeon's Law** holds for philosophy as it does for everything else, what, in my view, is the good stuff? First of all, the classics really are classics for a good reason. From Plato to Russell, the standard fare in history-of-philosophy courses holds up well even after centuries of examination, and the best of the secondary literature about this primary literature is also very valuable. You will get *something*—a lot, really—out of reading Aristotle or Kant or Nietzsche on your own, without any background, but you'll get a lot more if you accept some guidance from those who have specialized in these thinkers for their entire careers.

Not all historians of philosophy have the same goals and attitudes, and I for one see no good reason for disqualifying any of the contenders. Some insist on placing their thinkers in the historical context in which they wrote, which means, for instance, learning a lot of seventeenth-century science if you really want to understand Descartes, and a lot of seventeenth- and eighteenth-century political history if you really want to understand Locke or Hume, and always, of course, a lot of the philosophy of their lesser contemporaries as well. Why bother with the also-rans? There's a good reason. I found I never really appreciated many of the painters of the sixteenth and seventeenth centuries until I visited European museums where I could see room after room full of second-rate paintings of the same genres. If all you ever see is the good stuff—which is all you see in the introductory survey courses, and in the top museums—it's very hard to see just how wonderful the good stuff is. Do you know the difference between a good library and a great library? A good library has all the good books. A great library has all the books. If you really want to understand a great philosopher, you have to spend some time looking at the less great contemporaries and predecessors that are left in the shadows of the masters.

Other specialists touch only lightly on the historic contexts in which their heroes worked, and instead concentrate on showing how to translate the ideas into today's contexts. After all, Leibniz didn't write the *Monadology* to be an exemplary work of seventeenth-century rationalism; he wrote it to *get at the truth*. In the end, you're not taking any philosopher seriously until you ask whether or not what they say is *right*. Philosophy students—and professors—sometimes forget this, and concentrate on pigeonholing and engaging in "compare and contrast," as we say in examination questions. Whole philosophy departments sometimes fall into this vision of their goal. That's not philosophy; that's just *philosophy appreciation*. This is how I try to help my students break this habit:

> You've stumbled on a terrible secret—a plot to destroy the Statue of Liberty, say, or to bring down the national electric grid. You work feverishly to gather and marshal your evidence, and then compose a letter that draws on all your eloquence. You send copies to the police, the FBI, the *New York Times*, CNN, and this is the response you get: "Ah, another very clever example of post-9/11 conspiracy theory" and "a gripping read, actually, and quite plausible in its own way, with excellent touches" and "reminds me of Dom De Lillo, with echoes of Pynchon." Aaargh! Pay attention! I'm trying to tell you the *truth*! Respect the philosopher you are reading by asking yourself, about every sentence and paragraph, "Do I believe this, and if not, why not?"

In addition to the history of philosophy there is excellent work in the philosophy of science—mathematics, logic, physics, biology, psychology, economics, political theory. There is almost no work in the philosophy of chemistry or astronomy or geology or engineering as such, but there is good work on some of the conceptual issues that arise in these fields. And then there is ethics. In 1971 John Rawls published *A Theory of Justice*, a towering work that opened up a fruitful era of philosophers who approach the traditional topics of ethics with an eye on the social sciences, especially economics and political science, but also biology and psychology. Thanks largely to Rawls, philosophers working in ethics raised their game, and the result has been a bounty of valuable philosophical research, which deserves and receives attention from researchers in other disciplines—and politicians and social critics.

Finally, there are philosophers who are not interdisciplinary at all, and also lean lightly on the history of the field, specializing on contemporary problems that arise in the work of philosophers specializing on contemporary problems that arise in the work of other contemporary philosophers. Some of this, as I have already noted, succumbs to Hebb's rule: if it's not worth doing, it's not worth doing well. But some of it is excellent and valuable. I have mentioned quite a few contemporary philosophers in this book, and I wouldn't mention them if I didn't think their ideas were worth taking seriously, especially when I claim they are making a mistake. Aside from my targets, there are several-dozen other philosophers whose work I particularly admire, but I won't make the mistake of listing them. Several times in my career I have relied on the judgment of a colleague who told me not to bother with X's work because it was foolish junk, only to learn some time later that I had been misled into ignoring a thinker with valuable ideas whose contribution to my own thinking was delayed by the bum steer. I am painfully aware of how easily I could be read as excusing interested thinkers from reading some philosopher who didn't make it onto my list. So please treat this book as an open-ended introduction to *some* ways of doing philosophy, and if you find them useful, they can be a springboard into your own exploration of the questions and answers that have been worked on for so long by so many thinkers.

X.
USE THE TOOLS.
TRY HARDER.

"It's inconceivable!" That's what some people declare when they confront the "mystery" of consciousness, or the claim that life arose on this planet more than three billion years ago without any helping hand from an Intelligent Designer, for instance. When I hear this, I am always tempted to say, "Well of course it's inconceivable *to you*. You left your thinking tools behind and you're hardly trying." Recall William Bateson's firm declaration that a material basis for genes was inconceivable. Even schoolchildren have little difficulty conceiving of DNA today, and it's not because they are more brilliant than Bateson was. It's because in the last century we have devised and refined the thinking tools that make it a snap. Of course some people really don't want to conceive of these things. They want to protect the mysteries from even an attempt at explanation, for fear that an explanation might make the treasures disappear.

When other people start getting inquisitive, they find that "God works in mysterious ways" is a convenient anti-thinking tool. By hinting that the questioner is arrogant and overreaching, it can quench curiosity in an instant. It used to work well, and still works well in the communities where ignorance of science is regarded as a negligible flaw if not actually a virtue. I think we should stop treating this "pious" observation as any kind of wisdom and recognize it as the transparently defensive propaganda that it is. A positive response might be, "Oh good! I love a mystery. Let's see if we can solve this one, too. Do you have any ideas?"

Conceiving of something new is hard work, not just a matter of framing some idea in your mind, giving it a quick once-over and then endorsing it. What is inconceivable to us now may prove to be obviously conceivable when we've done some more work on it. And when we confidently declare that some things are truly impossible—a largest prime number, or a plane triangle with interior angles adding up to more than two right angles, or a married bachelor—it is not so much because we find these things inconceivable as that we find we have conceived of their components so well, so exhaustively, that the impossibility of their conjunction is itself clearly conceivable.

We haven't yet succeeded in fully conceiving how meaning could exist in the material world, or how life arose and evolved, or how consciousness works, or whether free will can be one of our endowments, but we've made progress: the questions we're posing and addressing now are better than the questions of yesteryear. We're hot on the trail of the answers.

XI

WHAT GOT LEFT OUT

Some readers of the draft of this book expressed surprise and disappointment that it didn't include some of my best-known intuition pumps. In fact, several dozen don't appear here, including some of my favorites. In a few cases I think an explanation is necessary.

"Where am I?" is probably my best-known intuition pump, but for that very reason it could be left out. It first appeared in *Brainstorms* in 1978, and then was included in *The Mind's I* in 1981. Translations have been published in about a dozen languages, and it has often been anthologized. The movie *Victim of the Brain* (1984) has a half-hour dramatization of it (with me playing the later Dennett body), and a scene also appears in a 1981 BBC documentary on consciousness and the brain. Then there was the Javanese shadow-puppet dramatization produced by the well-known puppeteer Lynn Jeffries at Harvard's Loeb Theater in 1984. Google leaves no doubt that it is readily available, along with a flood of commentaries.

"The Ballad of Shakey's Pizza Parlor" (in Dennett, 1982a) does serious work dismantling a set of presumptions about "*de re* and *de dicto* belief" that were once dominant in the thinking of some philosophers working on intentionality, but that were unfamiliar to everyone else. If I had included it here, I would first have had to infect all of you with some seductive but misguided intuitions so that I could then cure you with my intuition pump. Some philosophers have to know all about this, but others can remain blissfully ignorant without loss.

In the part on evolution I reluctantly left out my favorite new thinking tool, philosopher Peter Godfrey-Smith's Darwinian Spaces, the best use of a multidimensional space as a thinking tool in philosophy that I know, because it would have required too large a review of evolutionary theory and biological phenomena to make it effective. I explain it in somewhat technical terms for other philosophers, and exhibit some of its excellent uses, in my review essay "Homunculi Rule" (2010) on Godfrey-Smith's book *Population Thinking and Natural Selection* (2009). See also Godfrey-Smith's (2010) response.

My essay "Quining Qualia" (1988a) consists of no less than fourteen intuition pumps, designed to clarify, and then banish as hopelessly confused, the philosophical concept of qualia. Only one of those is included here, the **Curse of the Cauliflower,** to help introduce the concept and a major problem with qualia. "Quining Qualia" might be considered supplementary reading on the topic for anyone who still thinks the concept of qualia (as philosophers like to define it) is a good idea. The essay has often been anthologized and is readily available on the Internet, in several languages. My book *Sweet Dreams* (2005b) contains yet other arguments and intuition pumps on the topic. Others on consciousness are "curare-cum-amnestic" in "Why You Can't Make a Computer That Feels Pain" (Dennett, 1978c), "Swamp Mary and RoboMary" in "What RoboMary Knows" (Dennett, 2007d), and "Orwellian and Stalinesque" models of consciousness in *Consciousness Explained* (Dennett, 1991a). These all require more stage setting than I could comfortably provide if I was to keep this book relatively short.

I've also left out the various intuition pumps for thinking about religion that I introduced in *Breaking the Spell* (Dennett, 2006a), and my example of Superman tweaking the Burgess Shale in *Science and Religion: Are They Compatible?* (Dennett and Plantinga, 2011).

•

EXERCISE 1

PROGRAM 1:

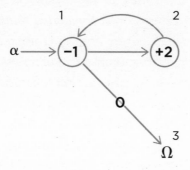

a. How many steps will it take the register machine to add 2 + 5 and get 7, running Program 1 (counting End as a step)?
Answer: Six steps: three decrements, two increments, one End (the last decrement is a branch on zero).

b. How many steps will it take to add 5 + 2?
Answer: Twelve steps: six decrements, five increments, and one End.
(What conclusion do you draw from this?)
Answer: The order of the contents can make a big difference, so you might think it would be good to have a rule of always putting the smaller number in register 1—but if you first had to test the two numbers to see which is smaller, you'd use up more steps than you'd spend doing the addition!

EXERCISE 2

a. Write the RAP program for this flow graph. (Note that since the program branches, you can number the steps in several different ways. It doesn't matter which way you choose as long as the "go to" commands point to the right steps.)

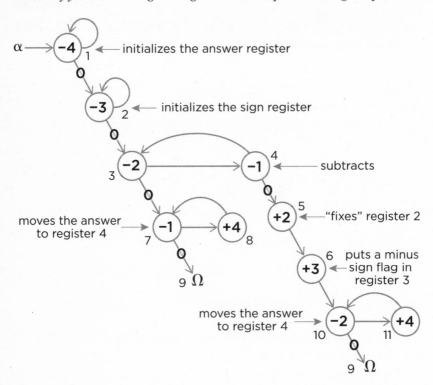

STEP	INSTRUCTION	REGISTER	GO TO STEP	[BRANCH TO STEP]
I.	*Deb*	4	I	2
2.	*Deb*	3	2	3
3.	*Deb*	2	4	7
4.	*Deb*	I	3	5
5.	*Inc*	2	6	
6.	*Inc*	3	10	
7.	*Deb*	I	8	9
8.	*Inc*	4	7	
9.	*End*			
10.	*Deb*	I	II	9
II.	*Inc*	4	10	

b. What happens when the program tries to subtract 3 from 3 or 4 from 4?
The program halts with 0 in register 4.

c. What possible error is prevented by zeroing out register 3 before trying the subtraction at step 3 instead of after step 4?
If there was a zero at the start in both registers 1 and 2, the answer when the program ended could be nonsensical (either –0, or some number other than 0 or 1 in the sign register).

EXERCISE 3

a. Draw a flow graph (and write the RAP program) for multiplying the content of register 1 by the content of register 3, putting the answer in register 5.

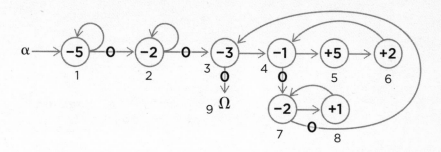

STEP	INSTRUCTION	REGISTER	GO TO STEP	[BRANCH TO STEP]
1.	*Deb*	5	1	2 [zeroes out
2.	*Deb*	2	2	3 buffers]
3.	*Deb*	3	4	9 [starts the countdown]
4.	*Deb*	1	5	7 [adds the
5.	*Inc*	5	6	contents of
6.	*Inc*	2	4	register 1
7.	*Deb*	2	8	to itself]
8.	*Inc*	1	7	
9.	*End*			

b. (Optional) Using Copy and Move, improve the multiplier you created in problem a: when it stops, the original contents of register 1 and register 3 are restored, so that you can easily check the inputs and output for correctness after a run.

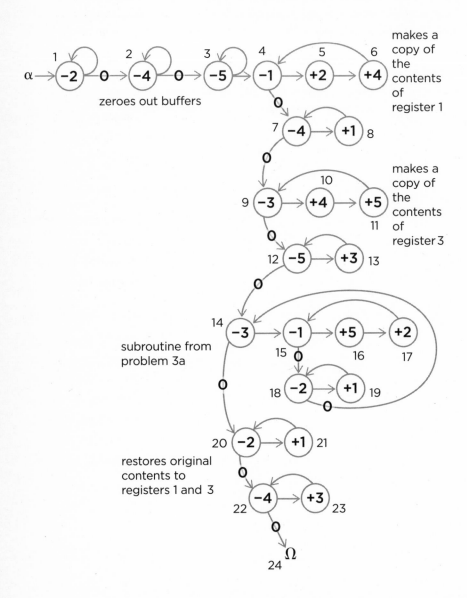

makes a copy of the contents of register 1

zeroes out buffers

makes a copy of the contents of register 3

subroutine from problem 3a

restores original contents to registers 1 and 3

STEP	INSTRUCTION	REGISTER	GO TO STEP	[BRANCH TO STEP]	
1.	Deb	2	1	2	[zeroes out 3 buffers]
2.	Deb	4	2	3	
3.	Deb	5	3	4	
4.	Deb	1	5	7	[makes a copy of
5.	Inc	2	6		contents of 1]
6.	Inc	4	4		
7.	Deb	4	8	9	
8.	Inc	1	7		
9.	Deb	3	10	12	[makes a copy of
10.	Inc	4	11		contents of 3]
11.	Inc	5	9		
12.	Deb	5	13	14	
13.	Inc	3	12		
14.	Deb	3	15	20	[this is just the code in
15.	Deb	1	16	18	exercise 3a with
16.	Inc	5	17		different line
17.	Inc	2	15		numbers]
18.	Deb	2	19	14	
19.	Inc	1	18		
20.	Deb	2	21	22	[restores the original
21.	Inc	1	20		values to registers 1
22.	Deb	4	23	24	and 3]
23.	Inc	3	22		
24.	End				

c. (Optional) Draw a flow graph and write a RAP program that examines the contents of register 1 and register 3 (without destroying them!) and writes the address (1 or 3) of the smaller content in register 2, and puts 2 in register 2 if the contents of registers 1 and 3 are equal. (After this program has executed, the contents of register 1 and register 3 should be unchanged, and register 2 should say if their contents are equal, and if not, which of those two registers has the smaller content.)

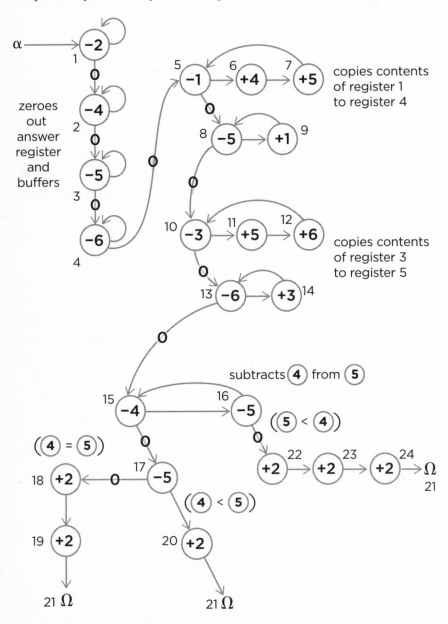

STEP	INSTRUCTION	REGISTER	GO TO STEP	[BRANCH TO STEP]	
1.	*Deb*	2	1	2	[zeroes out answer register]
2.	*Deb*	4	2	3	[zeroes out buffers]
3.	*Deb*	5	3	4	
4.	*Deb*	6	4	5	
5.	*Deb*	1	6	8	[copies contents of register 1 to register 4]
6.	*Inc*	4	7		
7.	*Inc*	5	5		
8.	*Deb*	5	9	10	
9.	*Inc*	1	8		
10.	*Deb*	3	11	13	[copies contents of register 3 to register 5]
11.	*Inc*	5	12		
12.	*Inc*	6	10		
13.	*Deb*	6	14	15	
14.	*Inc*	3	13		
15.	*Deb*	4	16	17	[subtracts register 4
16.	*Deb*	5	15	22	from register 5]
17.	*Deb*	5	20	18	[checks to see if contents of 4 = contents of 5]
18.	*Inc*	2	19		[contents are equal;
19.	*Inc*	2	21		puts 2 in register 2]
20.	*Inc*	2	21		[contents of 4 less than
21.	*End*				5; puts 1 in register 2]
22.	*Inc*	2	23		[contents of 5 less than
23.	*Inc*	2	24		4; puts 3 in register 2]
24.	*Inc*	2	21		

EXERCISE 4 (OPTIONAL)

Draw a flow graph, and write a RAP program that turns a register machine into a simple pocket calculator, as follows:

a. Use register 2 for the operation:

> 0 = add
> 1 = subtract
> 2 = multiply
> 3 = divide

b. Put the values to be acted on in registers 1 and 3.

(Thus 3 0 6 would mean 3 + 6, and 5 1 3 would mean 5 − 3, and 4 2 5 would mean 4 × 5, and 9 3 3 would mean 9 ÷ 3). Then put the results of the operation in registers 4 through 7, using register 4 for the sign (using 0 for + and 1 for −) and register 5 for the numerical answer, register 6 for any remainder in a case of division, and register 7 as an alarm, signaling a divide-by-zero mistake.

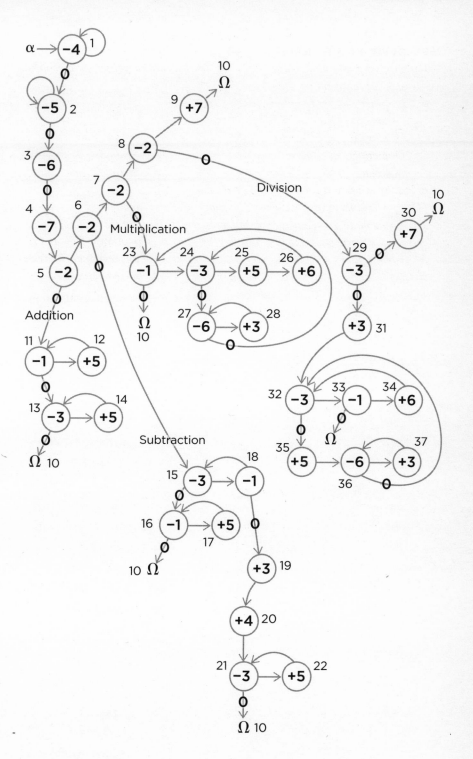

STEP	INSTRUCTION	REGISTER	GO TO STEP	[BRANCH TO STEP]	
1.	Deb	4	1	2	[zeroes out
2.	Deb	5	2	3	answer registers]
3.	Deb	6	3	4	
4.	Deb	7	4	5	
5.	Deb	2	6	11	[branches to addition]
6.	Deb	2	7	15	[branches to subtraction]
7.	Deb	2	8	23	[branches to multiplication]
8.	Deb	2	9	28	[branches to division]
9.	Inc	7	10		[flags improper opera-
10.	End				tion code entered in register 2 and stops]
11.	Deb	1	12	13	[begins addition]
12.	Inc	5	11		
13.	Deb	3	14	10	
14.	Inc	5	13		
15.	Deb	3	18	16	
16.	Deb	1	17	10	[begins and ends
17.	Inc	5	16		subtraction]
18.	Deb	1	15	19	
19.	Inc	3	20		[restores register 3]
20.	Inc	4	21		[puts minus sign in
21.	Deb	3	22	10	register 4]
22.	Inc	5	21		
23.	Deb	1	24	10	[begins and ends
24.	Deb	3	24	27	multiplication]
25.	Inc	5	26		
26.	Inc	6	24		
27.	Deb	6	28	23	
28.	Inc	3	27		
29.	Deb	3	31	30	[begins division, checks for divide-by-zero]

STEP	INSTRUCTION	REGISTER	GO TO STEP	[BRANCH TO STEP]
30.	*Inc*	7	10	[flags divide-by-zero error and stops]
31.	*Inc*	3	32	[restores register 3]
32.	*Deb*	3	33	35
33.	*Deb*	1	34	10 [ends division]
34.	*Inc*	6	32	
35.	*Inc*	5	36	
36.	*Deb*	6	37	32
37.	*Inc*	3	36	

SOURCES

I. INTRODUCTION
The whimsical jailer and the jewels in the trashcan are drawn with revisions from *Elbow Room* (Dennett, 1984a).

II. A DOZEN GENERAL THINKING TOOLS
1. "Making Mistakes" began as "How to Make Mistakes" (Dennett, 1995b).
2. " 'By Parody of Reasoning' " has not been published before.
3. "Rapoport's Rules." The rules were first presented by me in print in my reflections on Dawkins's *The God Delusion* in *Free Inquiry* (Dennett, 2007a).
4. "Sturgeon's Law." The law was discussed in "Holding a Mirror up to Dupré" (Dennett, 2004).
5. "Occam's Razor" has not been published before.
6. "Occam's Broom." The coinage is attributed on many websites to Sydney Brenner. Apparently he has not published anything about it.
7. "Using Lay Audiences as Decoys" has not been published before.
8. "Jootsing" includes material drawn from "I Could Not Have Done Otherwise—So What?" (Dennett, 1984b).
9. "Three Species of *Goulding*" is drawn from "Confusion over Evolution: An Exchange" (Dennett, 1993) and "Shall We Tango? No, But Thanks for Asking" (Dennett, 2011b).
10. "The 'Surely' Operator" grew out of remarks in "Get Real" (Dennett, 1994a).
11. "Rhetorical Questions" has not been published before.
12. "What Is a Deepity?" draws on material in "With a Little Help from My Friends" (Dennett, 2000).

III. TOOLS FOR THINKING ABOUT MEANING OR CONTENT
13. "Murder in Trafalgar Square" is drawn from "Three Kinds of Intentional Psychology" (Dennett, 1981).
14. "An Older Brother Living in Cleveland" is drawn from "Brain Writing and Mind Reading" (Dennett, 1975).
15. "'Daddy Is a Doctor'" is drawn from *Content and Consciousness* (Dennett, 1969).
16. "Manifest Image and Scientific Image" includes material drawn from "Expecting Ourselves to Expect" (Dennett, forthcoming); "Sakes and Dints" (Dennett, 2012); and "Kinds of Things" (Dennett, forthcoming). The discussion of anteaters and birds is drawn from *Elbow Room* (Dennett, 1984a).
17. "Folk Psychology" is drawn from "Three Kinds of Intentional Psychology" (Dennett, 1981).
18. "The Intentional Stance" is drawn from "Intentional Systems" (Dennett, 1971) and *The Intentional Stance* (Dennett, 1987) and is discussed in many other books and articles.
19. "The Personal/Sub-personal Distinction" is drawn from *Content and Consciousness* (Dennett, 1969).

20. "A Cascade of Homunculi" draws on *Brainstorms* (Dennett, 1978) and a piece on Edge.org (Dennett, 2008), later published in *What Have You Changed Your Mind About* (Brockman, 2009).
21. "The *Sorta* Operator" has not been published before, but themes in it are developed in "Turing's 'Strange Inversion of Reason' " (Dennett, forthcoming).
22. "Wonder Tissue." The term was first used in print in "Natural Freedom" (Dennett, 2005a). My thanks to Christof Koch for drawing my attention to the quotation from William Bateson.
23. "Trapped in the Robot Control Room" is drawn from "Current Issues in the Philosophy of Mind" (Dennett, 1978b).

IV. AN INTERLUDE ABOUT COMPUTERS
24. "The Seven Secrets of Computer Power Revealed" grew out of an introductory course in computer science that George Smith, David Isles, and I taught at Tufts, remarkably assisted by undergraduate computer science major Steve Barney. Steve became the lead programmer at the Curricular Software Studio at Tufts, a project funded by the Sloan Foundation after seeing the simulated computer, AESOP, created by Steve for that course. RodRego was inspired by AESOP, and first programmed in Logo by me in 1986—I called it Rego and the pointy-headed homunculus in the figure on p. 118 is a fossil trace of the Logo "turtle." It was then redone in more portable and robust versions, first by Rod Da Silva—RodRego— and then revised by Nikolai Shvertner at the Curricular Software Studio.
25. "Virtual Machines." These machines have been discussed by me in many places, including "Notes on Prosthetic Imagination" (Dennett, 1982d) (the manifesto that led to the creation of the Curricular Software Studio), *Consciousness Explained* (Dennett, 1991a), and "The Practical Requirements for Making a Conscious Robot" (Dennett, 1994b).
26. "Algorithms" draws on material from *Darwin's Dangerous Idea* (Dennett, 1995a).
27. "Automating the Elevator" was first presented by me in "Varieties of Content" at a symposium held at the University of Copenhagen in 2007 (Dennett, 2007c). It has not been published before.
The "Summary" includes ideas from "Turing's 'Strange Inversion of Reasoning' " (Dennett, forthcoming).

V. MORE TOOLS ABOUT MEANING
28. "A Thing about Redheads" is drawn from "Things about Things" (Dennett, 2001e).
29. "The Wandering Two-Bitser, Twin Earth, and the Giant Robot" is drawn with revisions from "Evolution, Error and Intentionality" (Dennett, 1988c).
30. "Radical Translation and a Quinian Crossword Puzzle" first appeared in "With a Little Help from My Friends" (Dennett, 2000).
31. "Semantic Engines and Syntactic Engines" is drawn with revisions from "Three Kinds of Intentional Psychology" (Dennett, 1981).
32. "Swampman Meets a Cow-Shark" includes material drawn with revisions from "Features of Intentional Action" (Dennett, 1968) and "Get Real" (Dennett, 1994a).
33. "Two Black Boxes" is drawn with revisions from *Darwin's Dangerous Idea* (Dennett, 1995a).

VI. TOOLS FOR THINKING ABOUT EVOLUTION

34. "Universal Acid" is drawn with revisions from *Darwin's Dangerous Idea* (Dennett, 1995a).

35. "The Library of Mendel: *Vast* and *Vanishing*" is drawn with revisions from *Darwin's Dangerous Idea* (Dennett, 1995a).

36. "Genes as Words or as Subroutines" is new, inspired by Richard Dawkins's *The Ancestor's Tale* (2004) and including a lengthy quotation from that book.

37. "The Tree of Life" is new; the figure is the creation of Leonard Eisenberg. On his website, http://evogeneao.com/tree.html, you will find lucid explanations of how to use the diagram, and you can order posters, T-shirts, hoodies, and other items.

38. "Cranes and Skyhooks, Lifting in Design Space" is drawn with revisions from *Darwin's Dangerous Idea* (Dennett, 1995a).

39. "Competence without Comprehension" is drawn with revisions from "Darwin's 'Strange Inversion of Reasoning'" (Dennett, 2009a).

40. "Free-Floating Rationales." Free-floating rationales were introduced in "Intentional Systems in Cognitive Ethology: The 'Panglossian Paradigm' Defended" (Dennett, 1983) and have been discussed in many other essays.

41. "Do Locusts Understand Prime Numbers?" is drawn with revisions from *Darwin's Dangerous Idea* (Dennett, 1995a).

42. "How to Explain Stotting" is new.

43. "Beware of the Prime Mammal" is drawn with revisions from *Darwin's Dangerous Idea* (Dennett, 1995a).

44. "When Does Speciation Occur?" is drawn with revisions from "The Multiple Drafts Model" (Dennett and Akins, 2008).

45. "Widowmakers, Mitochondrial Eve, and Retrospective Coronations" is drawn with revisions from *Darwin's Dangerous Idea* (1995a).

46. "Cycles" is drawn with revisions from "Cycles" (Dennett, 2011a), my answer to the Edge Question 2011 "What Scientific Concept Would Improve Everybody's Cognitive Toolkit?" later published in *This Will Make You Smarter* (Brockman, 2012).

47. "What *Does* the Frog's Eye Tell the Frog's Brain?" is drawn with revisions from *Darwin's Dangerous Idea* (Dennett, 1995a).

48. "Leaping through Space in the Library of Babel" is drawn with revisions from *Darwin's Dangerous Idea* (Dennett, 1995a).

49. "Who Is the Author of *Spamlet*?" is drawn with revisions from my presidential address to the Eastern Division of the American Philosophical Association, titled "In Darwin's Wake, Where Am I?" (Dennett, 2001d).

50. "Noise in the Virtual Hotel" is drawn with revisions from "Collision-Detection, Muselot, and Scribble: Some Reflections on Creativity" (Dennett, 2001a).

51. "Herb, Alice, and Hal, the Baby" is drawn with revisions from "Homunculi Rule: Reflections on *Darwinian Populations and Natural Selection* by Peter Godfrey-Smith, Oxford University Press, 2009" (Dennett, 2010).

52. "Memes" draws on various publications on memes listed in the essay.

VII. TOOLS FOR THINKING ABOUT CONSCIOUSNESS

53. "Two Counter-images" includes material drawn from *Consciousness Explained* (Dennett, 1991a) and *Sweet Dreams* (Dennett, 2005b).

54. "The Zombic Hunch." The Zombic Hunch was defined in *Sweet Dreams* (Dennett, 2005b).

55. "Zombies and Zimboes" draws with revisions on material in *Consciousness Explained* (Dennett, 1991a).

56. "The Curse of the Cauliflower" draws with revisions on material from "Quining Qualia" (Dennett, 1988a).

57. "Vim: How Much Is That in 'Real Money'?" is drawn with revisions from "Consciousness: 'How Much Is That in Real Money?'" (Dennett, 2001b).

58. "The Sad Case of Mr. Clapgras" is drawn with revisions from *Sweet Dreams* (Dennett 2005b).

59. "The Tuned Deck" is drawn with revisions from "Explaining the 'Magic' of Consciousness" (Dennett, 2001c).

60. "The Chinese Room" draws with revisions on material in *The Mind's I* (Hofstadter and Dennett, 1981) and *The Intentional Stance* (Dennett, 1987).

61. "The Teleclone Fall from Mars to Earth" is drawn with revisions from *The Mind's I* (Hofstadter and Dennett, 1981).

62. "The Self as the Center of Narrative Gravity." This tool was first described in "Why Everyone Is a Novelist" (Dennett, 1988b).

63. "Heterophenomenology." Heterophenomenology was first described in "How to Study Consciousness Empirically: or Nothing Comes to Mind" (Dennett, 1982b). This was further elaborated in a chapter of *Consciousness Explained* (Dennett, 1991a). A special issue of *Phenomenology and Cognitive Science* (vol. 6, nos. 1 and 2), guest-edited by Alva Noë, is devoted to heterophenomenology, and comprises most of the best subsequent thinking on the topic. It includes my reply to the essays, "Heterophenomenology Reconsidered" (Dennett, 2007b).

64. "Mary the Color Scientist: A Boom Crutch Unveiled" draws with revisions on *Consciousness Explained* (Dennett, 1991a) and "What RoboMary Knows" (Dennett, 2007d), which appears in the second of the two anthologies devoted to "Mariology," the first one being Ludlow, Nagasawa, and Stoljar, 2004.

VIII. TOOLS FOR THINKING ABOUT FREE WILL

65. "A Truly Nefarious Neurosurgeon" is drawn from my Erasmus Lecture, "Erasmus: Sometimes a Spin-Doctor Is Right" in 2012.

66. "A Deterministic Toy: Conway's Game of Life." Martin Gardner introduced the game of Life to a wide audience in two of his "Mathematical Games" columns in *Scientific American*, in October 1970 and February 1971. Poundstone (1985) provides an excellent exploration of the game and its philosophical implications. There's also a decent Wikipedia article on it, with lots of links. I've often used the game of Life in my writing. This version is drawn with revisions from the account in *Freedom Evolves* (Dennett, 2003).

67. "Rock, Paper, and Scissors" has not previously been published.

68. "Two Lotteries" is drawn with revisions from *Elbow Room* (Dennett, 1984a).

69. "Inert Historical Facts" is drawn with revisions from "Get Real" (Dennett, 1994a). Tanmoy Bhattacharya drew my attention to the quantum complications.

70. "A Computer Chess Marathon" is drawn from *Freedom Evolves* (Dennett, 2003).

71. "Ultimate Responsibility" has not been published before.

72. "Sphexishness" has not been published before.

73. "The Boys from Brazil: Another Boom Crutch" has not been published before.

IX. WHAT IS IT LIKE TO BE A PHILOSOPHER?

74. "A Faustian Bargain" is drawn with revisions from my review of Thomas Nagel's book *Other Minds: Critical Essays, 1969–1994* (Dennett, 1996b).

75. "Philosophy as Naïve Auto-anthropology" is drawn with revisions from "Sakes and Dints" (Dennett, 2012), and "Kinds of Things" (Dennett, forthcoming).

76. "Higher-Order Truths of Chmess" is drawn, with revisions, from "The Higher-Order Truths about Chmess" (Dennett, 2006c).

77. "The 10 Percent That's Good" has not been published before.

BIBLIOGRAPHY

ABBOTT, EDWIN A., (1884) 1983, *Flatland: A Romance in Many Dimensions* (reprint of 1963 fifth edition with foreword by Isaac Asimov). New York: HarperCollins.

ALAIN, CHARTIER, (1908) 1956, *Propos d'un Normand 1906–1914*. Paris: Gallimard. Quoted in Deborah S. Rogers and Paul R. Ehrlich, 2008, "Natural Selection and Cultural Rates of Change." *Proceedings of the National Academy of Sciences*, vol. 105, pp. 3416–3420.

AUSTIN, J. L., 1961, *Philosophical Papers*. Oxford: Oxford University Press.

AXELROD, ROBERT, 1984, *The Evolution of Cooperation*. New York: Basic Books.

AXELROD, ROBERT, and WILLIAM HAMILTON, 1981, "The Evolution of Cooperation." *Science*, vol. 211, pp. 1390–1396.

BARRETT, JUSTIN, 2000, "Exploring the Natural Foundations of Religion." *Trends in Cognitive Science*, vol. 4, pp. 29–34.

BATESON, WILLIAM, 1916, Review of the *Mechanisms of Mendelian Heredity* by T. H. Morgan (1914).

BEHE, MICHAEL J., 1996, *Darwin's Black Box: The Biochemical Challenge to Evolution*. New York: Free Press.

BENNETT, MAX, DANIEL DENNETT, P. M. S. HACKER, and JOHN SEARLE, 2009, *Neuroscience and Philosophy: Brain, Mind, and Language*. New York: Columbia University Press.

BENNETT, MAX, and P. M. S. HACKER, 2003, *Philosophical Foundations of Neuroscience*. Malden, Mass.: Wiley-Blackwell.

BLOCK, NED, 1978, "Troubles with Functionalism." In W. Savage, ed., *Perception and Cognition: Issues in the Foundations of Psychology*. Minnesota Studies in the Philosophy of Science, vol. 9. Minneapolis: University of Minnesota Press, pp. 261–326.

————, 1994, "What Is Dennett's Theory a Theory of?" *Philosophical Topics*, vol. 22 (special issue on the philosophy of Daniel Dennett), pp. 23–40.

BOBROW, DANIEL, 1985, *Qualitative Reasoning about Physical Systems*. Cambridge, Mass.: MIT Press.

BORGES, J. L., 1962, *Labyrinths: Selected Stories and Other Writings*. New York: New Directions.

BRAY, DENNIS, 2009, *Wetware*. New Haven, Conn.: Yale University Press.

BROCKMAN, J., ed., 2009, *What Have You Changed Your Mind About*. New York: HarperCollins.

————, 2012, *This Will Make You Smarter*. New York: Harper Torchbook.

BROOKS, R. A., 1987, *Planning Is Just a Way of Avoiding Figuring Out What to Do Next*. Technical report, MIT Artificial Intelligence Laboratory, Cambridge, Mass. Available at http://people.csail.mit.edu/brooks/papers/Planning%20is%20Just.pdf.

BROOKS, RODNEY, 1991, "Intelligence without Representation." *Artificial Intelligence*, vol. 47, pp. 139–159.

CANN, REBECCA L., MARK STONEKING, and ALLAN C. WILSON, 1987, "Mitochondrial DNA and Human Evolution." *Nature*, vol. 325, pp. 31–36.

CHALMERS, DAVID, 1995, "Facing Up to the Problem of Consciousness." *Journal of Consciousness Studies*, vol. 2, no. 3, pp. 200–219.

CLARK, A., 2013, "Whatever Next? Predictive Brains, Situated Agents, and the Future of Cognitive Science." *Behavioral and Brain Sciences*.

CLEGG, LIAM, 2012, *Protean Free Will*. California Institute of Technology, Pasadena. Available at http://authors.library.caltech.edu/29887/.

COPE, DAVID, 2000, *The Algorithmic Composer*. Middleton, Wisc.: A-R Editions.

————, 2001, *Virtual Music: Computer Synthesis of Musical Style*. Cambridge, Mass.: MIT Press.

CRONIN, HELENA, 1991, *The Ant and the Peacock*. Cambridge: Cambridge University Press.

DAMIAAN, DENYS, MARISKA MANTIONE, MARTIJN FIGEE, PEPIJN VAN DEN MUNCKHOF, FRANK KOERSELMAN, HERMAN WESTENBERG, ANDRIES BOSCH, and RICK SCHUURMAN, 2010, "Deep Brain Stimulation of the Nucleus Accumbens for Treatment-Refractory Obsessive-Compulsive Disorder." *Archives of General Psychiatry*, vol. 67, no. 10, pp. 1061–1068.

DAVIDSON, DONALD, 1987,"Knowing One's Own Mind." *Proceedings and Addresses of the American Philosophical Association*, vol. 60, pp. 441–458. Reprinted in Davidson, Donald, 2001, *Subjective, Intersubjective, Objective*. New York: Oxford University Press, pp. 15–38.

DAWKINS, RICHARD, 1976, *The Selfish Gene*. Oxford: Oxford University Press. Rev. ed. 1989.

————, 1982, *The Extended Phenotype: The Gene as the Unit of Selection*. Oxford: Oxford University Press.

————, 1986, *The Blind Watchmaker*. London: Longmans.

————, 1996, *Climbing Mount Improbable*. London: Viking Penguin.

————, 2004, *The Ancestor's Tale: A Pilgrimage to the Dawn of Time*. London: Weidenfeld & Nicolson.

DE VRIES, PETER, 1953, *The Vale of Laughter*. Boston: Little, Brown.

DEHAENE, S., and J. F. MARQUES, 2002, "Cognitive Euroscience: Scalar Variability in Price Estimation and the Cognitive Consequences of Switching to the Euro." *Quarterly Journal of Experimental Psychology*, vol. 55, pp. 705–731.

DENNETT, DANIEL C., 1968, "Features of Intentional Action." *Philosophy and Phenomenological Research*, vol. 29 (December), pp. 232–244.

————, 1969, *Content and Consciousness*. London: Routledge & Kegan Paul.

————, 1971, "Intentional Systems." *Journal of Philosophy*, vol. 68, pp. 87–106.

————, 1975, "Brain Writing and Mind Reading." In K. Gunderson, ed., *Language, Mind and Knowledge*. Minnesota Studies in the Philosophy of Science, vol. 7. Minneapolis: University of Minnesota Press, pp. 403–416. Reprinted in Dennett 1978a.

————, 1978a, *Brainstorms*. Cambridge, Mass.: MIT Press/A Bradford Book.

————, 1978b, "Current Issues in the Philosophy of Mind." *American Philosophical Quarterly*, vol. 15, pp. 249–261.

————, 1978c, "Why You Can't Make a Computer That Feels Pain." *Synthese*, vol. 38 (August), pp. 415–456.

————, 1980, "The Milk of Human Intentionality" (commentary on Searle). *Behavioral and Brain Sciences*, vol. 3, pp. 428–430.

————, 1981, "Three Kinds of Intentional Psychology." In R. Healey, ed., *Reduction, Time and Reality.* Cambridge: Cambridge University Press, pp. 37–61.

————, 1982a, "Beyond Belief." In A. Woodfield, ed., *Thought and Object: Essays on Intentionality.* Oxford: Oxford University Press. Reprinted in Dennett, 1987.

————, 1982b, "How to Study Consciousness Empirically: or Nothing Comes to Mind." *Synthese*, vol. 53, pp. 159–180.

————, 1982c, "The Myth of the Computer: An Exchange" (reply to John Searle's review of *The Mind's I*). *New York Review of Books*, vol. 29 (June 24), pp. 56–57.

————, 1982d, "Notes on Prosthetic Imagination." *New Boston Review*, vol. 7 (June), pp. 3–7. Reprinted in "30 Years of Boston Review." *Boston Review*, vol. 30, no. 5 (September/October 2005), p. 40.

————, 1983, "Intentional Systems in Cognitive Ethology: The 'Panglossian Paradigm' Defended." *Behavioral and Brain Sciences*, vol. 6, pp. 343–390.

————, 1984a, *Elbow Room: The Varieties of Free Will Worth Wanting.* Cambridge, Mass.: MIT Press.

————, 1984b, "I Could Not Have Done Otherwise—So What?" *Journal of Philosophy*, vol. 81, pp. 553–565.

————, 1986, "The Logical Geography of Computational Approaches: A View from the East Pole." In Robert M. Harnish and M. Brand, eds., *The Representation of Knowledge and Belief.* Tucson: University of Arizona Press, pp. 59–79.

————, 1987, *The Intentional Stance.* Cambridge, Mass.: MIT Press.

————, 1988a, "Quining Qualia." In A. Marcel and E. Bisiach, eds., *Consciousness in Modern Science.* Oxford: Oxford University Press, pp. 42–77.

————, 1988b, "Why Everyone Is a Novelist." *Times Literary Supplement*, vol. 4 (September 16–22), p. 459.

————, 1988c, "Evolution, Error and Intentionality." In Y. Wilks and D. Partridge, eds., *Sourcebook on the Foundations of Artificial Intelligence.* Albuquerque: University of New Mexico Press, pp. 190–211.

————, 1990, "Memes and the Exploitation of Imagination." *Journal of Aesthetics and Art Criticism*, vol. 48, pp. 127–135.

————, 1991a, *Consciousness Explained.* Boston: Little, Brown.

————, 1991b, "Real Patterns." *Journal of Philosophy*, vol. 88, pp. 27–51.

————, 1993, "Confusion over Evolution: An Exchange." *New York Review of Books*, January 14, pp. 43–44.

————, 1994a, "Get Real" (reply to my critics). *Philosophical Topics*, vol. 22 (special issue on the philosophy of Daniel Dennett), pp. 505–556.

————, 1994b, "The Practical Requirements for Making a Conscious Robot." *Proceedings of the Royal Society, A*, vol. 349, pp. 133–146.

————, 1995a, *Darwin's Dangerous Idea: Evolution and the Meanings of Life.* New York: Simon & Schuster.

————, 1995b, "How to Make Mistakes." In J. Brockman and K. Matson, eds., *How Things Are.* New York: William Morrow, pp. 137–144.

—————, 1996a, *Kinds of Minds: Towards an Understanding of Consciousness*. New York: Basic Books.

—————, 1996b, "Review of *Other Minds: Critical Essays, 1969–1994* by Thomas Nagel, 1995." *Journal of Philosophy*, vol. 63, no. 8 (August), pp. 425–428.

—————, 2000, "With a Little Help from My Friends." In Don Ross, Andrew Brook, and David Thompson, eds., *Dennett's Philosophy: A Comprehensive Assessment*. Cambridge, Mass.: MIT Press, pp. 327–388.

—————, 2001a, "Collision-Detection, Muselot, and Scribble: Some Reflections on Creativity." In Cope, 2001, pp. 283–291.

—————, 2001b, "Consciousness: How Much Is That in Real Money?" In R. Gregory, ed., *The Oxford Companion to the Mind*, 2nd ed. Oxford: Oxford University Press.

—————, 2001c, "Explaining the 'Magic' of Consciousness." In *Exploring Consciousness, Humanities, Natural Science, Religion, Proceedings of the International Symposium, Milano, November 19-20, 2001* (published in December 2002, Fondazione Carlo Erba), pp. 47–58.

—————, 2001d, "In Darwin's Wake, Where Am I?" (American Philosophical Association Presidential Address). *Proceedings and Addresses of the American Philosophical Association*, vol. 75, no. 2 (November), pp. 13–30. Reprinted in J. Hodge and G. Radick, eds., 2003, *The Cambridge Companion to Darwin*. Cambridge: Cambridge University Press, pp. 357–376.

—————, 2001e, "Things about Things." In Joao Branquinho, ed., *The Foundations of Cognitive Science*. Oxford: Clarendon Press, pp. 133–149.

—————, 2002, "The New Replicators." In Mark Pagel, ed., *The Encyclopedia of Evolution*, vol. 1. Oxford: Oxford University Press, pp. E83–E92.

—————, 2003, *Freedom Evolves*. New York: Viking Penguin.

—————, 2004, "Holding a Mirror up to Dupré" (commentary on John Dupré, *Human Nature and the Limits of Science*). *Philosophy and Phenomenological Research*, vol. 69, no. 2 (September), pp. 473–483.

—————, 2005a, "Natural Freedom." *Metaphilosophy*, vol. 36, no. 4 (July), pp. 449–459.

—————, 2005b, *Sweet Dreams: Philosophical Obstacles to a Science of Consciousness*. Cambridge, Mass.: MIT Press.

—————, 2006a, *Breaking the Spell: Religion as a Natural Phenomenon*. New York: Viking Penguin.

—————, 2006b, "From Typo to Thinko: When Evolution Graduated to Semantic Norms." In S. Levinson and P. Jaisson, eds., *Evolution and Culture*. Cambridge, Mass.: MIT Press, pp. 133–145.

—————, 2006c, "The Higher-Order Truths about Chmess." *Topoi*, pp. 39–41.

—————, 2007a, "The God Delusion by Richard Dawkins." *Free Inquiry*, vol. 27, no. 1 (December/January 2007).

—————, 2007b, "Heterophenomenology Reconsidered." *Phenomenology and Cognitive Science*, vol. 6, nos. 1 and 2 (special issue on heterophenomenology, Alva Noë, ed.), pp. 247–270.

—————, 2007c, "Varieties of Content." Presentation at Concepts: Content and Constitution, A Symposium, University of Copenhagen, Amager, Denmark, May 12.

————, 2007d, "What RoboMary Knows." In T. Alter and S. Walter, eds., *Phenomenal Concepts and Phenomenal Knowledge: New Essays on Consciousness and Physicalism*. Oxford: Oxford University Press, pp. 15–31.

————, 2008, "Competition in the Brain." World Question Center. Edge.org, December, later published in Brockman, 2009.

————, 2009a, "Darwin's 'Strange Inversion of Reasoning.'" *Proceedings of the National Academy of the Sciences of the United States of America*, vol. 106, suppl. 1, pp. 10061–10065.

————, 2009b, "Heterophenomenology." In T. Bayne, A. Cleeremans, and P. Wilken, eds., *The Oxford Companion to Consciousness*. Oxford: Oxford University Press, pp. 345–346.

————, 2009c, "Intentional Systems Theory." In B. McLaughlin, A. Beckermann, and S. Walter, eds., *The Oxford Handbook of Philosophy of Mind*. Oxford: Oxford University Press, pp. 339–350.

————, 2010, "Homunculi Rule: *Reflections on Darwinian Populations and Natural Selection* by Peter Godfrey-Smith, Oxford University Press, 2009." *Biology and Philosophy* (published online December 21). Available at http://ase .tufts.edu/cogstud/papers/homunculi.pdf.

————, 2011a, "Cycles" (as an answer to the Edge Question 2011, "What Scientific Concept Would Improve Everybody's Cognitive Toolkit?"). World Question Center. Edge.org, later published in Brockman, 2012, pp. 81–88.

————, 2011b, "Shall We Tango? No, but Thanks for Asking" (commentaries on Evan Thompson, *Mind in Life*, with replies). *Journal of Consciousness Studies*, vol. 18, nos. 5 and 6 (special issue on Evan Thompson), pp. 23–34.

————, 2012, "Sakes and Dints." *Times Literary Supplement*, March 2, pp. 12–14.

————, forthcoming, "The Evolution of Reasons." In BANA BASHOUR and HANS D. MULLER, eds., *Contemporary Philosophical Naturalism and Its Implications*. New York: Routledge.

————, forthcoming, "Expecting Ourselves to Expect" (commentary on Clark). *Behavioral and Brain Sciences*.

————, forthcoming, "Kinds of Things." In Don Ross, James Ladyman, and Harold Kincaid, eds., *Does Scientific Philosophy Exclude Metaphysics?* Oxford: Oxford University Press.

————, forthcoming, "Turing's 'Strange Inversion of Reasoning.'" In Barry Cooper, ed., *Alan Turing—His Work and Impact*. Elsevier.

DENNETT, DANIEL C., and KATHLEEN AKINS, 2008, "The Multiple Drafts Model." *Scholarpedia*, vol. 3, no. 4, 4321. http://www.scholarpedia.org/wiki/ index.php?title=Multiple_drafts_model.

DENNETT, DANIEL C., and ALVIN PLANTINGA, 2011, *Science and Religion: Are They Compatible?* Oxford: Oxford University Press.

DENNETT, DANIEL C., and C. F. WESTBURY, 2000, "Mining the Past to Construct the Future: Memory and Belief as Forms of Knowledge." In D. Schacter and E. Scarry, eds., *Memory, Brain, and Belief.* Cambridge, Mass.: Harvard University Press, pp. 11–32.

DENTON, MICHAEL, 1985, *Evolution: A Theory in Crisis*. London: Burnett Books.

DEWDNEY, A. K., 1984, *The Planiverse: Computer Contact with a Two-Dimensional World*. New York: Poseidon Press.

EIGEN, MANFRED, 1992, *Steps towards Life*. Oxford: Oxford University Press.

ELLIS, HAYDN, and ANDREW YOUNG, 1990, "Accounting for Delusional Misidentifications." *British Journal of Psychiatry*, vol. 157, pp. 239–248.

FEYNMAN, RICHARD, 1985, *"Surely You're Joking, Mr. Feynman!": Adventures of a Curious Character*. New York: W. W. Norton.

FITCH, TECUMSEH, 2008, "Nano-Intentionality: A Defense of Intrinsic Intentionality." *Biology and Philosophy*, vol. 23, pp. 157–177.

FITZGIBBON, C. D., and J. H. FANSHAWE, 1988, "Stotting in Thomson's Gazelles: An Honest Signal of Condition." *Behavioral Ecology and Sociobiology*, vol. 23, no. 2 (August), pp. 69–74.

FODOR, JERRY, 1975, *The Language of Thought*. Hassocks, Sussex: Harvester Press.

————, 2003, "Why Would Mother Nature Bother?" (review of *Freedom Evolves*). *London Review of Books*, vol. 25, no. 5, pp. 17–18.

————, 2008, *LOT 2: The Language of Thought Revisited*. Oxford: Oxford University Press.

FODOR, JERRY, and E. LEPORE, 1992, *Holism: A Shopper's Guide*. Oxford: Blackwell.

FODOR, JERRY, and M. PIATELLI-PALMERINI, 2010, *What Darwin Got Wrong*. New York: Farrar, Straus & Giroux.

FRANKFURT, HARRY, 1969, "Alternate Possibilities and Moral Responsibility." *Journal of Philosophy*, vol. 65, pp. 829–833.

GELL-MAN, MURRAY, 1995, *The Quark and the Jaguar: Adventures in the Simple and the Complex*. New York: St. Martin's.

GIBSON, J. J., 1979, *The Ecological Approach to Visual Perception*. Boston: Houghton Mifflin.

GODFREY-SMITH, PETER, 2009, *Darwinian Populations and Natural Selection*. Oxford: Oxford University Press.

————, 2011, "Agents and Acacias: Replies to Dennett, Sterelny, and Queller" (replies to reviews of *Darwinian Populations and Natural Selection*). *Biology and Philosophy*, vol. 26, pp. 501–515.

GOFFMAN, ERVING, 1959, *The Presentation of Self in Everyday Life*. Edinburgh: University of Edinburgh Social Sciences Research Centre.

GOULD, STEPHEN JAY, 1977, *Ever since Darwin*. New York: W. W. Norton.

————, 1989a, "Tires to Sandals." *Natural History*, April, pp. 8-15.

————, 1989b, *Wonderful Life: The Burgess Shale and the Nature of History*. New York: W. W. Norton.

————, 1992a, "The Confusion over Evolution." *New York Review of Books*, November 19.

————, 1992b, "Life in a Punctuation." *Natural History*, October, pp. 10–21.

————, 1993, "Confusion over Evolution: An Exchange." *New York Review of Books*, January 14, pp. 43–44.

GRAHAM, GEORGE, and TERENCE HORGAN, 2000, "Mary Mary Quite Contrary." *Philosophical Studies*, vol. 99, pp. 59–87.

GREENE, JOSHUA, and JONATHAN COHEN, 2004, "For the Law, Neuroscience Changes Everything and Nothing." *Philosophical Transactions of the Royal Society*, vol. 359, pp. 1775–1785.

HARRIS, SAM, 2012, *Free Will*. New York: Free Press.

HAUGELAND, JOHN, 1981, *Mind Design*. Cambridge, Mass.: MIT Press/Bradford Book.

————, 1985, *Artificial Intelligence: The Very Idea*. Cambridge, Mass.: MIT Press.

HAWKING, STEPHEN W., 1988, *A Brief History of Time*. New York: Bantam.

HAYES, PATRICK, 1978, "The Naïve Physics Manifesto." In D. Michie, ed., *Expert Systems in the Microelectronic Age*. Edinburgh: Edinburgh University Press.

HEIDER, F., and M. SIMMEL, 1944, "An Experimental Study of Apparent Behavior." *American Journal of Psychology*, vol. 57, no. 2, pp. 243–259.

HILLIARD, JOHN NORTHERN, 1938, *Card Magic*. Minneapolis: Carl W. Jones.

HOFSTADTER, DOUGLAS, 1979, *Gödel Escher Bach*. New York: Basic Books.

————, 1982, "Metamagical Themas: Can Inspiration Be Mechanized?" *Scientific American*, September, pp. 18–34. Reprinted as "On the Seeming Paradox of Mechanizing Creativity," in Hofstadter, 1985, pp. 526–546.

————, 1985, *Metamagical Themas: Questing for the Essence of Mind and Pattern*. New York: Basic Books.

————, 1997, *Le Ton Beau de Marot: In Praise of the Music of Language*. New York: Basic Books.

————, 2007, *I Am a Strange Loop*. New York: Basic Books.

HOFSTADTER, DOUGLAS, and DANIEL DENNETT, eds., 1981, *The Mind's I*. New York: Basic Books.

HOLLAND, JOHN, 1975, *Adaptation in Natural and Artificial Systems*. Ann Arbor: University of Michigan Press.

HUME, DAVID, (1739) 1964, *A Treatise of Human Nature* (L. A. Selby-Bigge, ed.). Oxford: Clarendon.

HUMPHREY, NICHOLAS, 1987, "Scientific Shakespeare." *The Guardian* (London), August 26.

HUMPHREY, NICHOLAS, and DANIEL DENNETT, 1989, "Speaking for Our Selves: An Assessment of Multiple Personality Disorder." *Raritan: A Quarterly Review*, vol. 9 (Summer), pp. 68–98. Reprinted (with footnotes), Occasional Paper 8, Center on Violence and Human Survival, John Jay College of Criminal Justice, City University of New York, 1991.

HURLEY, MATTHEW, DANIEL DENNETT, and REGINALD B. ADAMS JR., 2011, *Inside Jokes: Using Humor to Reverse-Engineer the Mind*. Cambridge, Mass.: MIT Press.

JACKENDOFF, RAY, 1987, *Consciousness and the Computational Mind*. Cambridge, Mass.: MIT Press/Bradford Book.

————, 1993, *Patterns in the Mind: Language and Human Nature*. Harlow, Essex: Harvester Wheatsheaf; New York: Basic Books, 1994.

JACKSON, FRANK, 1982, "Epiphenomenal Qualia." *Philosophical Quarterly*, vol. 32, pp. 127–136.

KANE, ROBERT, 1996, *The Significance of Free Will*. Oxford: Oxford University Press.

KNOBE, J., and NICHOLS, S., eds., 2008, *Experimental Philosophy*. Oxford: Oxford University Press.

LEIBNIZ, GOTTFRIED, (1714) 1898, *Monadology*. In *The Monadology and Other Philosophical Writings*, Robert Latta, trans. Oxford: Oxford University Press.

LENAT, DOUGLAS B., and R. V. GUHA, 1990, *Building Large Knowledge-Based Systems: Representation and Inference in the CYC Project*. Reading, Mass.: Addison-Wesley.

LETTVIN, J. Y., U. MATURANA, W. McCULLOCH, and W. PITTS, 1959, "What the Frog's Eye Tells the Frog's Brain." In *Proceedings of the Institute of Radio Engineers*, vol. 47, pp. 1940–1951.

LEVINE, JOSEPH, 1994, "Out of the Closet: A Qualophile Confronts Qualophobia." *Philosophical Topics*, vol. 22, pp. 107–126.

LEWIS, DAVID, 1978, "Truth in Fiction." *American Philosophical Quarterly*, vol. 15, pp. 37–46.

LLOYD, M., and DYBAS, H. S., 1966, "The Periodical Cicada Problem." *Evolution*, vol. 20, pp. 132–149.

LLOYD MORGAN, CONWY, 1894, *An Introduction to Comparative Psychology*. London: W. Scott.

LUDLOW, PETER, YUJIN NAGASAWA, and DANIEL STOLJAR, eds., 2004, *There's Something about Mary: Essays on Phenomenal Consciousness and Frank Jackson's Knowledge Argument*. Cambridge, Mass.: MIT Press/Bradford Books.

MacKENZIE R. B., 1868, *The Darwinian Theory of the Transmutation of Species Examined*. London: Nisbet.

MAYNARD SMITH, JOHN, 1978, *The Evolution of Sex*. Cambridge: Cambridge University Press.

McCLELLAND, JAY, DAVID RUMELHART, and THE PDP RESEARCH GROUP, 1986, *Parallel Distributed Processing: Explorations in the Microstructure of Cognition*, vol. 2. Cambridge, Mass.: MIT Press.

MENABREA, LUIGI FEDERICO, 1842, "Sketch of the Analytic Engine Invented by Charles Babbage." In the *Bibliothèque Universelle de Genève*, no. 82 (October). Translated by Augusta Ada King, Countess of Lovelace, 1843, with notes, in *Scientific Memoirs*, vol. 3, pp. 666–731.

MEYER, STEPHEN C., 2009, *Signature in the Cell: DNA and the Evidence for Intelligent Design*. New York: HarperOne.

MILLIKAN, RUTH, 1984, *Language, Thought and Other Biological Categories*. Cambridge, Mass.: MIT Press.

————, 1993, *White Queen Psychology and Other Essays for Alice*. Cambridge, Mass.: MIT Press.

NAGEL, THOMAS, 1974, "What Is It Like to Be a Bat?" *Philosophical Review*, vol. 83, pp. 435–450.

————, 2009, Recommendation for Book of the Year. *Times Literary Supplement*, November 27.

————, 2010, Letter to the editor. *Times Literary Supplement*, January 1.

NEUGEBAUER, OTTO, 1989, "A Babylonian Lunar Ephemeris from Roman Egypt." In E. Leichty, M. de J. Ellis, and P. Gerardi, eds., *A Scientific Humanist: Studies in Honor of Abraham Sachs*. Philadelphia: Occasional Publications of the Samuel Noah Kramer Fund no. 9, pp. 301–304.

PINKER, STEVEN, 2002, *The Blank Slate: The Modern Denial of Human Nature*. New York: Viking.

POPEK, GERALD J., and ROBERT P. GOLDBERG, 1974, "Formal Requirements for Virtualizable Third Generation Architectures." *Communications of the ACM*, vol. 17, no. 7, pp. 412–421. doi:10.1145/361011.361073. Available at http://doi.acm.org/10.1145/361011.361073.

POUNDSTONE, WILLIAM, 1985, *The Recursive Universe: Cosmic Complexity and the Limits of Scientific Knowledge*. New York: William Morrow.

PUTNAM, HILARY, 1975, "The Meaning of 'Meaning.' " In K. Gunderson, ed., *Language, Mind and Knowledge*. Minnesota Studies in the Philosophy of Science, vol. 7. Minneapolis: University of Minnesota Press. Reprinted in Putnam, 1975, *Mind, Language and Reality (Philosophical Papers*, vol. 2). Cambridge: Cambridge University Press.

QUINE, W. V. O., 1960, *Word and Object*. Cambridge, Mass.: MIT Press.

————, 1987, "Universal Library." In *Quiddities: An Intermittently Philosophical Dictionary*. Cambridge, Mass.: Harvard University Press.

RAPOPORT, ANATOL, 1960, *Fights, Games, and Debates*. Ann Arbor: University of Michigan Press.

————, 1961, "Three Modes of Conflict." *Management Science*, vol. 3, p. 210.

RIDLEY, MATT, 1993, *The Red Queen: Sex and the Evolution of Human Nature*. New York: Macmillan.

————, 2004, *Nature via Nurture*. London: Fourth Estate. Also published under the title *The Agile Gene: How Nature Turns on Nurture*. New York: HarperCollins.

ROSS, AMBER, 2013, "Inconceivable Minds." Philosophy PhD dissertation, University of North Carolina at Chapel Hill.

RUINA, ANDY, 2011, "Cornell Ranger, 2011, 4-Legged Bipedal Robot." ruina.tam. cornell.edu/research/topics/locomotion_and_robotics/ranger/Ranger 2011/.

RUMELHART, D. E., J. L. MCCLELLAND, and THE PDP RESEARCH GROUP, 1986, *Parallel Distributed Processing: Explorations in the Microstructure of Cognition*, vol. 1. Cambridge, Mass.: MIT Press.

RYDER, DAN, JUSTINE KINGSBURY, and KENNETH WILLIFORD, eds., 2013, *Millikan and Her Critics*. Oxford: Wiley-Blackwell.

SANFORD, DAVID, 1975, "Infinity and Vagueness." *Philosophical Review*, vol. 84, pp. 520–535.

SCHÖNBORN, CHRISTOPH, 2005, "Finding Design in Nature." *New York Times*, July 7.

SEARLE, JOHN, 1980, "Minds, Brains and Programs." *Behavioral and Brain Sciences*, vol. 3, pp. 417–458.

————, 1982, "The Myth of the Computer" (review of *The Mind's I*). *New York Review of Books*, vol. 29 (April 29).

————, 1988, "Turing the Chinese Room." In T. Singh, ed., *Synthesis of Science and Religion, Critical Essays and Dialogues*. San Francisco: Bhaktivedanta Institute.

SELLARS, WILFRID, 1962, "Philosophy and the Scientific Image of Man." In *Science, Perception and Reality*. London: Routledge & Kegan Paul.

SEUNG, SEBASTIAN, 2007, "The Once and Future Science of Neural Networks." Presented at the Society for Neuroscience meeting, San Diego, November 4.

SIEGEL, LEE, 1991, *Net of Magic: Wonders and Deceptions in India*. Chicago: University of Chicago Press.

SIMS, KARL, 1994, *Evolved Virtual Creatures*. http://www.karlsims.com/evolved -virtual-creatures.html.

STRAWSON, GALEN, 2003, "Evolution Explains It All for You" (review of Dennett, 2003). *New York Times*, March 2.

————, 2010, "Your Move: The Maze of Free Will," The Stone, *New*

York Times online, July 22, 2010. http://www.scribd.com/doc/86763712/Week-2-Strawson-The-Maze-of-Free-Will.

THOMPSON, EVAN, 2007, *Mind in Life*. Cambridge, Mass.: Belknap Press, Harvard University Press.

VOHS, KATHLEEN D., and JONATHAN W. SCHOOLER, 2008, "The Value of Believing in Free Will: Encouraging a Belief in Determinism Increases Cheating." *Psychological Science*, pp. 49–54.

VON NEUMANN, JOHN, 1966, *Theory of Self-Reproducing Automata* (Arthur Burks, ed.). Champaign-Urbana: University of Illinois Press.

VON NEUMANN, JOHN, and OSKAR MORGENSTERN, 1944, *Theory of Games and Economic Behavior*. Princeton, N.J.: Princeton University Press.

VON UEXKÜLL, JAKOB, (1934) 1957, "A Stroll through the Worlds of Animals and Men: A Picture Book of Invisible Worlds." In Claire H. Schiller, ed. and trans., *Instinctive Behavior: The Development of a Modern Concept*. New York: International Universities Press.

WANG, HAO, 1957, "A Variant to Turing's Theory of Computing Machines." *Journal of the Association for Computing Machinery*, pp. 63–92.

WIGGINS, DAVID, 1973, "Towards a Reasonable Libertarianism." In T. Honderich, ed., *Essays on Freedom of Action*. London: Routledge & Kegan Paul, pp. 31–63.

WIMSATT, WILLIAM C., 1980, "Randomness and Perceived Randomness in Evolutionary Biology." *Synthese*, vol. 43, pp. 287–290.

WOLFE, TOM, 2000, "Sorry, But Your Soul Just Died." In *Hooking Up*. New York: Farrar, Straus & Giroux.

WOOLDRIDGE, DEAN, 1963, *The Machinery of the Brain*. New York: McGraw-Hill.

WRIGHT, ROBERT, 2000, *Nonzero: The Logic of Human Destiny*. New York: Pantheon.

ZAHAVI, A., 1987, "The Theory of Signal Selection and Some of Its Implications." In V. P. Delfino, ed., *Bari, 9-14 April 1985*. Bari: Adriatici Editrici, pp. 305–327.

CREDITS